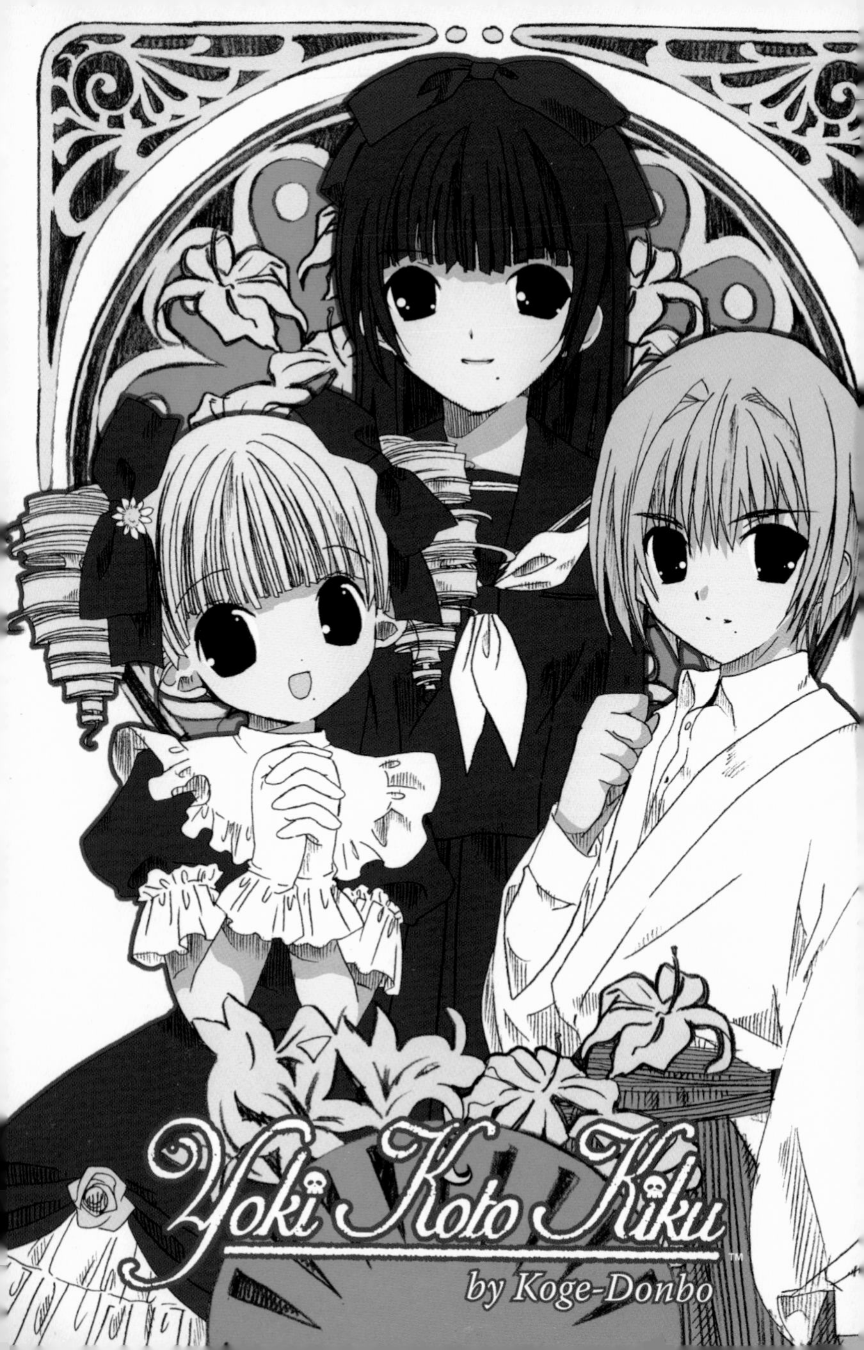
Yoki Koto Kiku™
by Koge-Donbo

☠ Characters ☠

Yoki (Yokiko Nekogami)
13 years old.
The eldest of the Nekogami triplets.
She attends a music school. A *yamato nadeshiko* who dreams of becoming a star, she hopes to overcome her shyness by getting on stage and performing.

Koto (Kotosuke Nekogami)
13 years old.
The second of the Nekogami triplets.
He is a kind and gentle boy, but becomes scary when mad. He is an expert koto player.

Kiku (Kikuno Nekogami)
13 years old.
The third of the Nekogami triplets.
She is dainty and bashful and is proud of her ribbons and curly hair. She likes to arrange flowers.

Tamayo
14 years old.
She works as a maid in the Nekogami household.
The eldest of the Nekogami, Sukekiyo, fell in love with her and she is now his fiancée. The creature on her shoulder is Saruzou.

☠ Table of Contents ☠

Yoki Koto Kiku

by Koge-Donbo

brought to you by
BROCCOLI BOOKS
A DIVISION OF BROCCOLI INTERNATIONAL USA

Other titles available from Broccoli Books

E'S
❑Volume 1 (ongoing)
❑Volume 2

Disgaea® 2
❑Volume 1 (ongoing)

Galaxy Angel II
❑Volume 1 (ongoing)

KAMUI
❑Volume 1 (of 11)
❑Volume 2
❑Volume 3
❑Volume 4
❑Volume 5
❑Volume 6

Murder Princess
❑Volume 1 (of 2)

Aquarian Age – Juvenile Orion
❑Volume 1 (of 5)
❑Volume 2
❑Volume 3
❑Volume 4
❑Volume 5

Galaxy Angel
❑Volume 1 (of 5)
❑Volume 2
❑Volume 3
❑Volume 4
❑Volume 5

Di Gi Charat Theater
❑Dejiko's Summer Vacation
❑Piyoko is Number One!

Galaxy Angel Beta
❑Volume 1 (of 3)
❑Volume 2
❑Volume 3

**Di Gi Charat Theater –
Dejiko's Adventure**
❑Volume 1 (of 3)

Galaxy Angel Party
❑Volume 1 (ongoing)
❑Volume 2

Disgaea®
❑Volume 1 (of 1)

For more information about Broccoli Books titles,
check out **bro-usa.com**!

Yoki Koto Kiku™

English Adaptation Staff
Translation: Satsuki Yamashita
English Adaptation: Jason R. Grissom
Touch-Up & Lettering: Fawn Lau
Cover & Graphic Supervision: Chris McDougall
Graphic Assistant: Krystal Sae Eua

Editor: Dietrich Seto
Sales Manager: Ardith D. Santiago
Managing Editor: Shizuki Yamashita
Publisher: Kaname Tezuka

Email: editor@broccolibooks.com
Website: www.broccolibooks.com

A BROCCOLI BOOKS Manga
Broccoli Books is a division of Broccoli International USA, Inc.
1728 S. La Cienega Blvd., Los Angeles, CA 90035

ISBN-13: 978-1-5974-1025-0
ISBN-10: 1-5974-1025-X

Published by Broccoli International USA, Inc.
First printing, June 2006
Second printing, February 2007
All illustrations by Koge-Donbo.

Distributed by Publishers Group West

ANIME GAMERS BROCCOLI INTERNATIONAL USA
www.bro-usa.com

10 9 8 7 6 5 4 3 2
Printed in Canada

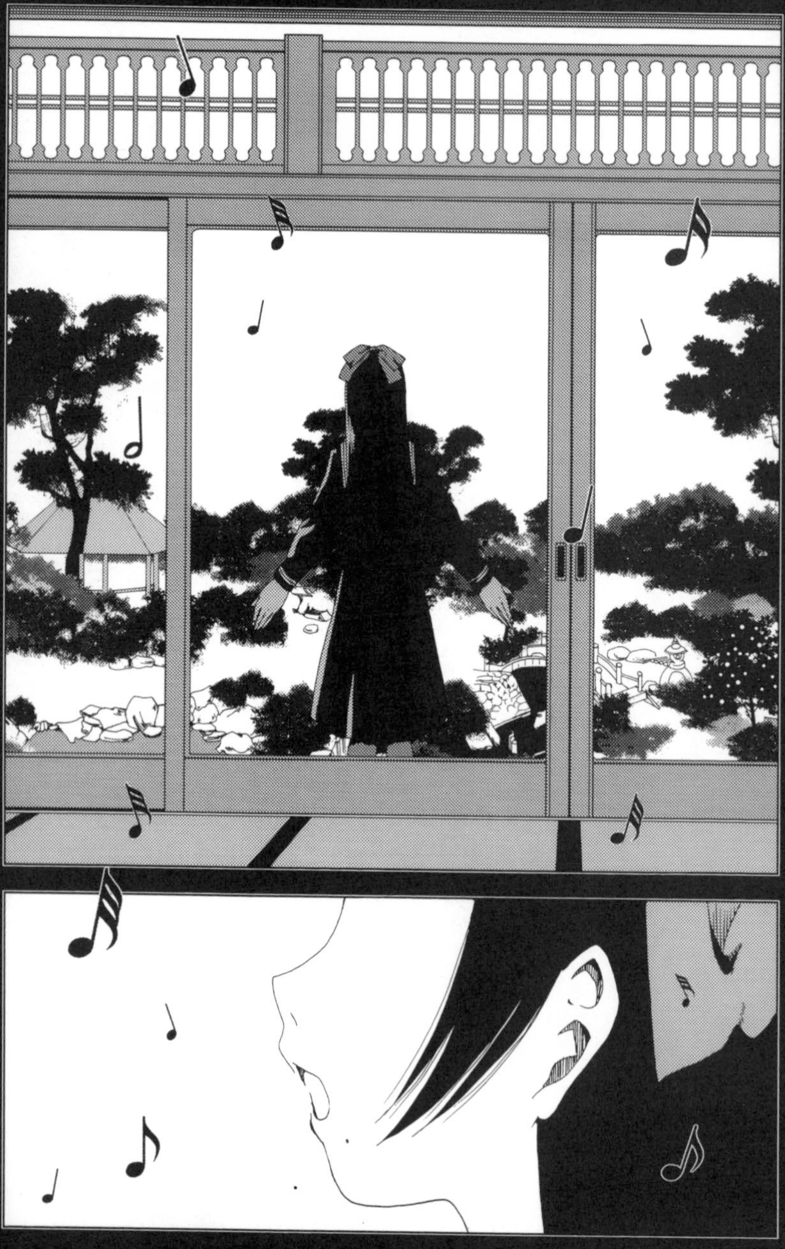

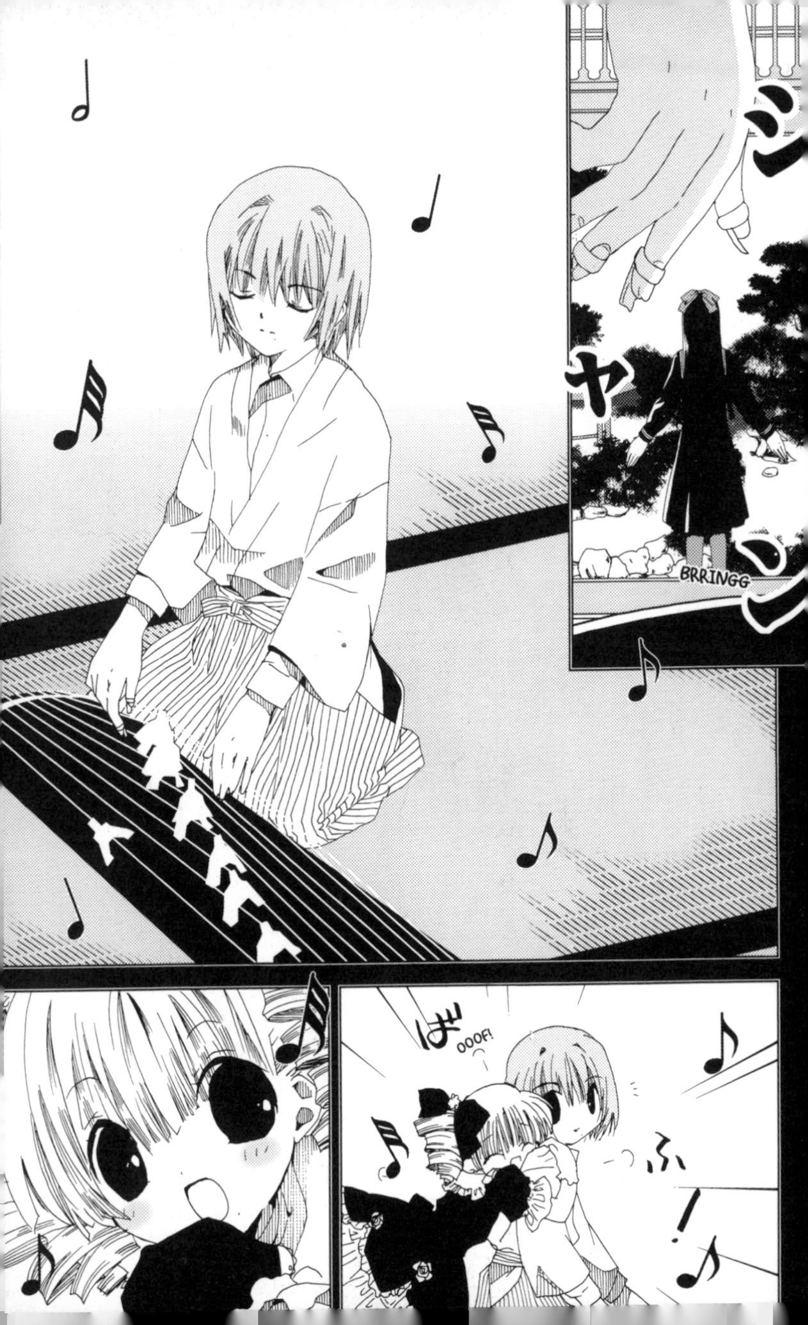
BRRINGG
OOOF!

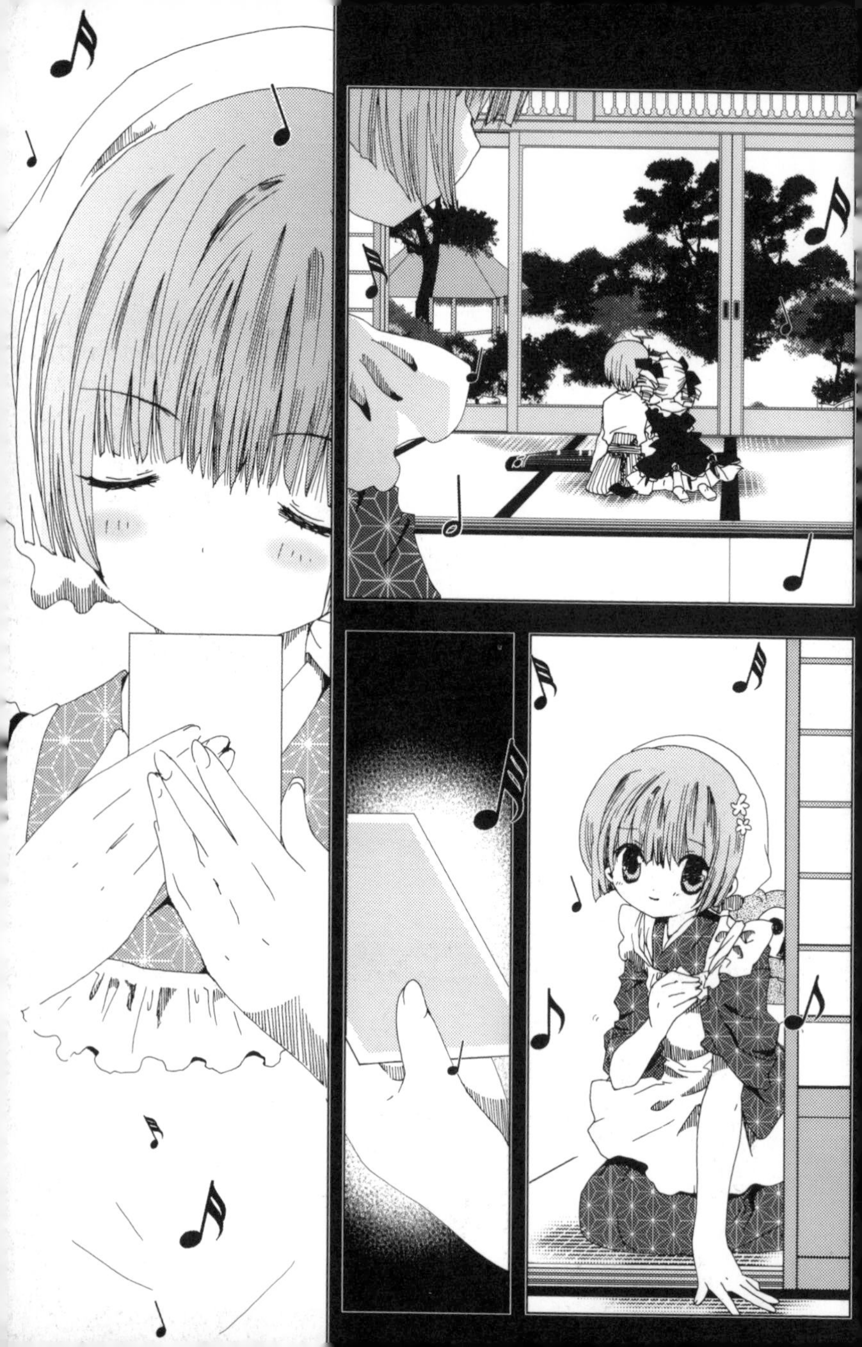

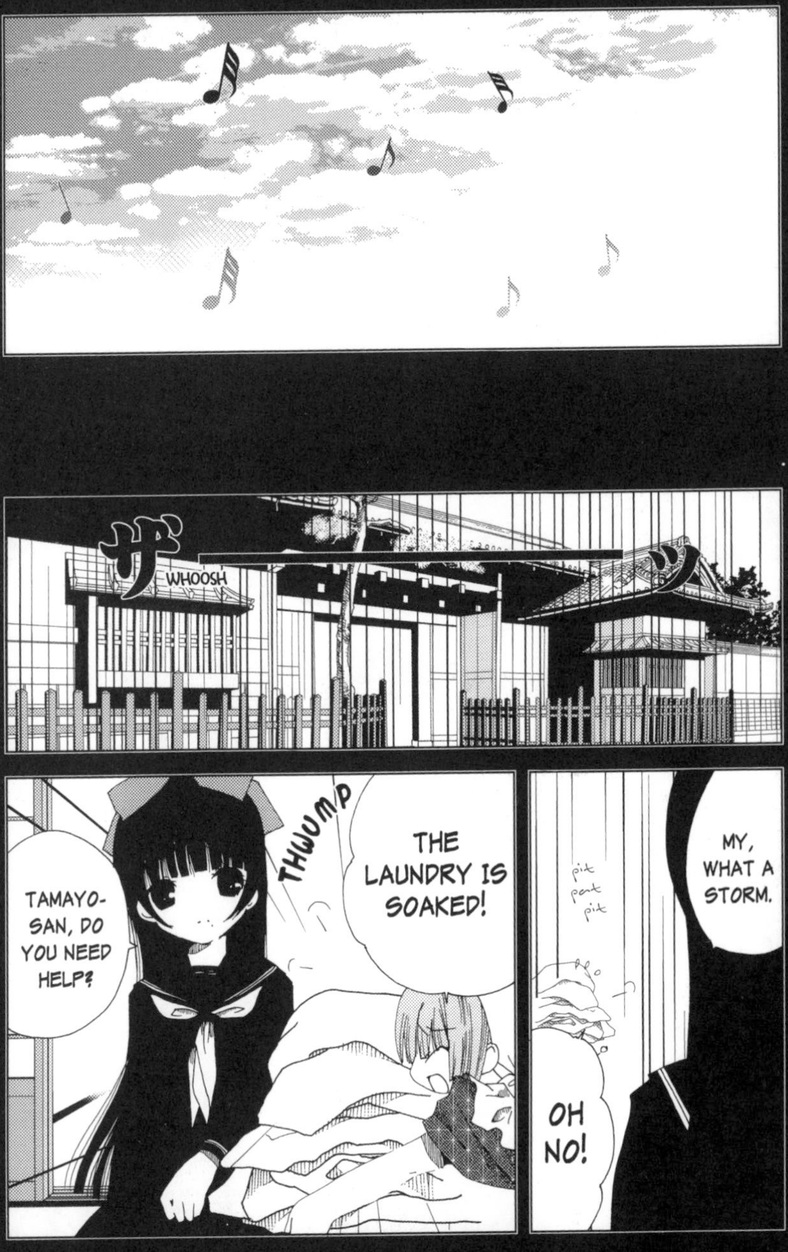
ザーッ
WHOOSH
MY, WHAT A STORM.
pit pat pit
OH NO!
THE LAUNDRY IS SOAKED!
THWUMP
TAMAYO-SAN, DO YOU NEED HELP?

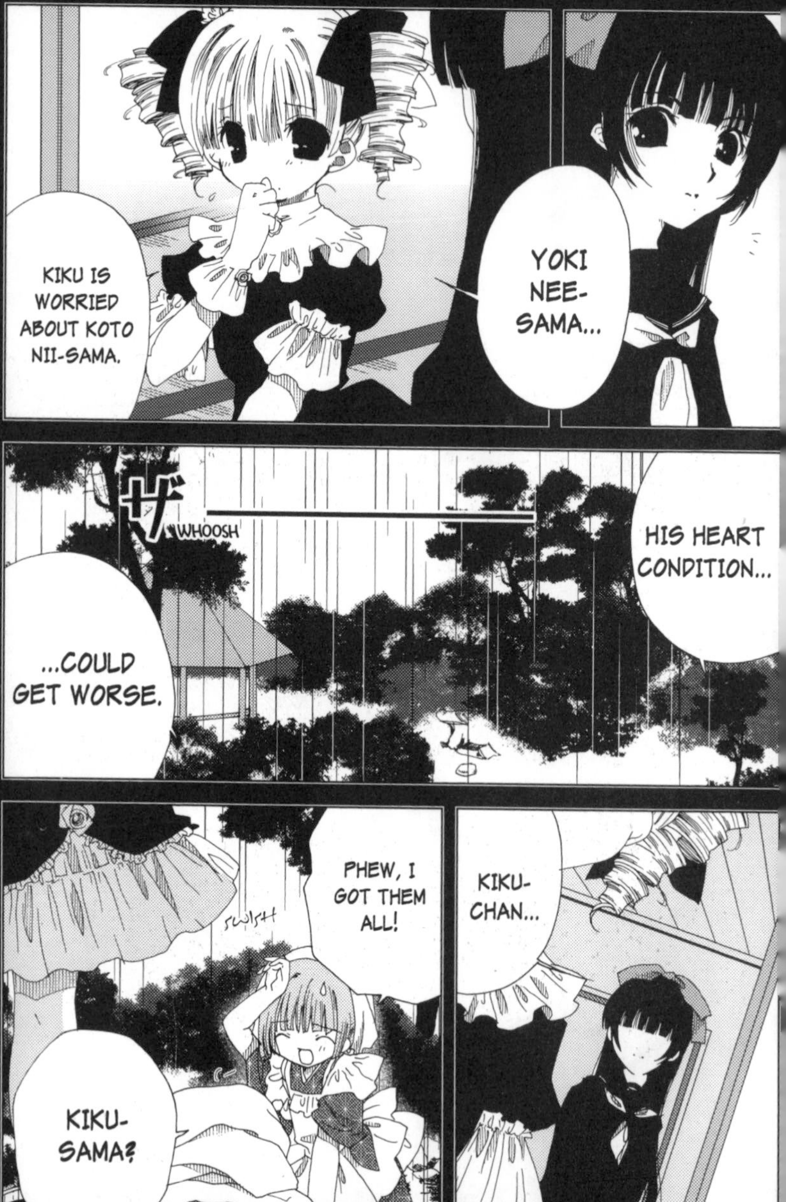
YOKI NEE-SAMA...
KIKU IS WORRIED ABOUT KOTO NII-SAMA.
HIS HEART CONDITION...
ザ
WHOOSH
...COULD GET WORSE.
KIKU-CHAN...
PHEW, I GOT THEM ALL!
SWISH
KIKU-SAMA?

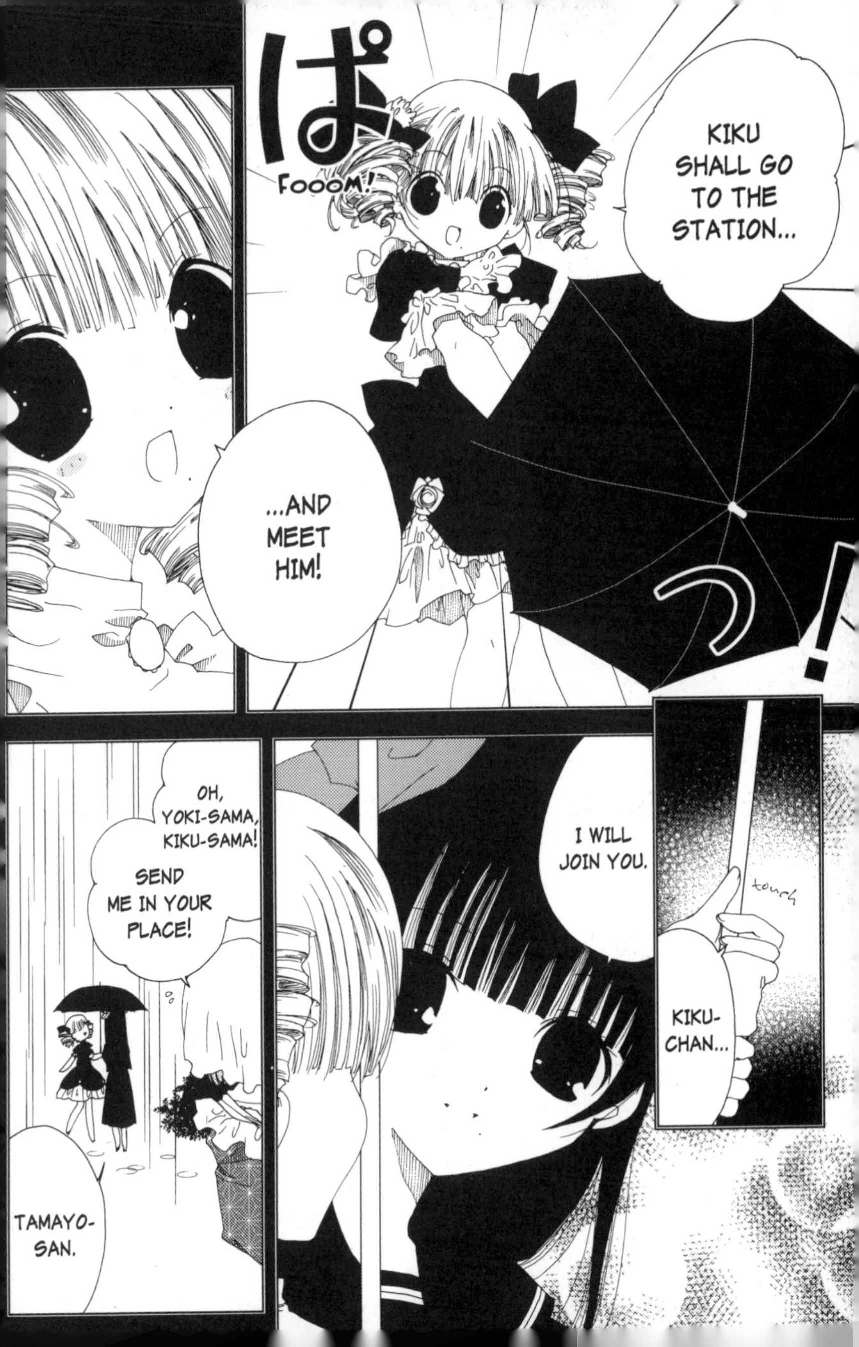
ぱ
Foooom!
KIKU SHALL GO TO THE STATION...
つ!
...AND MEET HIM!
touch
KIKU-CHAN...
I WILL JOIN YOU.
OH, YOKI-SAMA, KIKU-SAMA!
SEND ME IN YOUR PLACE!
TAMAYO-SAN.

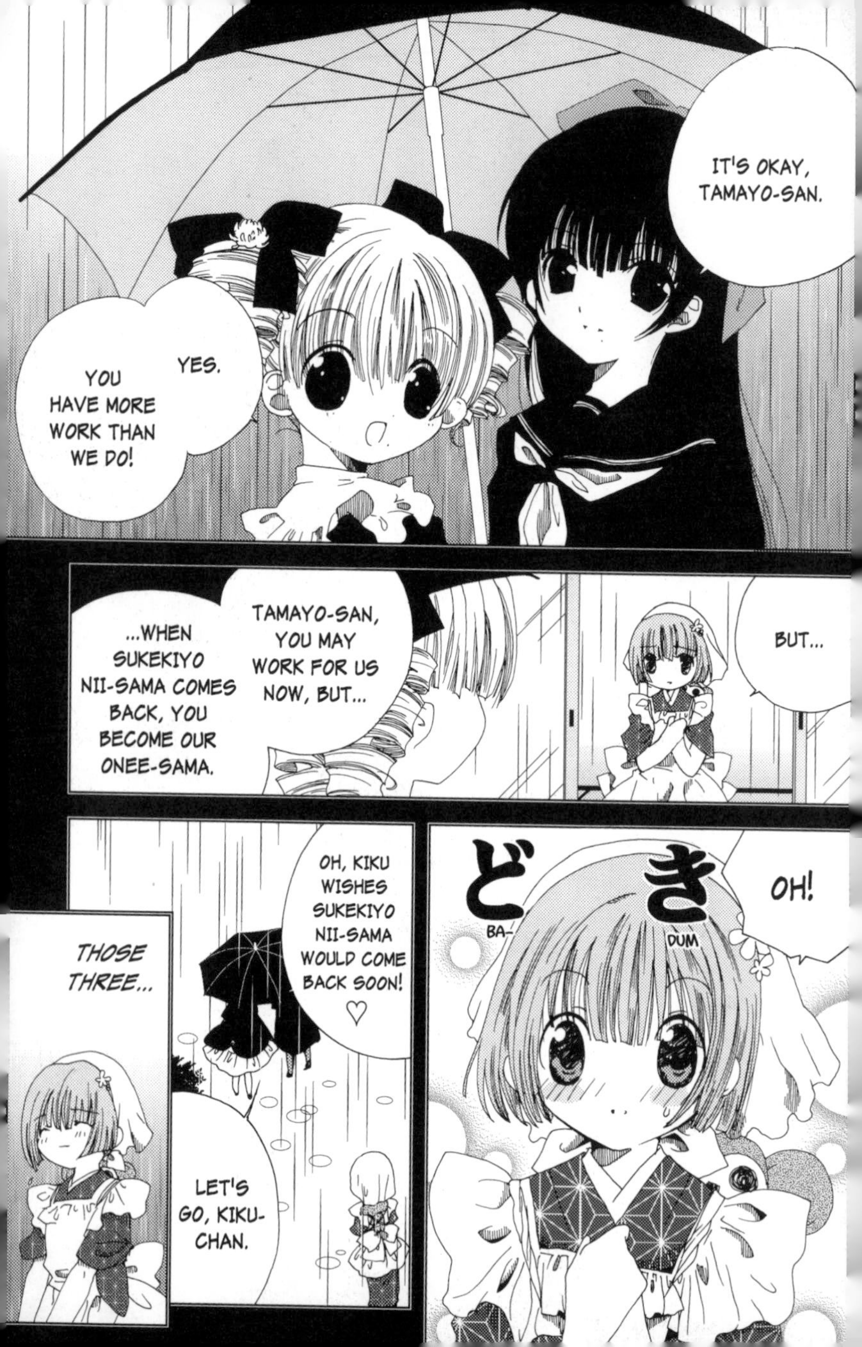
IT'S OKAY, TAMAYO-SAN.
YES.
YOU HAVE MORE WORK THAN WE DO!
BUT...
TAMAYO-SAN, YOU MAY WORK FOR US NOW, BUT...
...WHEN SUKEKIYO NII-SAMA COMES BACK, YOU BECOME OUR ONEE-SAMA.
OH!
どき
BA-DUM
OH, KIKU WISHES SUKEKIYO NII-SAMA WOULD COME BACK SOON! ♡
LET'S GO, KIKU-CHAN.
THOSE THREE...

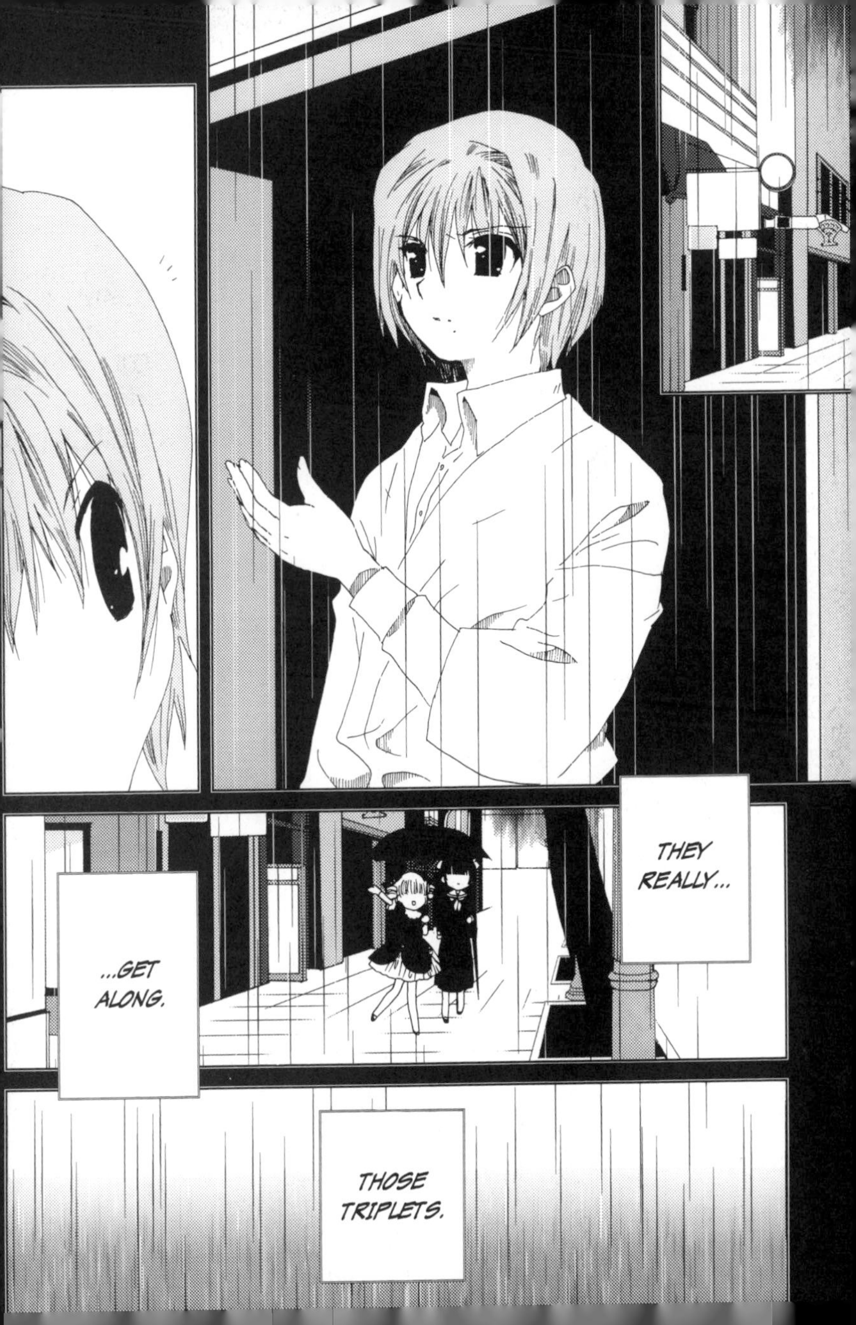
THEY REALLY...
...GET ALONG.
THOSE TRIPLETS.

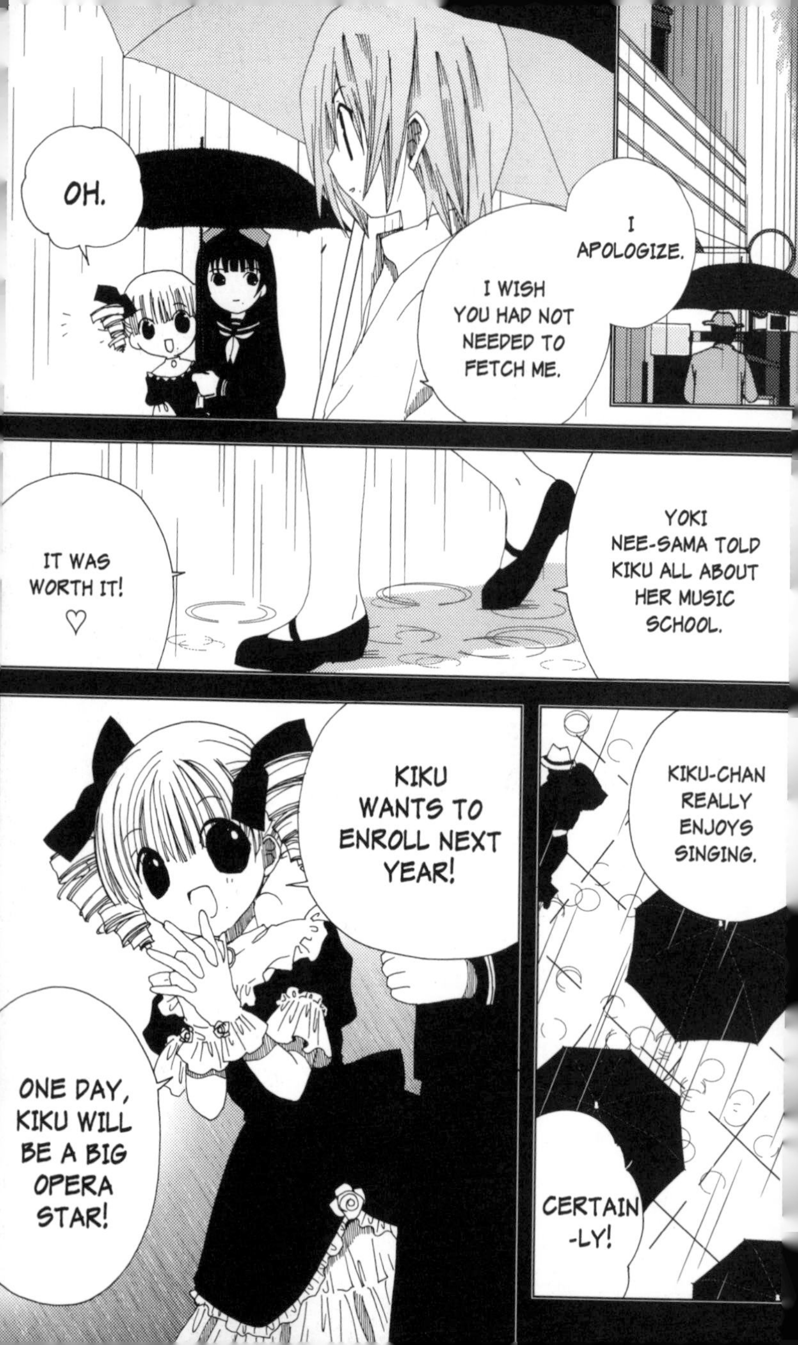
I APOLOGIZE.
I WISH YOU HAD NOT NEEDED TO FETCH ME.
OH.
YOKI NEE-SAMA TOLD KIKU ALL ABOUT HER MUSIC SCHOOL.
IT WAS WORTH IT! ♡
KIKU-CHAN REALLY ENJOYS SINGING.
CERTAIN -LY!
KIKU WANTS TO ENROLL NEXT YEAR!
ONE DAY, KIKU WILL BE A BIG OPERA STAR!

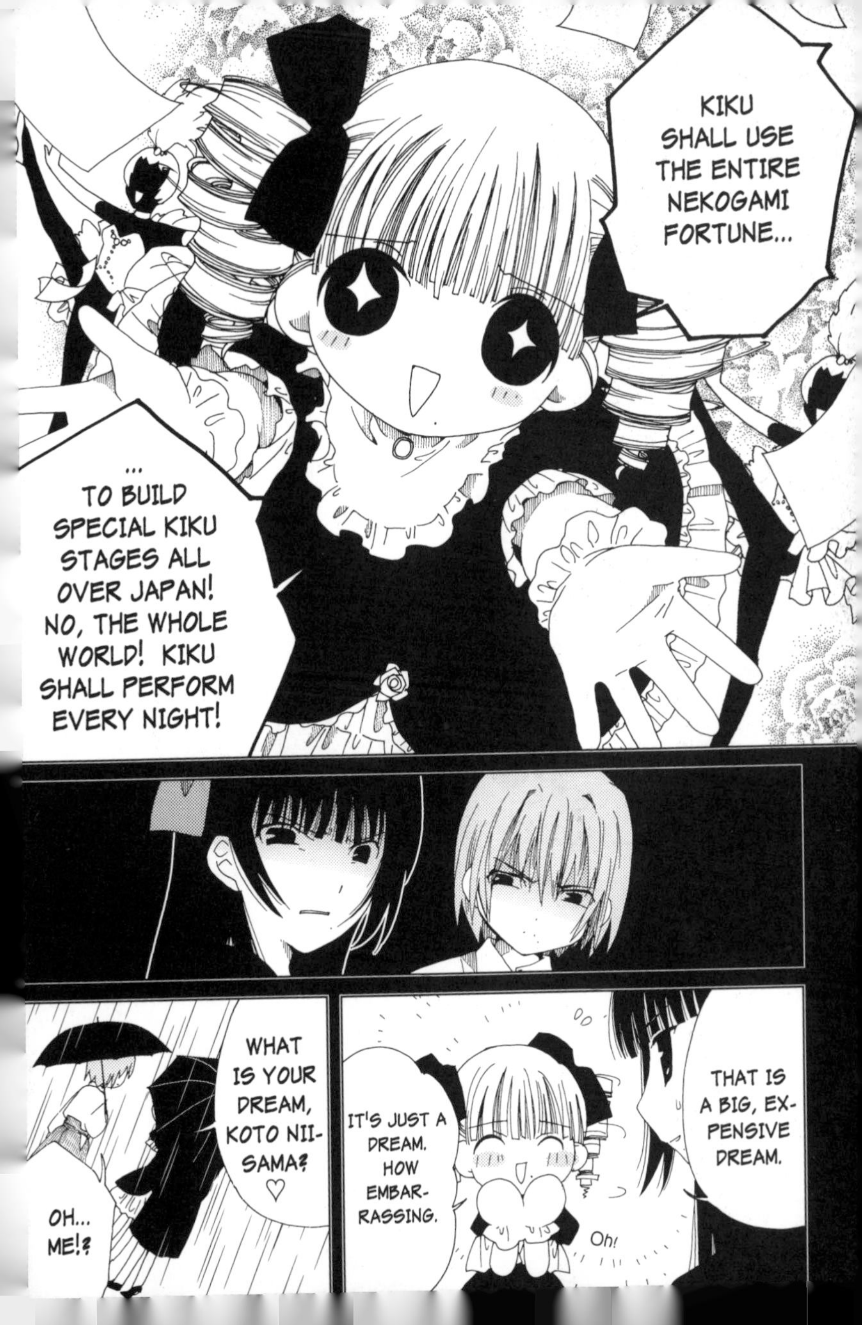
KIKU SHALL USE THE ENTIRE NEKOGAMI FORTUNE...
... TO BUILD SPECIAL KIKU STAGES ALL OVER JAPAN! NO, THE WHOLE WORLD! KIKU SHALL PERFORM EVERY NIGHT!
THAT IS A BIG, EX-PENSIVE DREAM.
IT'S JUST A DREAM. HOW EMBAR-RASSING.
Oh!
WHAT IS YOUR DREAM, KOTO NII-SAMA? ♡
OH... ME!?

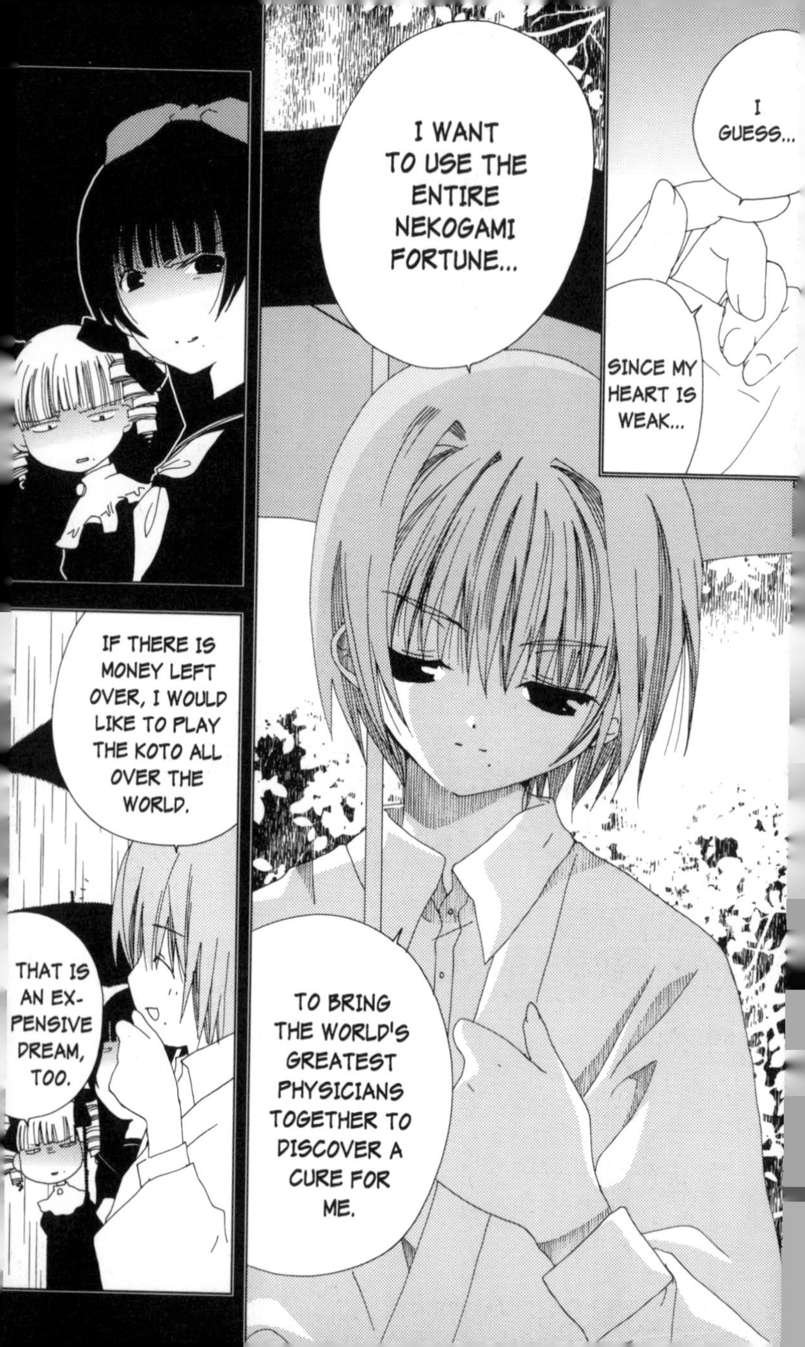
I GUESS...
SINCE MY HEART IS WEAK...
I WANT TO USE THE ENTIRE NEKOGAMI FORTUNE...
TO BRING THE WORLD'S GREATEST PHYSICIANS TOGETHER TO DISCOVER A CURE FOR ME.
IF THERE IS MONEY LEFT OVER, I WOULD LIKE TO PLAY THE KOTO ALL OVER THE WORLD.
THAT IS AN EX-PENSIVE DREAM, TOO.

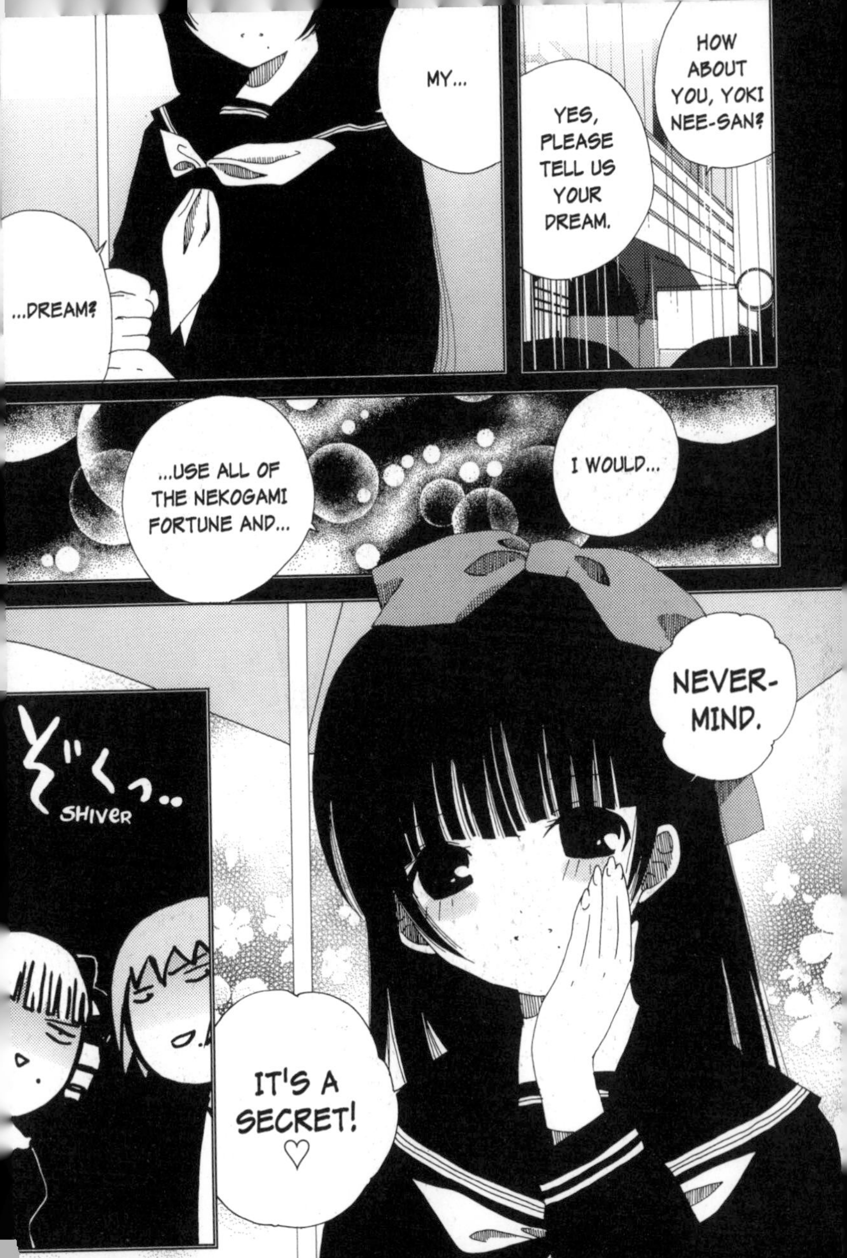
HOW ABOUT YOU, YOKI NEE-SAN?
YES, PLEASE TELL US YOUR DREAM.
MY...
...DREAM?
I WOULD...
...USE ALL OF THE NEKOGAMI FORTUNE AND...
NEVER-MIND.
IT'S A SECRET! ♡
ぞくっ..
SHIVER

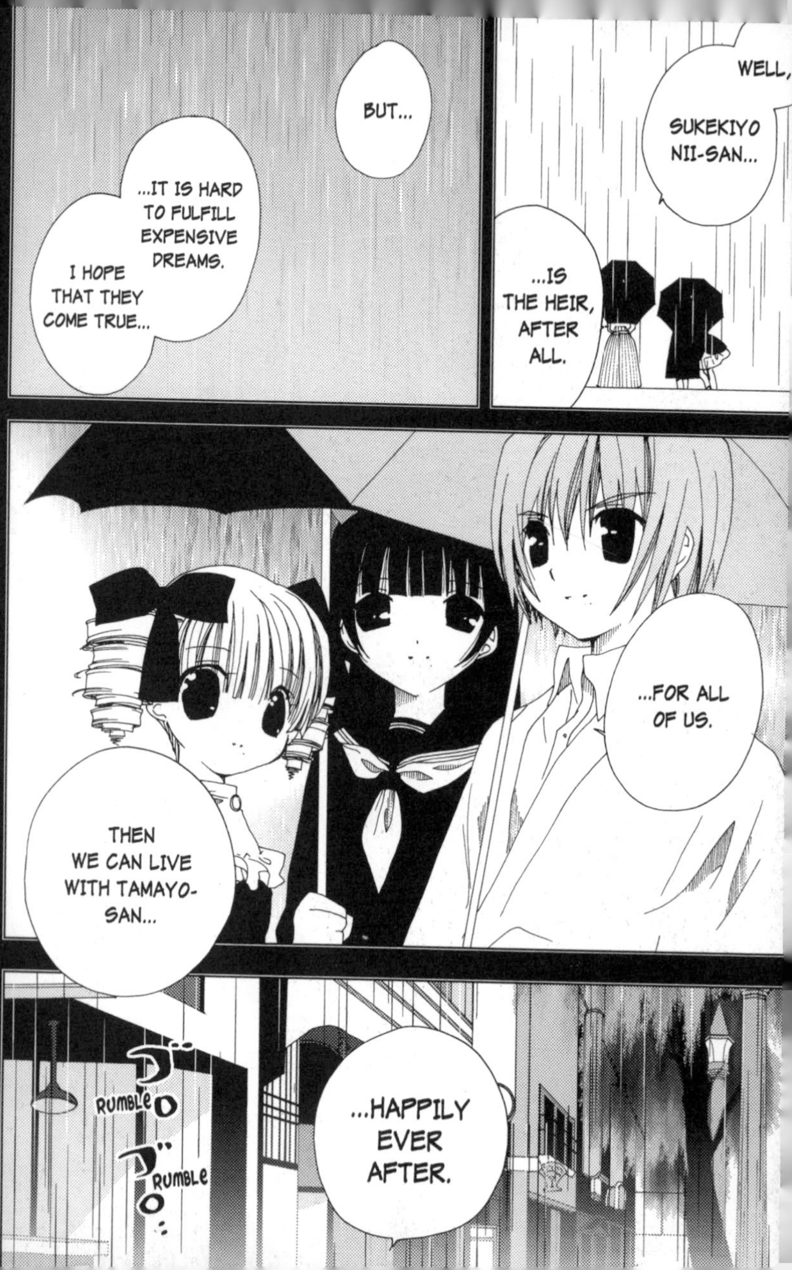
WELL,
SUKEKIYO NII-SAN...
...IS THE HEIR, AFTER ALL.
BUT...
...IT IS HARD TO FULFILL EXPENSIVE DREAMS.
I HOPE THAT THEY COME TRUE...
...FOR ALL OF US.
THEN WE CAN LIVE WITH TAMAYO-SAN...
...HAPPILY EVER AFTER.
RUMBLE
RUMBLE

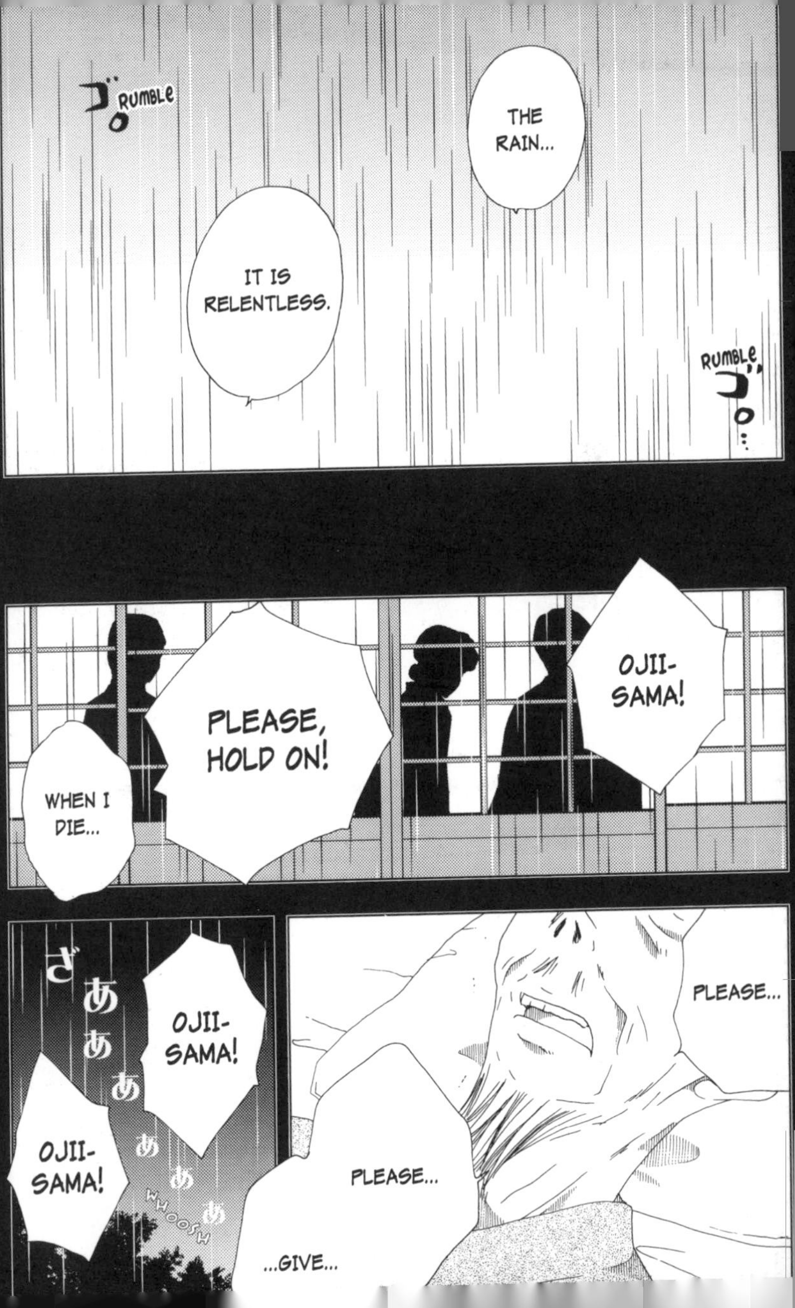
THE RAIN...
IT IS RELENTLESS.
ゴ RUMBLE
RUMBLE ゴ...
OJII-SAMA!
PLEASE, HOLD ON!
WHEN I DIE...
PLEASE...
PLEASE...
...GIVE...
ざあああああああ
OJII-SAMA!
OJII-SAMA!
WHOOSH

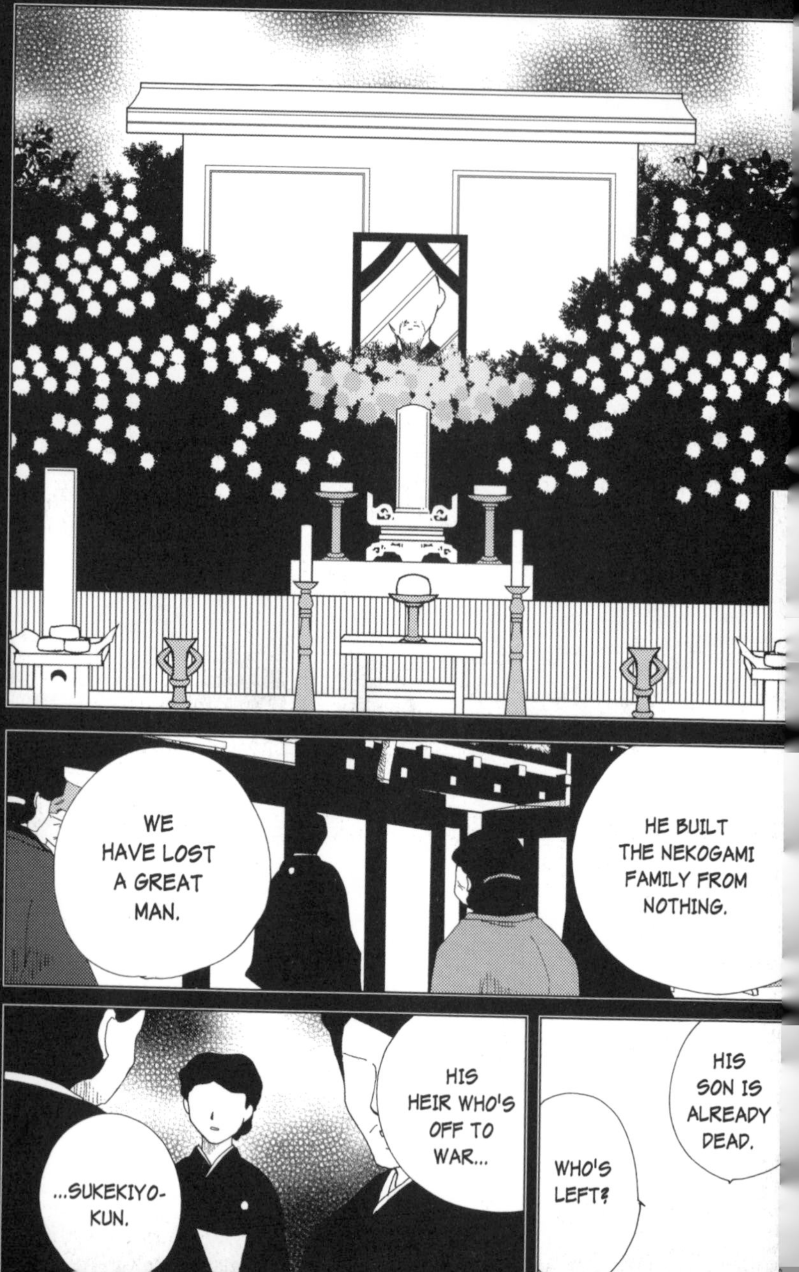
HE BUILT THE NEKOGAMI FAMILY FROM NOTHING.
WE HAVE LOST A GREAT MAN.
HIS SON IS ALREADY DEAD.
WHO'S LEFT?
HIS HEIR WHO'S OFF TO WAR...
...SUKEKIYO-KUN.

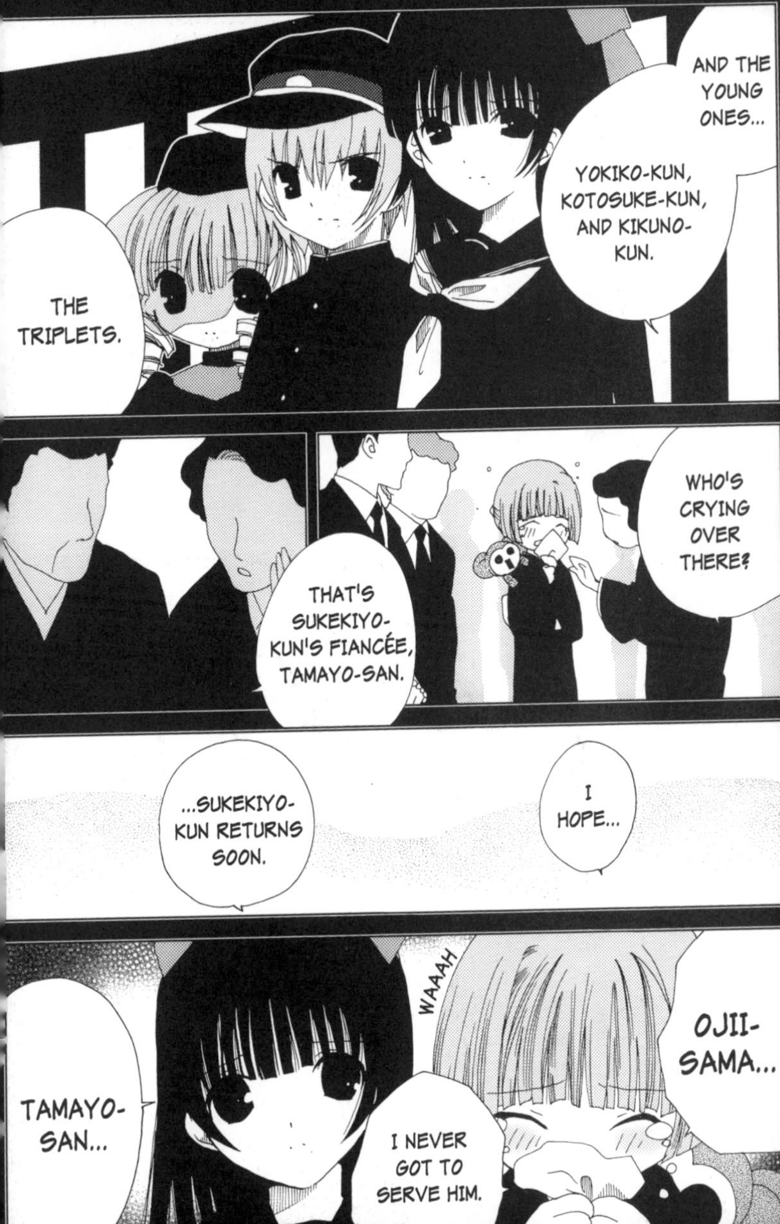
AND THE YOUNG ONES...
YOKIKO-KUN, KOTOSUKE-KUN, AND KIKUNO-KUN.
THE TRIPLETS.
WHO'S CRYING OVER THERE?
THAT'S SUKEKIYO-KUN'S FIANCÉE, TAMAYO-SAN.
I HOPE...
...SUKEKIYO-KUN RETURNS SOON.
OJII-SAMA...
WAAAH
I NEVER GOT TO SERVE HIM.
TAMAYO-SAN...

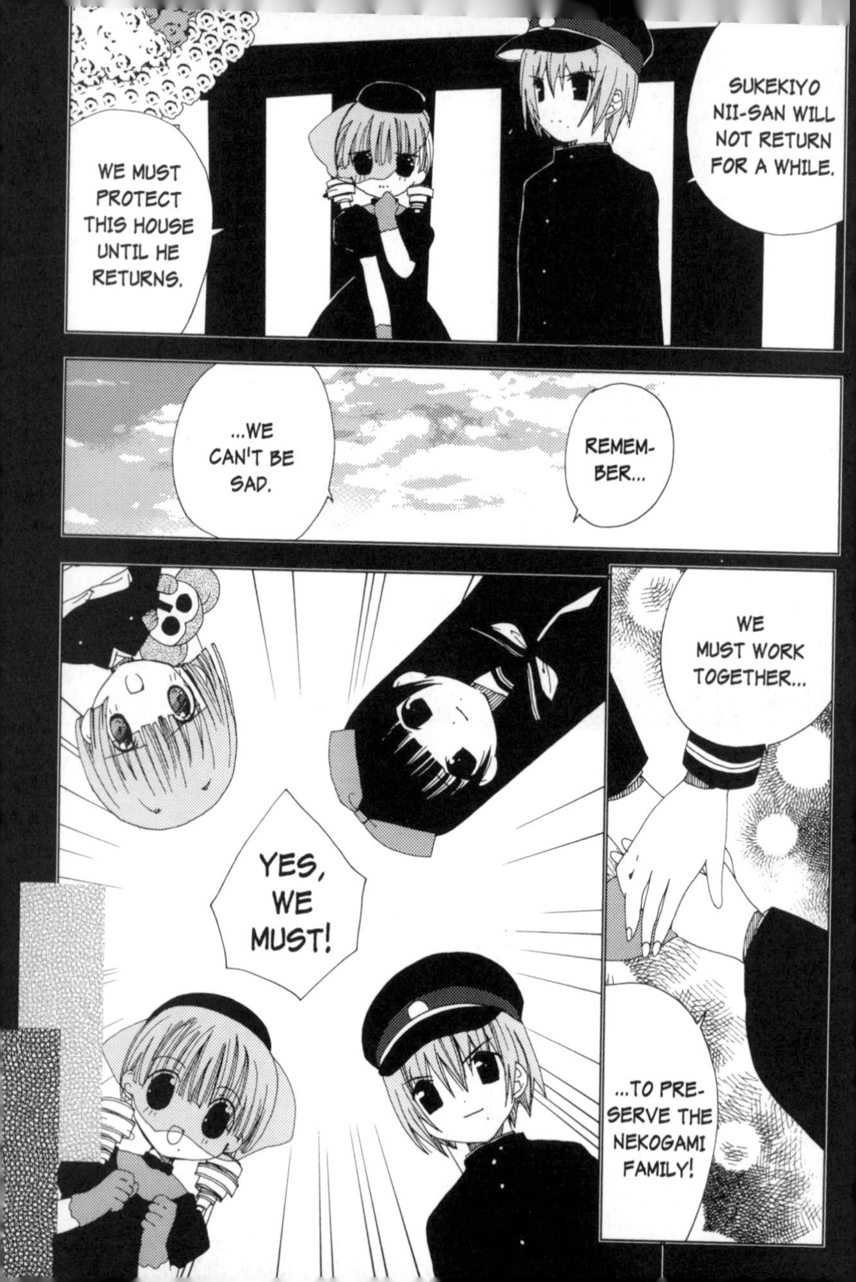
SUKEKIYO NII-SAN WILL NOT RETURN FOR A WHILE.
...
WE MUST PROTECT THIS HOUSE UNTIL HE RETURNS.
REMEM-BER...
...WE CAN'T BE SAD.
WE MUST WORK TOGETHER...
...TO PRE-SERVE THE NEKOGAMI FAMILY!
YES, WE MUST!

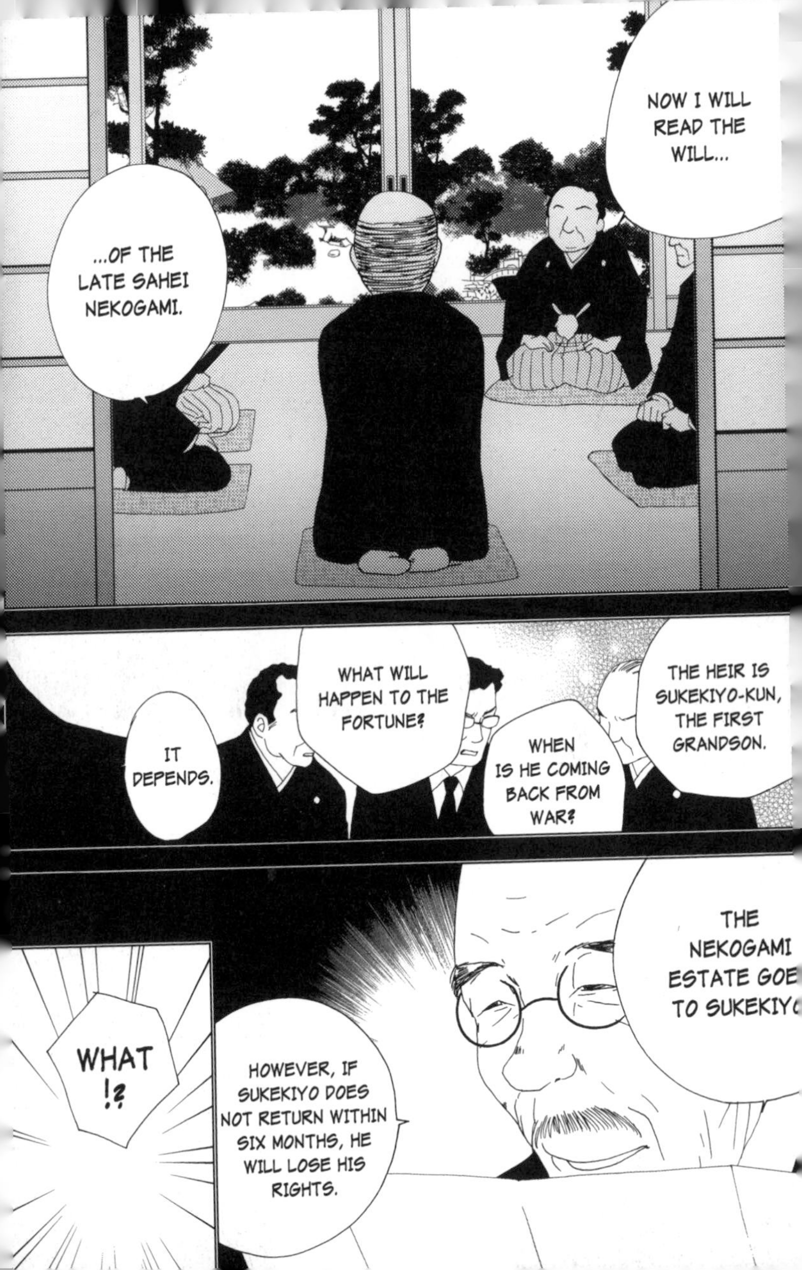
NOW I WILL READ THE WILL...
...OF THE LATE SAHEI NEKOGAMI.
THE HEIR IS SUKEKIYO-KUN, THE FIRST GRANDSON.
WHEN IS HE COMING BACK FROM WAR?
WHAT WILL HAPPEN TO THE FORTUNE?
IT DEPENDS.
THE NEKOGAMI ESTATE GOE TO SUKEKIY
HOWEVER, IF SUKEKIYO DOES NOT RETURN WITHIN SIX MONTHS, HE WILL LOSE HIS RIGHTS.
WHAT !?

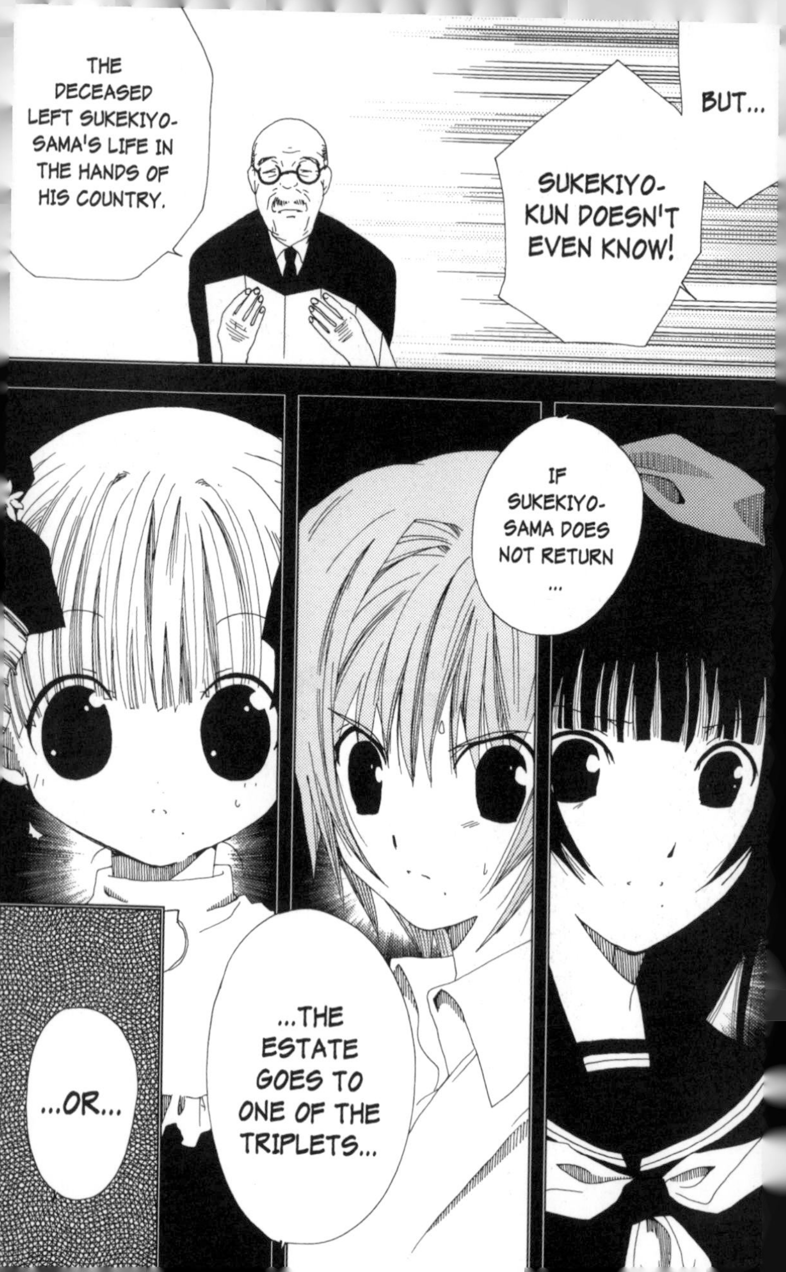
THE DECEASED LEFT SUKEKIYO-SAMA'S LIFE IN THE HANDS OF HIS COUNTRY.
BUT...
SUKEKIYO-KUN DOESN'T EVEN KNOW!
IF SUKEKIYO-SAMA DOES NOT RETURN ...
...THE ESTATE GOES TO ONE OF THE TRIPLETS...
...OR...

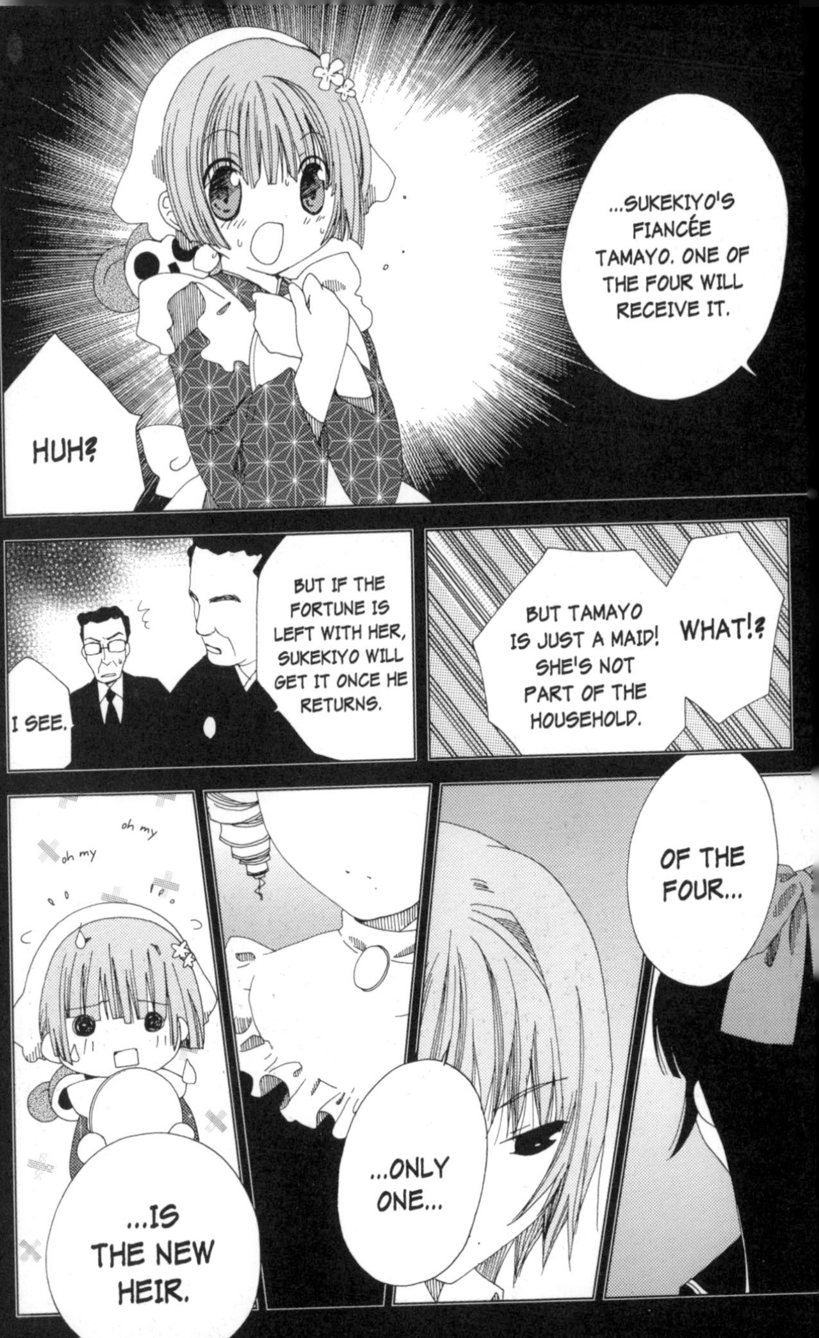
...SUKEKIYO'S FIANCÉE TAMAYO. ONE OF THE FOUR WILL RECEIVE IT.
HUH?
WHAT!?
BUT TAMAYO IS JUST A MAID! SHE'S NOT PART OF THE HOUSEHOLD.
BUT IF THE FORTUNE IS LEFT WITH HER, SUKEKIYO WILL GET IT ONCE HE RETURNS.
I SEE.
OF THE FOUR...
...ONLY ONE...
oh my
oh my
...IS THE NEW HEIR.

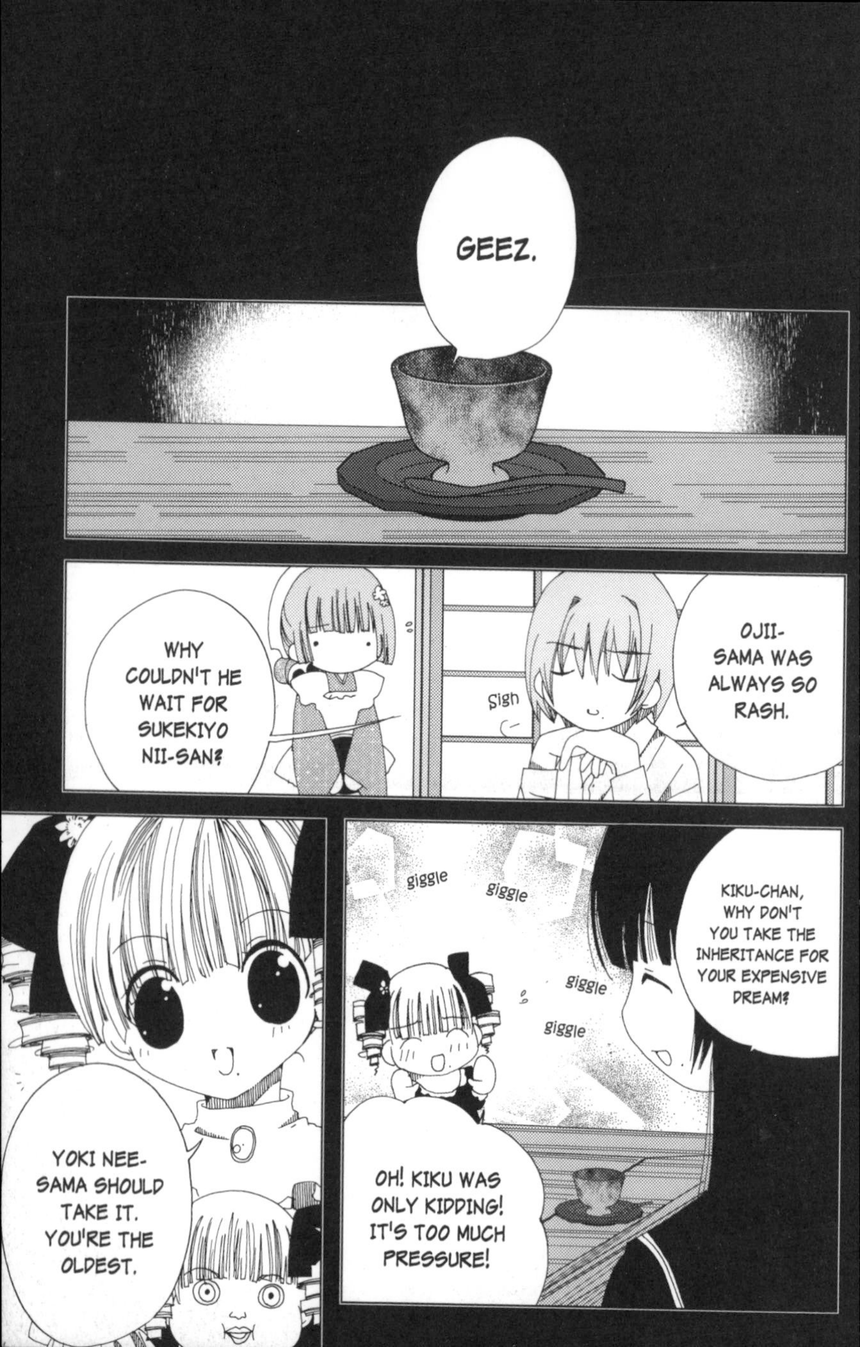
GEEZ.
OJII-SAMA WAS ALWAYS SO RASH.
Sigh
WHY COULDN'T HE WAIT FOR SUKEKIYO NII-SAN?
KIKU-CHAN, WHY DON'T YOU TAKE THE INHERITANCE FOR YOUR EXPENSIVE DREAM?
giggle
giggle
giggle
giggle
OH! KIKU WAS ONLY KIDDING! IT'S TOO MUCH PRESSURE!
YOKI NEE-SAMA SHOULD TAKE IT. YOU'RE THE OLDEST.

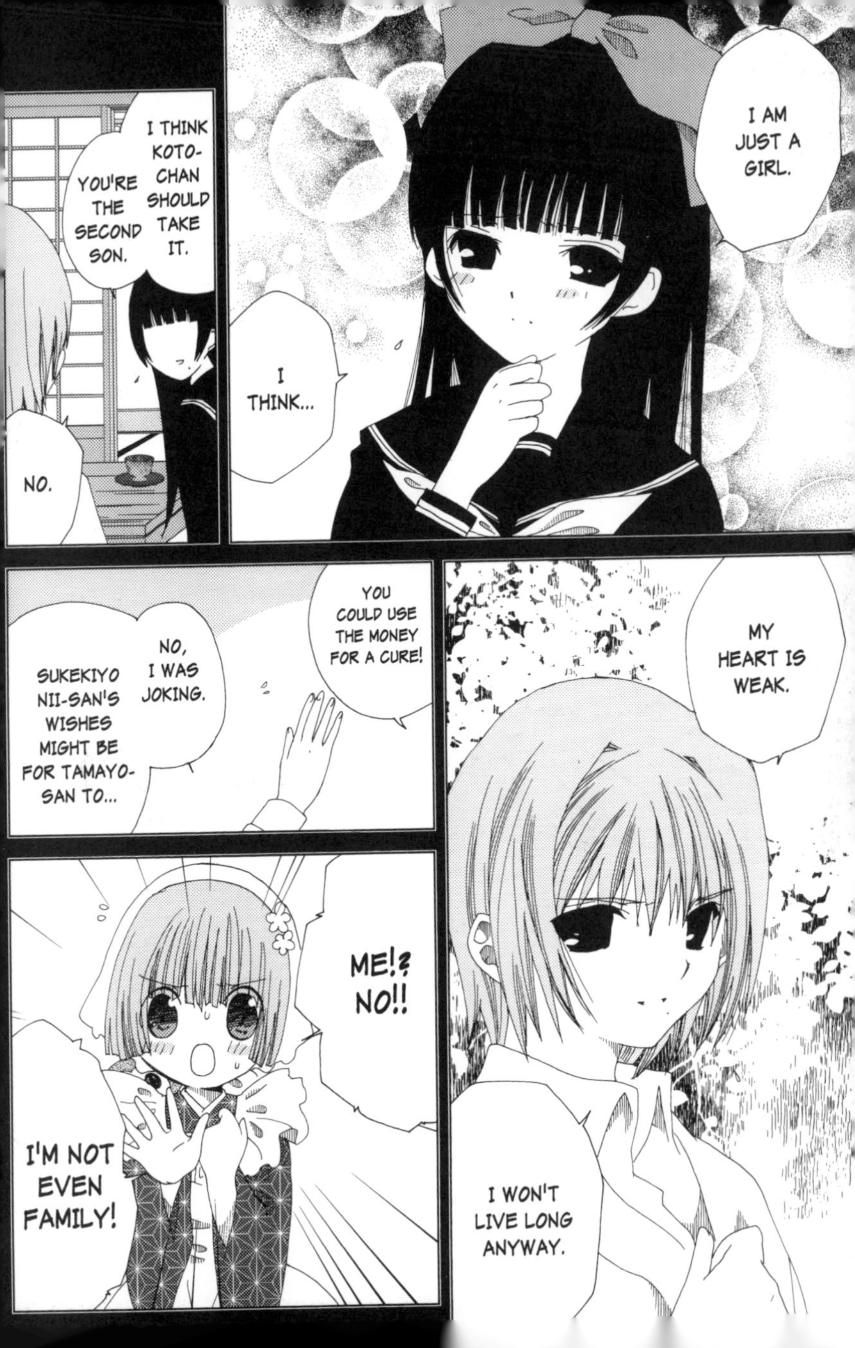

I AM JUST A GIRL.
I THINK...
I THINK KOTO-CHAN SHOULD TAKE IT.
YOU'RE THE SECOND SON.
NO.
MY HEART IS WEAK.
I WON'T LIVE LONG ANYWAY.
YOU COULD USE THE MONEY FOR A CURE!
NO, I WAS JOKING.
SUKEKIYO NII-SAN'S WISHES MIGHT BE FOR TAMAYO-SAN TO...
ME!? NO!!
I'M NOT EVEN FAMILY!

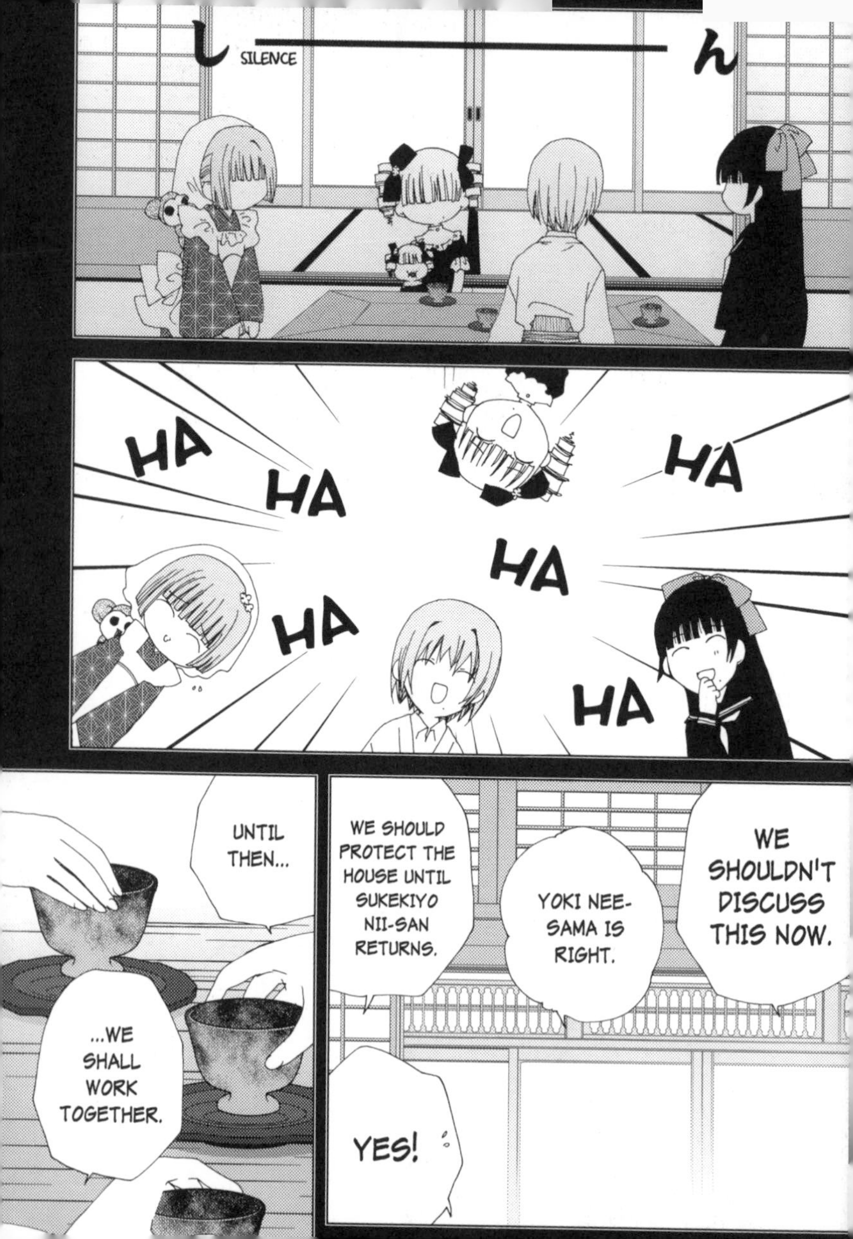
し——ん
SILENCE
HA
HA
HA
HA
HA
HA
WE SHOULDN'T DISCUSS THIS NOW.
YOKI NEE-SAMA IS RIGHT.
WE SHOULD PROTECT THE HOUSE UNTIL SUKEKIYO NII-SAN RETURNS.
YES!
UNTIL THEN...
...WE SHALL WORK TOGETHER.

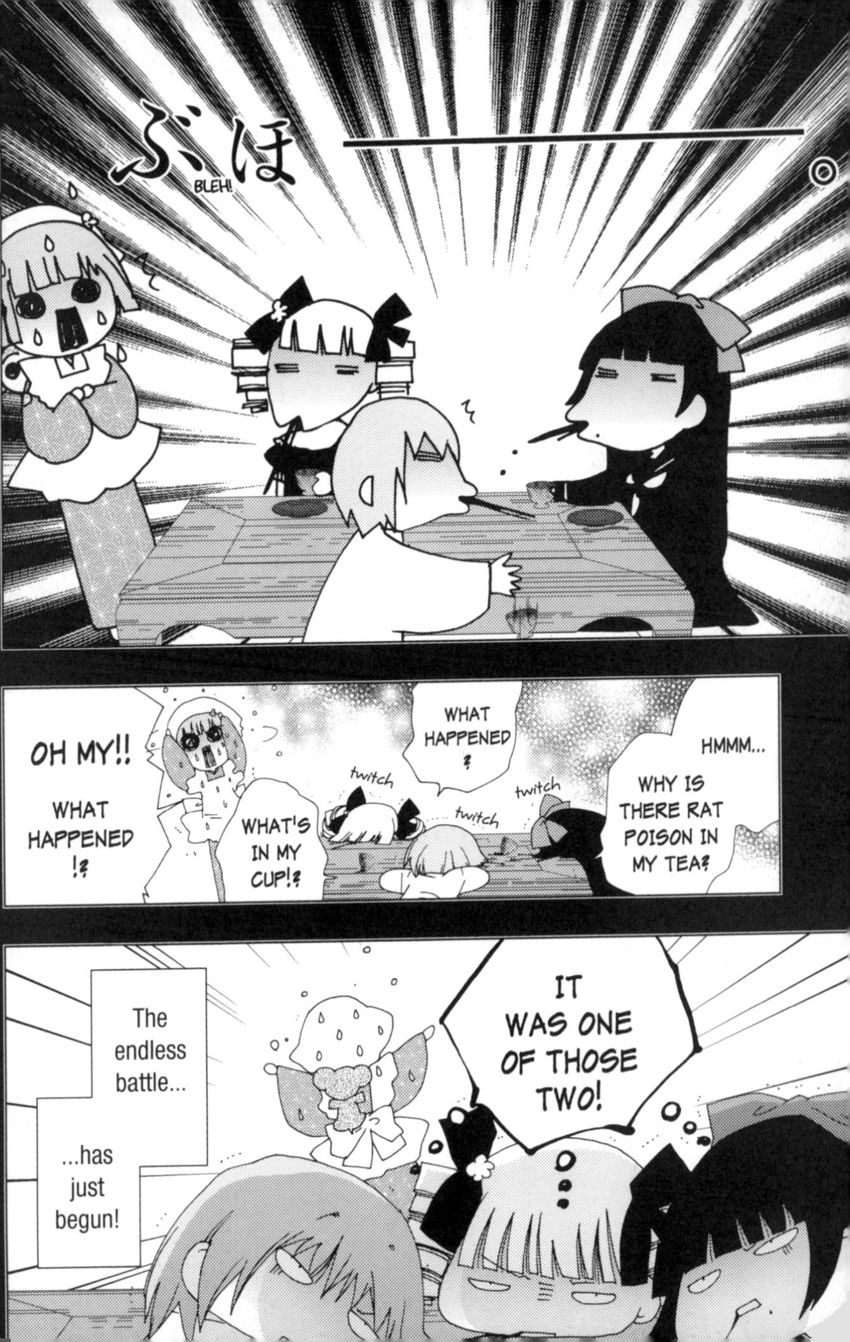
ぶほ
BLEH!
HMMM...
WHY IS THERE RAT POISON IN MY TEA?
twitch
WHAT HAPPENED?
twitch
twitch
WHAT'S IN MY CUP!?
OH MY!!
WHAT HAPPENED!?
IT WAS ONE OF THOSE TWO!
The endless battle...
...has just begun!

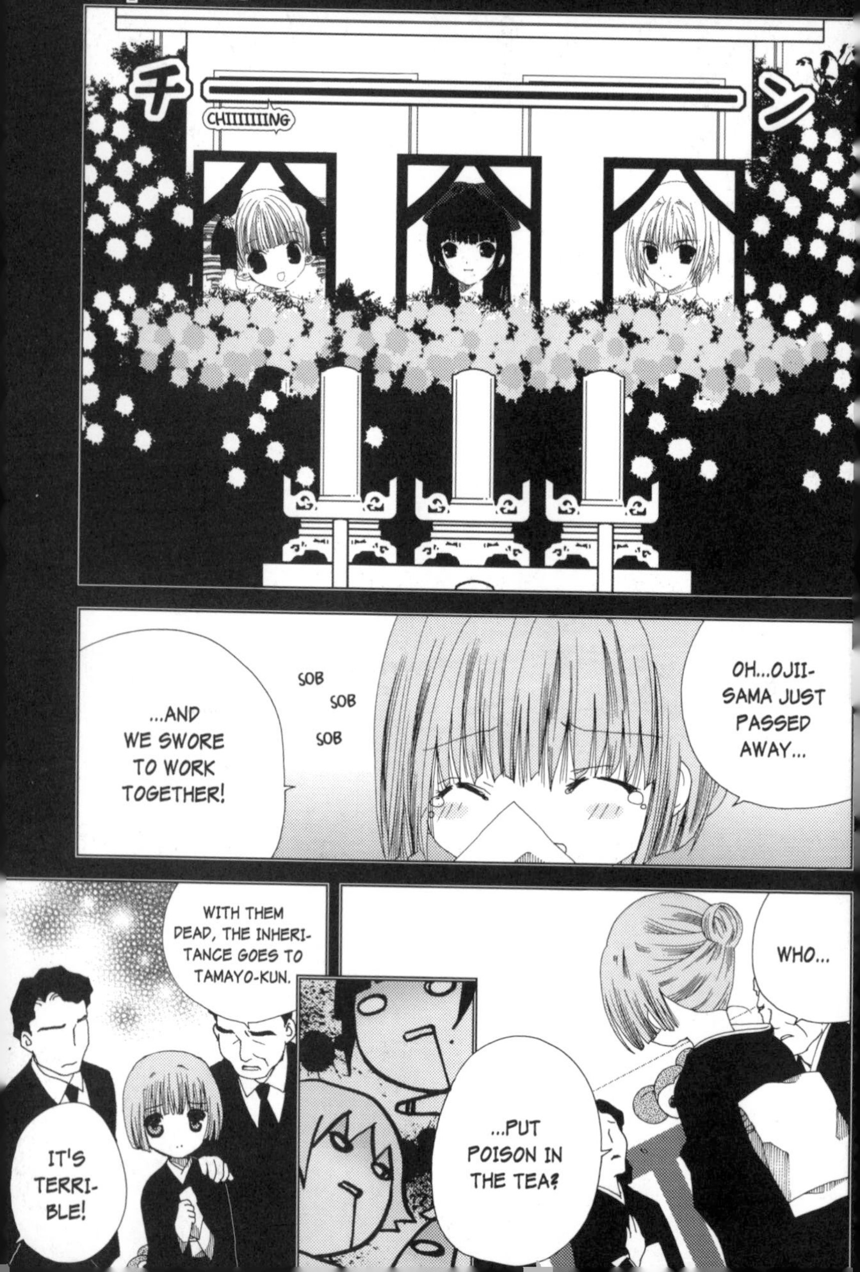
チーン
CHIIIIIIING
OH...OJII-SAMA JUST PASSED AWAY...
SOB SOB SOB
...AND WE SWORE TO WORK TOGETHER!
WHO...
...PUT POISON IN THE TEA?
WITH THEM DEAD, THE INHERITANCE GOES TO TAMAYO-KUN.
IT'S TERRIBLE!

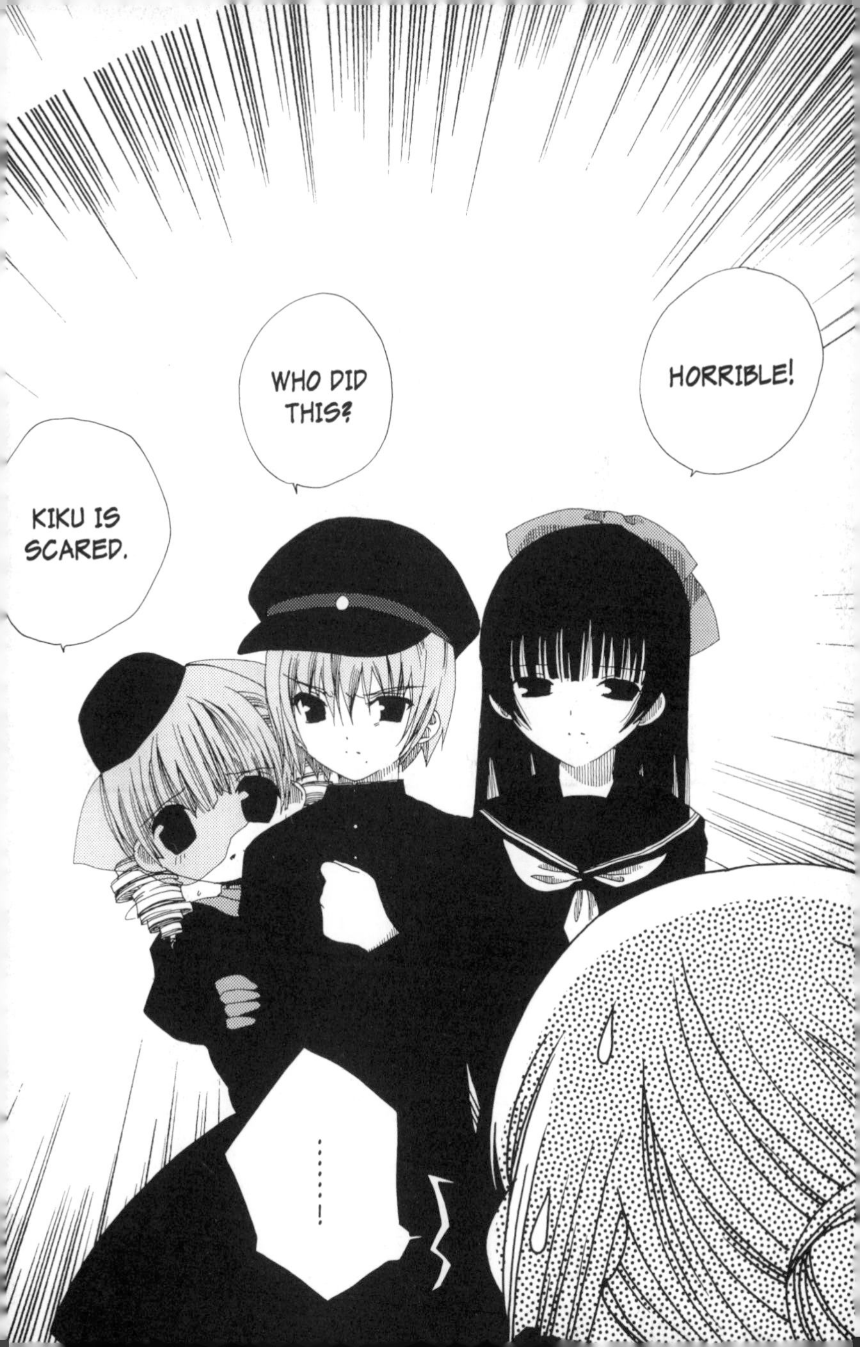
HORRIBLE!
WHO DID THIS?
KIKU IS SCARED.
......!

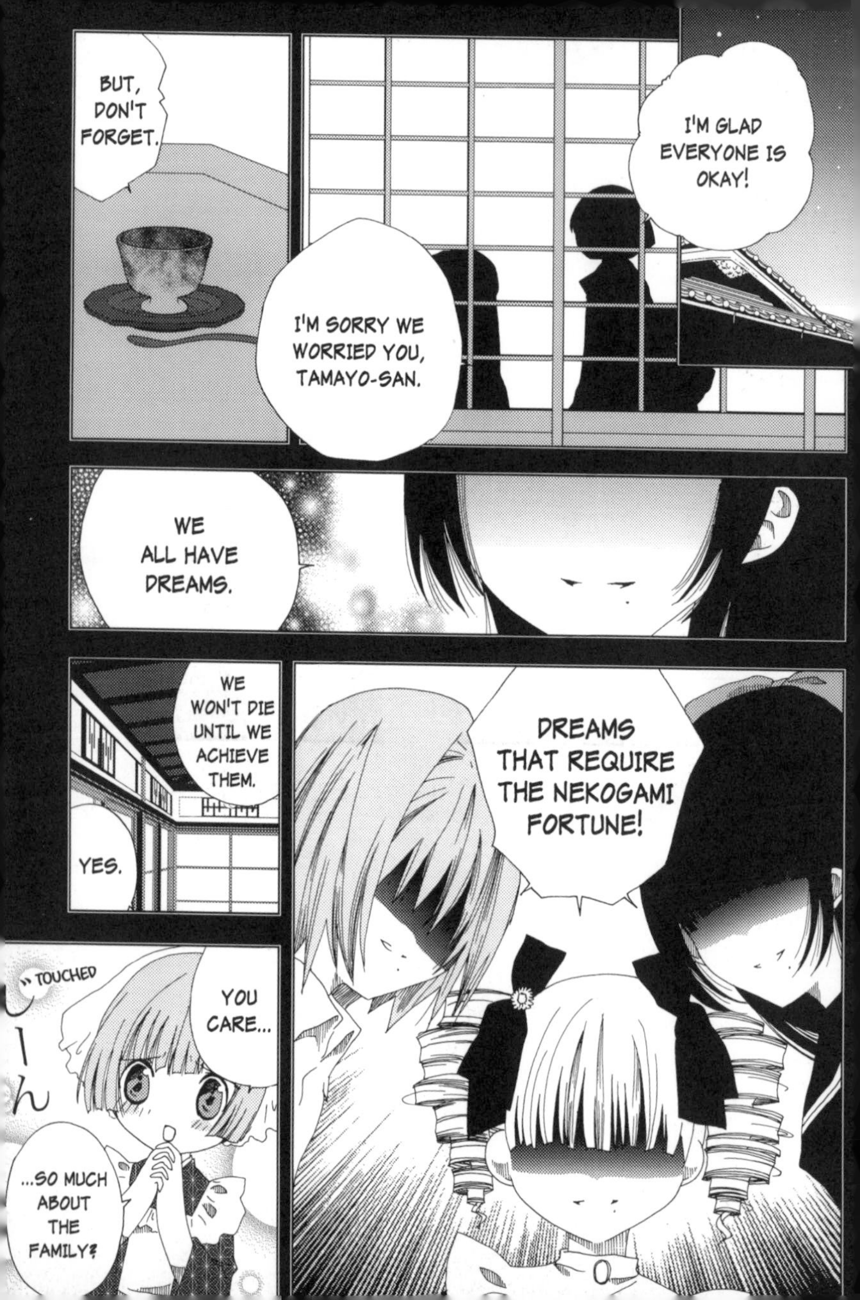

I'M GLAD EVERYONE IS OKAY!
I'M SORRY WE WORRIED YOU, TAMAYO-SAN.
BUT, DON'T FORGET.
WE ALL HAVE DREAMS.
DREAMS THAT REQUIRE THE NEKOGAMI FORTUNE!
WE WON'T DIE UNTIL WE ACHIEVE THEM.
YES.
TOUCHED
YOU CARE...
...SO MUCH ABOUT THE FAMILY?

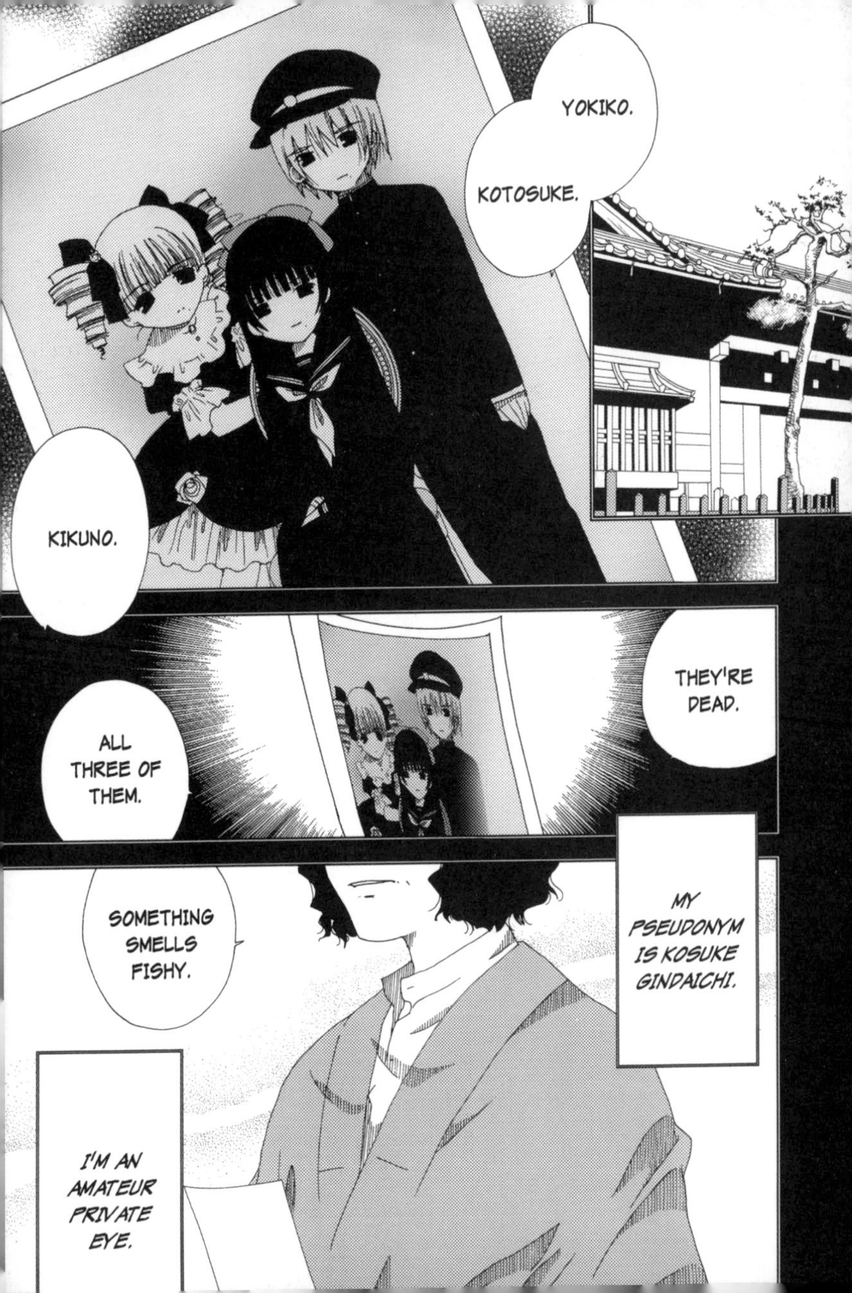
YOKIKO.
KOTOSUKE.
KIKUNO.
THEY'RE DEAD.
ALL THREE OF THEM.
MY PSEUDONYM IS KOSUKE GINDAICHI.
SOMETHING SMELLS FISHY.
I'M AN AMATEUR PRIVATE EYE.

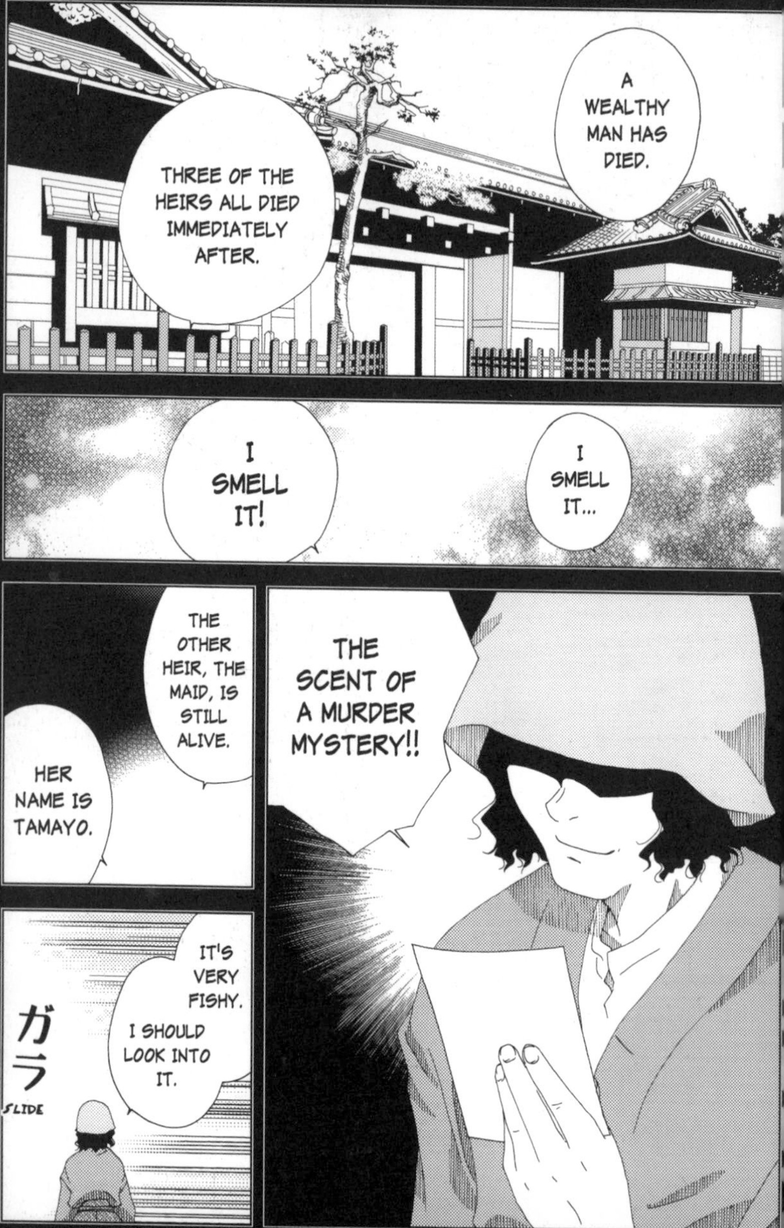
A WEALTHY MAN HAS DIED.
THREE OF THE HEIRS ALL DIED IMMEDIATELY AFTER.
I SMELL IT...
I SMELL IT!
THE SCENT OF A MURDER MYSTERY!!
THE OTHER HEIR, THE MAID, IS STILL ALIVE.
HER NAME IS TAMAYO.
IT'S VERY FISHY.
I SHOULD LOOK INTO IT.
ガラ
SLIDE

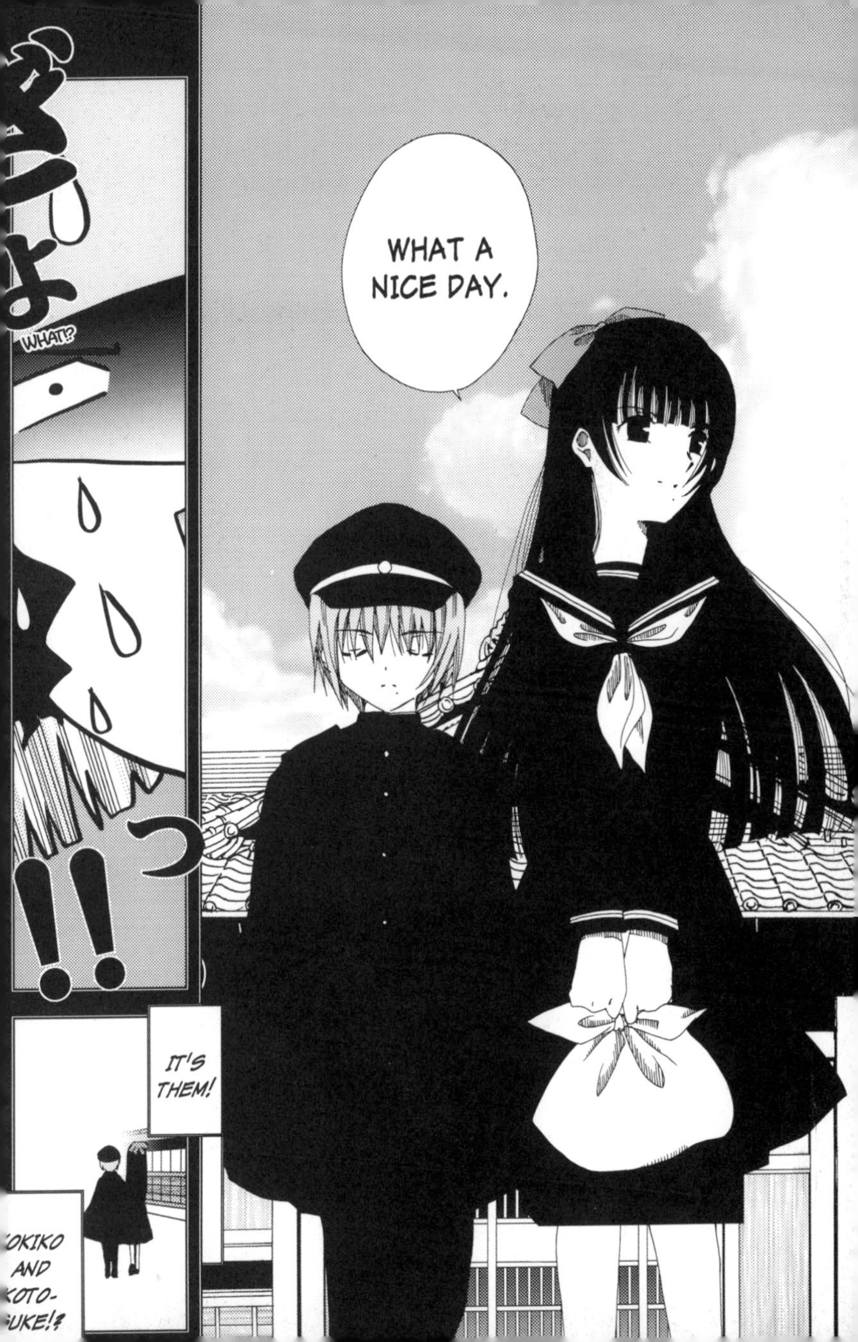
WHAT A NICE DAY.
WHAT!?
IT'S THEM!
OKIKO AND KOTO- UKE!?

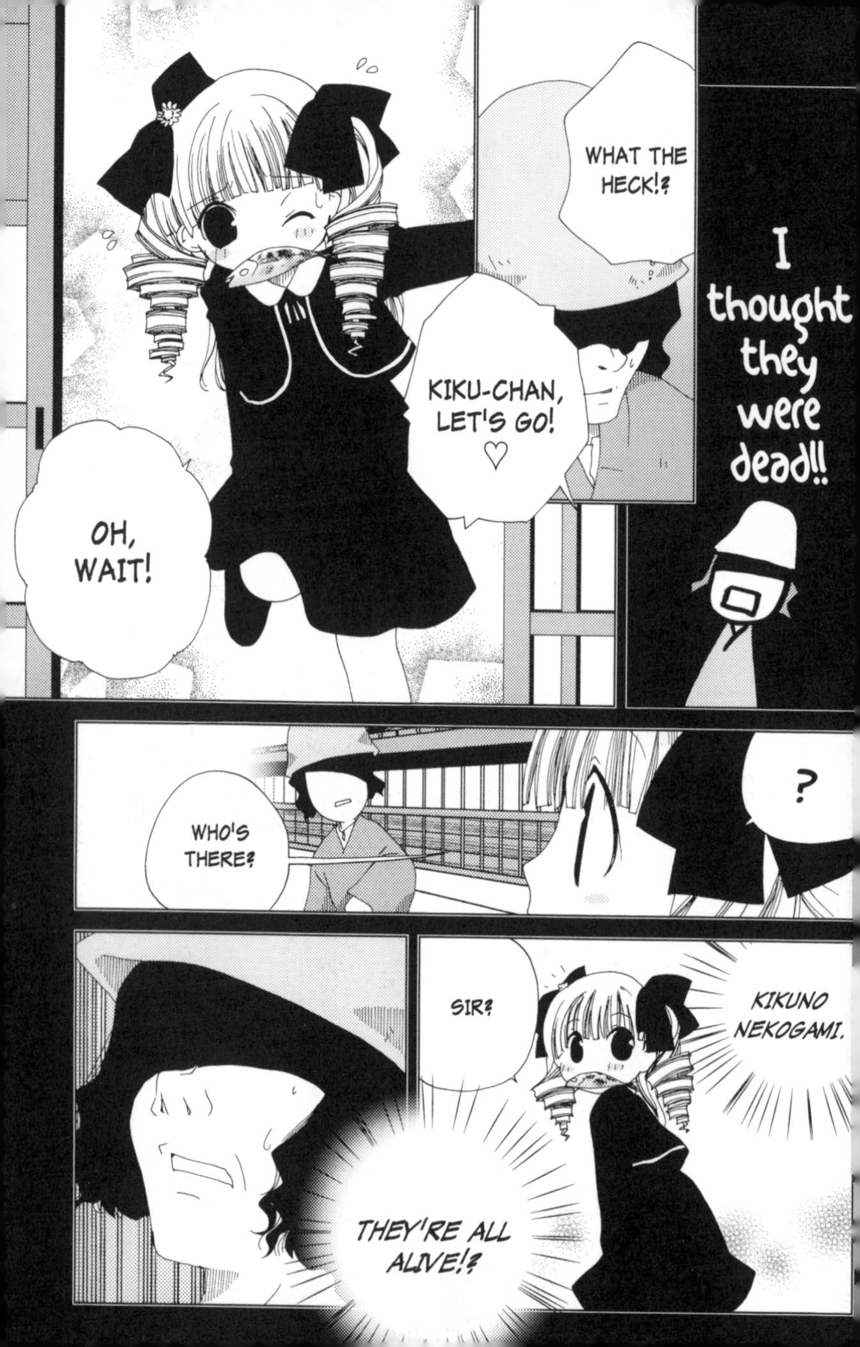
WHAT THE HECK!?
I thought they were dead!!
KIKU-CHAN, LET'S GO! ♡
OH, WAIT!
?
WHO'S THERE?
KIKUNO NEKOGAMI.
SIR?
THEY'RE ALL ALIVE!?

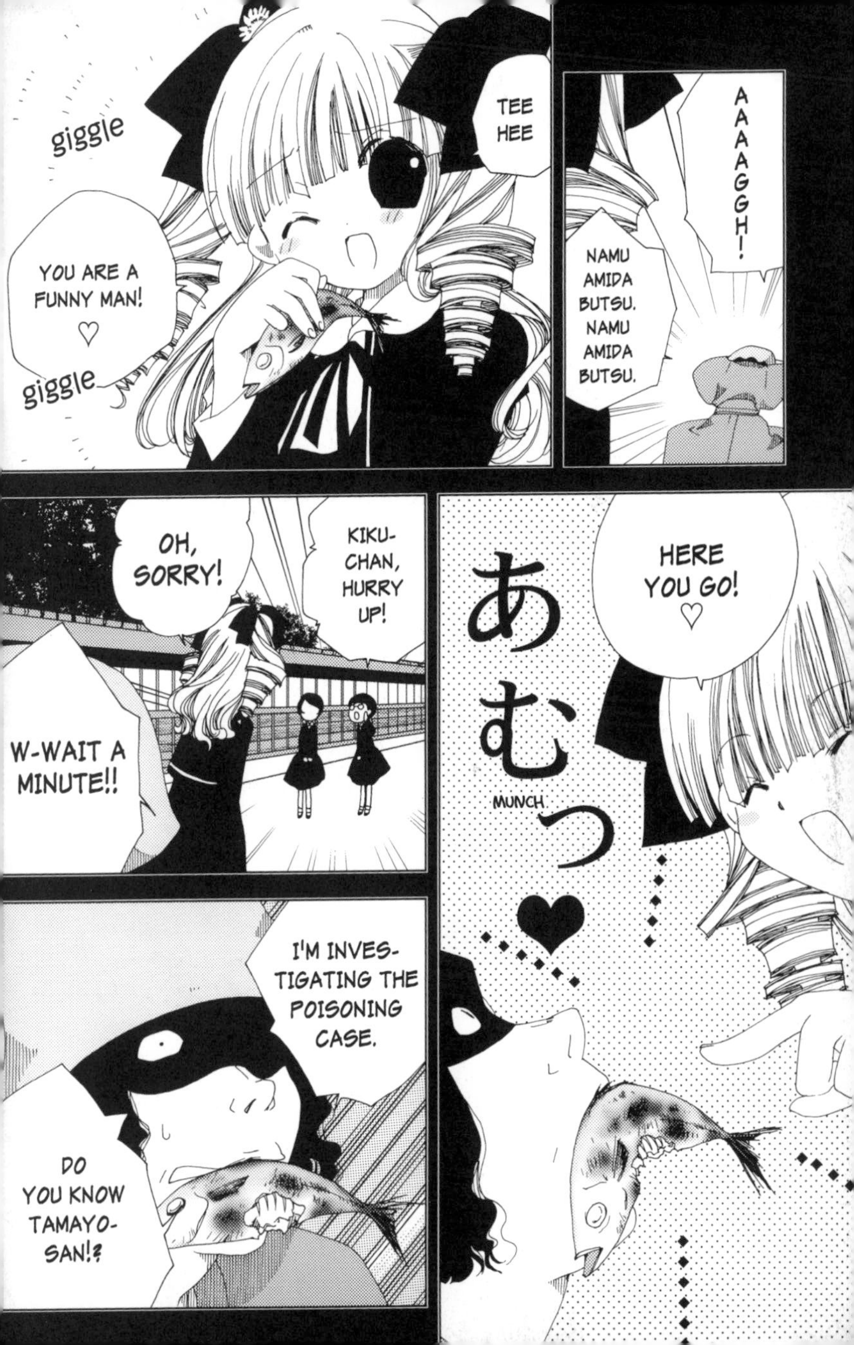
AAAAAGH!
NAMU AMIDA BUTSU. NAMU AMIDA BUTSU.
TEE HEE
giggle
YOU ARE A FUNNY MAN! ♡
giggle
HERE YOU GO! ♡
あむっ
MUNCH
KIKU-CHAN, HURRY UP!
OH, SORRY!
W-WAIT A MINUTE!!
I'M INVES-TIGATING THE POISONING CASE.
DO YOU KNOW TAMAYO-SAN!?

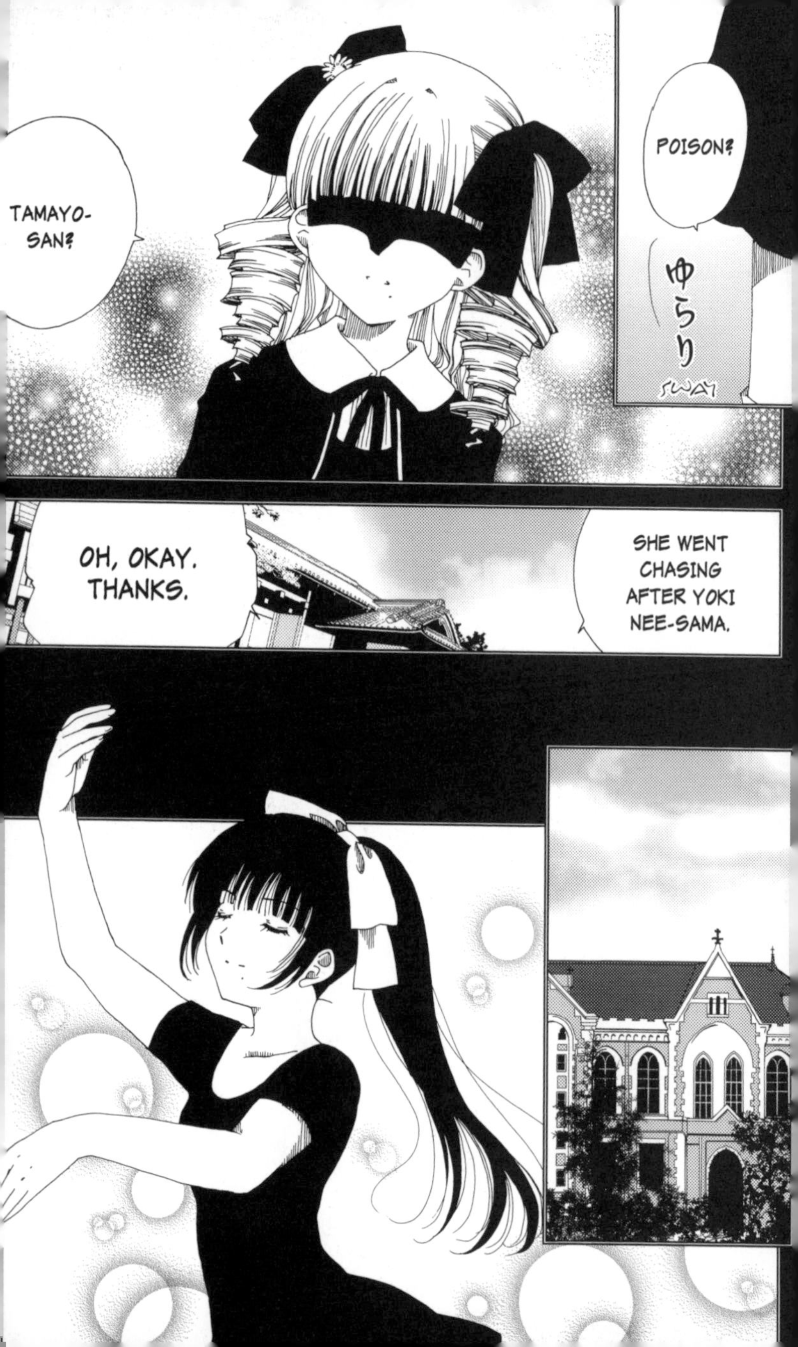
POISON?
ゆらり
SWAY
TAMAYO-SAN?
SHE WENT CHASING AFTER YOKI NEE-SAMA.
OH, OKAY. THANKS.

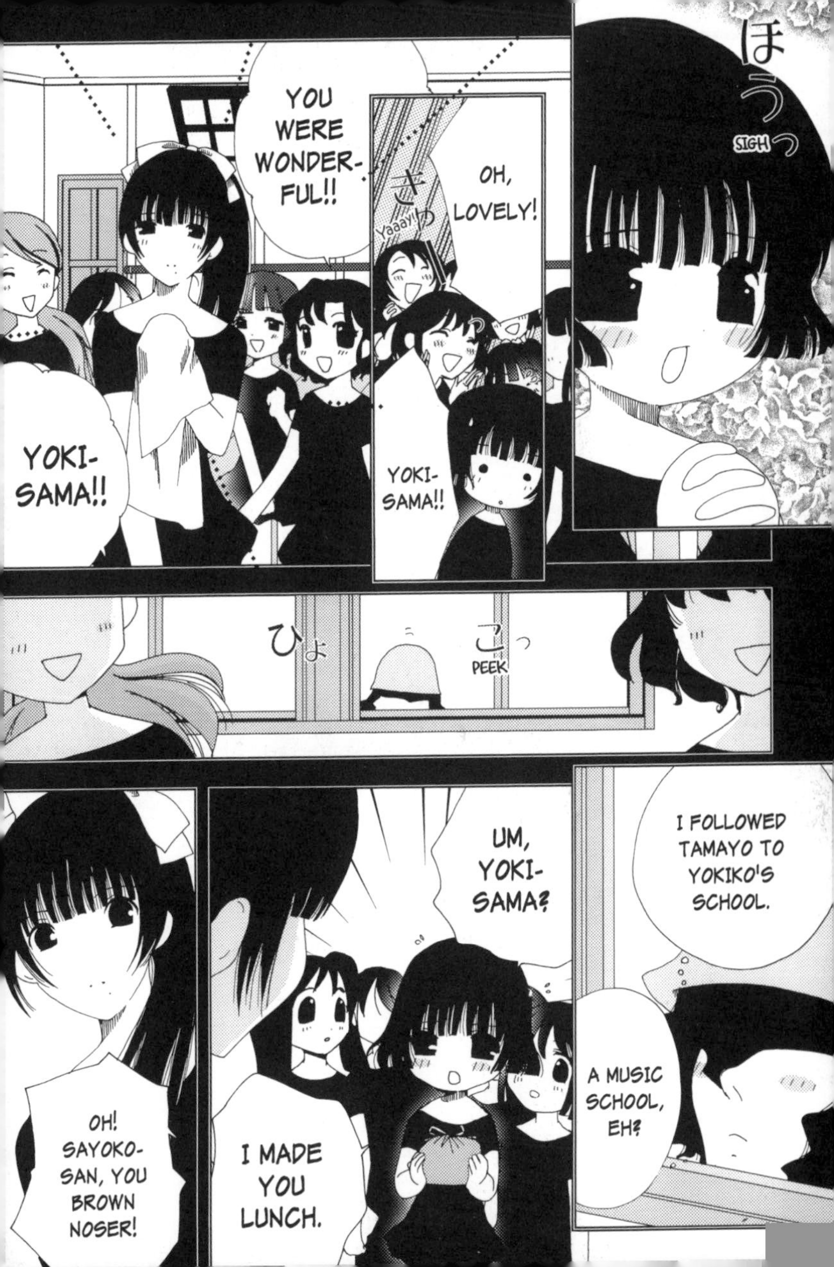
ほうっ
SIGH
きゃ
Yaaay!
OH, LOVELY!
YOKI-SAMA!!
YOU WERE WONDERFUL!!
YOKI-SAMA!!
ひょこっ
PEEK
I FOLLOWED TAMAYO TO YOKIKO'S SCHOOL.
A MUSIC SCHOOL, EH?
UM, YOKI-SAMA?
I MADE YOU LUNCH.
OH! SAYOKO-SAN, YOU BROWN NOSER!

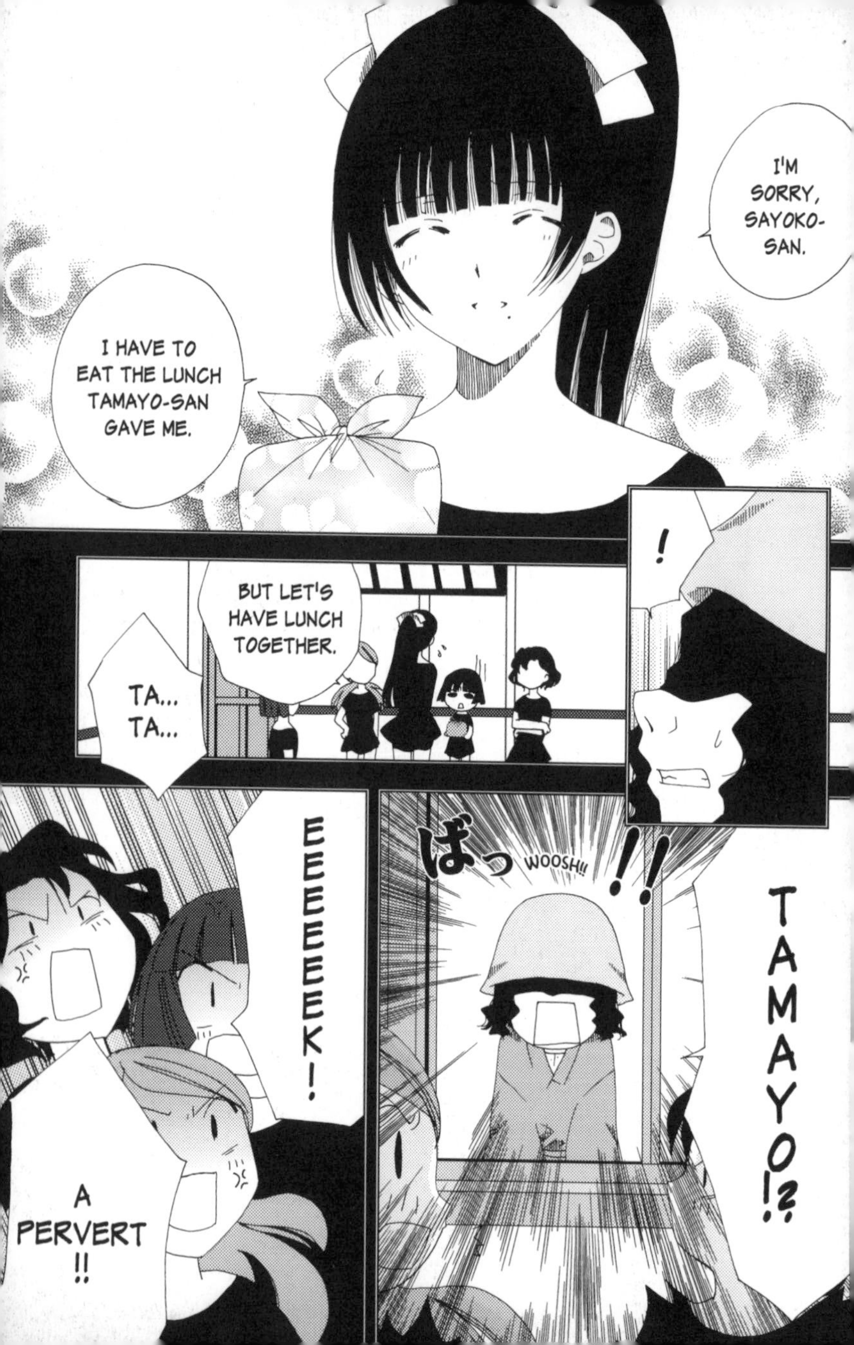
I'M SORRY, SAYOKO-SAN.
I HAVE TO EAT THE LUNCH TAMAYO-SAN GAVE ME.
!
BUT LET'S HAVE LUNCH TOGETHER.
TA... TA...
ばっ
WOOSH!!
!!
TAMAYO!?
EEEEEEEK!
A PERVERT!!

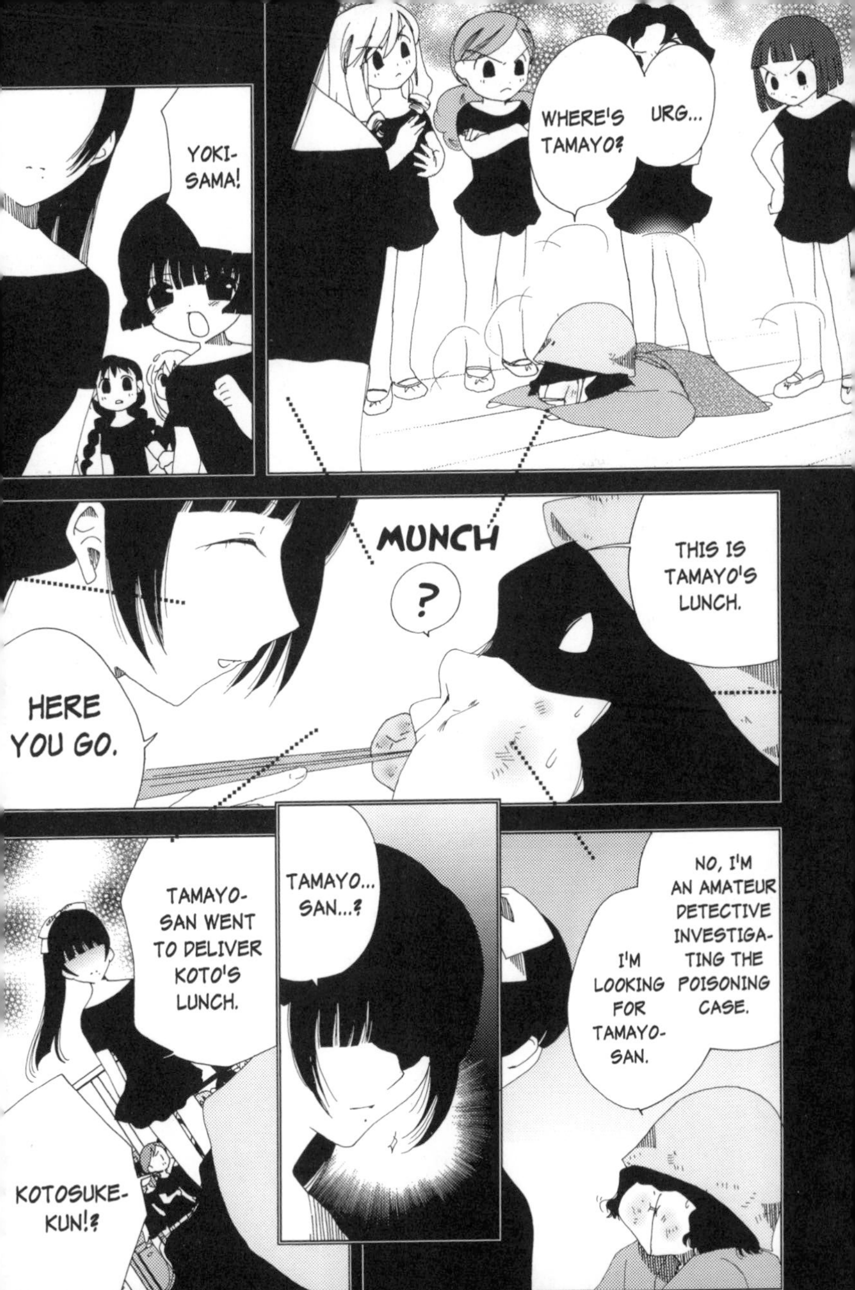
URG...
WHERE'S TAMAYO?
YOKI-SAMA!
THIS IS TAMAYO'S LUNCH.
MUNCH
?
HERE YOU GO.
NO, I'M AN AMATEUR DETECTIVE INVESTIGA-TING THE POISONING CASE.
I'M LOOKING FOR TAMAYO-SAN.
TAMAYO... SAN...?
TAMAYO-SAN WENT TO DELIVER KOTO'S LUNCH.
KOTOSUKE-KUN!?

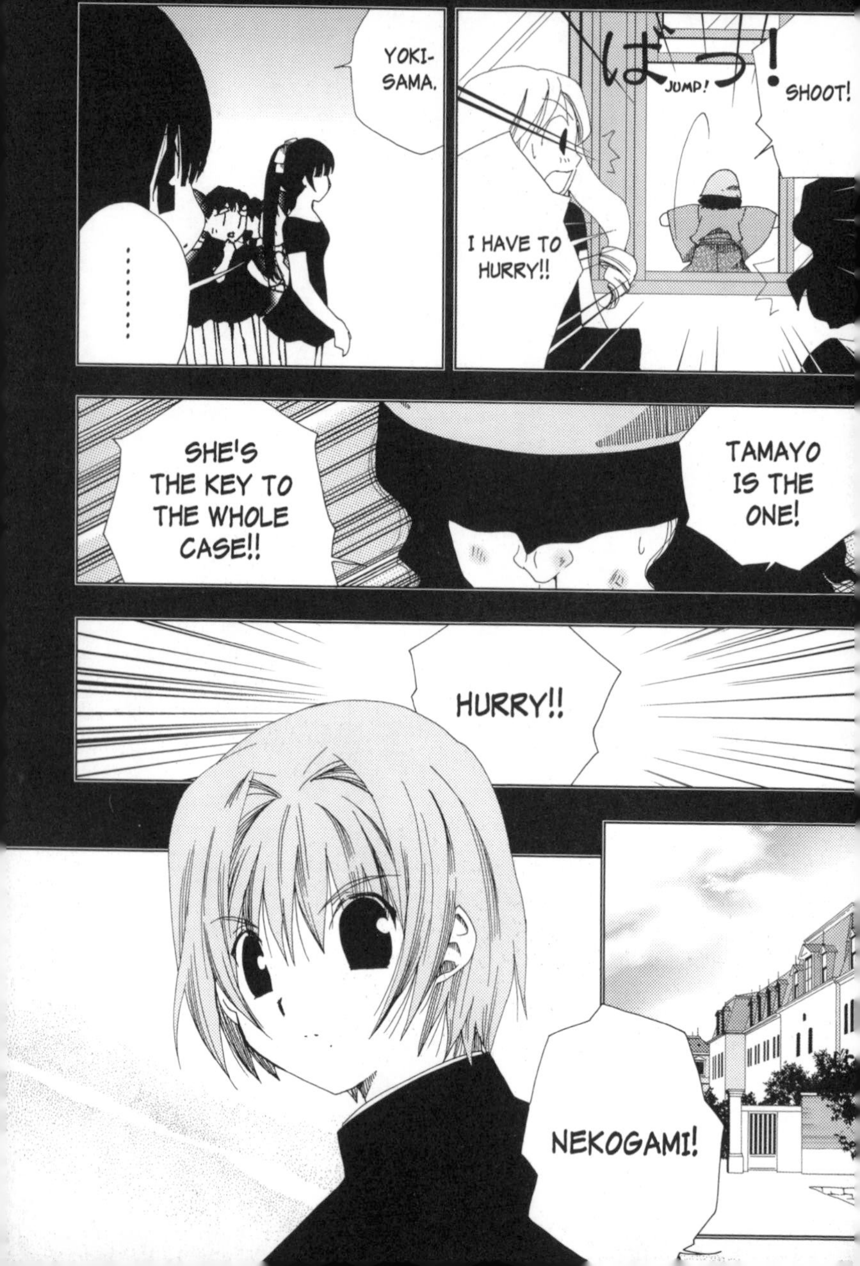

ばっ!
JUMP!
SHOOT!
I HAVE TO HURRY!!
YOKI-SAMA.
......
TAMAYO IS THE ONE!
SHE'S THE KEY TO THE WHOLE CASE!!
HURRY!!
NEKOGAMI!

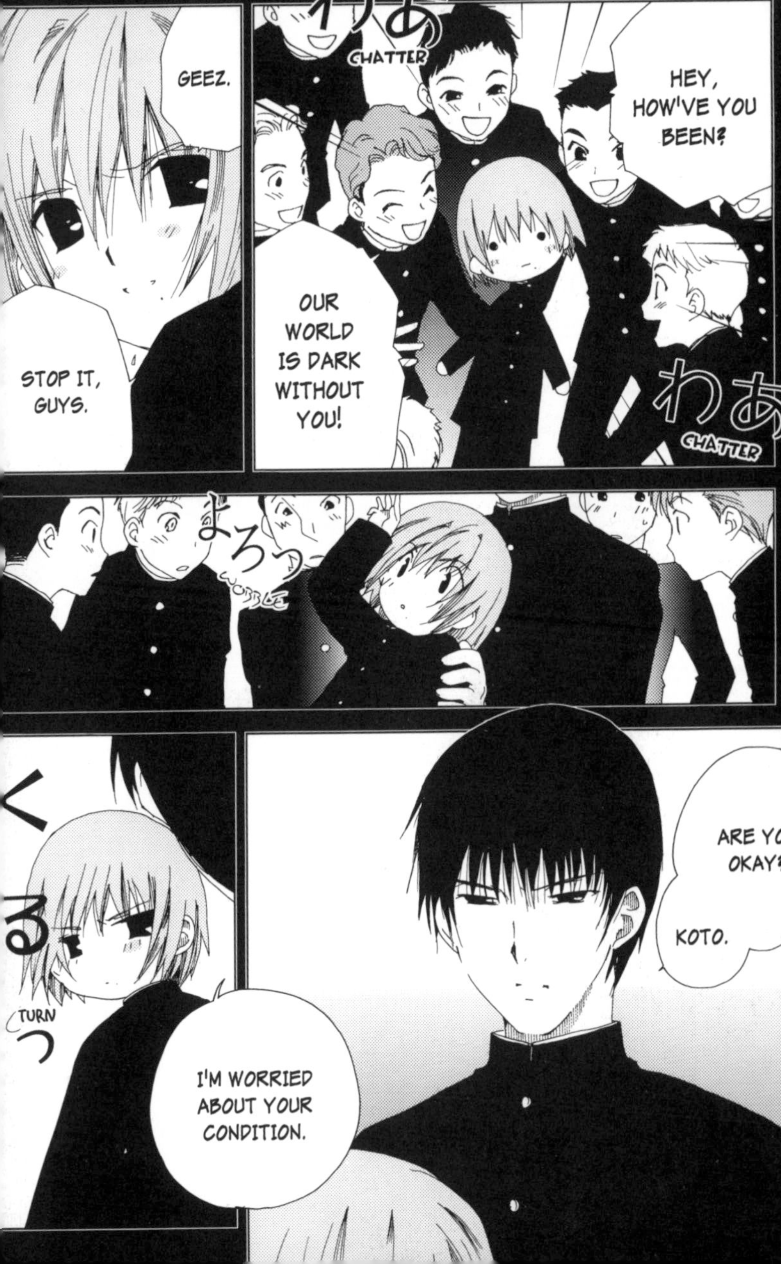
HEY, HOW'VE YOU BEEN?
わあ
CHATTER
わあ
CHATTER
OUR WORLD IS DARK WITHOUT YOU!
GEEZ.
STOP IT, GUYS.
よろっ
WOBBLE
ARE YOU OKAY?
KOTO.
くるっ
TURN
I'M WORRIED ABOUT YOUR CONDITION.

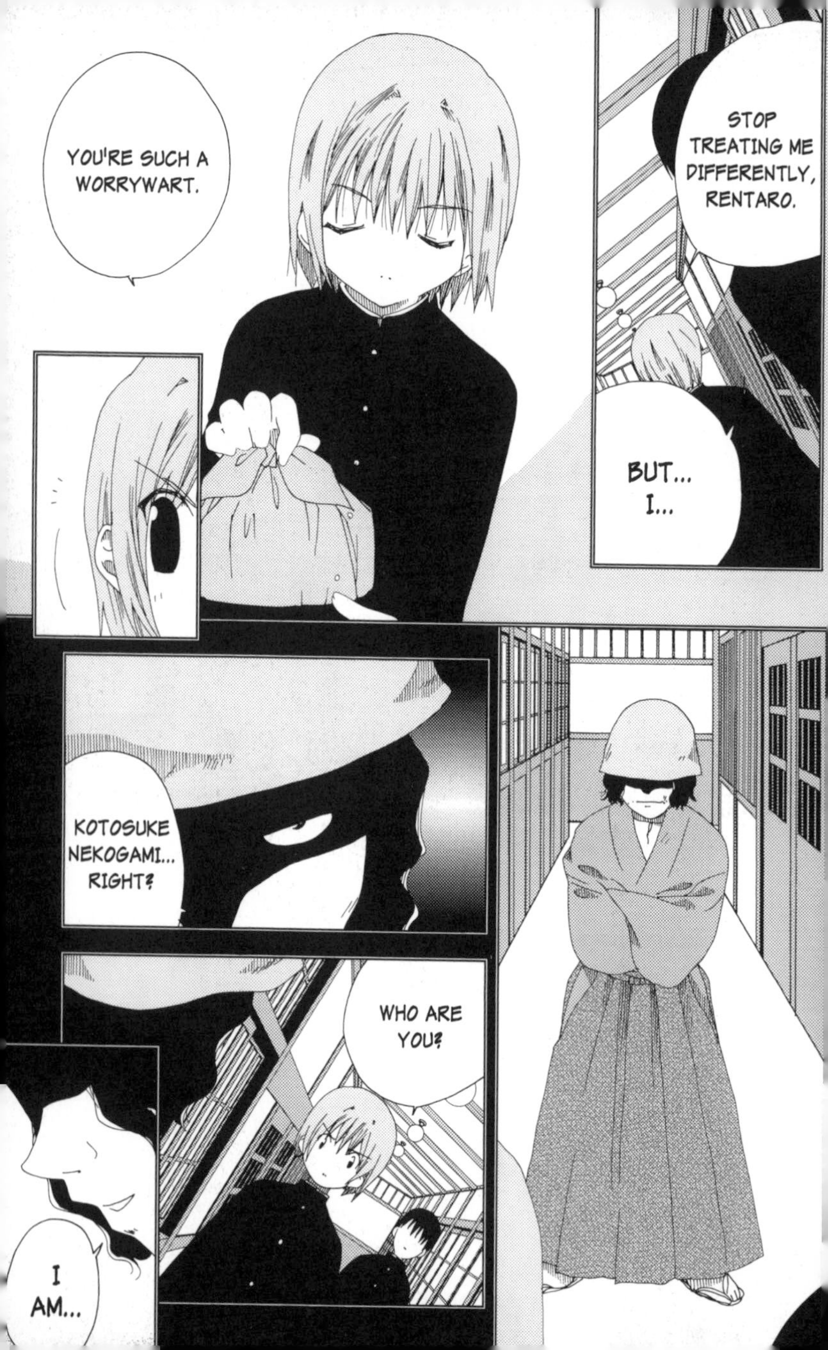
STOP TREATING ME DIFFERENTLY, RENTARO.
BUT... I...
YOU'RE SUCH A WORRYWART.
KOTOSUKE NEKOGAMI... RIGHT?
WHO ARE YOU?
I AM...

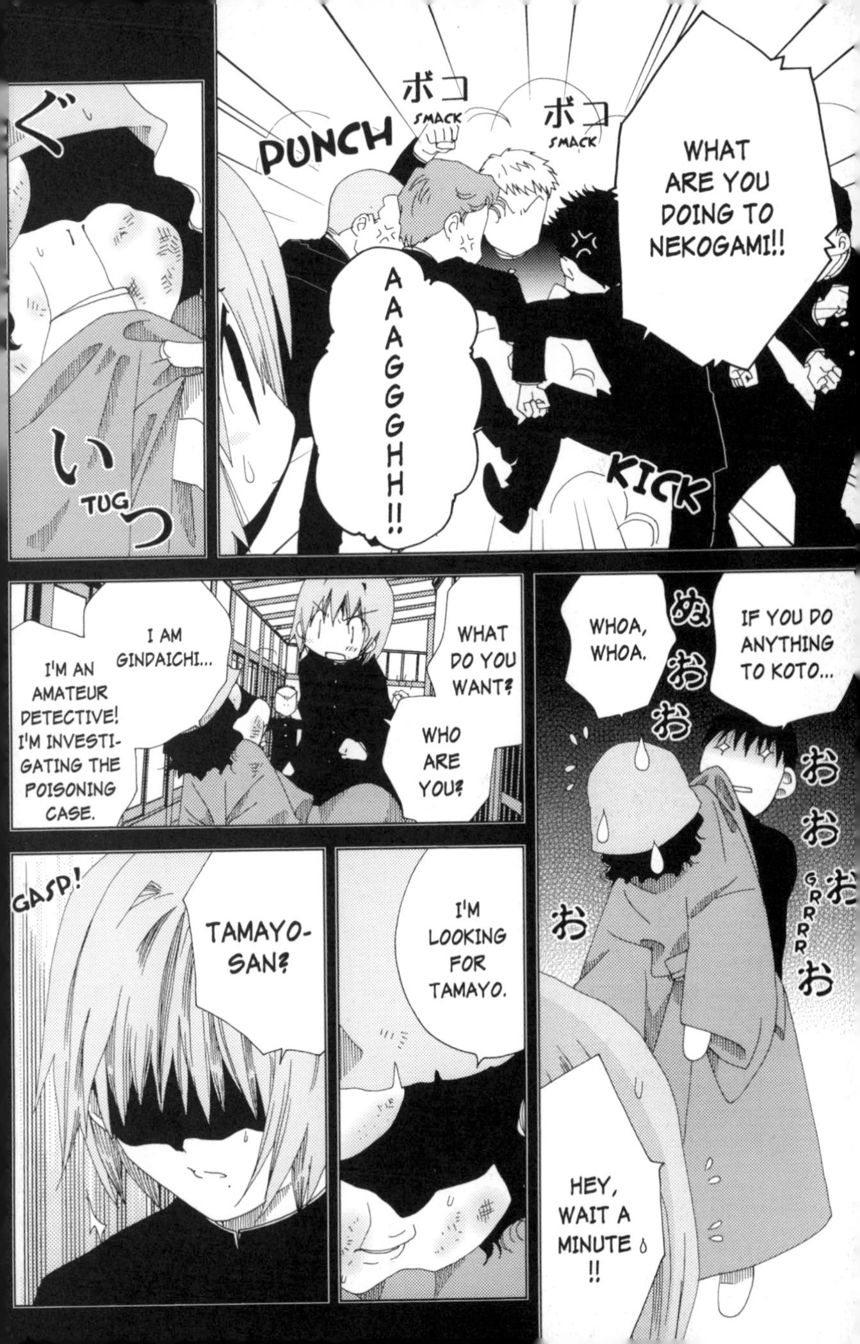
WHAT ARE YOU DOING TO NEKOGAMI!!
ボコ
SMACK
ボコ
SMACK
PUNCH
AAAAGGGHH!!
KICK
ぐ
い
TUG
つ
IF YOU DO ANYTHING TO KOTO...
WHOA, WHOA.
ぬおおおおおおおお
GRRRR
HEY, WAIT A MINUTE!!
WHAT DO YOU WANT?
WHO ARE YOU?
I AM GINDAICHI...
I'M AN AMATEUR DETECTIVE! I'M INVESTI-GATING THE POISONING CASE.
I'M LOOKING FOR TAMAYO.
GASP!
TAMAYO-SAN?

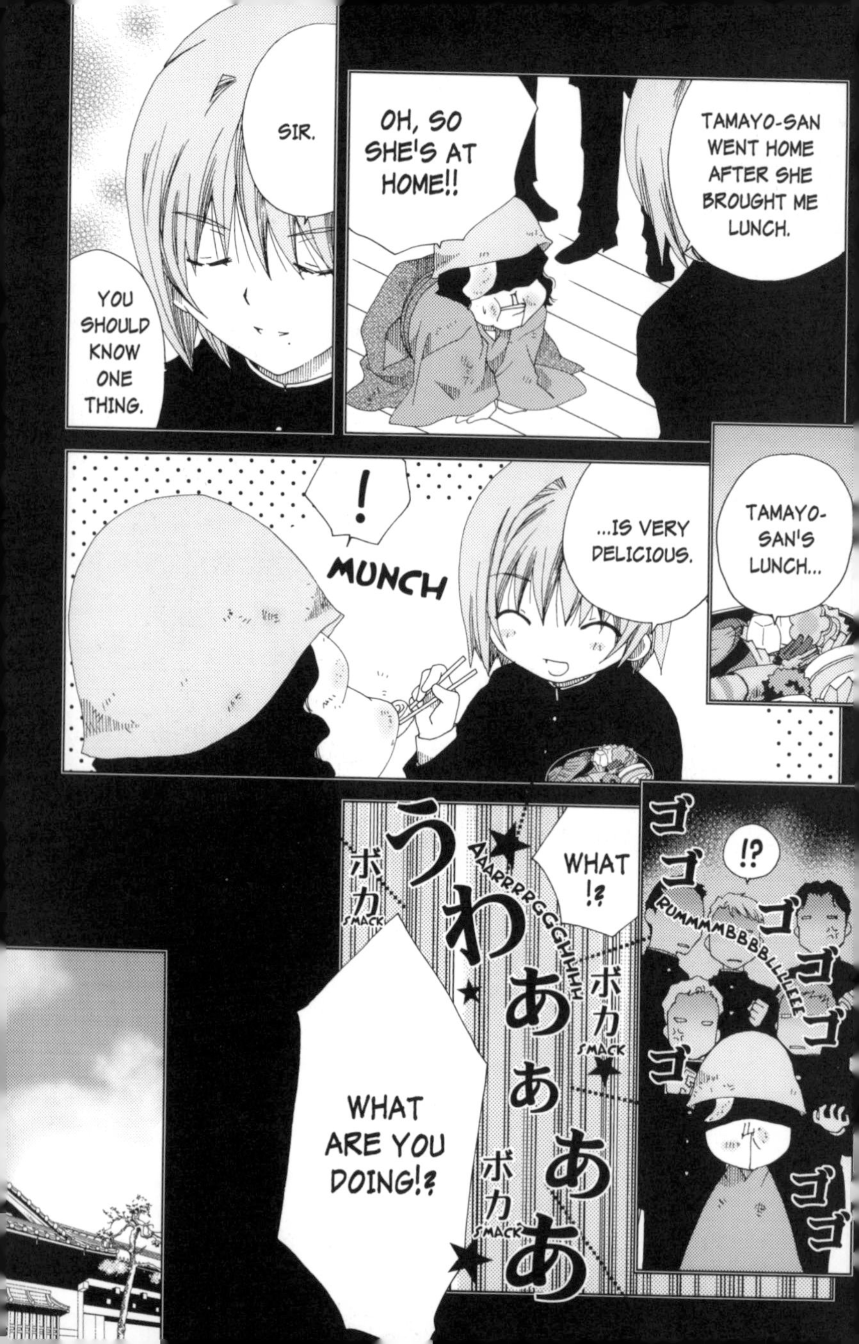
TAMAYO-SAN WENT HOME AFTER SHE BROUGHT ME LUNCH.
OH, SO SHE'S AT HOME!!
SIR.
YOU SHOULD KNOW ONE THING.
TAMAYO-SAN'S LUNCH...
...IS VERY DELICIOUS.
!
MUNCH
!?
ゴゴゴ
ゴゴゴ
RUMMMMBBBBLLLEEE
WHAT!?
うわあぁああ
AAARRRRGGGHHHH
ボカ SMACK
ボカ SMACK
ボカ SMACK
WHAT ARE YOU DOING!?

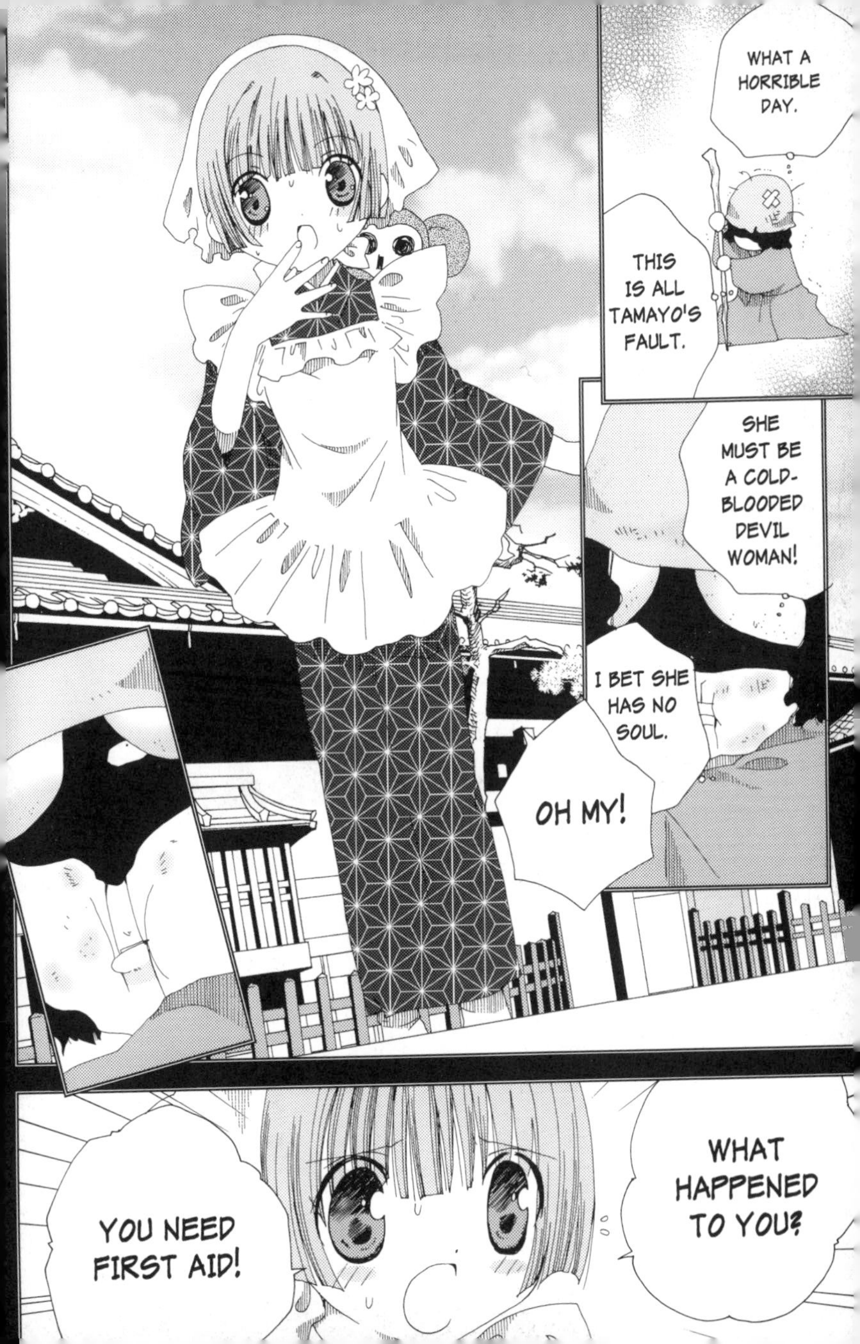
WHAT A HORRIBLE DAY.
THIS IS ALL TAMAYO'S FAULT.
SHE MUST BE A COLD-BLOODED DEVIL WOMAN!
I BET SHE HAS NO SOUL.
OH MY!
WHAT HAPPENED TO YOU?
YOU NEED FIRST AID!

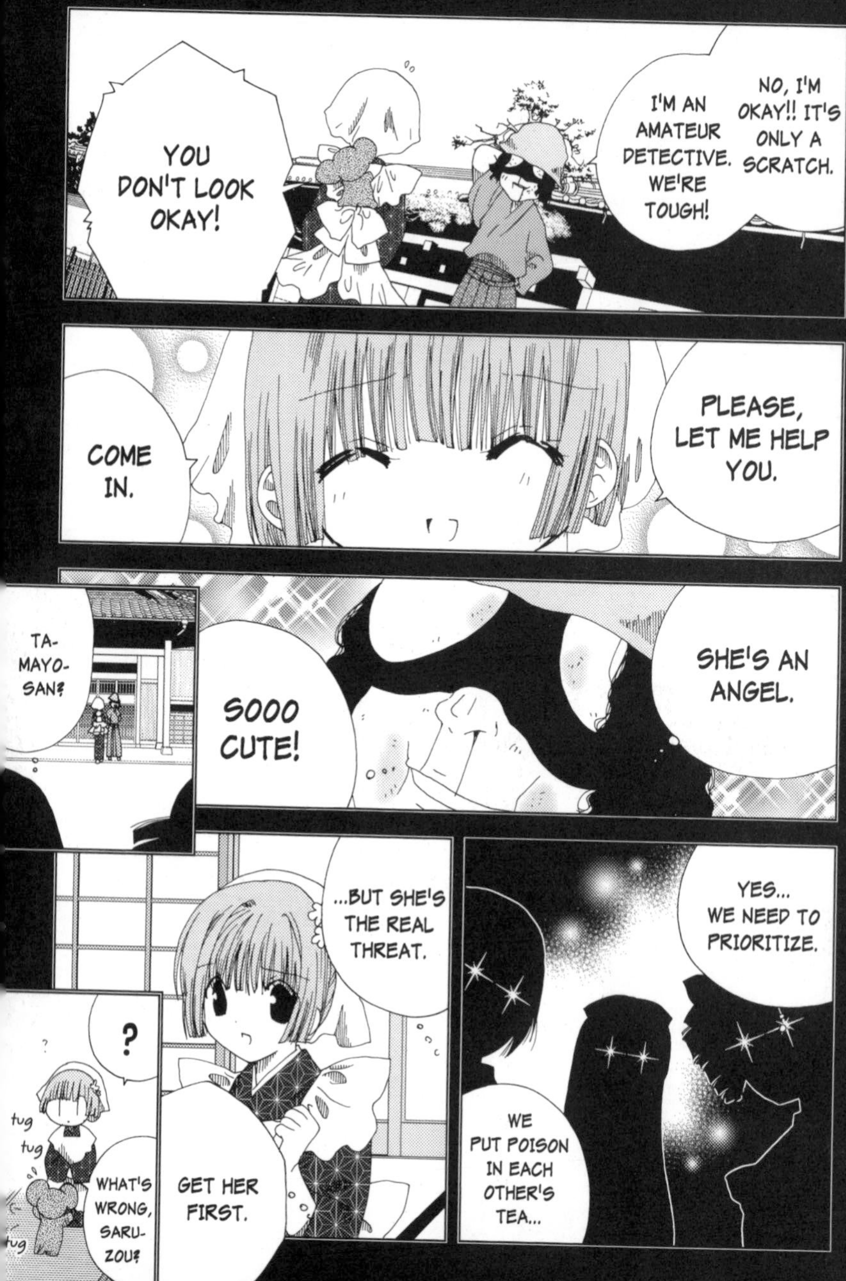
NO, I'M OKAY!! IT'S ONLY A SCRATCH.
I'M AN AMATEUR DETECTIVE. WE'RE TOUGH!
YOU DON'T LOOK OKAY!
PLEASE, LET ME HELP YOU.
COME IN.
SHE'S AN ANGEL.
SOOO CUTE!
TA-MAYO-SAN?
YES... WE NEED TO PRIORITIZE.
WE PUT POISON IN EACH OTHER'S TEA...
...BUT SHE'S THE REAL THREAT.
GET HER FIRST.
?
tug tug tug
WHAT'S WRONG, SARU-ZOU?

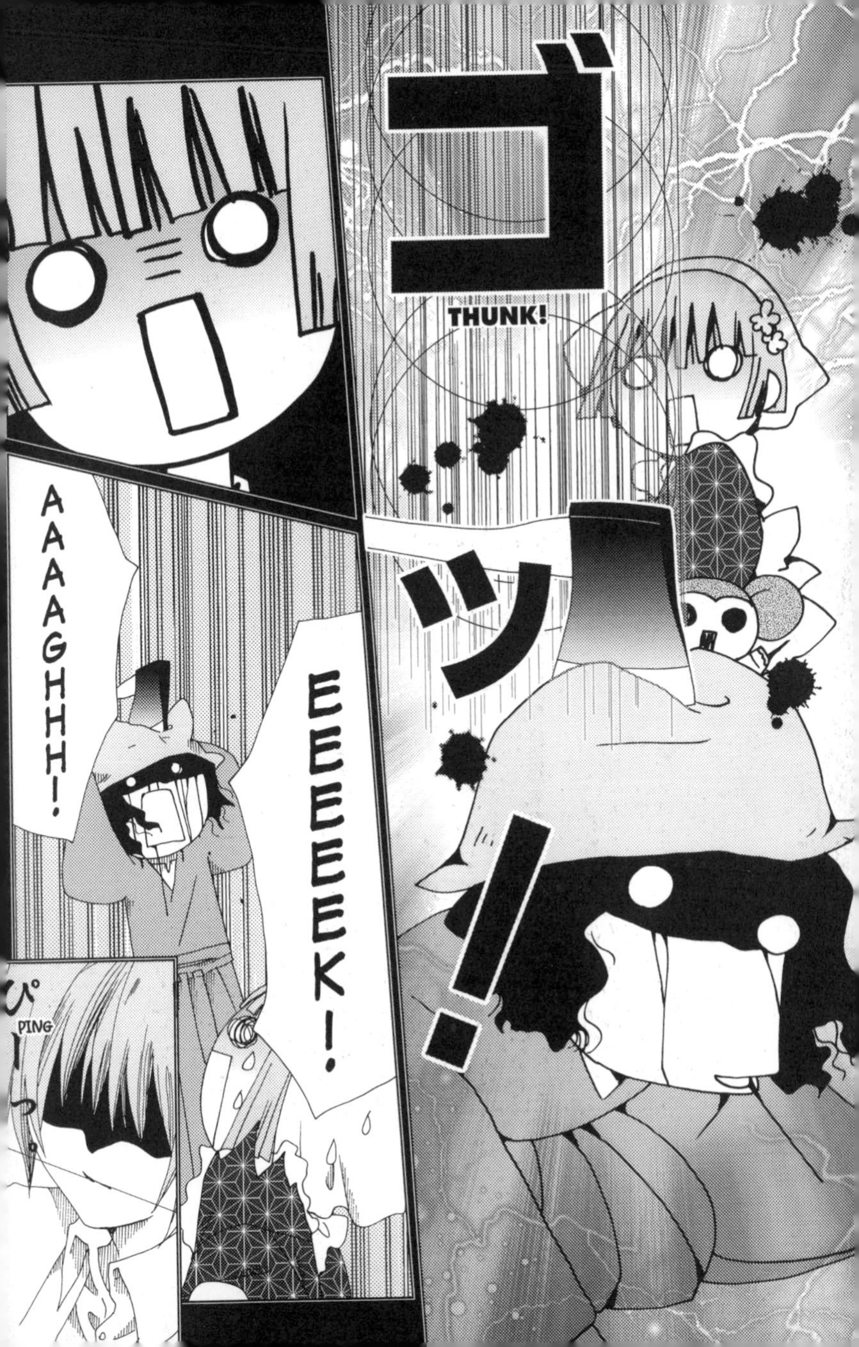
ゴッ!!
THUNK!
AAAAGHHH!
EEEEEK!
ぴーっ。
PING

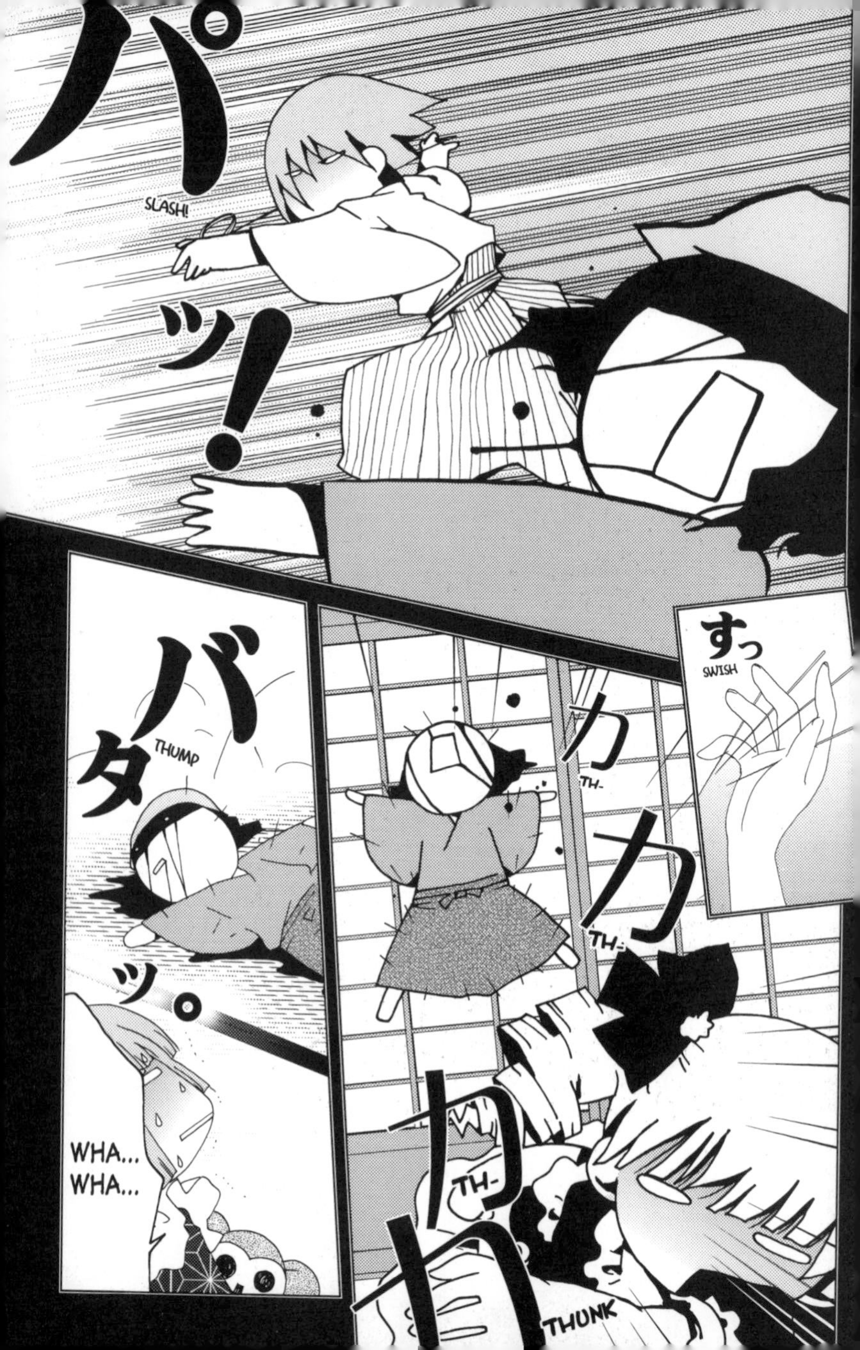
パッ!
SLASH!
すっ
SWISH
カ
TH-
カ
TH-
カ
TH-
THUNK
バタッ。
THUMP
WHA...
WHA...

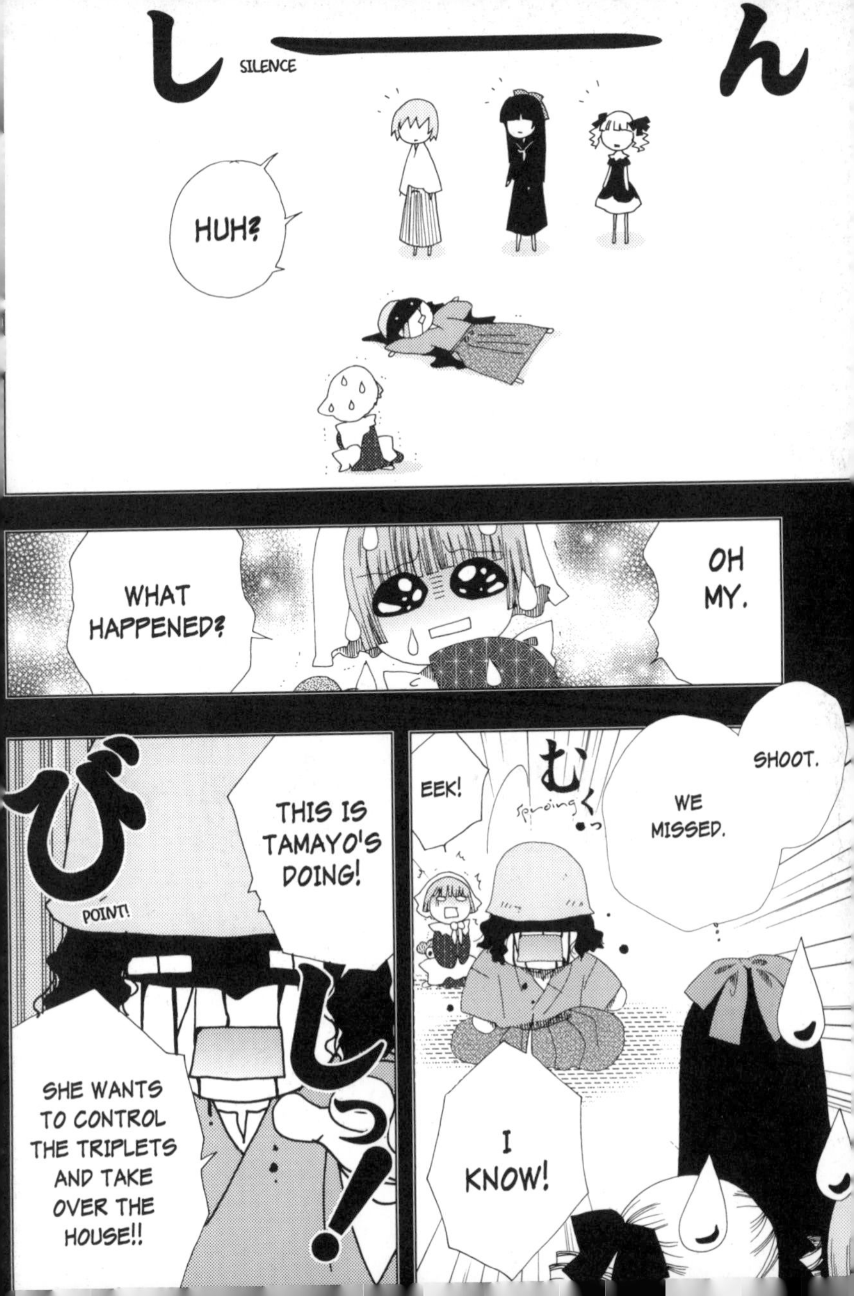

しーん
SILENCE
HUH?
OH MY.
WHAT HAPPENED?
SHOOT.
WE MISSED.
EEK!
むくっ
Sproing
I KNOW!
THIS IS TAMAYO'S DOING!
びしっ!
POINT!
SHE WANTS TO CONTROL THE TRIPLETS AND TAKE OVER THE HOUSE!!

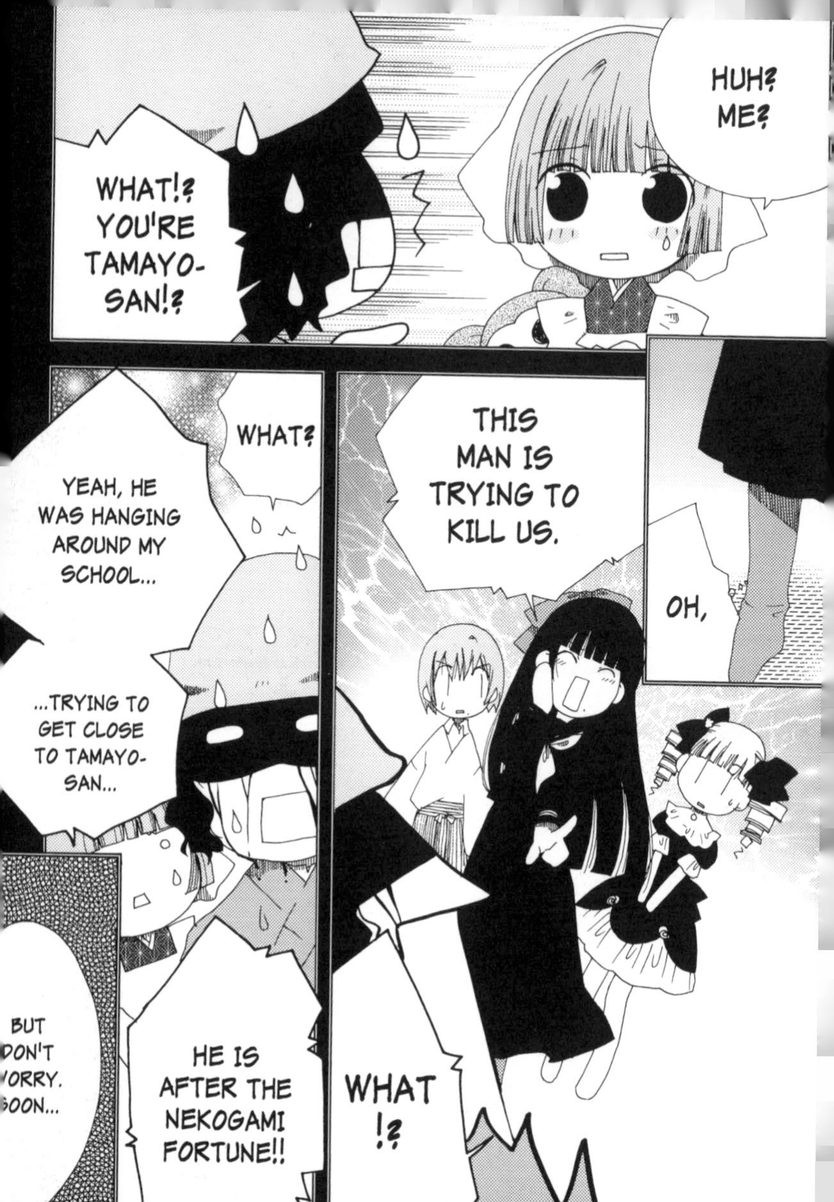
HUH? ME?
WHAT!? YOU'RE TAMAYO-SAN!?
OH,
THIS MAN IS TRYING TO KILL US.
WHAT?
YEAH, HE WAS HANGING AROUND MY SCHOOL...
...TRYING TO GET CLOSE TO TAMAYO-SAN...
HE IS AFTER THE NEKOGAMI FORTUNE!!
WHAT !?
BUT DON'T ORRY. OON...

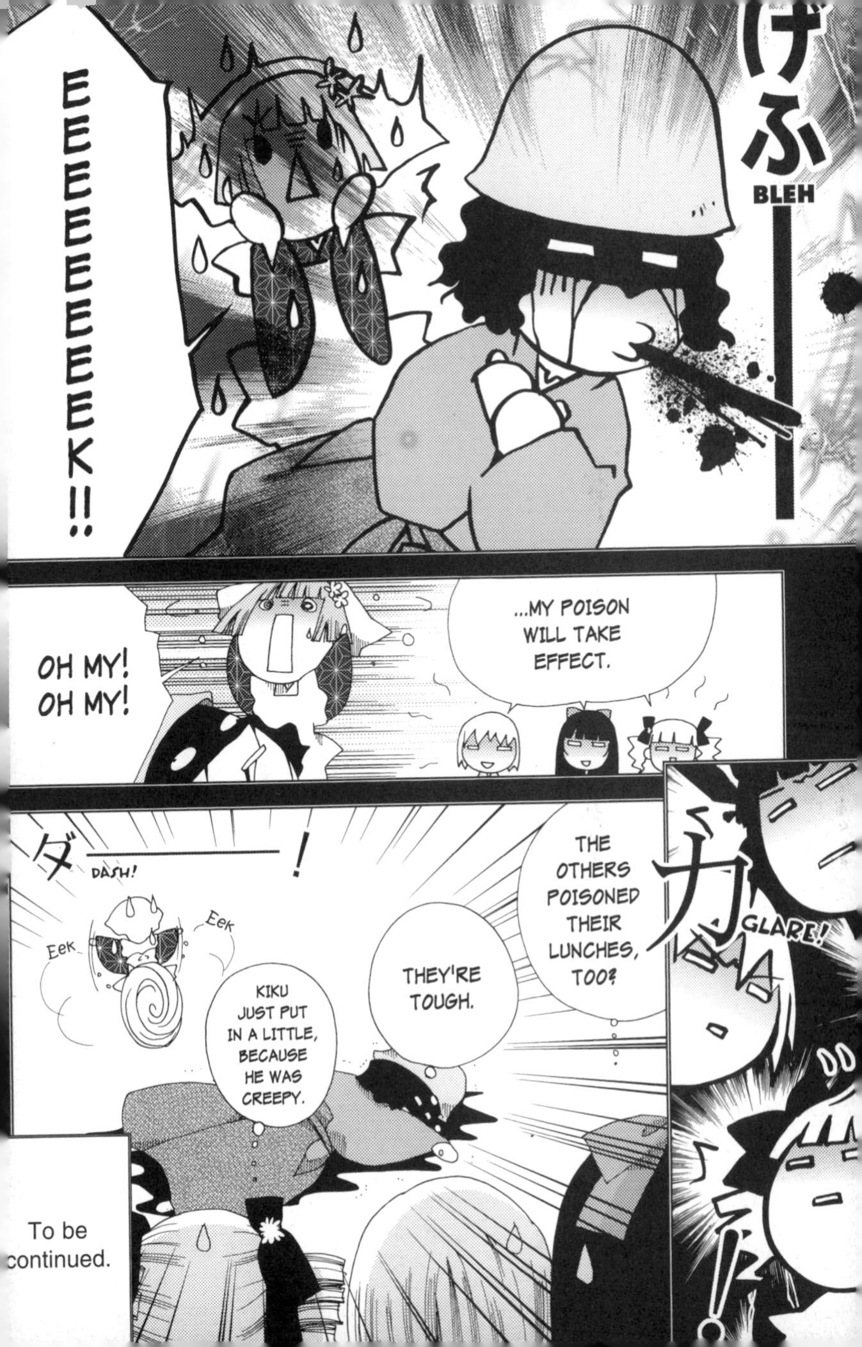
げふ
BLEH
EEEEEEEEEEEK!!
...MY POISON WILL TAKE EFFECT.
OH MY! OH MY!
ガ
GLARE!
THE OTHERS POISONED THEIR LUNCHES, TOO?
ダ
DASH!
THEY'RE TOUGH.
KIKU JUST PUT IN A LITTLE, BECAUSE HE WAS CREEPY.
Eek
Eek
To be continued.

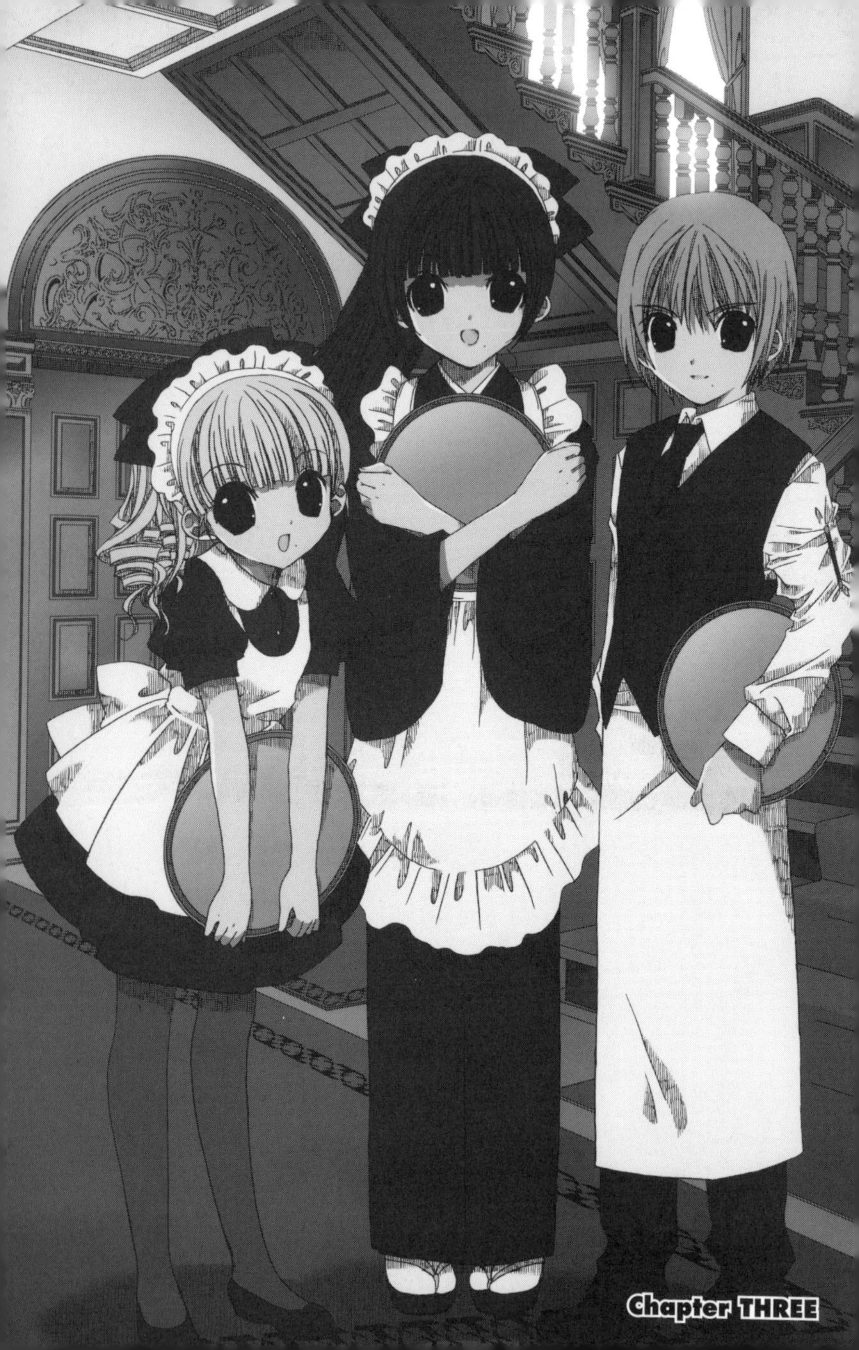
Chapter THREE

Yoki Koto Kiku

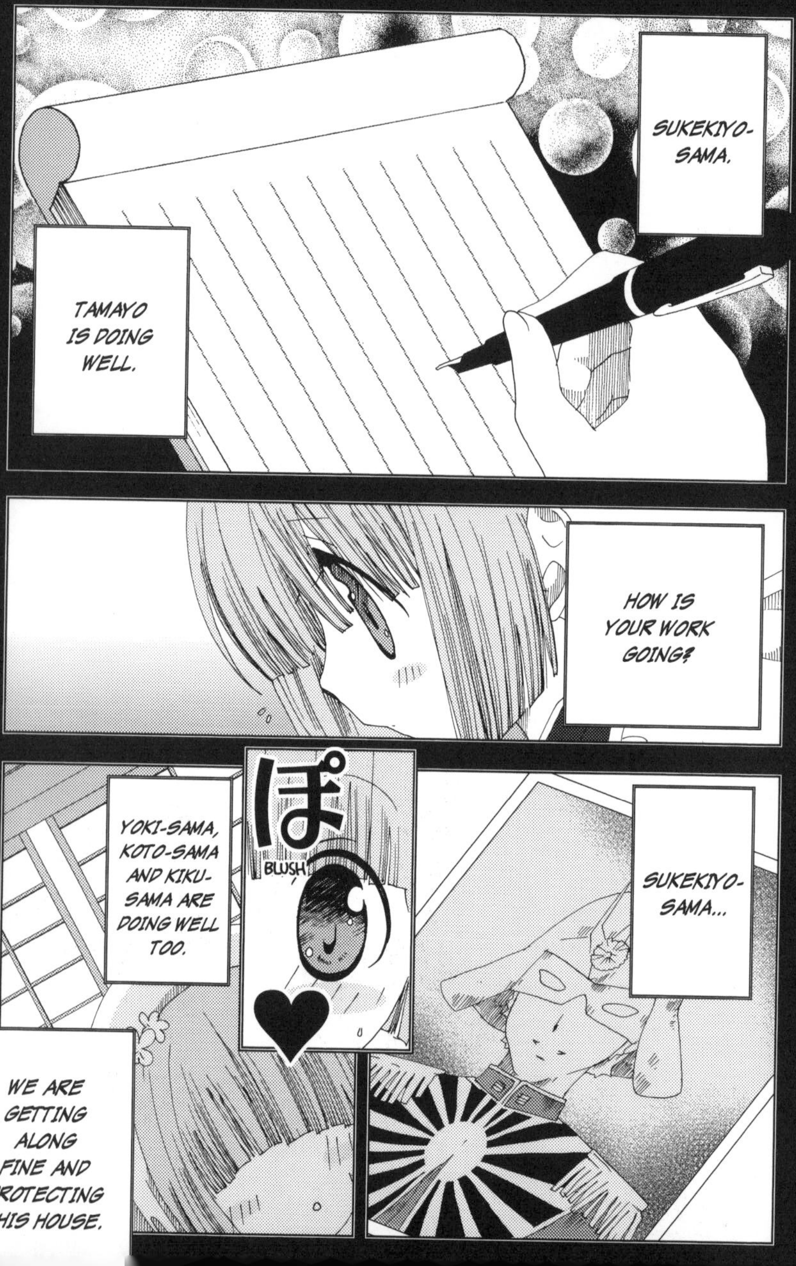
SUKEKIYO-SAMA.
TAMAYO IS DOING WELL.
HOW IS YOUR WORK GOING?
SUKEKIYO-SAMA...
ぽ
BLUSH
YOKI-SAMA, KOTO-SAMA AND KIKU-SAMA ARE DOING WELL TOO.
WE ARE GETTING ALONG FINE AND PROTECTING THIS HOUSE.

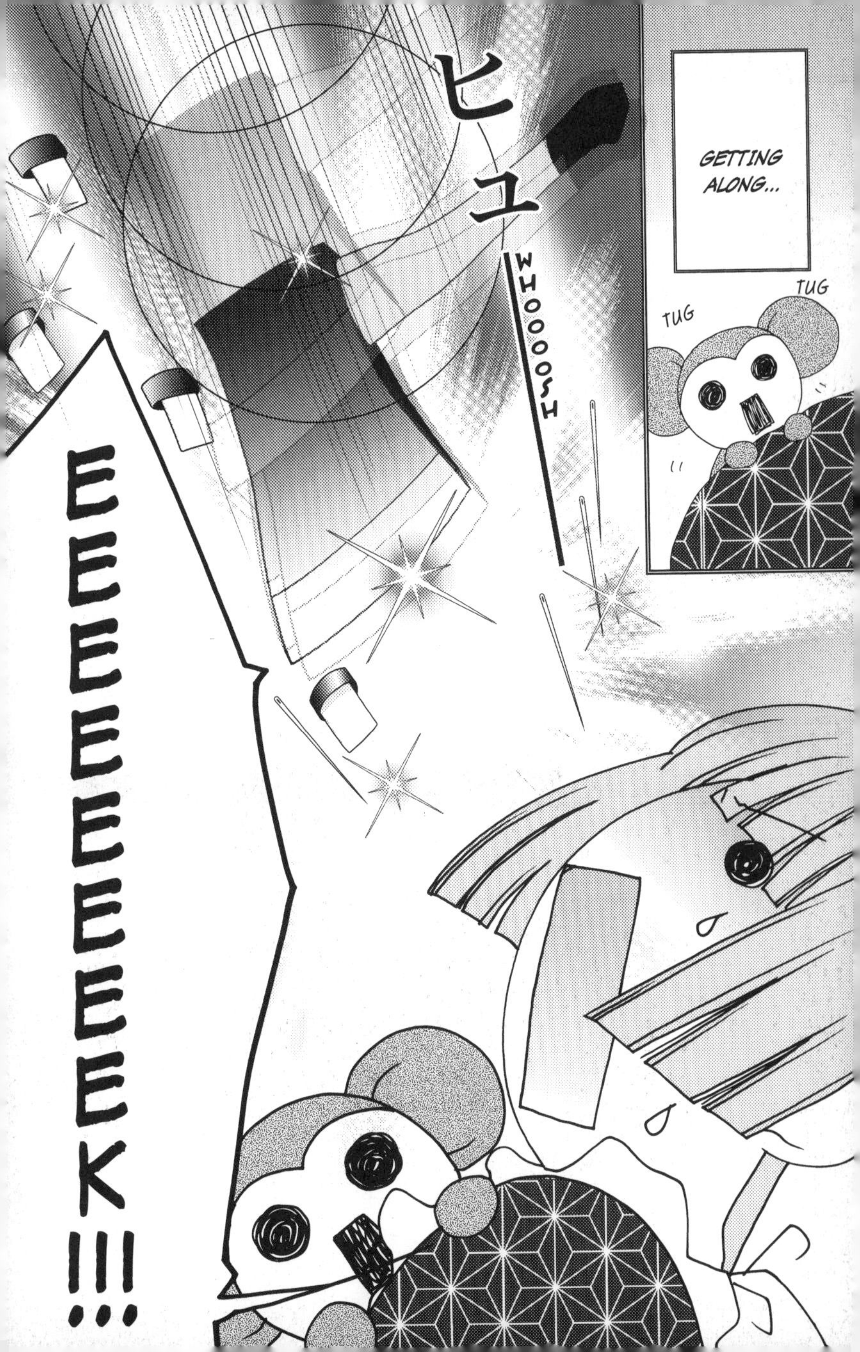
GETTING ALONG...
TUG
TUG
ヒュ
WHOOOOSH
EEEEEEEEK!!!

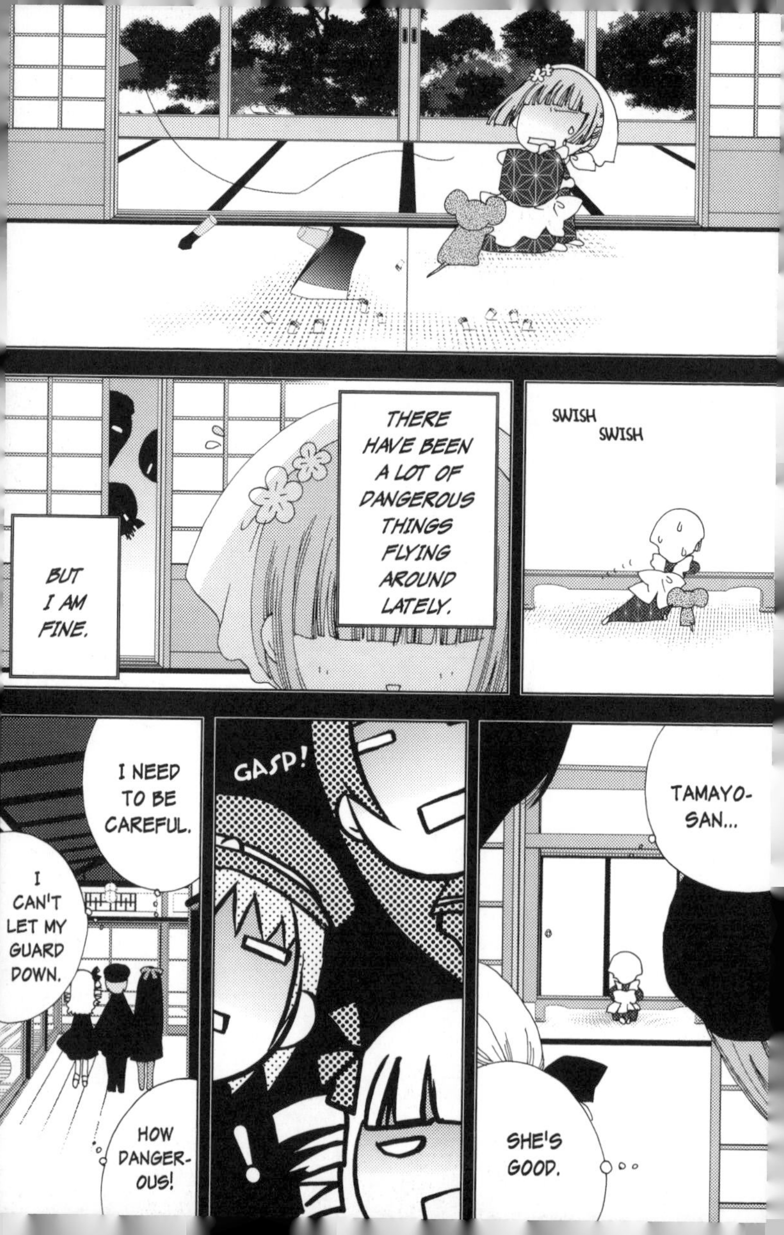
SWISH SWISH
THERE HAVE BEEN A LOT OF DANGEROUS THINGS FLYING AROUND LATELY.
BUT I AM FINE.
TAMAYO-SAN...
SHE'S GOOD.
GASP!
I NEED TO BE CAREFUL.
I CAN'T LET MY GUARD DOWN.
HOW DANGER-OUS!

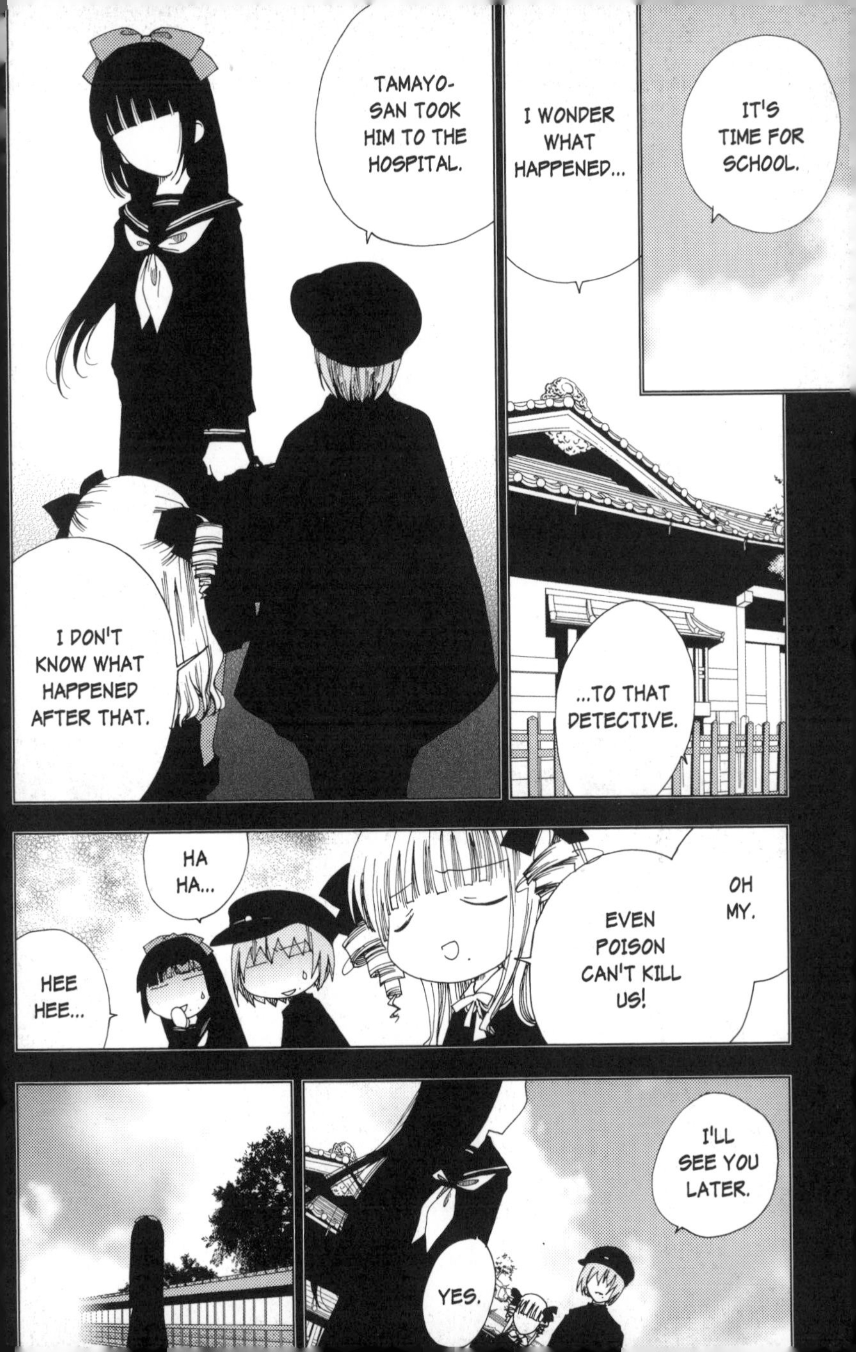
IT'S TIME FOR SCHOOL.
I WONDER WHAT HAPPENED...
...TO THAT DETECTIVE.
TAMAYO-SAN TOOK HIM TO THE HOSPITAL.
I DON'T KNOW WHAT HAPPENED AFTER THAT.
OH MY.
EVEN POISON CAN'T KILL US!
HA HA...
HEE HEE...
I'LL SEE YOU LATER.
YES.

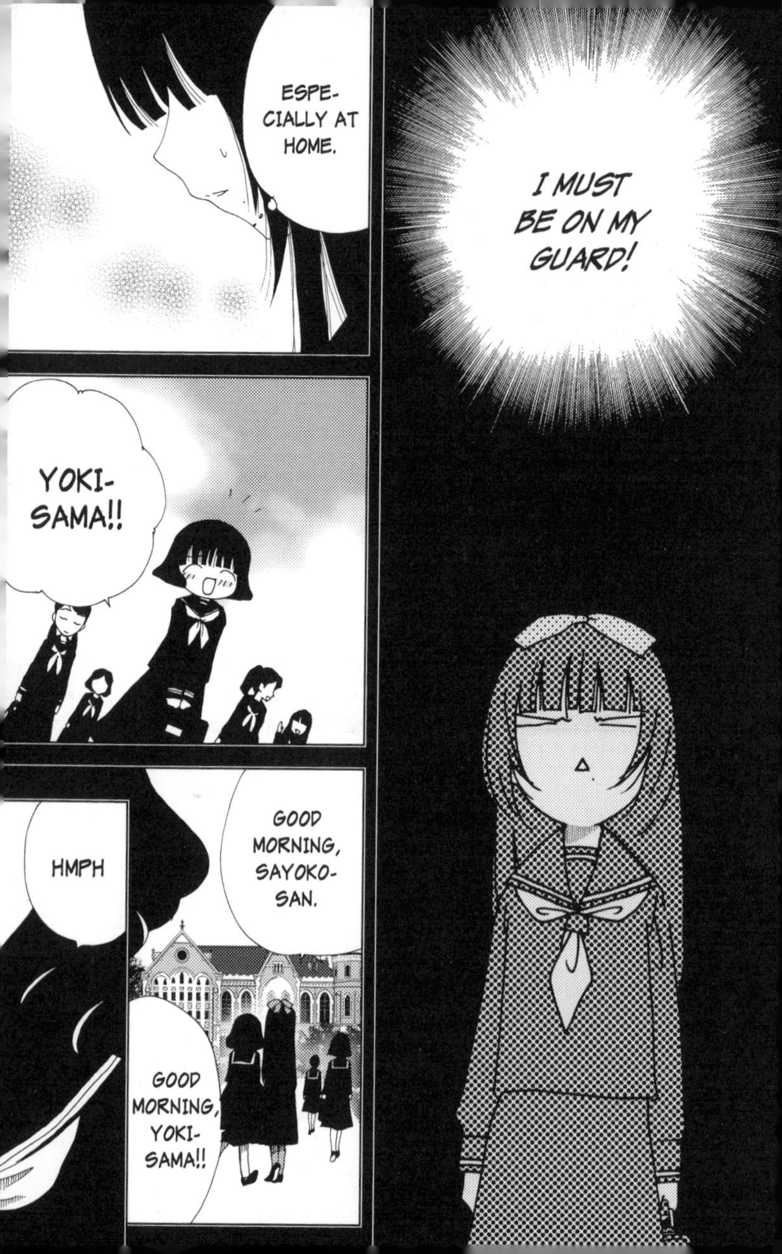
I MUST BE ON MY GUARD!
ESPE-CIALLY AT HOME.
YOKI-SAMA!!
GOOD MORNING, SAYOKO-SAN.
HMPH
GOOD MORNING, YOKI-SAMA!!

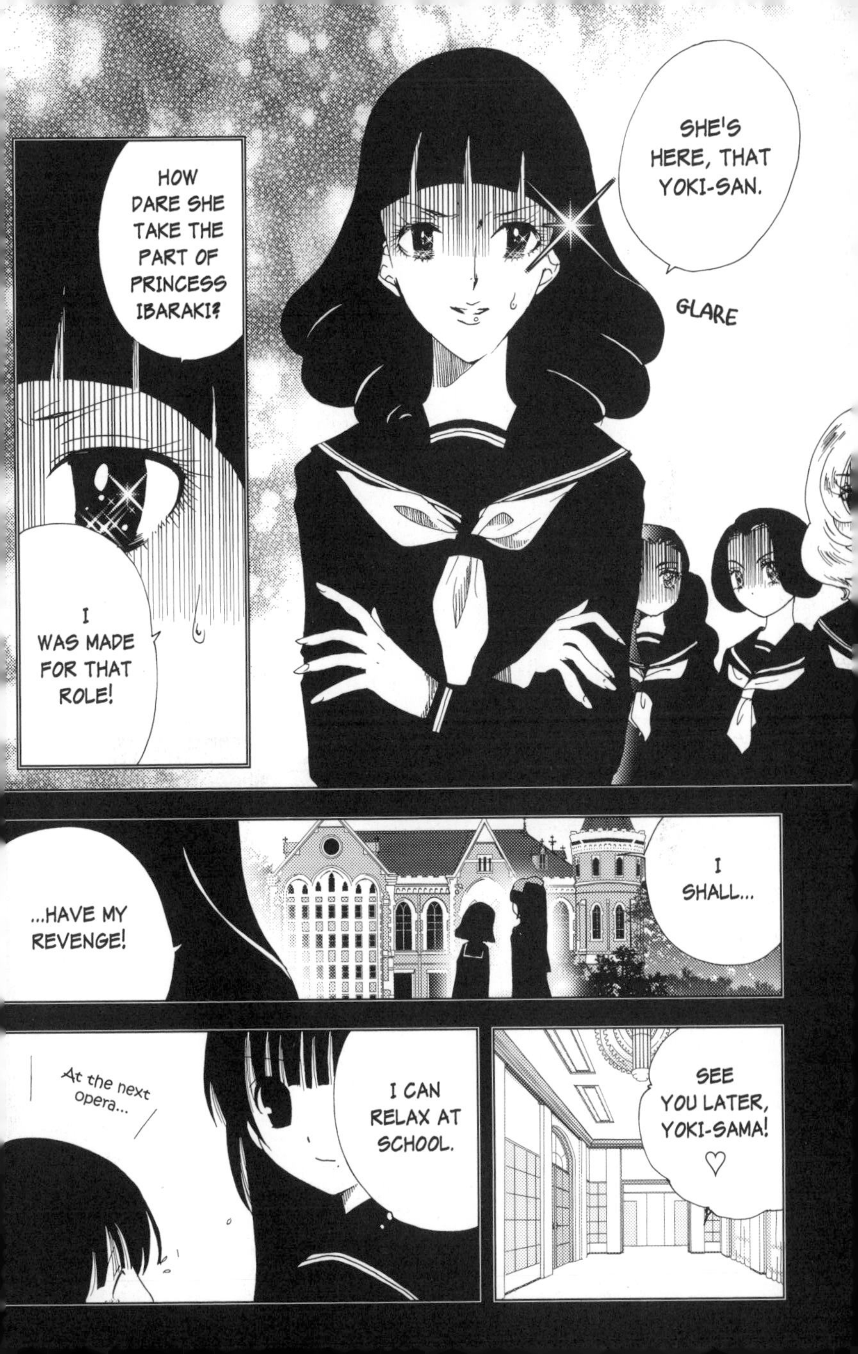
SHE'S HERE, THAT YOKI-SAN.
GLARE
HOW DARE SHE TAKE THE PART OF PRINCESS IBARAKI?
I WAS MADE FOR THAT ROLE!
I SHALL...
...HAVE MY REVENGE!
SEE YOU LATER, YOKI-SAMA! ♡
I CAN RELAX AT SCHOOL.
At the next opera...

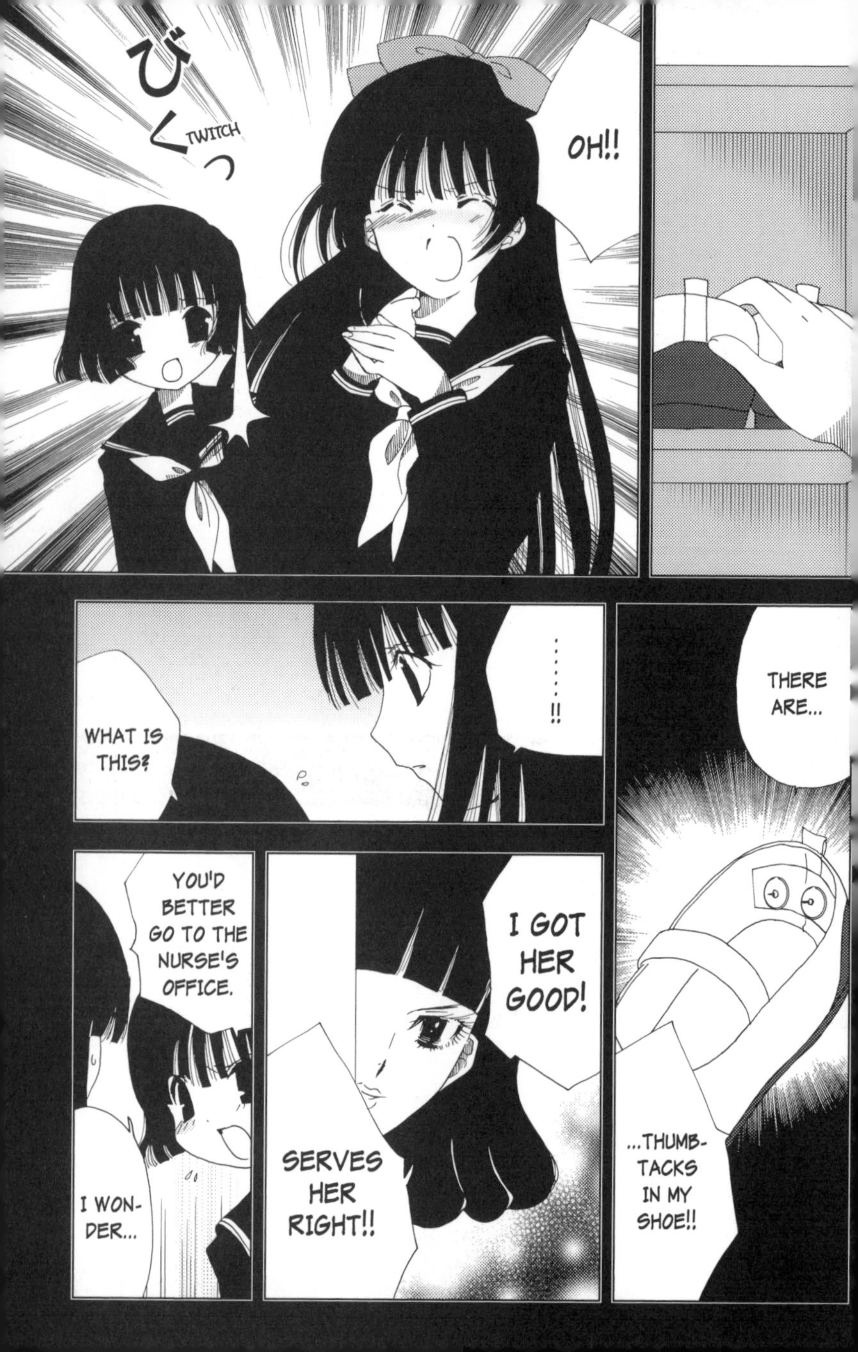
OH!!
びくっ
TWITCH
THERE ARE...
...THUMB-TACKS IN MY SHOE!!
......!!
WHAT IS THIS?
I GOT HER GOOD!
SERVES HER RIGHT!!
YOU'D BETTER GO TO THE NURSE'S OFFICE.
I WON-DER...

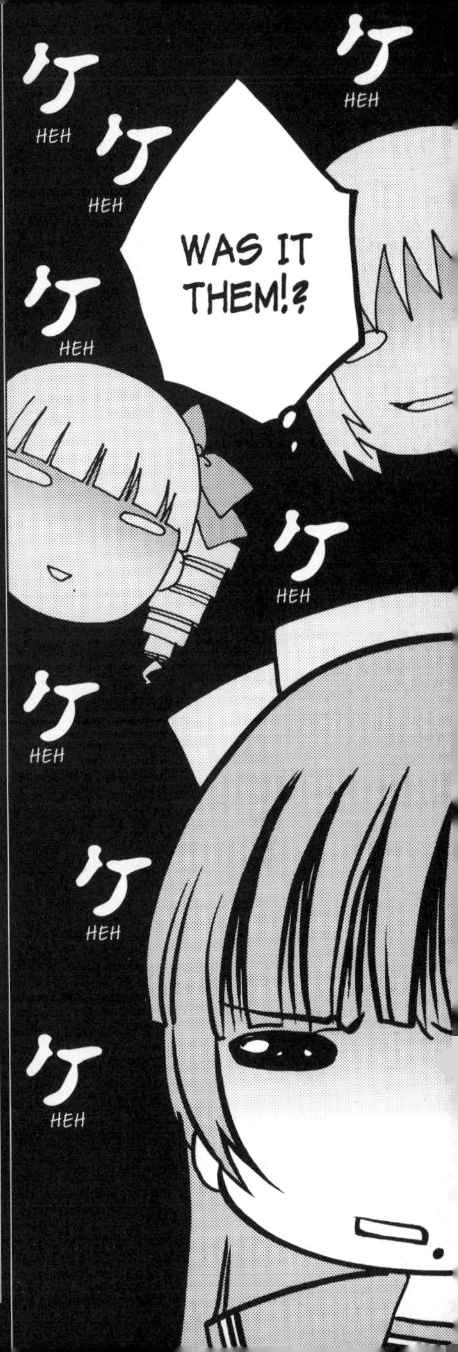
ケ
HEH
WAS IT THEM!?
ケ
HEH
ケ
HEH
ケ
HEH
ケ
HEH
ケ
HEH
ケ
HEH
ケ
HEH

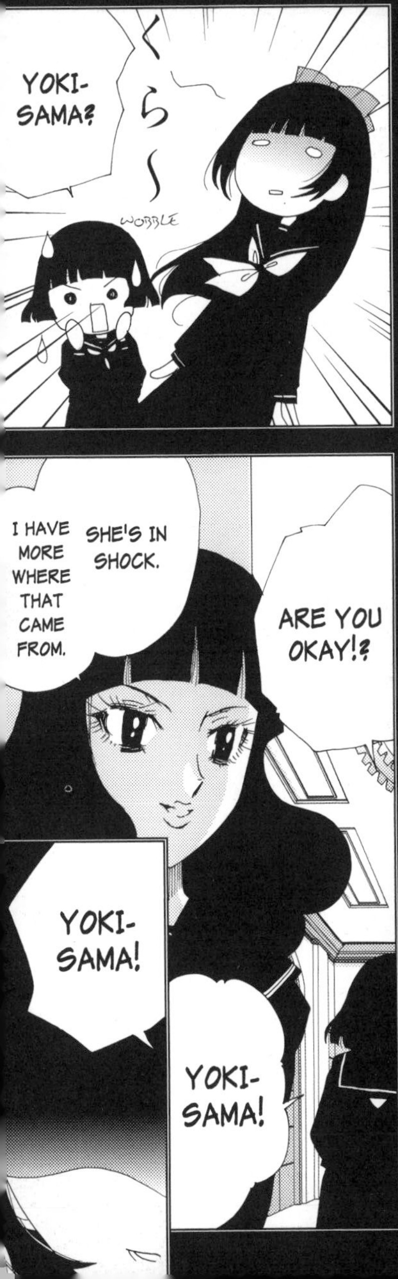
YOKI-SAMA?
くら
WOBBLE
ARE YOU OKAY!?
SHE'S IN SHOCK.
I HAVE MORE WHERE THAT CAME FROM.
YOKI-SAMA!
YOKI-SAMA!

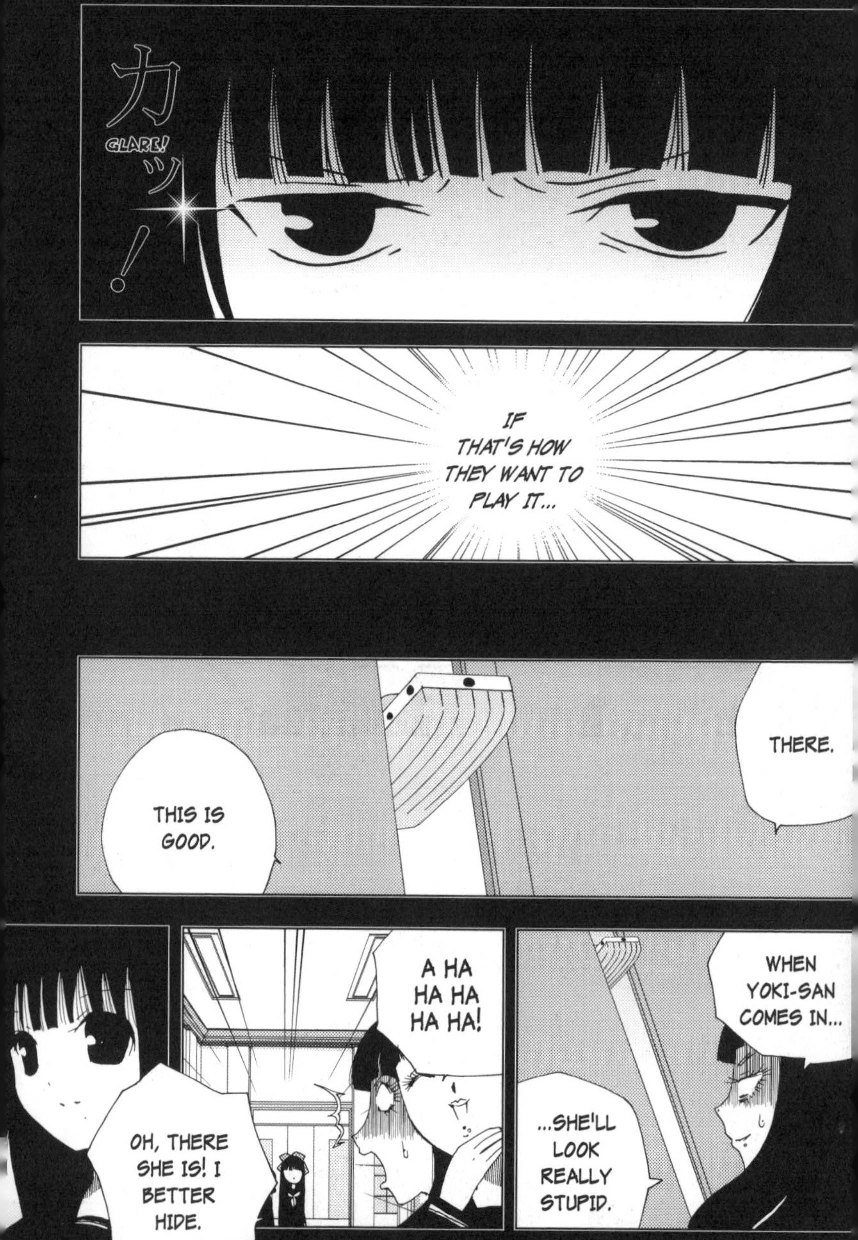
カッ!
GLARE!
IF THAT'S HOW THEY WANT TO PLAY IT...
THERE.
THIS IS GOOD.
WHEN YOKI-SAN COMES IN...
...SHE'LL LOOK REALLY STUPID.
A HA HA HA HA HA!
OH, THERE SHE IS! I BETTER HIDE.

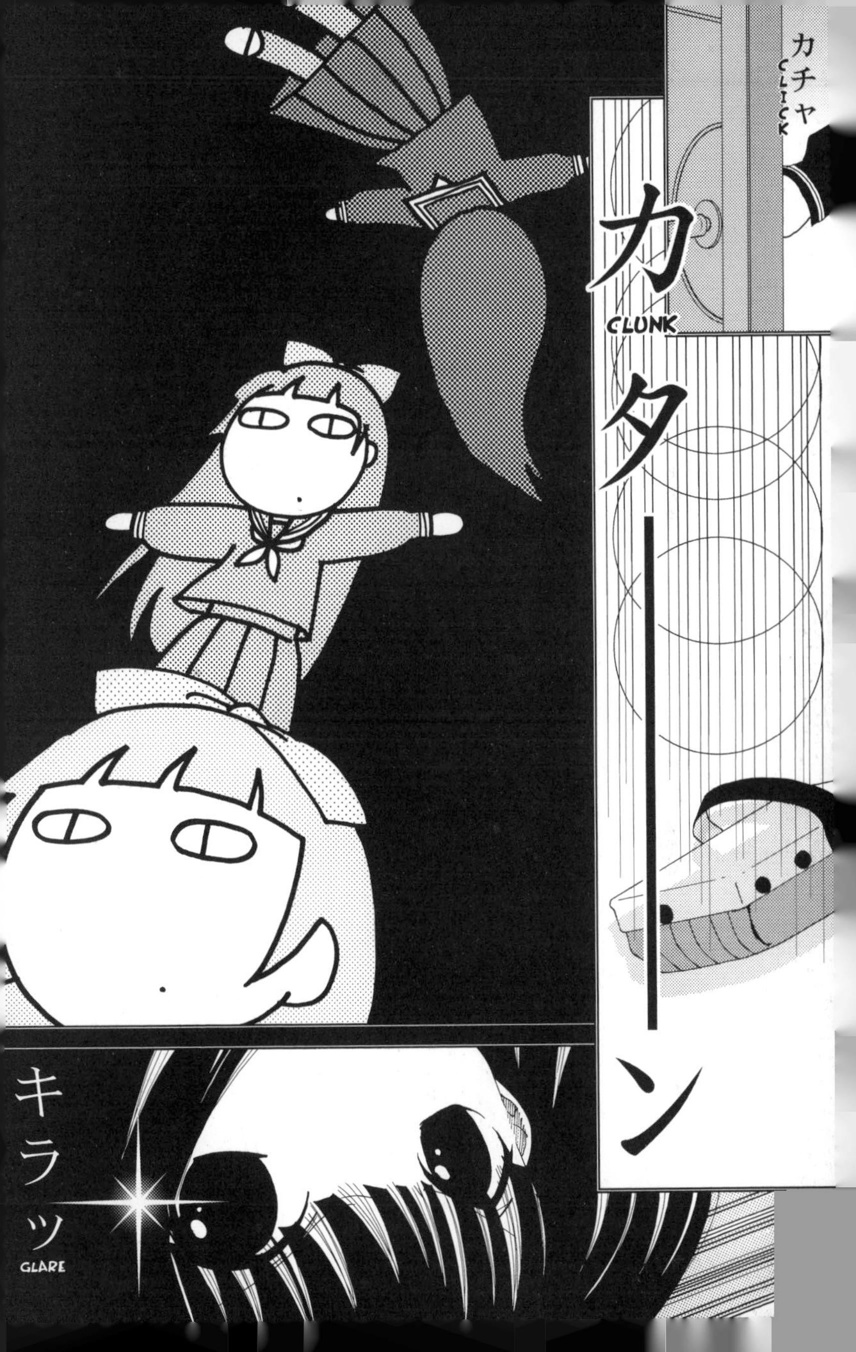
カチャ
CLICK
カタ―ン
CLUNK
キラッ
GLARE

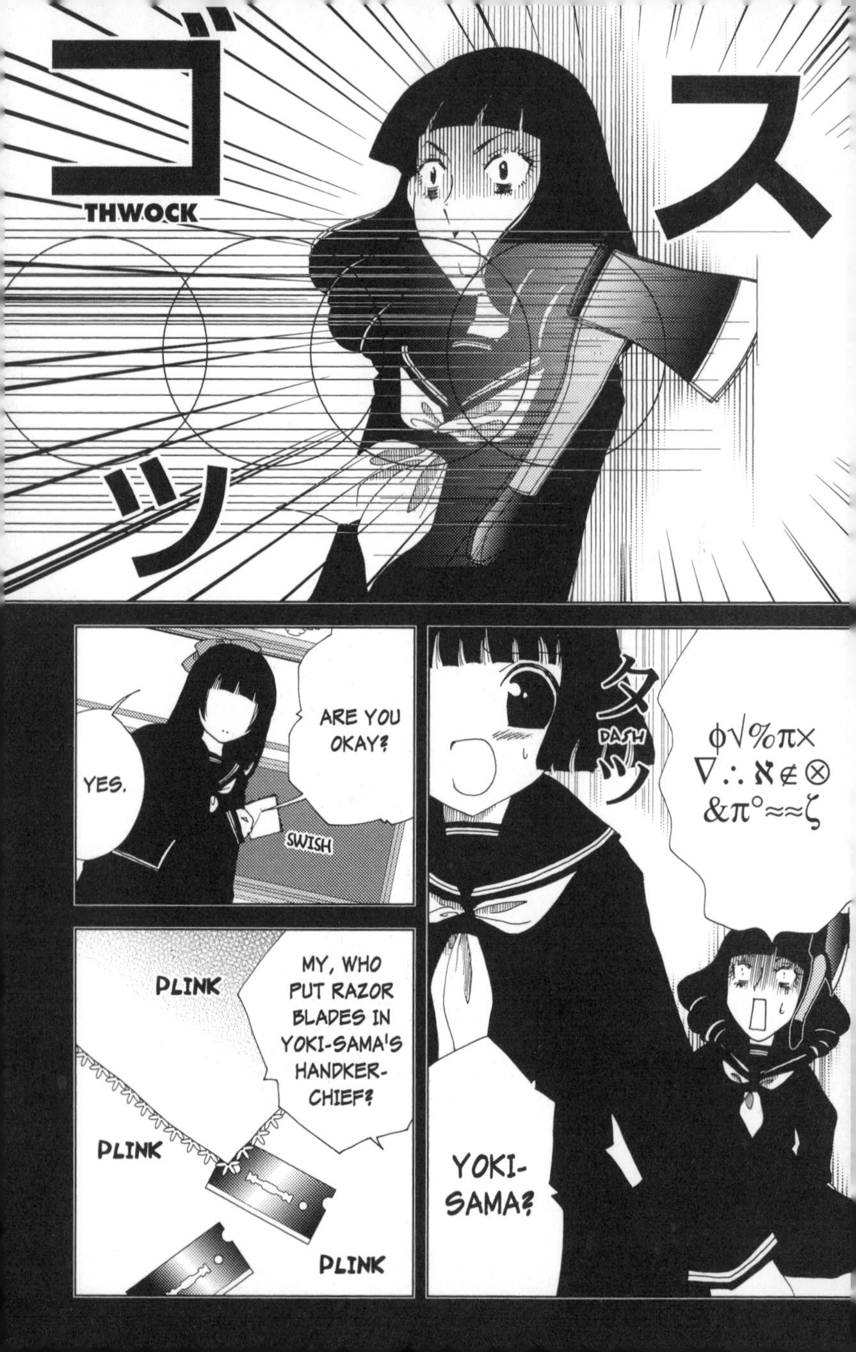
ゴス
THWOCK
ッ
φ√%π×
∇∴ℵ∉⊗
&π°≈≈ζ
タ
DASH
ッ
YOKI-SAMA?
ARE YOU OKAY?
YES.
SWISH
MY, WHO PUT RAZOR BLADES IN YOKI-SAMA'S HANDKER-CHIEF?
PLINK
PLINK
PLINK

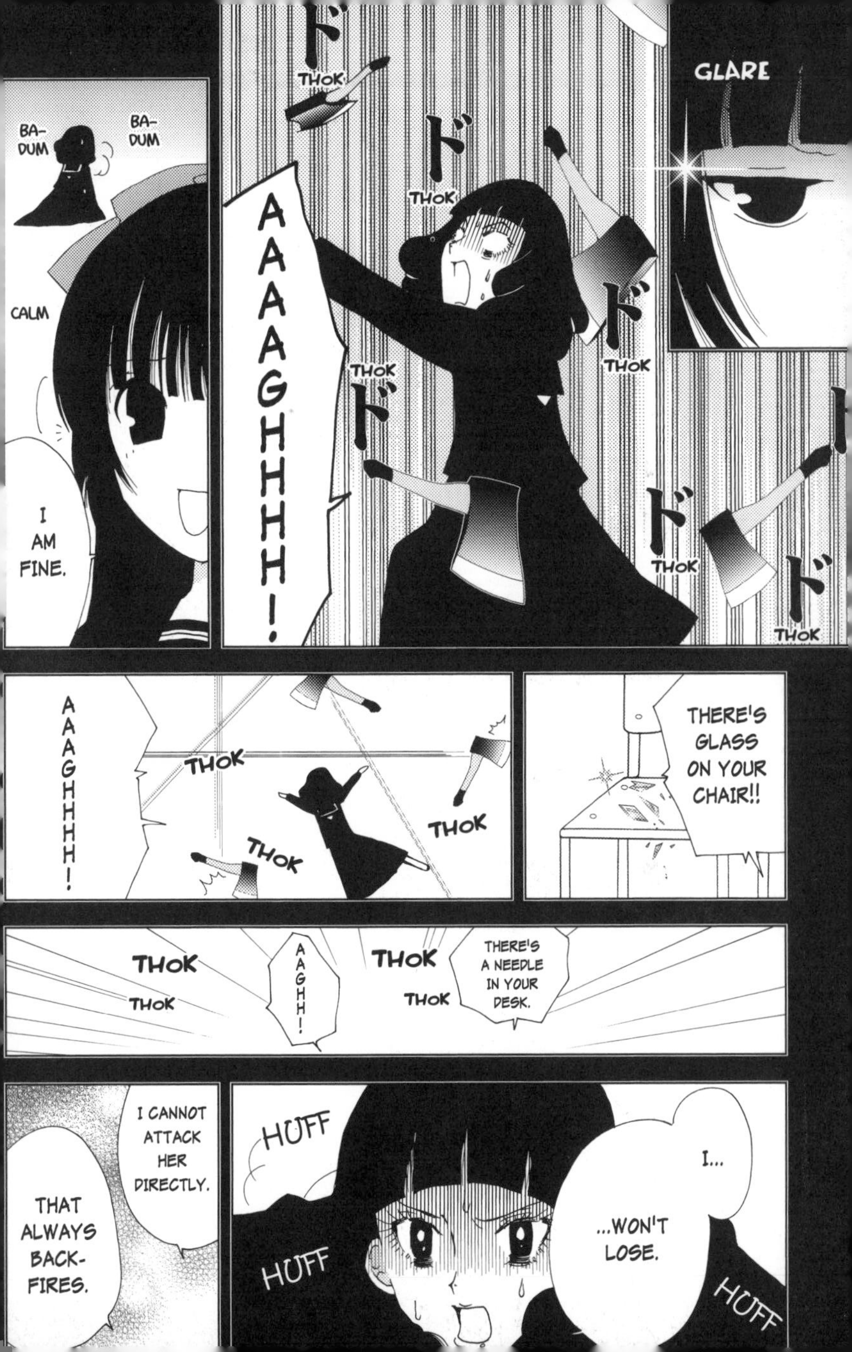
GLARE
ド
THOK
ド
THOK
ド
THOK
ド
THOK
ド
THOK
ド
THOK
AAAAGHHHHH!
BA-DUM
BA-DUM
CALM
I AM FINE.
THERE'S GLASS ON YOUR CHAIR!!
THOK
THOK
THOK
AAAGHHHHH!
THERE'S A NEEDLE IN YOUR DESK.
THOK
THOK
AAGHH!
THOK
THOK
I...
...WON'T LOSE.
HUFF
HUFF
HUFF
I CANNOT ATTACK HER DIRECTLY.
THAT ALWAYS BACKFIRES.

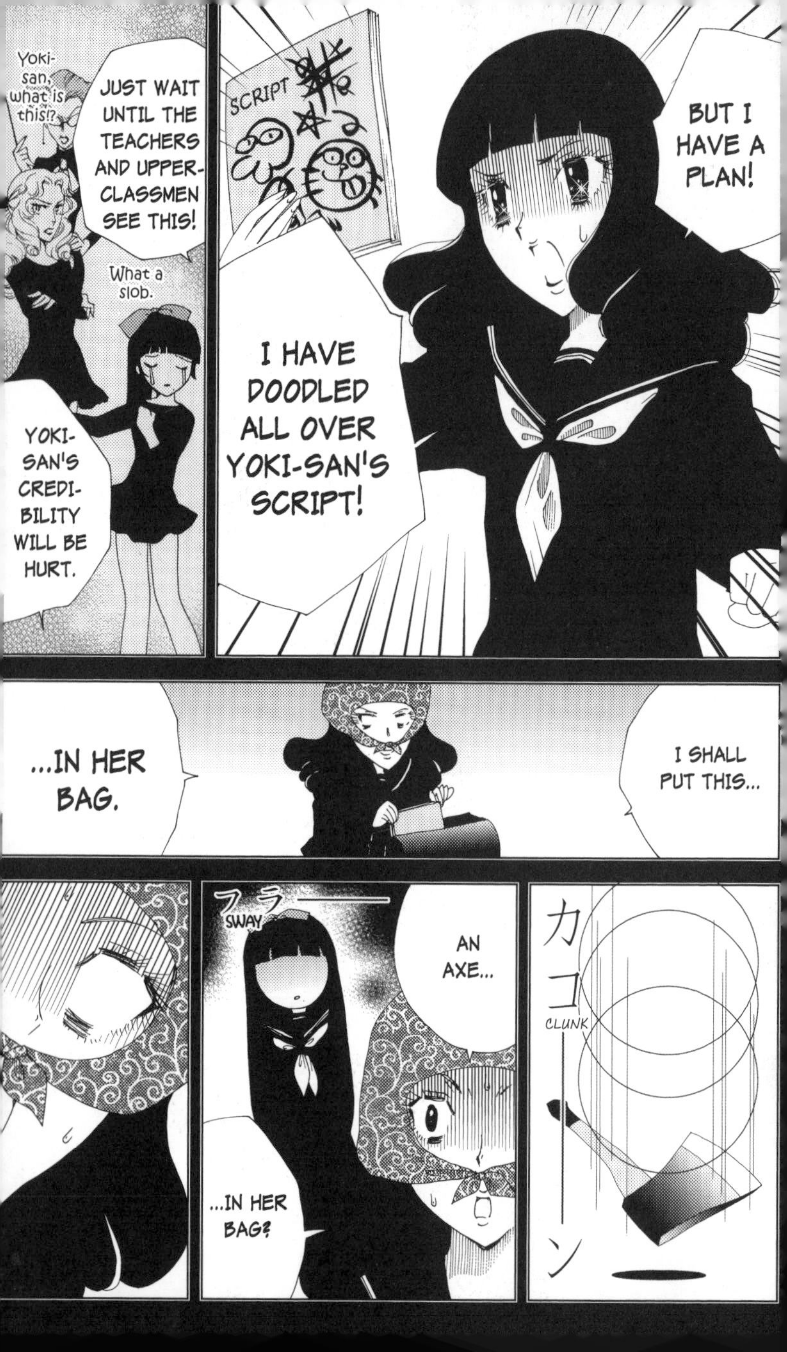
SCRIPT
BUT I HAVE A PLAN!
I HAVE DOODLED ALL OVER YOKI-SAN'S SCRIPT!
JUST WAIT UNTIL THE TEACHERS AND UPPER-CLASSMEN SEE THIS!
Yoki-san, what is this!?
What a slob.
YOKI-SAN'S CREDI-BILITY WILL BE HURT.
I SHALL PUT THIS...
...IN HER BAG.
カコン
CLUNK
フラー
SWAY
AN AXE...
...IN HER BAG?

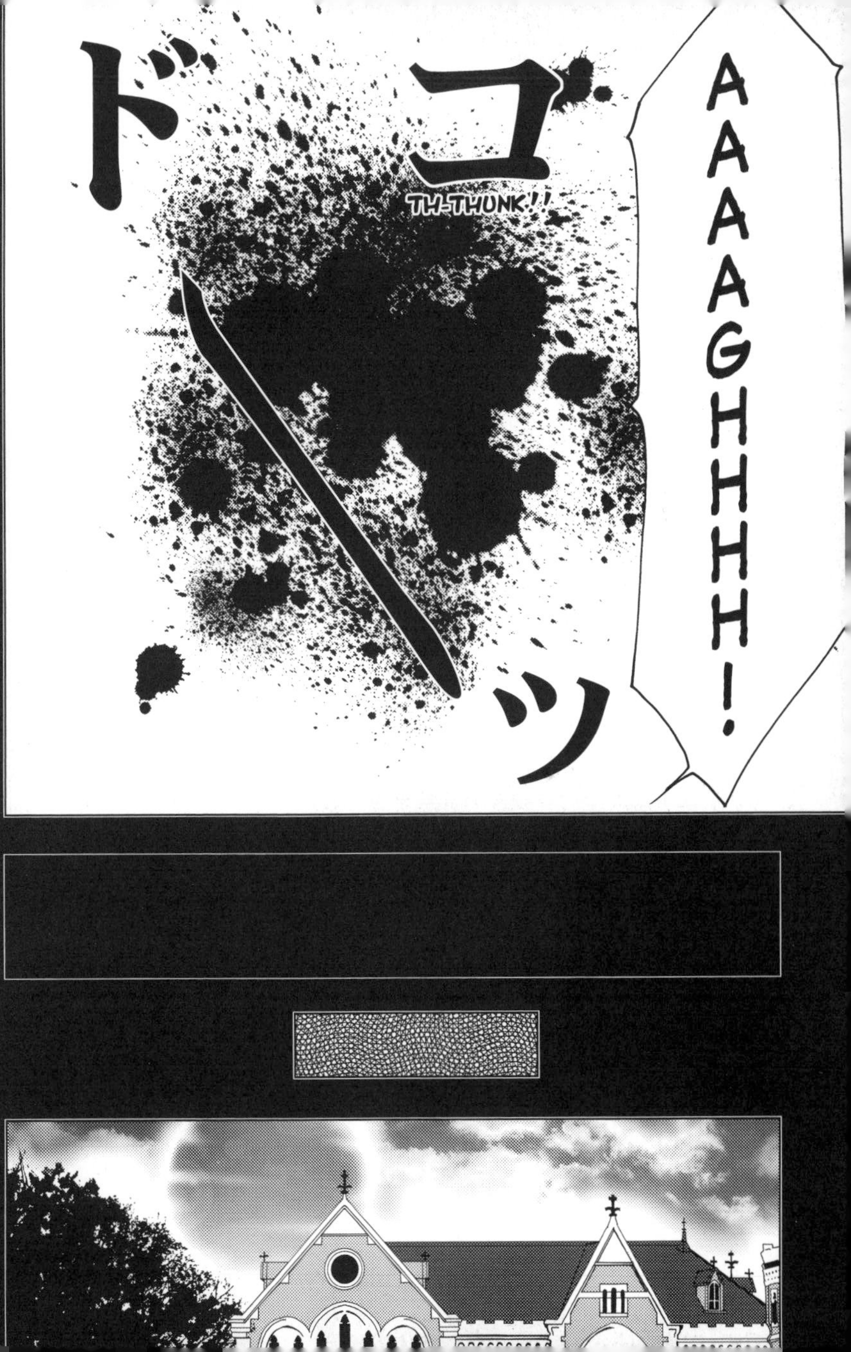
AAAAAGHHHHH!
ドゴッ
TH-THUNK!!

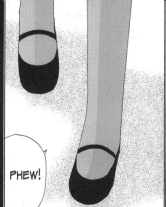

TODAY WAS TIRING.

PHEW!

I WON'T GIVE UP.

I MUST ACHIEVE MY DREAM!

BUT...

WELCOME HOME!

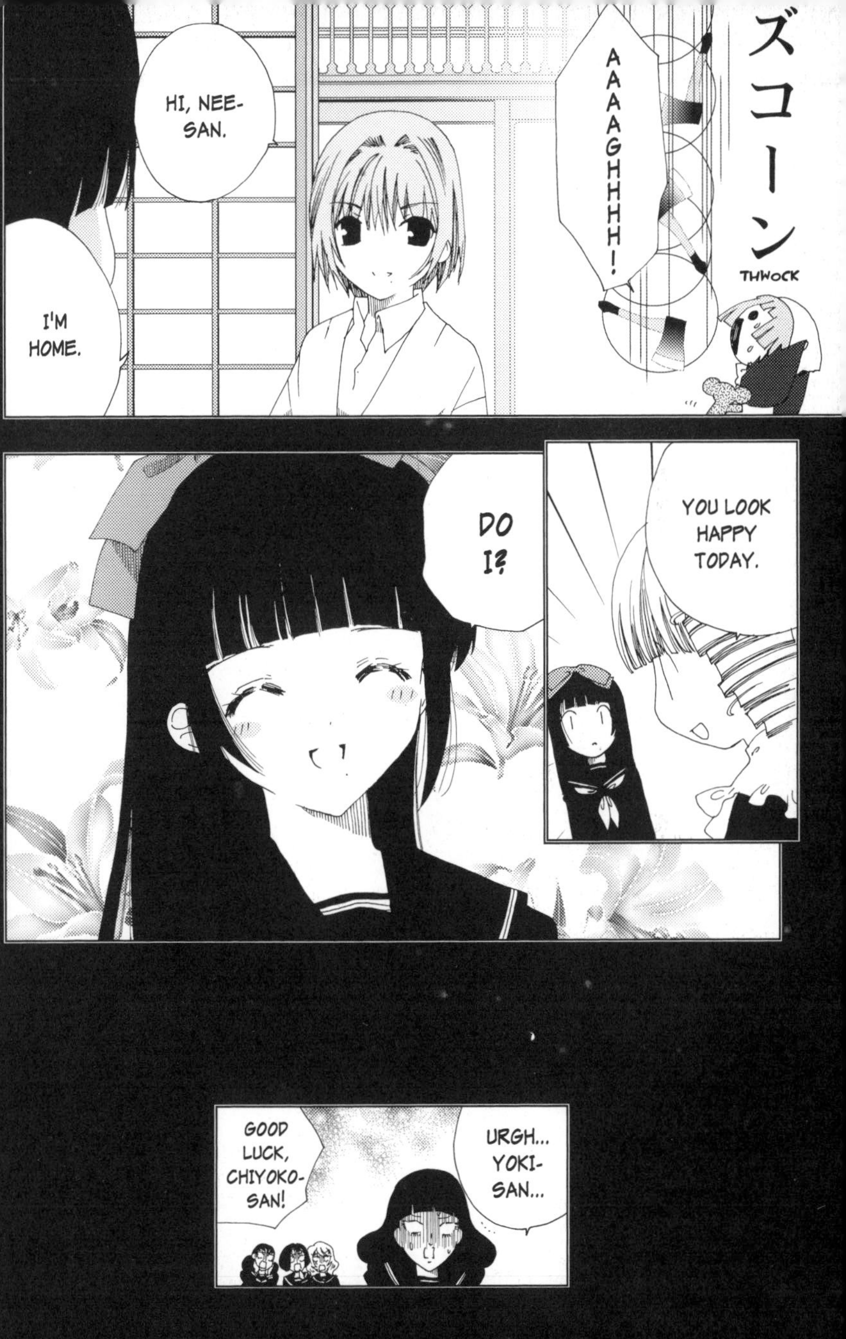
ズコーン
THWOCK
AAAAGHHHH!
HI, NEE-SAN.
I'M HOME.
YOU LOOK HAPPY TODAY.
DO I?
URGH... YOKI-SAN...
GOOD LUCK, CHIYOKO-SAN!

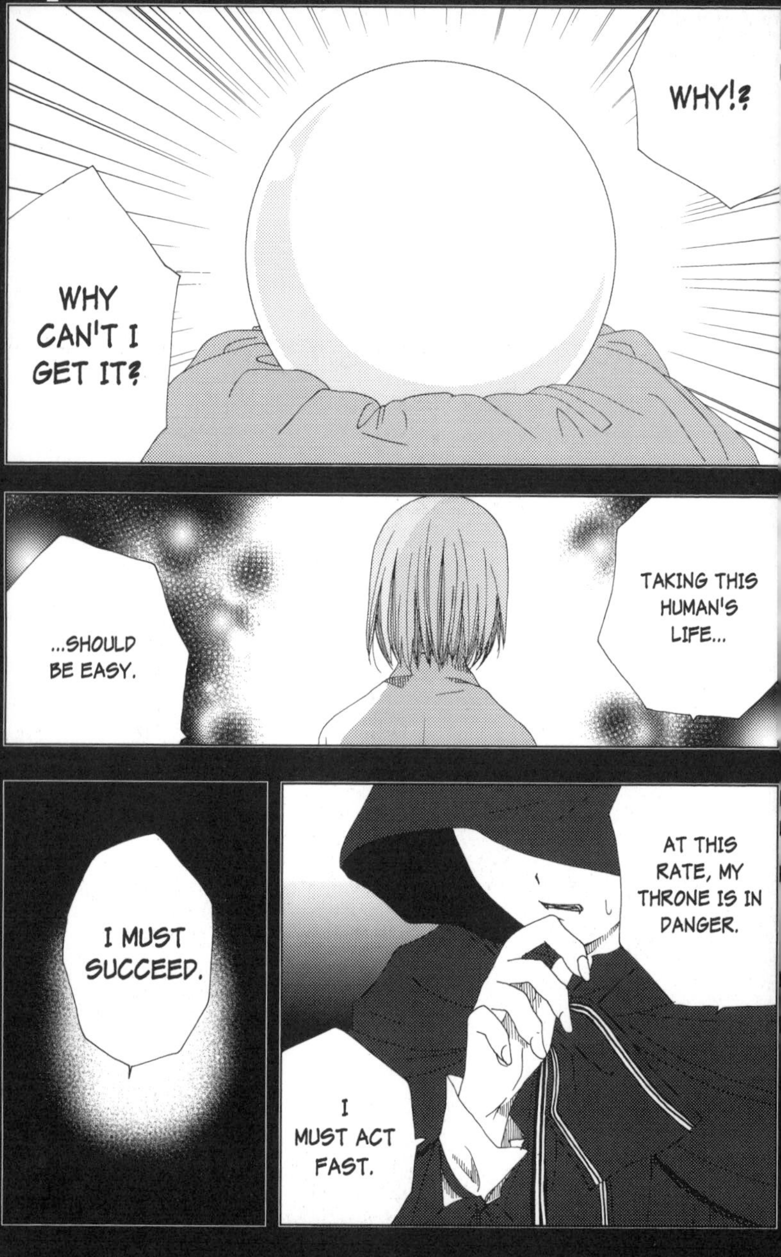
WHY!?
WHY CAN'T I GET IT?
TAKING THIS HUMAN'S LIFE...
...SHOULD BE EASY.
AT THIS RATE, MY THRONE IS IN DANGER.
I MUST ACT FAST.
I MUST SUCCEED.

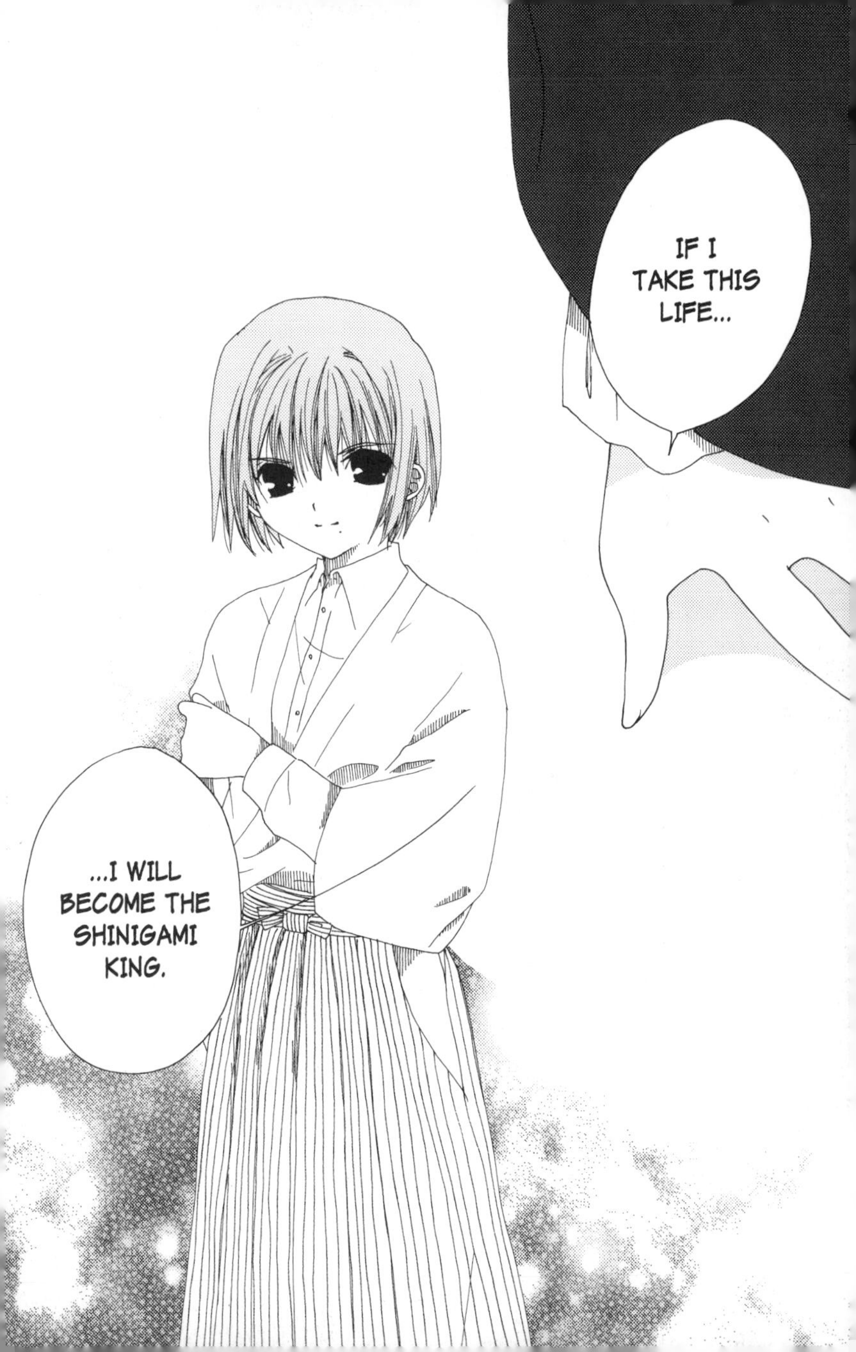
IF I TAKE THIS LIFE...
...I WILL BECOME THE SHINIGAMI KING.

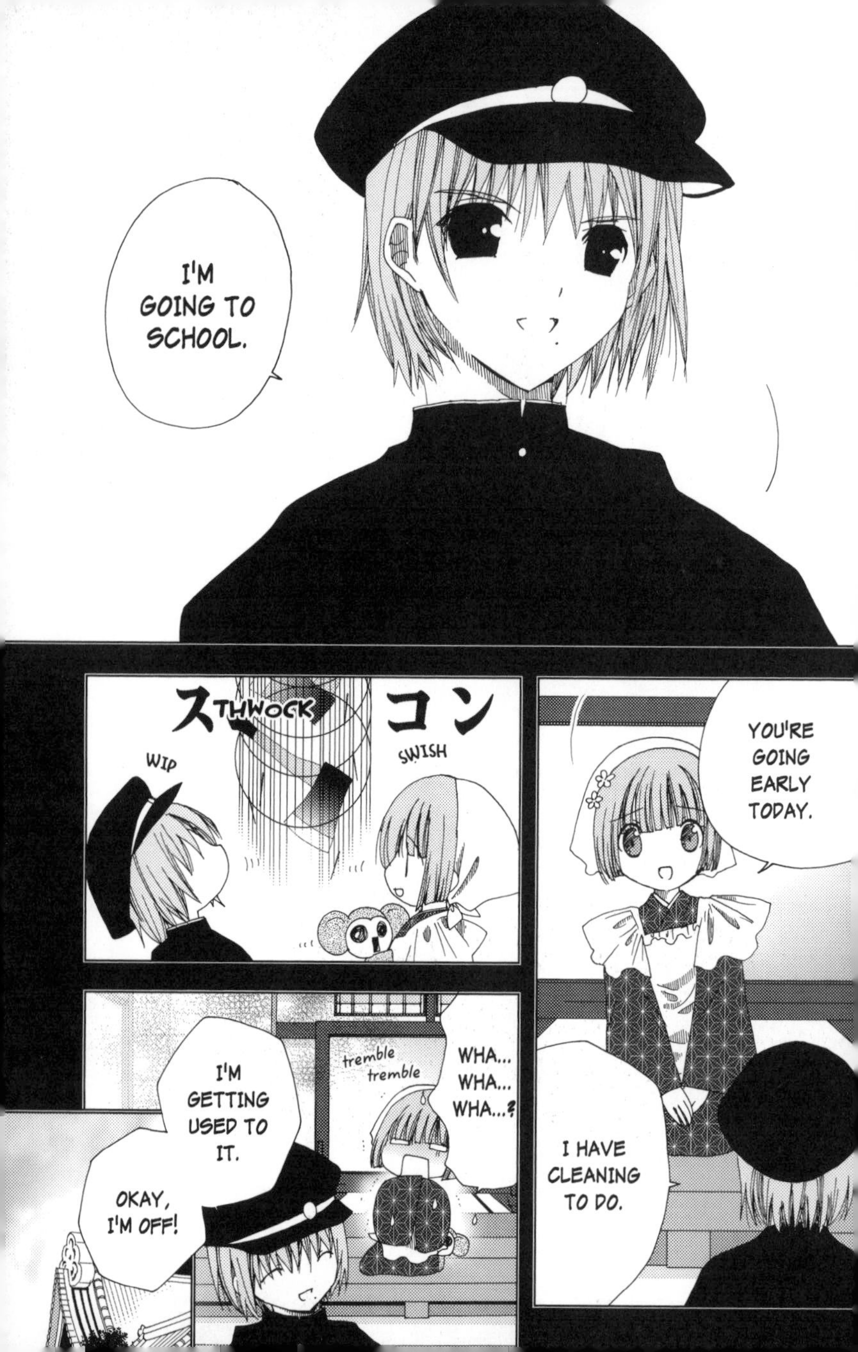
I'M GOING TO SCHOOL.
YOU'RE GOING EARLY TODAY.
I HAVE CLEANING TO DO.
スコン
THWOCK
SWISH
WIP
WHA... WHA... WHA...?
tremble tremble
I'M GETTING USED TO IT.
OKAY, I'M OFF!

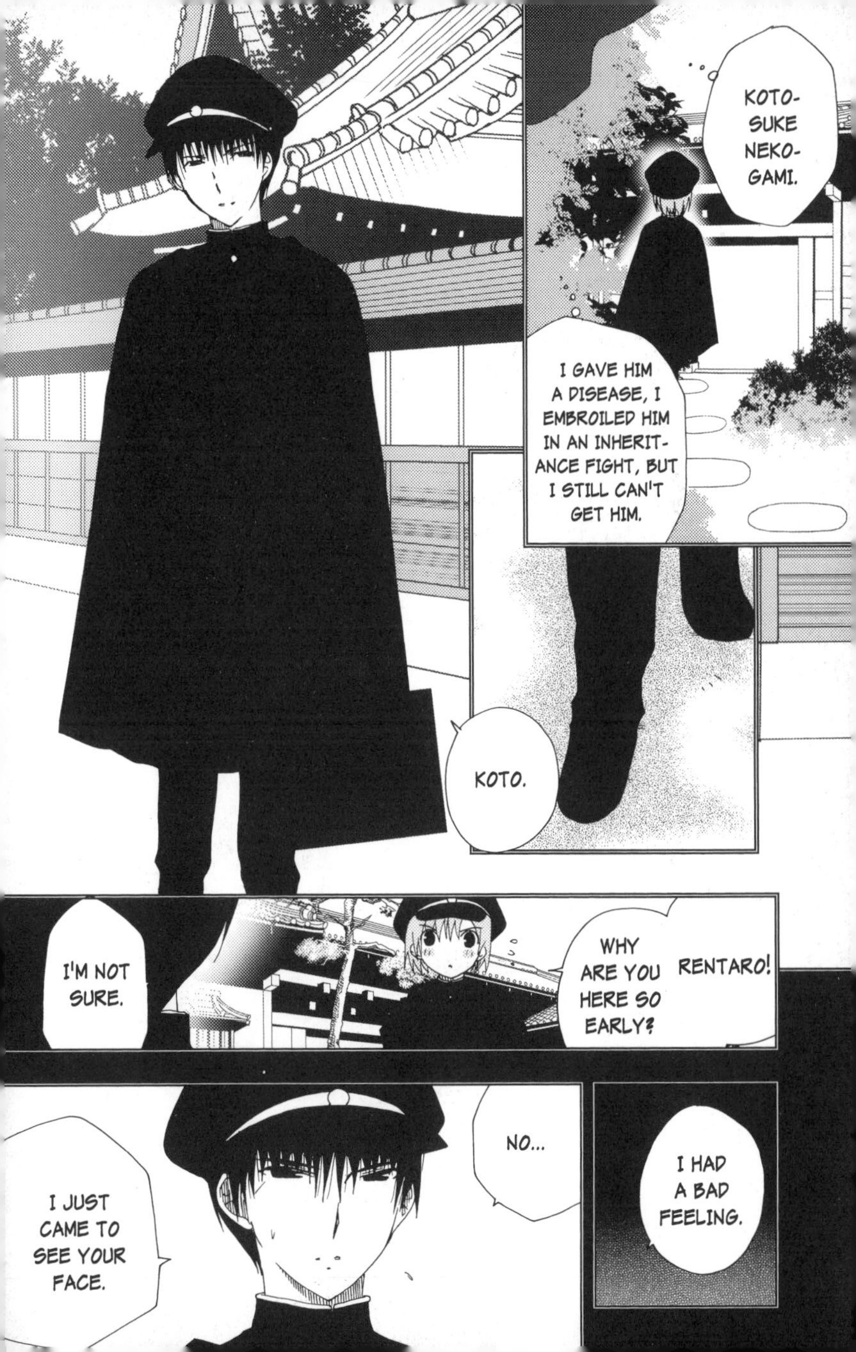
KOTO-SUKE NEKO-GAMI.
I GAVE HIM A DISEASE, I EMBROILED HIM IN AN INHERIT-ANCE FIGHT, BUT I STILL CAN'T GET HIM.
KOTO.
RENTARO!
WHY ARE YOU HERE SO EARLY?
I'M NOT SURE.
I HAD A BAD FEELING.
NO...
I JUST CAME TO SEE YOUR FACE.

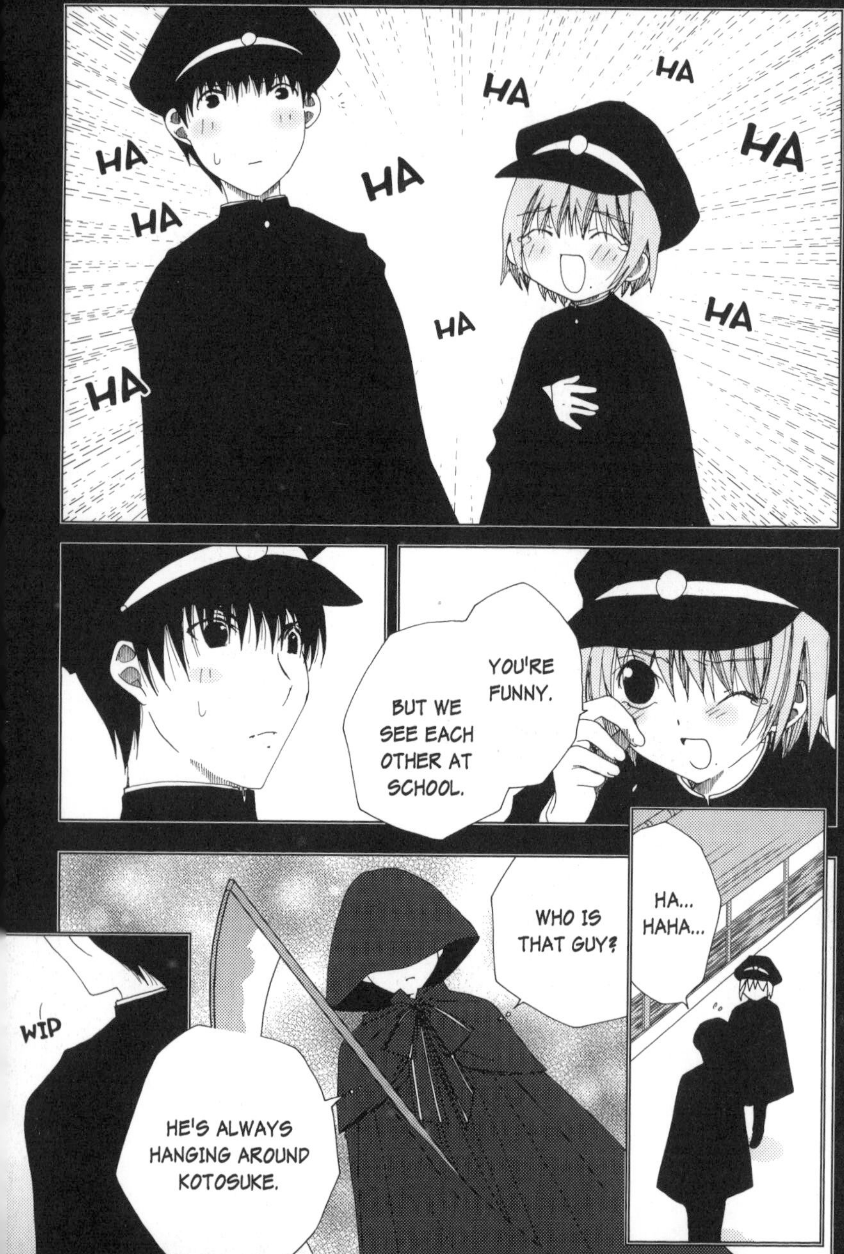
HA
HA
HA
HA
HA
HA
HA
HA
HA
YOU'RE FUNNY.
BUT WE SEE EACH OTHER AT SCHOOL.
HA... HAHA...
WHO IS THAT GUY?
HE'S ALWAYS HANGING AROUND KOTOSUKE.
WIP

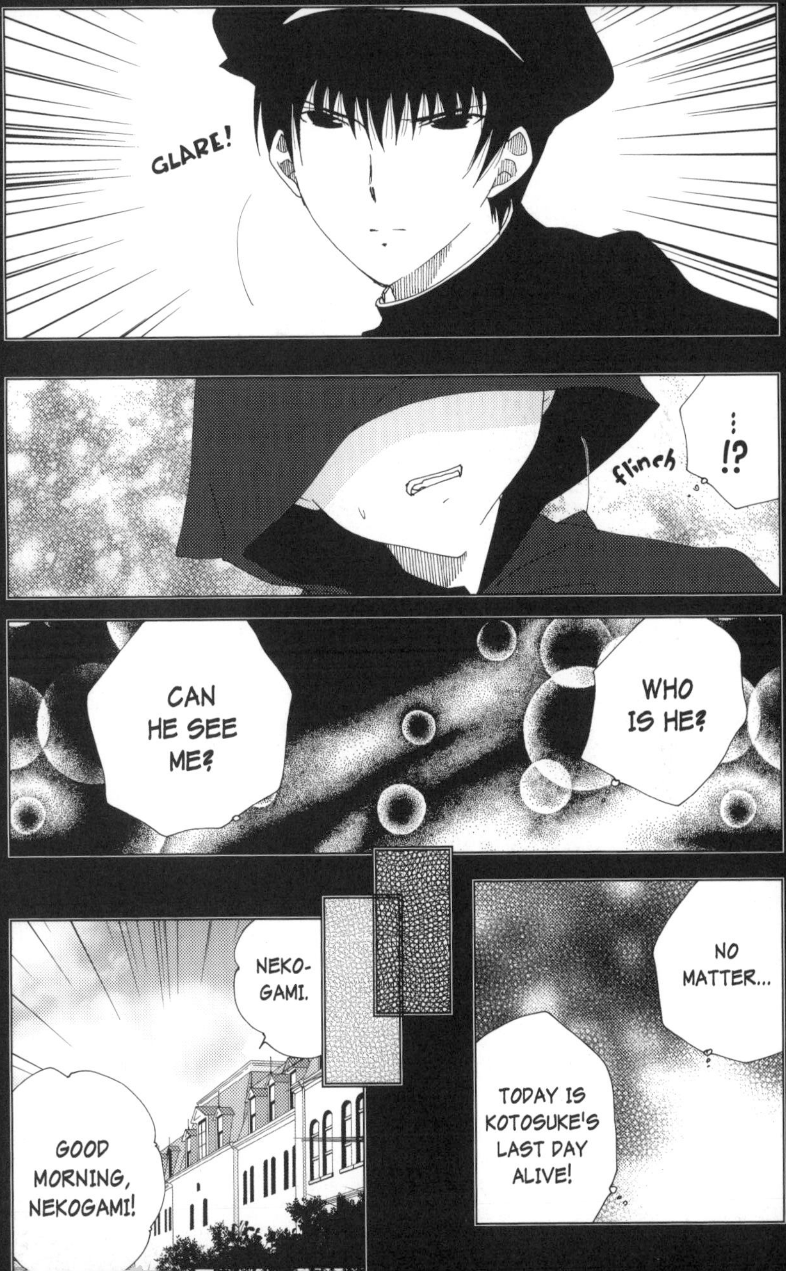
GLARE!
flinch
...!?
WHO IS HE?
CAN HE SEE ME?
NO MATTER...
TODAY IS KOTOSUKE'S LAST DAY ALIVE!
NEKO-GAMI.
GOOD MORNING, NEKOGAMI!

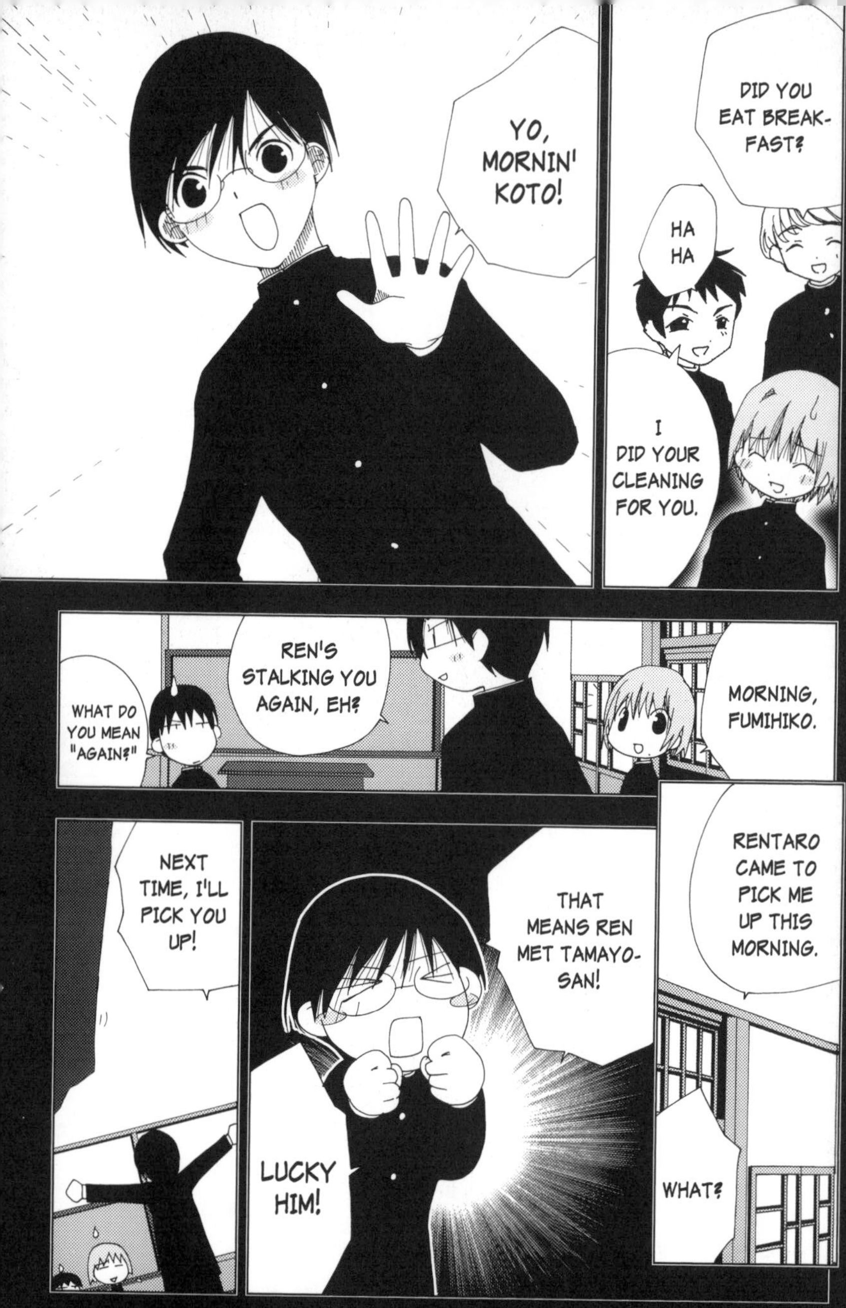
DID YOU EAT BREAK-FAST?
HA HA
I DID YOUR CLEANING FOR YOU.
YO, MORNIN' KOTO!
MORNING, FUMIHIKO.
REN'S STALKING YOU AGAIN, EH?
WHAT DO YOU MEAN "AGAIN?"
RENTARO CAME TO PICK ME UP THIS MORNING.
WHAT?
THAT MEANS REN MET TAMAYO-SAN!
LUCKY HIM!
NEXT TIME, I'LL PICK YOU UP!

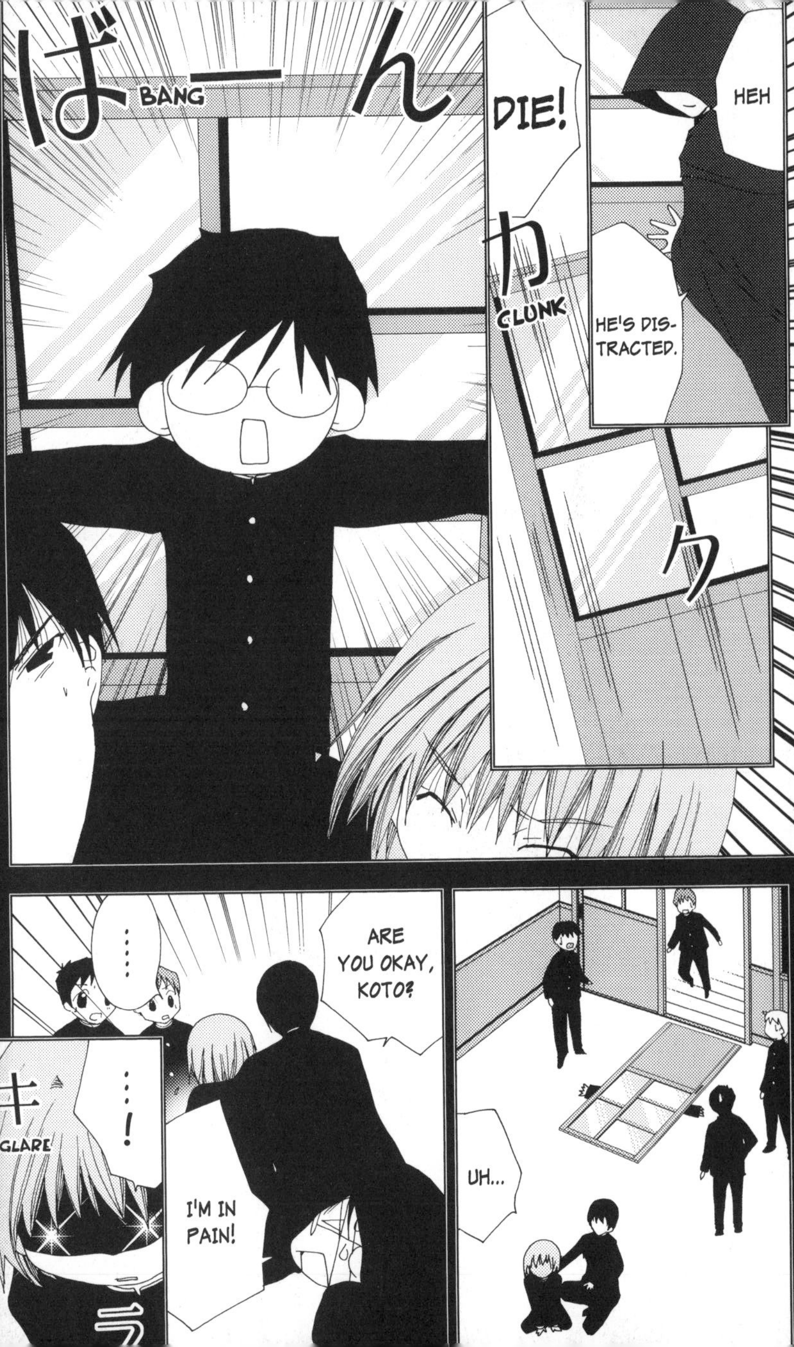
HEH
HE'S DIS-
TRACTED.
DIE!
カ
CLUNK
ク
ばーん
BANG
UH...
ARE YOU OKAY, KOTO?
......
I'M IN PAIN!
...!
キ
GLARE
ラ

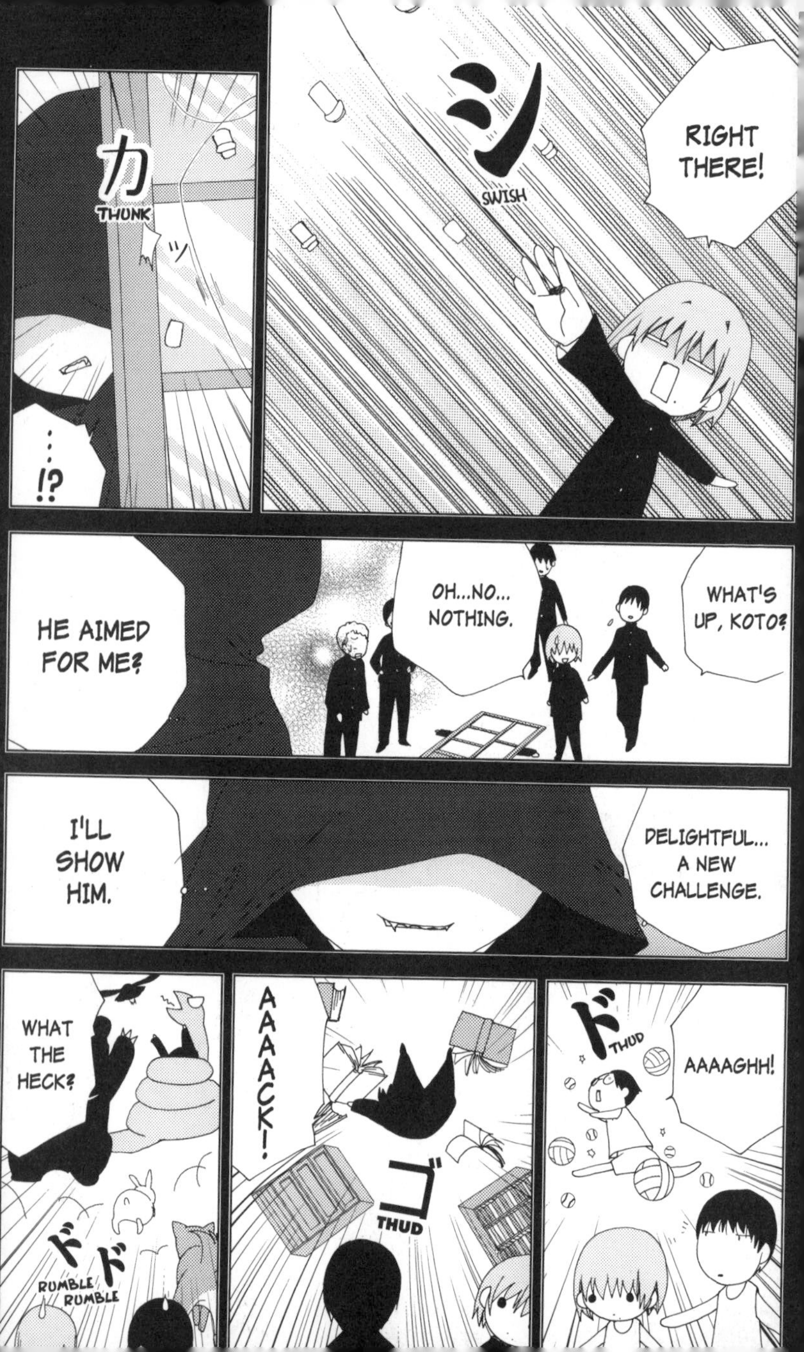
シ
SWISH
RIGHT THERE!
カ
THUNK
ツ
...!?
WHAT'S UP, KOTO?
OH...NO... NOTHING.
HE AIMED FOR ME?
DELIGHTFUL... A NEW CHALLENGE.
I'LL SHOW HIM.
ド
THUD
AAAAGHH!
AAAACK!
ゴ
THUD
WHAT THE HECK?
ドド
RUMBLE RUMBLE

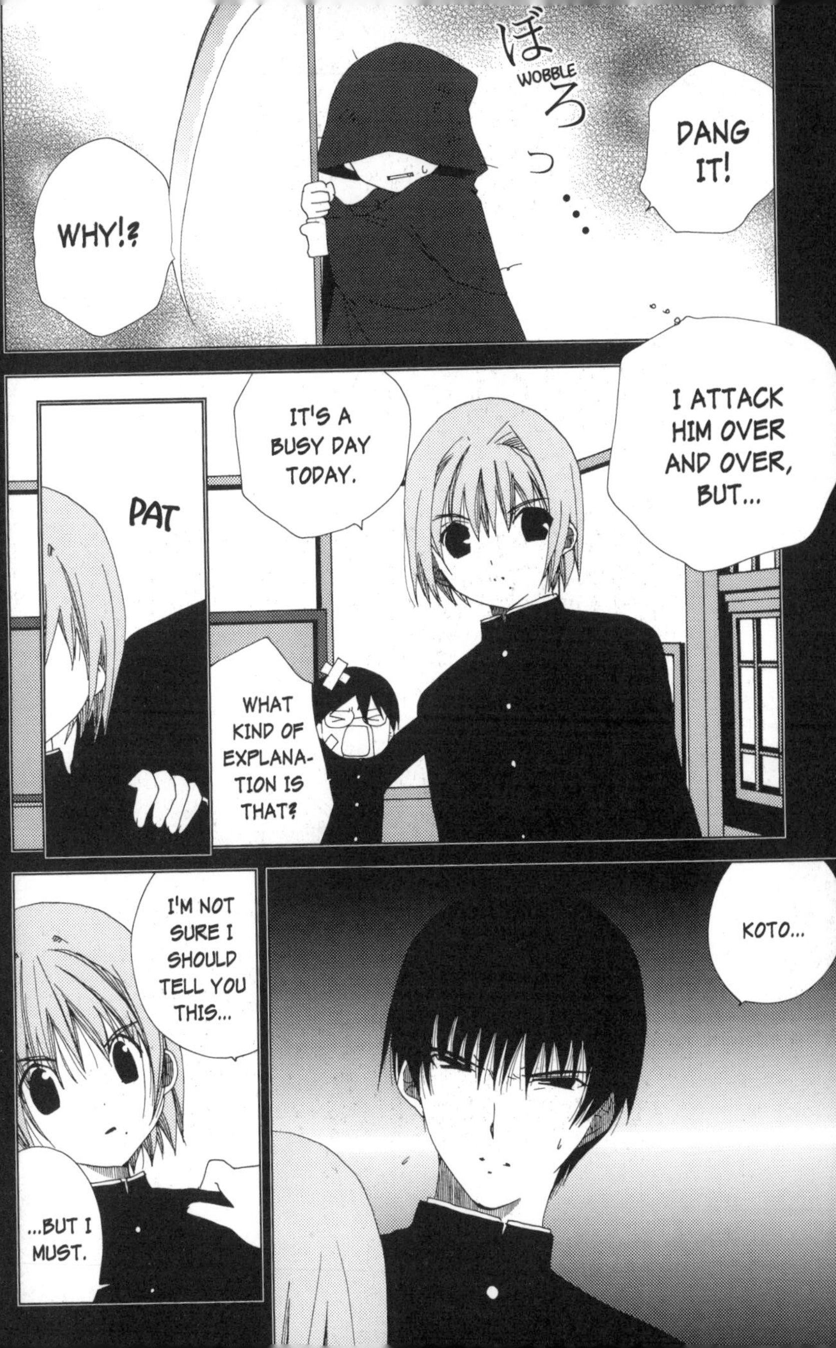
DANG IT!
ぼろっ
WOBBLE
...
WHY!?
I ATTACK HIM OVER AND OVER, BUT...
IT'S A BUSY DAY TODAY.
WHAT KIND OF EXPLANATION IS THAT?
PAT
KOTO...
I'M NOT SURE I SHOULD TELL YOU THIS...
...BUT I MUST.

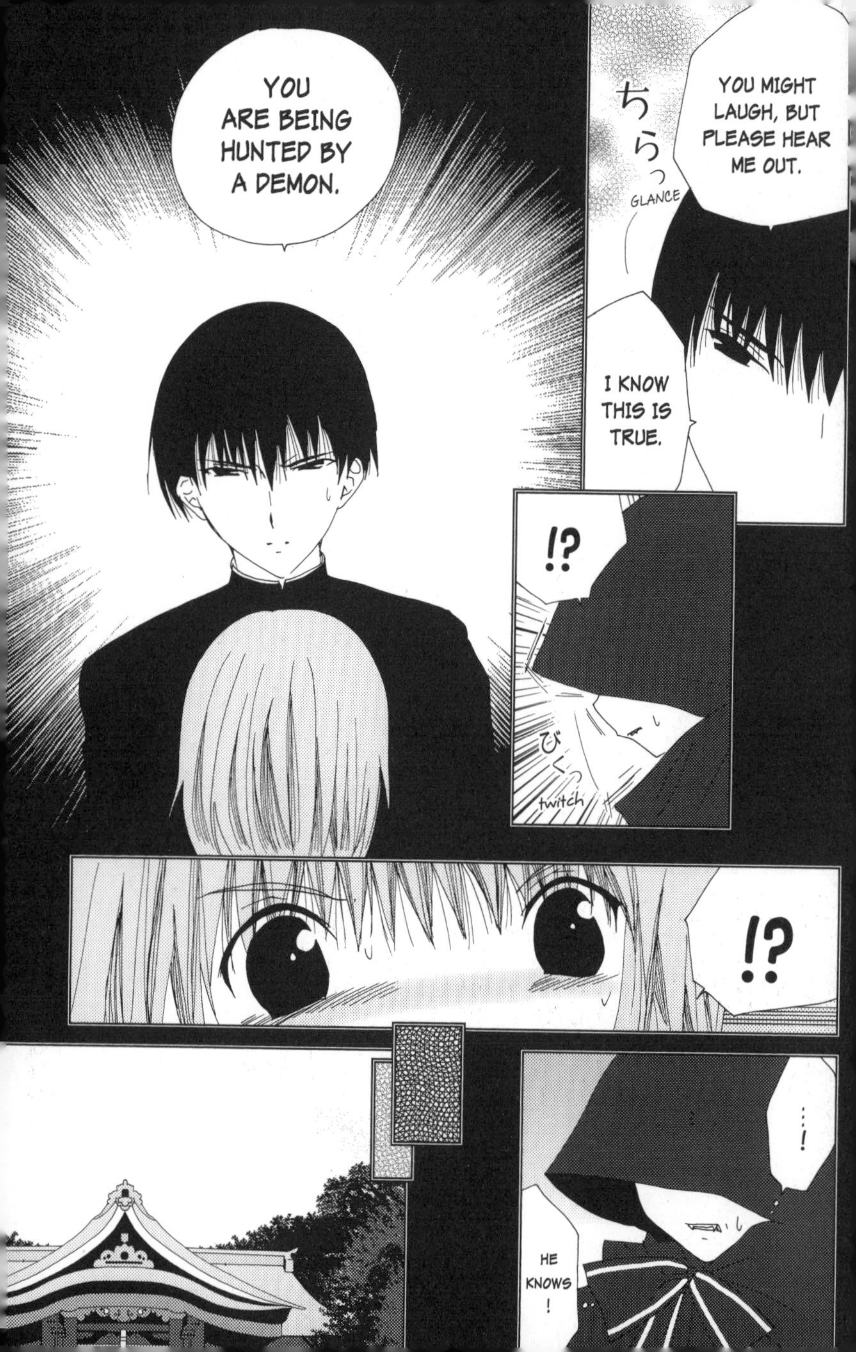
YOU MIGHT LAUGH, BUT PLEASE HEAR ME OUT.
ちらっ
GLANCE
I KNOW THIS IS TRUE.
!?
びくっ
twitch
YOU ARE BEING HUNTED BY A DEMON.
!?
...!
HE KNOWS!

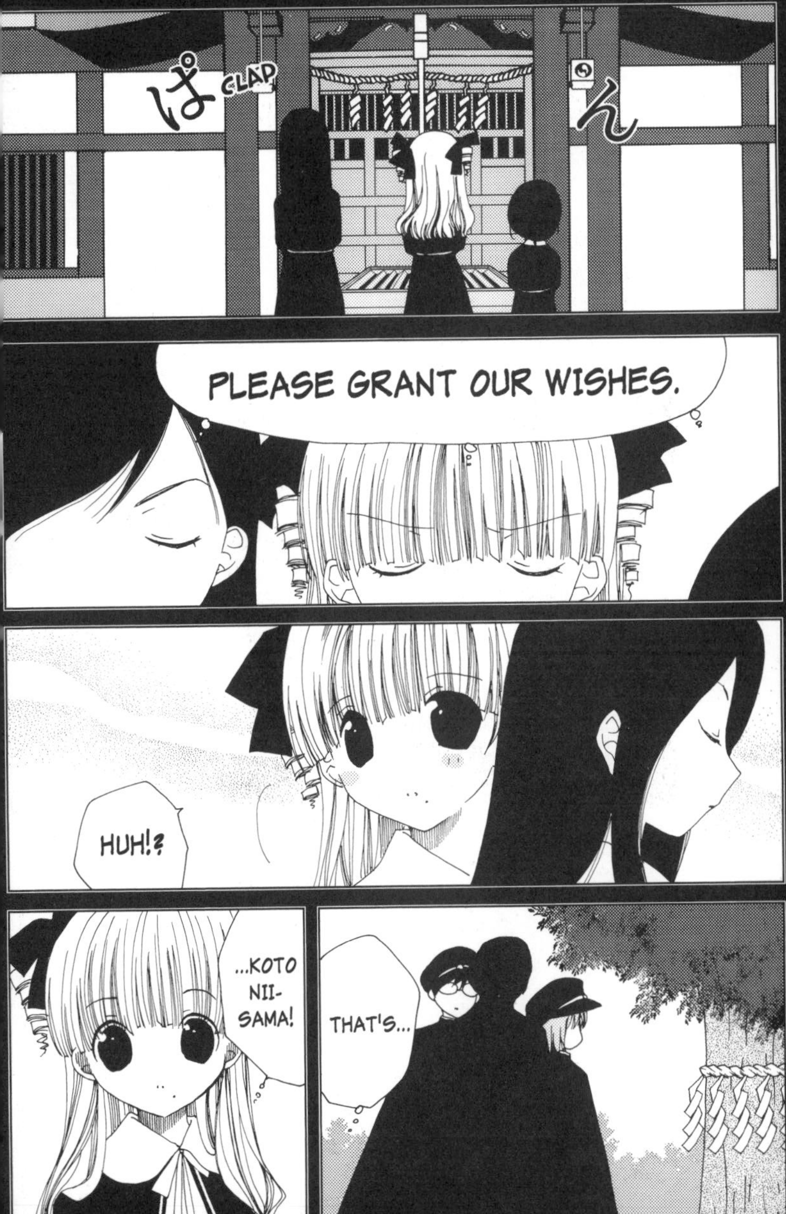
ぱ CLAP ん
PLEASE GRANT OUR WISHES.
HUH!?
THAT'S...
...KOTO NII-SAMA!

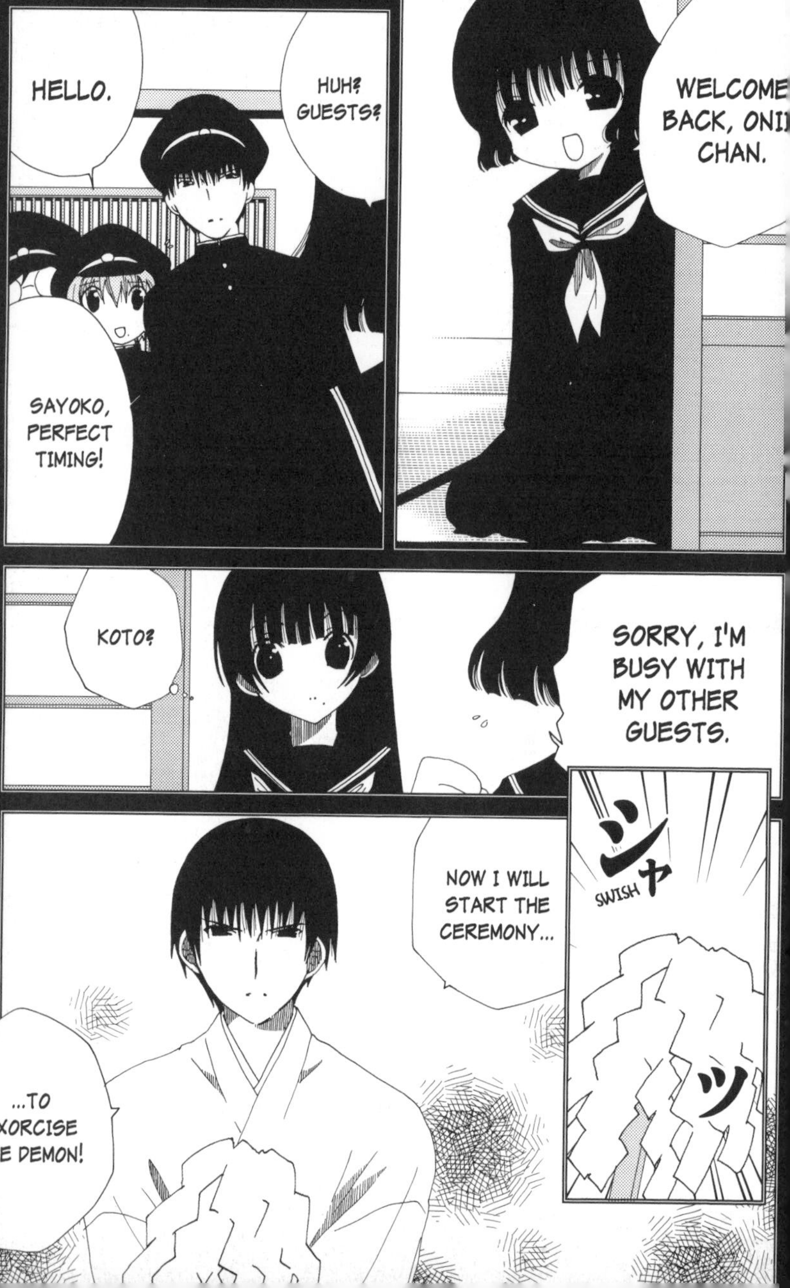
WELCOME BACK, ONII CHAN.
HUH? GUESTS?
HELLO.
SAYOKO, PERFECT TIMING!
SORRY, I'M BUSY WITH MY OTHER GUESTS.
KOTO?
シャ
SWISH
ッ
NOW I WILL START THE CEREMONY...
...TO EXORCISE THE DEMON!

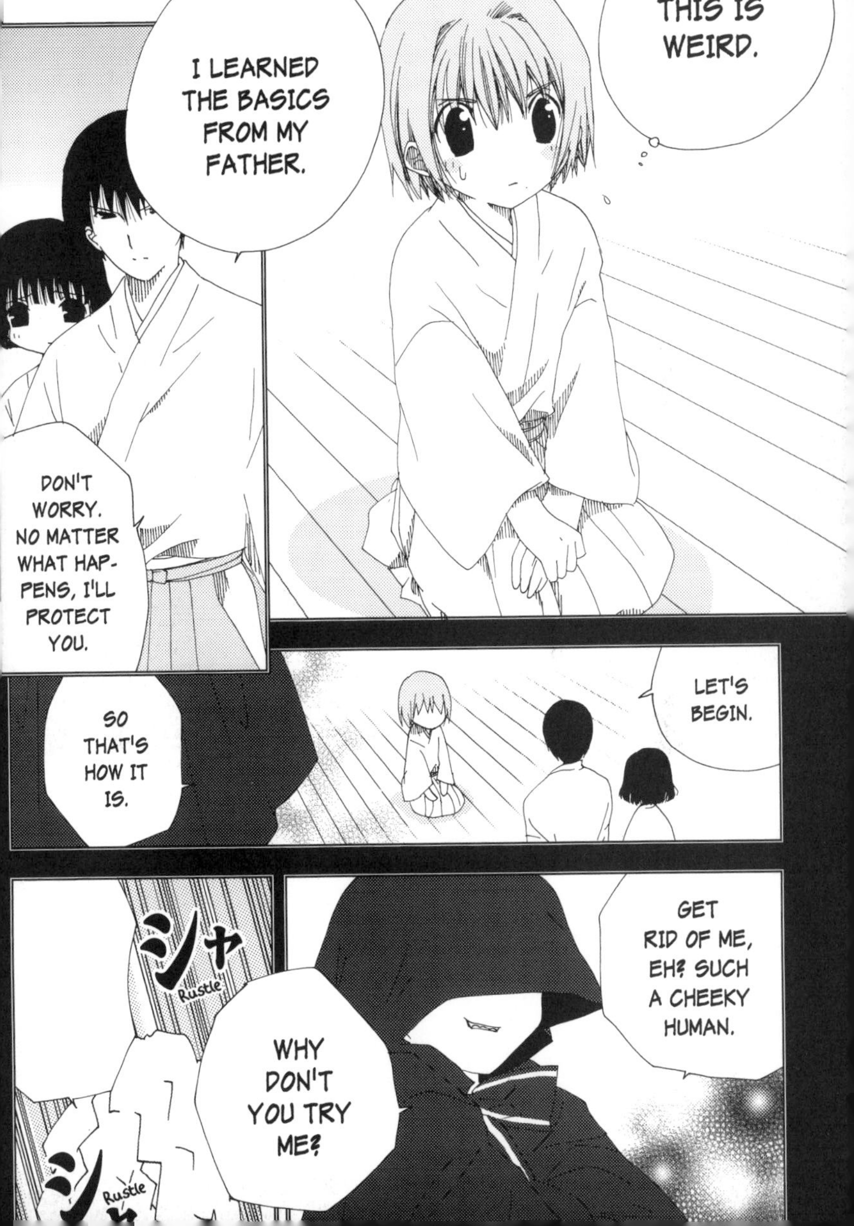
THIS IS WEIRD.
I LEARNED THE BASICS FROM MY FATHER.
DON'T WORRY. NO MATTER WHAT HAP-PENS, I'LL PROTECT YOU.
LET'S BEGIN.
SO THAT'S HOW IT IS.
GET RID OF ME, EH? SUCH A CHEEKY HUMAN.
WHY DON'T YOU TRY ME?
シャ
Rustle
シ
Rustle

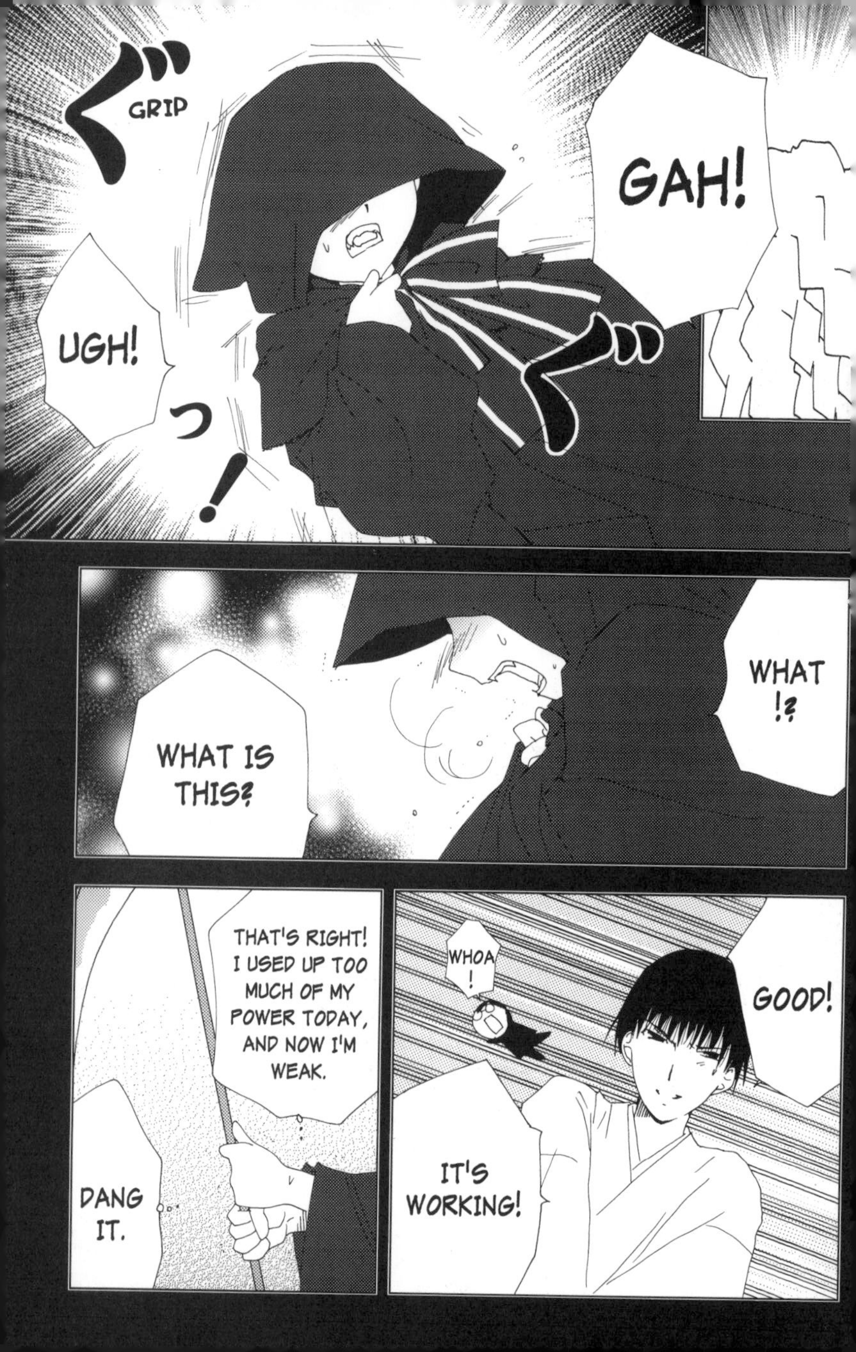
GAH!
GRIP
UGH!
WHAT !?
WHAT IS THIS?
GOOD!
WHOA !
IT'S WORKING!
THAT'S RIGHT! I USED UP TOO MUCH OF MY POWER TODAY, AND NOW I'M WEAK.
DANG IT.

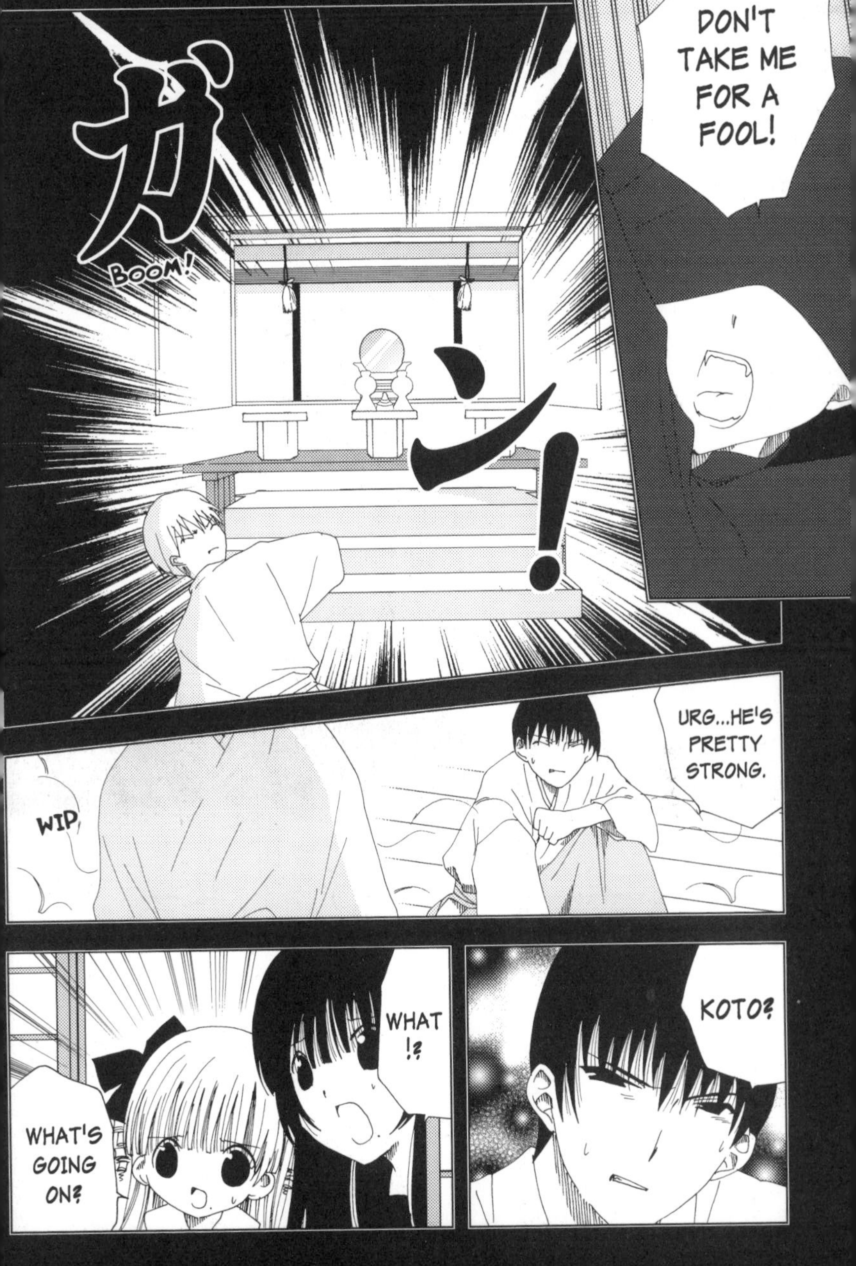
DON'T TAKE ME FOR A FOOL!
カン!
BOOM!
URG...HE'S PRETTY STRONG.
WIP
KOTO?
WHAT !?
WHAT'S GOING ON?

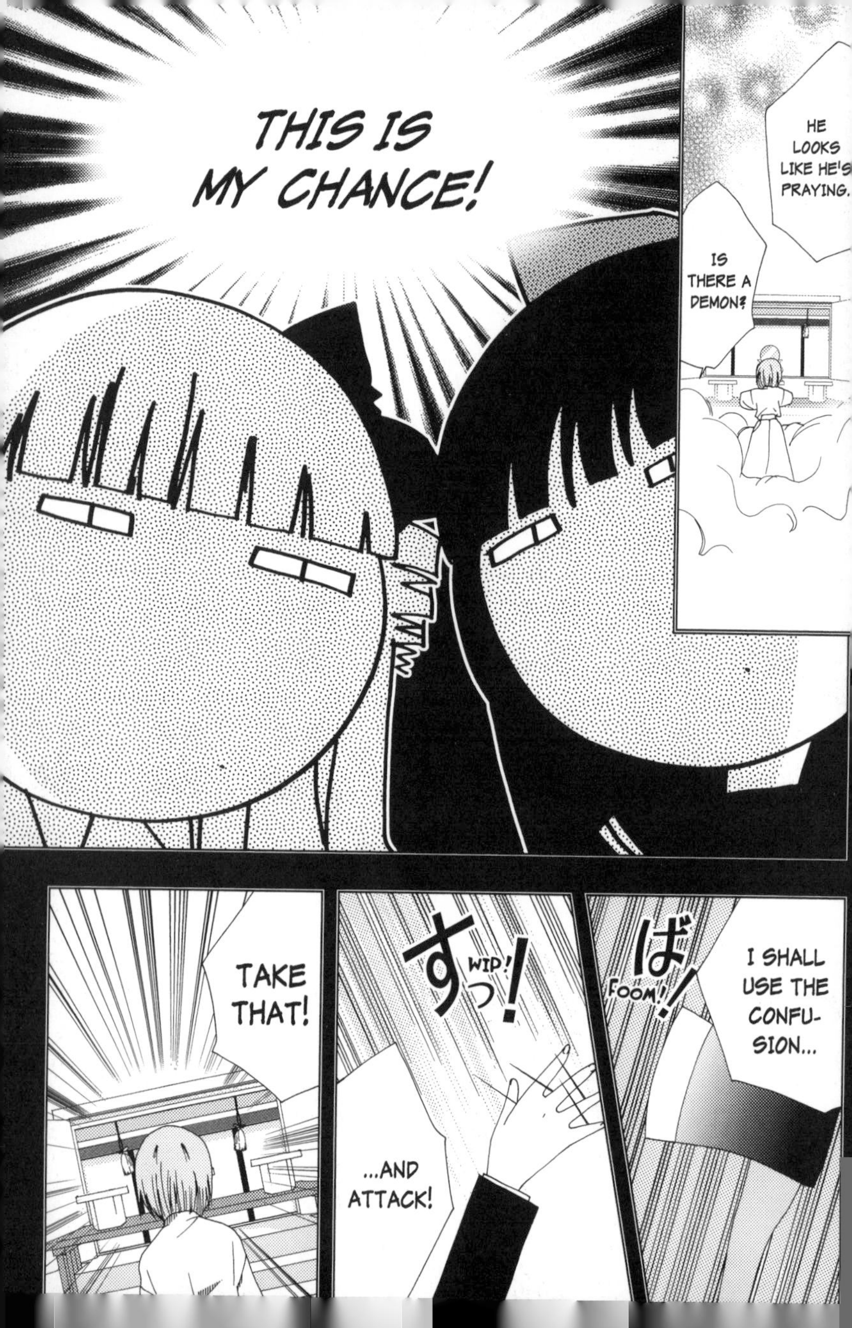
HE LOOKS LIKE HE'S PRAYING.
IS THERE A DEMON?
THIS IS MY CHANCE!
I SHALL USE THE CONFU-SION...
ば FOOM!!
すっ WIP!!
...AND ATTACK!
TAKE THAT!

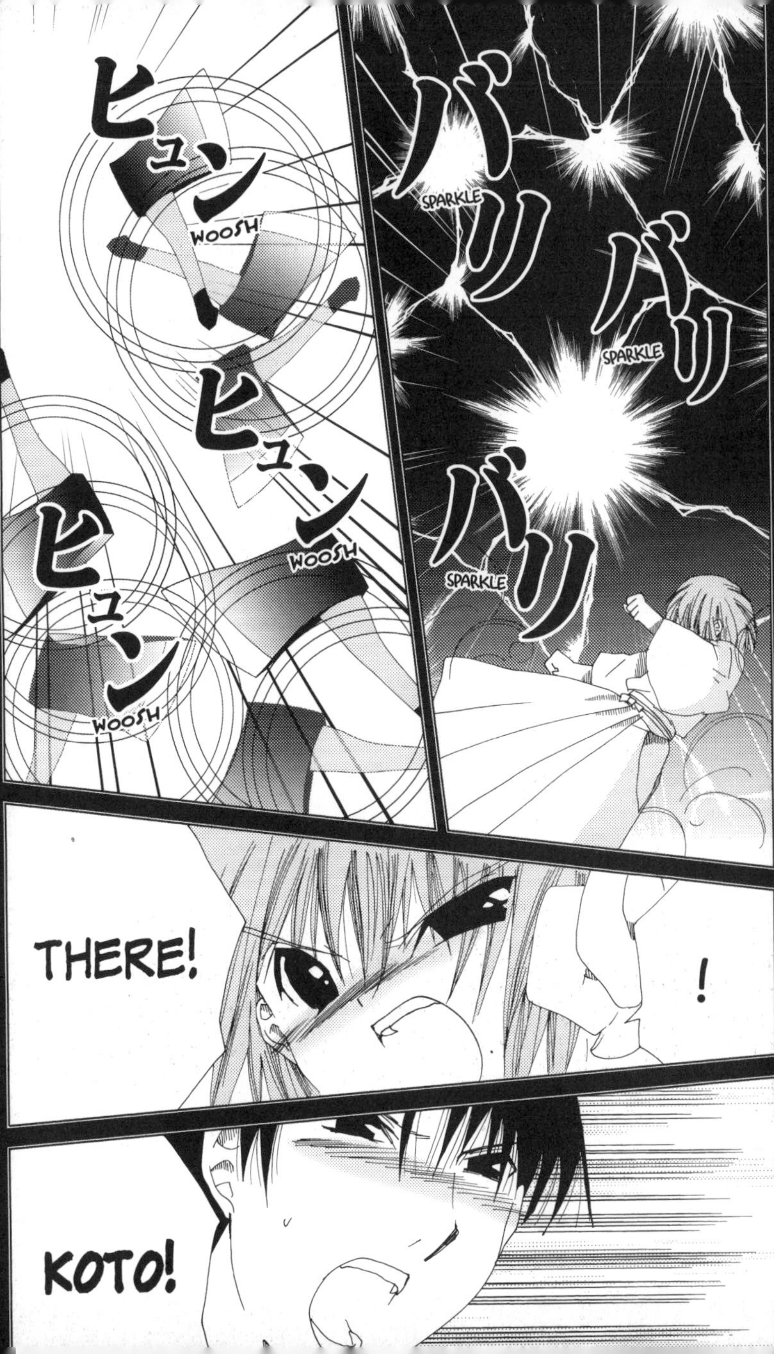
バリ
SPARKLE
バリ
SPARKLE
バリ
SPARKLE
ヒュン
WOOSH
ヒュン
WOOSH
ヒュン
WOOSH
!
THERE!
KOTO!

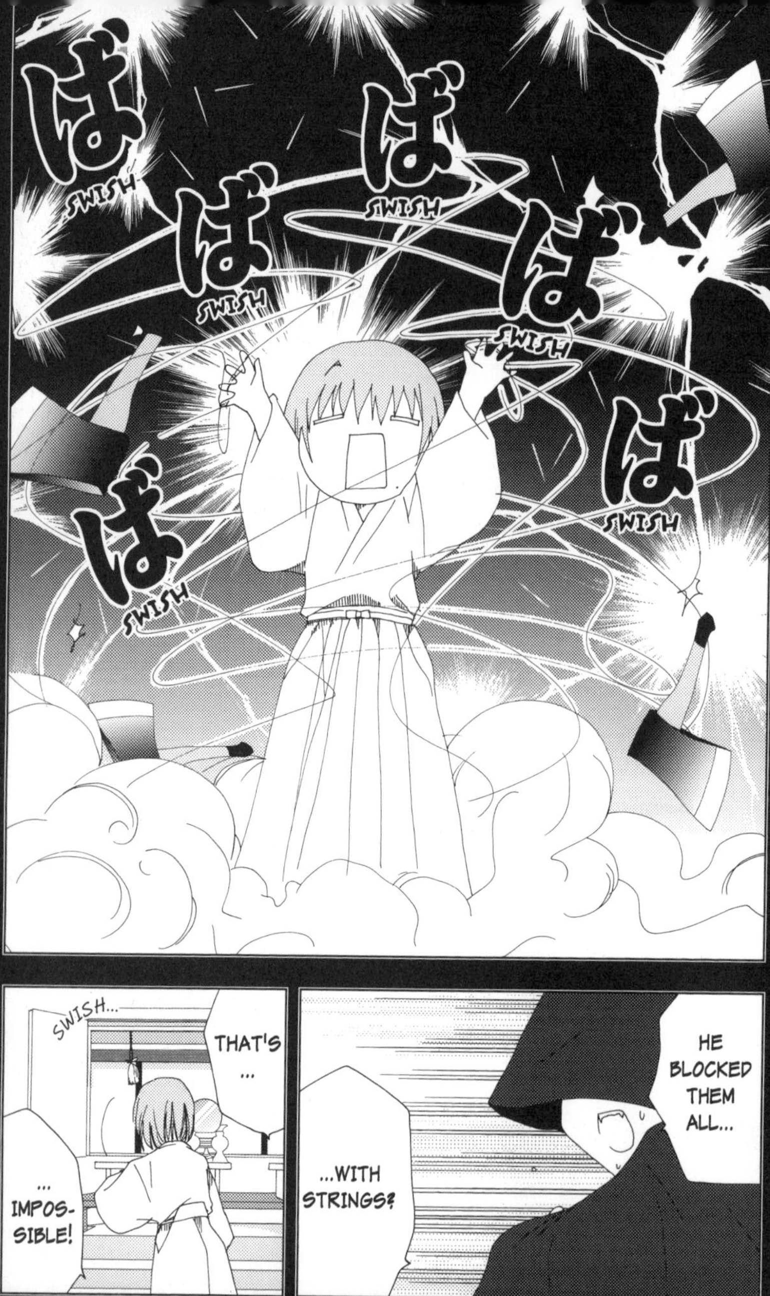
ば SWISH
ば SWISH
ば SWISH
ば SWISH
ば SWISH
ば SWISH
HE BLOCKED THEM ALL...
...WITH STRINGS?
SWISH...
THAT'S ...
... IMPOSSIBLE!

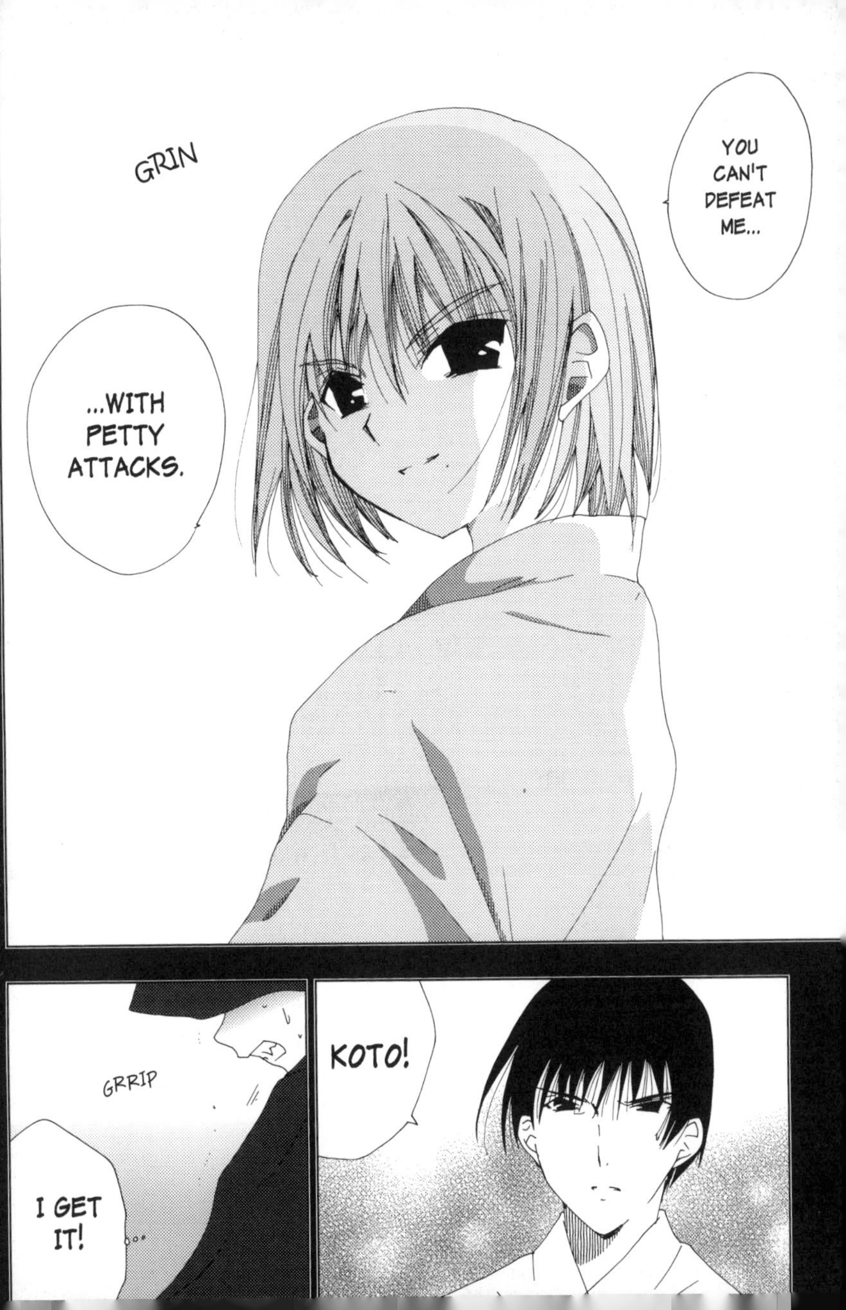
YOU CAN'T DEFEAT ME...
GRIN
...WITH PETTY ATTACKS.
KOTO!
GRRIP
I GET IT!

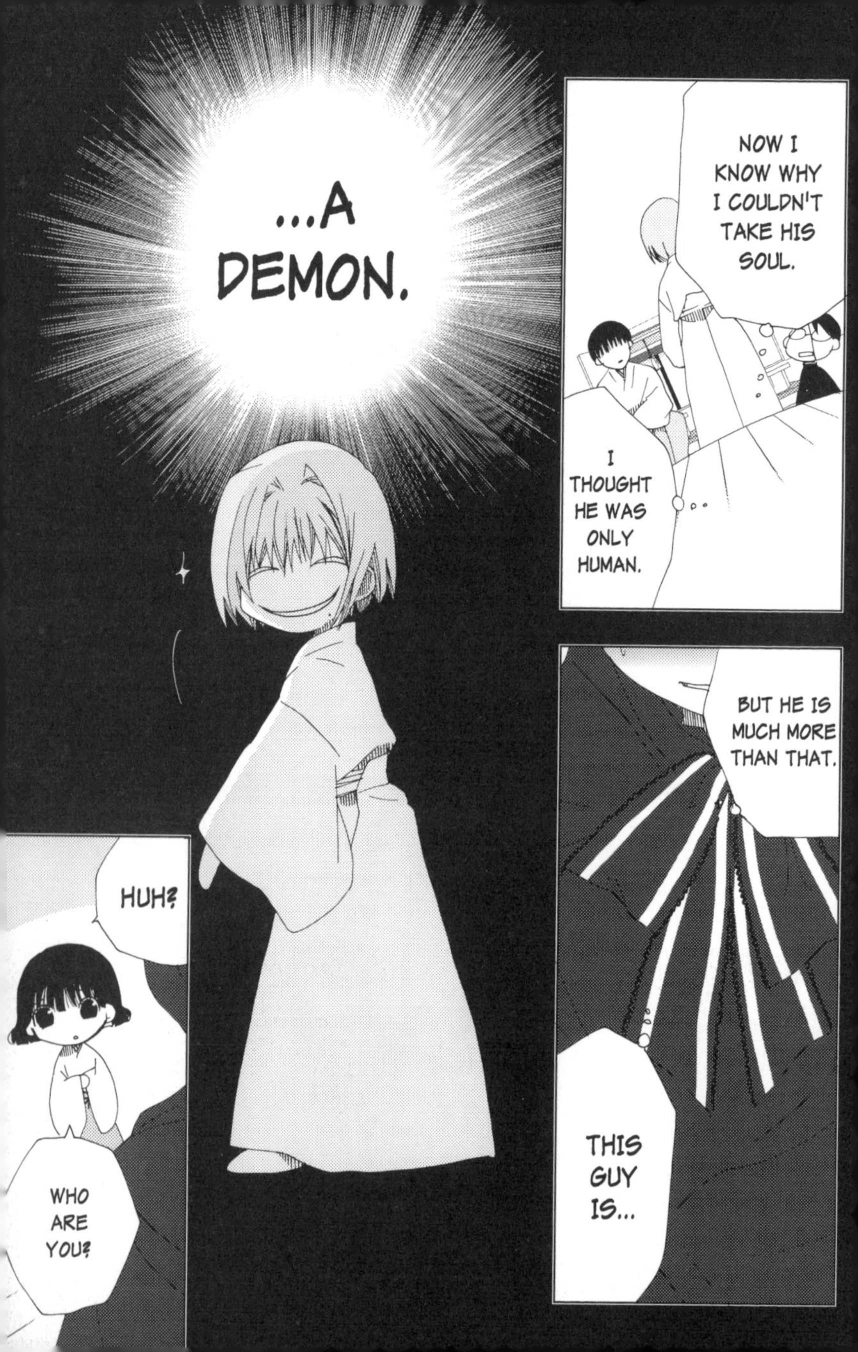
NOW I KNOW WHY I COULDN'T TAKE HIS SOUL.
I THOUGHT HE WAS ONLY HUMAN.
BUT HE IS MUCH MORE THAN THAT.
THIS GUY IS...
...A DEMON.
HUH?
WHO ARE YOU?

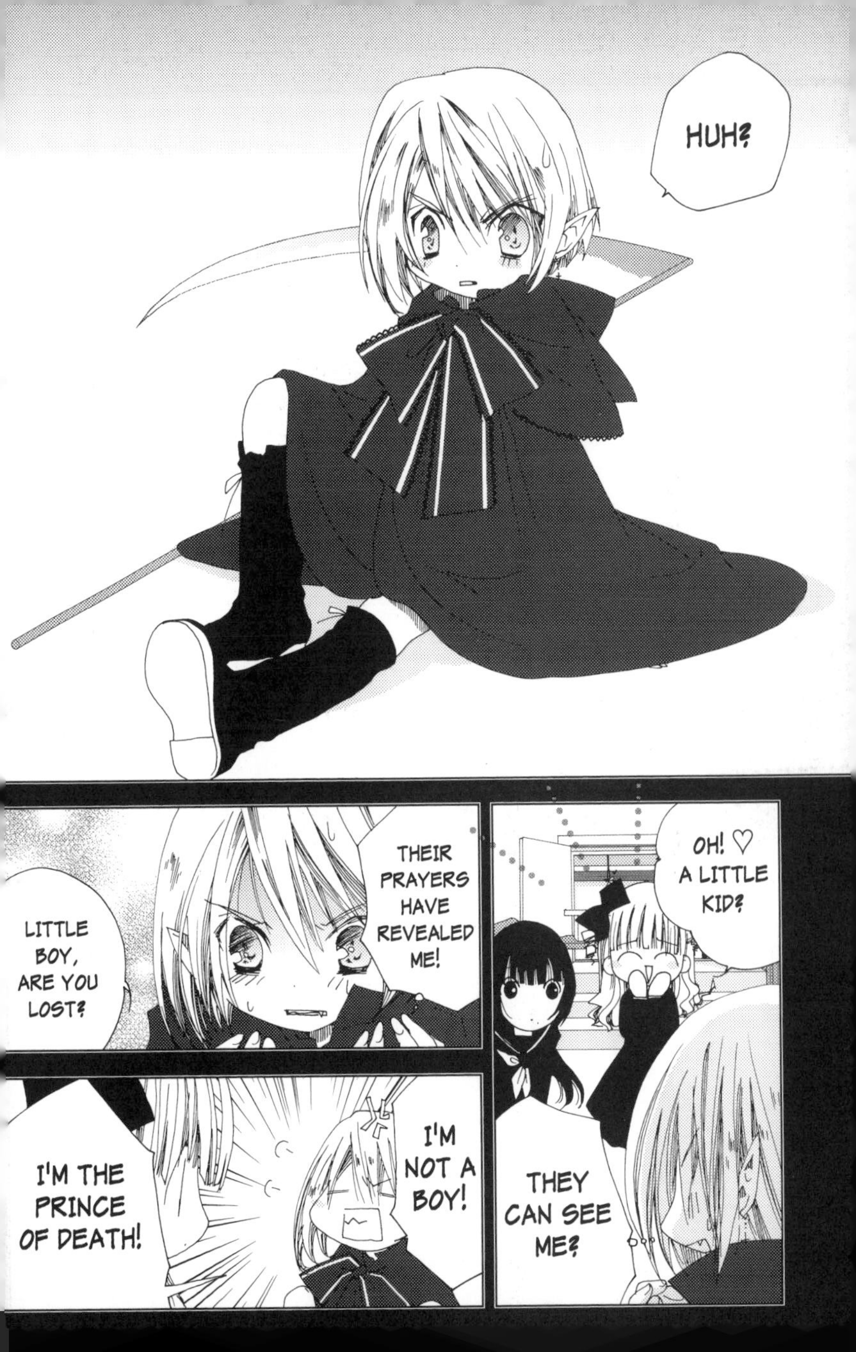
HUH?
OH! ♡ A LITTLE KID?
THEY CAN SEE ME?
THEIR PRAYERS HAVE REVEALED ME!
LITTLE BOY, ARE YOU LOST?
I'M NOT A BOY!
I'M THE PRINCE OF DEATH!

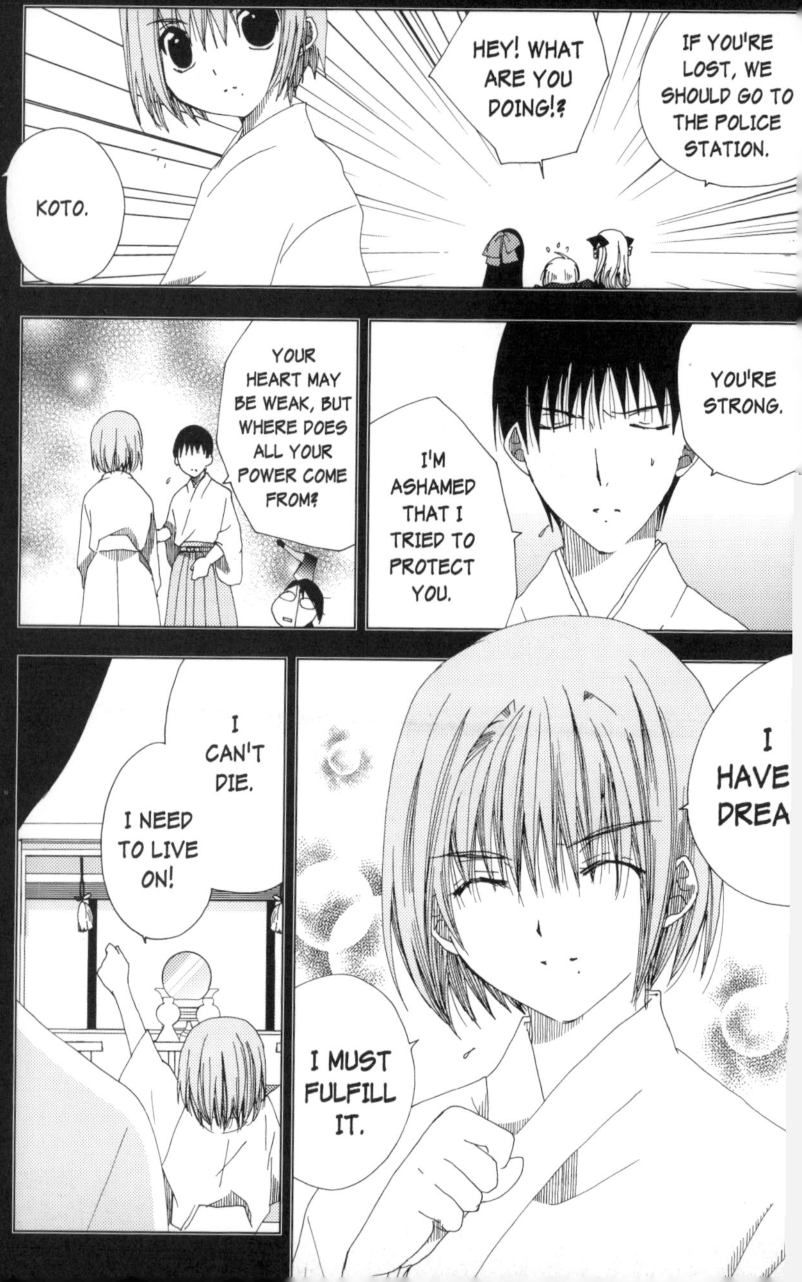
IF YOU'RE LOST, WE SHOULD GO TO THE POLICE STATION.
HEY! WHAT ARE YOU DOING!?
KOTO.
YOU'RE STRONG.
I'M ASHAMED THAT I TRIED TO PROTECT YOU.
YOUR HEART MAY BE WEAK, BUT WHERE DOES ALL YOUR POWER COME FROM?
I HAVE DREA
I MUST FULFILL IT.
I CAN'T DIE.
I NEED TO LIVE ON!

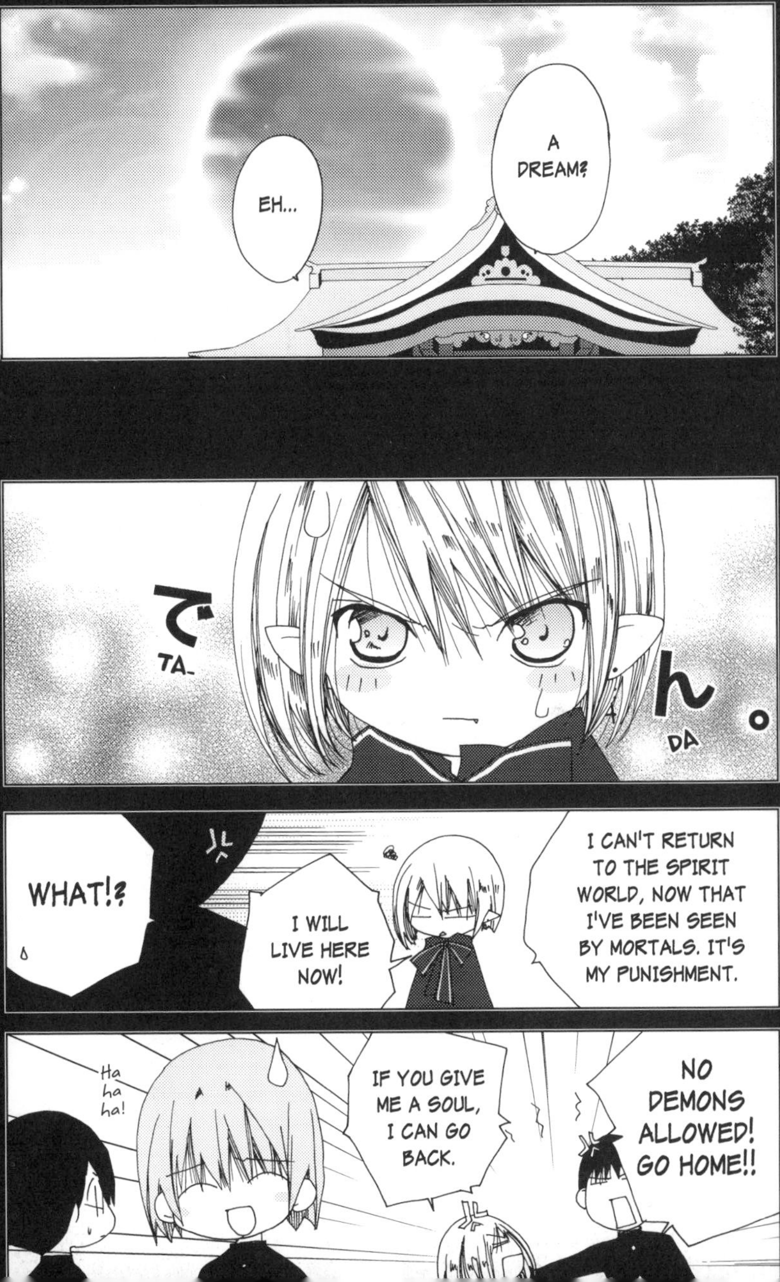
A DREAM?
EH...
で
TA-
ん。
DA
I CAN'T RETURN TO THE SPIRIT WORLD, NOW THAT I'VE BEEN SEEN BY MORTALS. IT'S MY PUNISHMENT.
I WILL LIVE HERE NOW!
WHAT!?
NO DEMONS ALLOWED! GO HOME!!
IF YOU GIVE ME A SOUL, I CAN GO BACK.
Ha ha ha!

Chapter FIVE

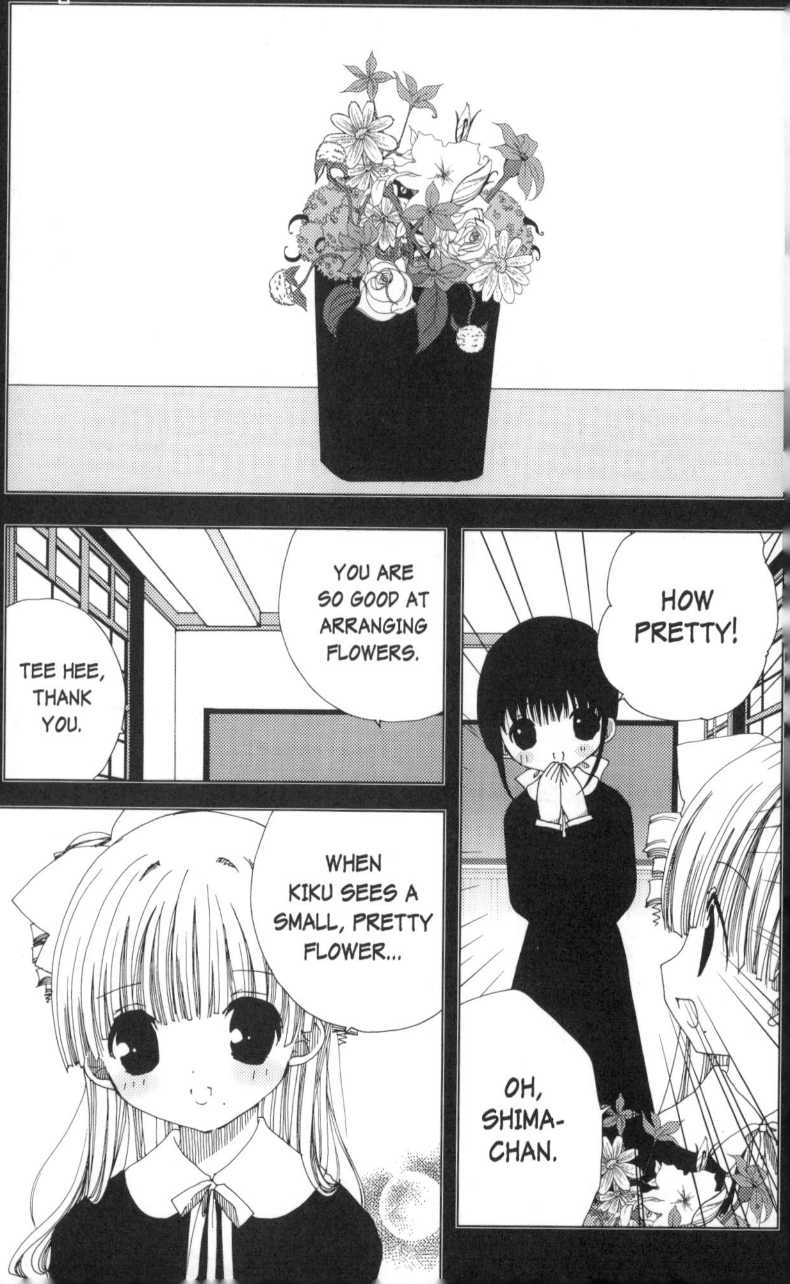
HOW PRETTY!
OH, SHIMA-CHAN.
YOU ARE SO GOOD AT ARRANGING FLOWERS.
TEE HEE, THANK YOU.
WHEN KIKU SEES A SMALL, PRETTY FLOWER...

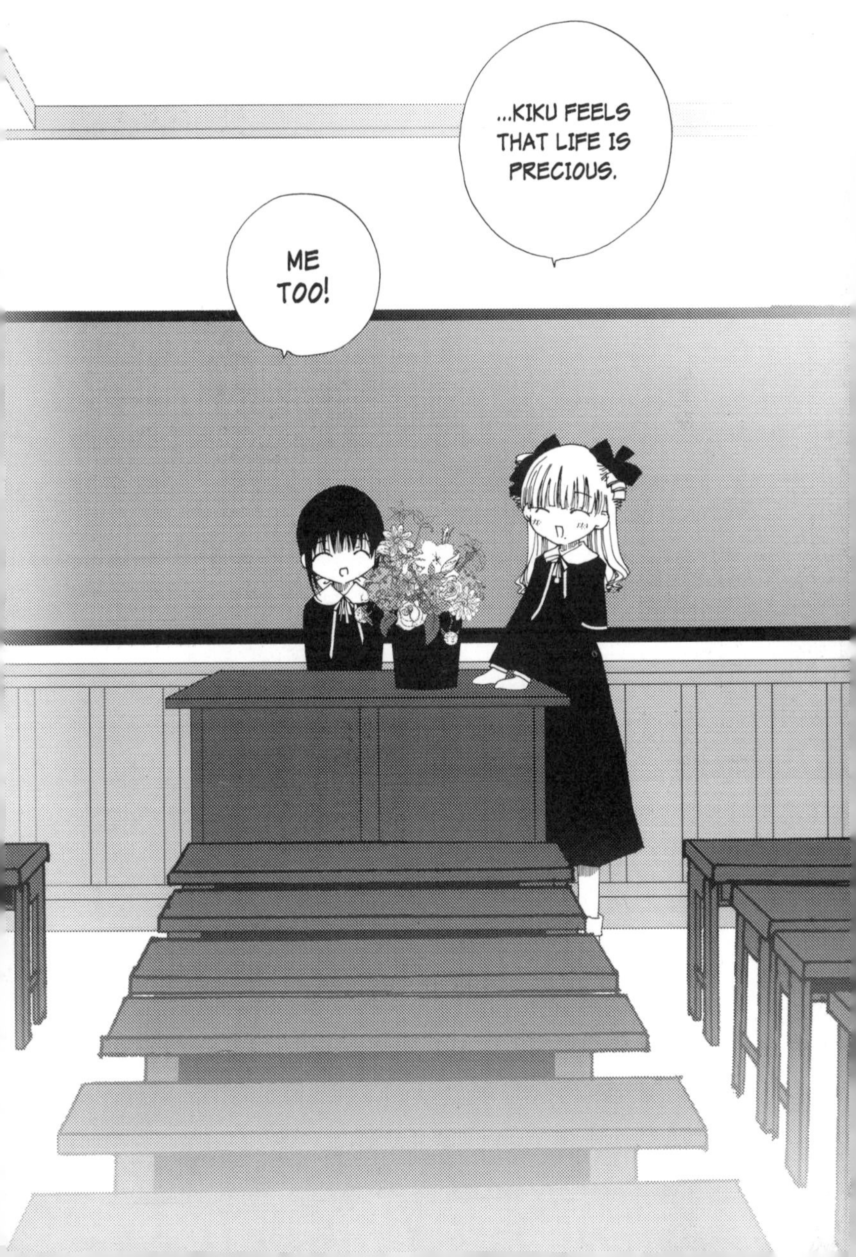
...KIKU FEELS THAT LIFE IS PRECIOUS.
ME TOO!

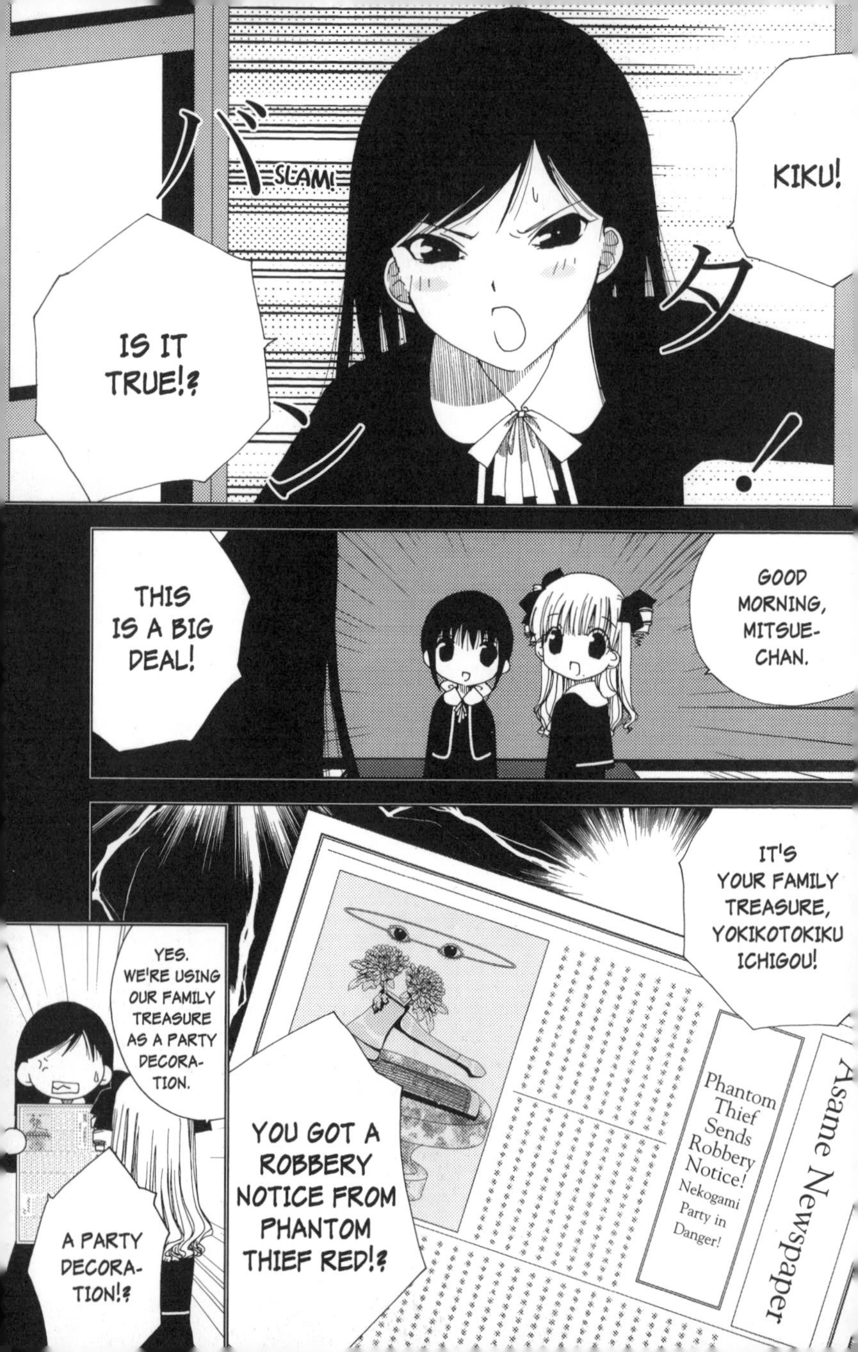
KIKU!
バタン!
SLAM!
IS IT TRUE!?
GOOD MORNING, MITSUE-CHAN.
THIS IS A BIG DEAL!
IT'S YOUR FAMILY TREASURE, YOKIKOTOKIKU ICHIGOU!
Asame Newspaper
Phantom Thief Sends Robbery Notice!
Nekogami Party in Danger!
YOU GOT A ROBBERY NOTICE FROM PHANTOM THIEF RED!?
YES. WE'RE USING OUR FAMILY TREASURE AS A PARTY DECORATION.
A PARTY DECORATION!?

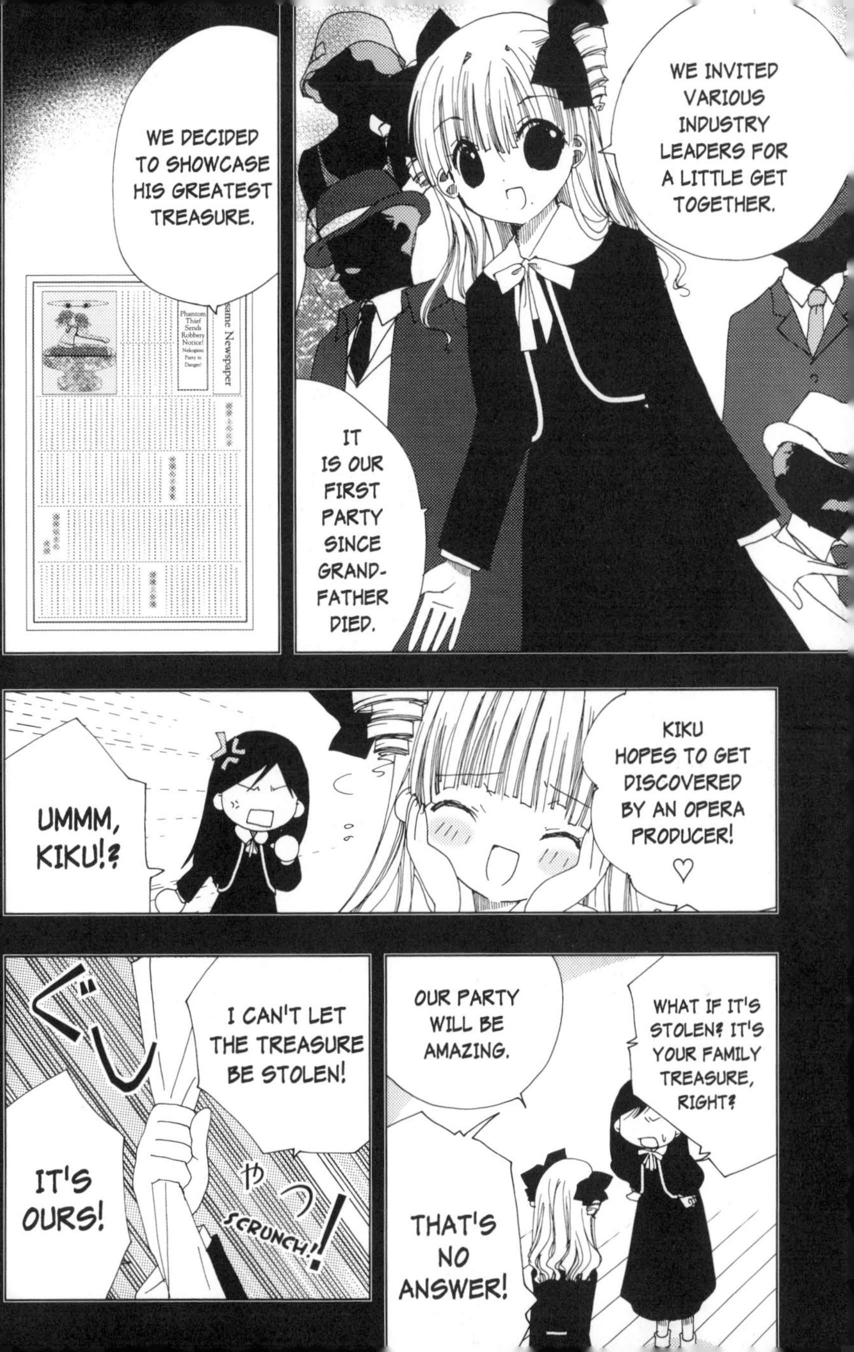
WE INVITED VARIOUS INDUSTRY LEADERS FOR A LITTLE GET TOGETHER.
IT IS OUR FIRST PARTY SINCE GRAND-FATHER DIED.
WE DECIDED TO SHOWCASE HIS GREATEST TREASURE.
Phantom Thief Sends Robbery Notice! Nekogami Party in Danger!
KIKU HOPES TO GET DISCOVERED BY AN OPERA PRODUCER! ♡
UMMM, KIKU!?
WHAT IF IT'S STOLEN? IT'S YOUR FAMILY TREASURE, RIGHT?
OUR PARTY WILL BE AMAZING.
THAT'S NO ANSWER!
I CAN'T LET THE TREASURE BE STOLEN!
IT'S OURS!
SCRUNCH!!

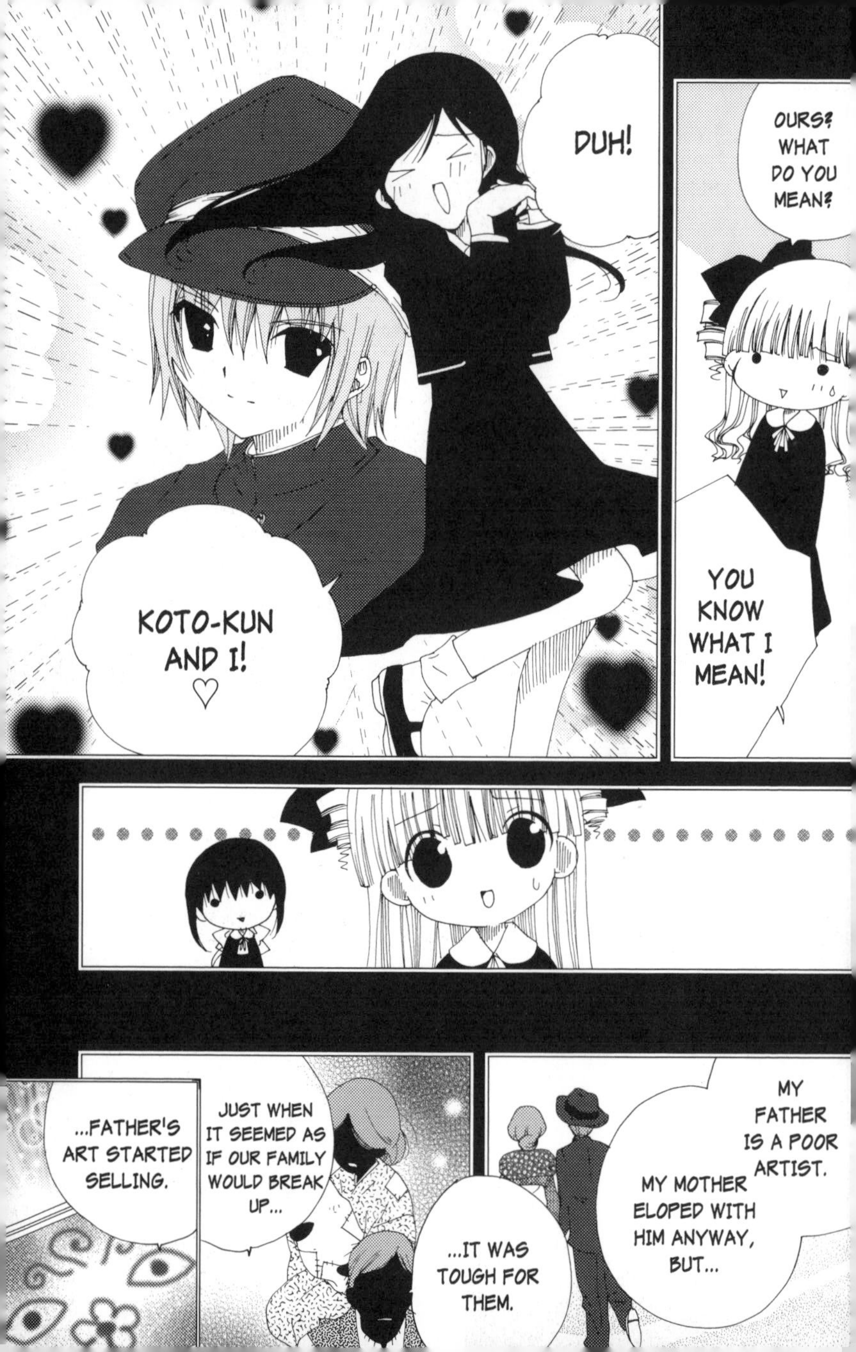
OURS? WHAT DO YOU MEAN?
YOU KNOW WHAT I MEAN!
DUH!
KOTO-KUN AND I! ♡
MY FATHER IS A POOR ARTIST.
MY MOTHER ELOPED WITH HIM ANYWAY, BUT...
...IT WAS TOUGH FOR THEM.
JUST WHEN IT SEEMED AS IF OUR FAMILY WOULD BREAK UP...
...FATHER'S ART STARTED SELLING.

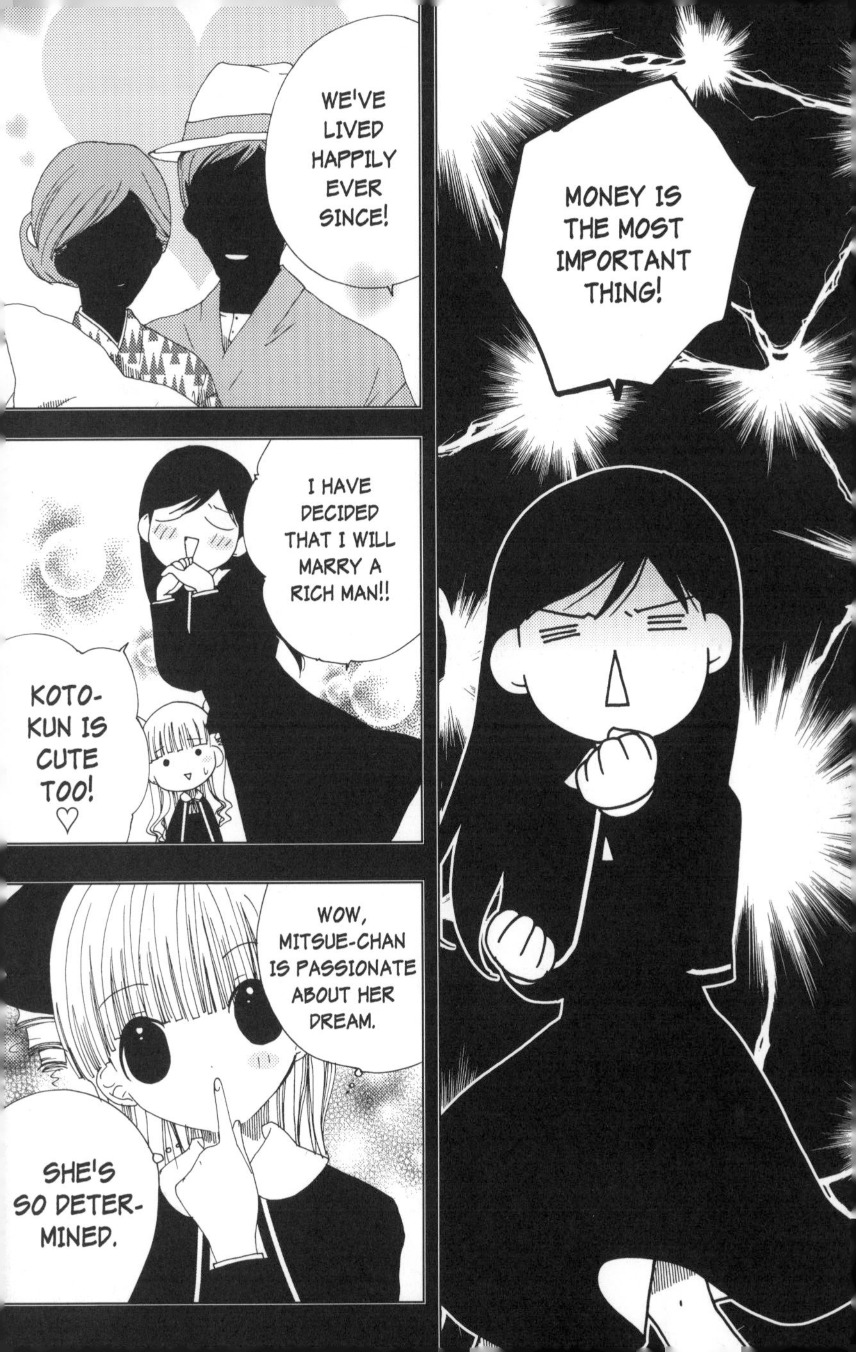
MONEY IS THE MOST IMPORTANT THING!
WE'VE LIVED HAPPILY EVER SINCE!
I HAVE DECIDED THAT I WILL MARRY A RICH MAN!!
KOTO-KUN IS CUTE TOO! ♡
WOW, MITSUE-CHAN IS PASSIONATE ABOUT HER DREAM.
SHE'S SO DETER-MINED.

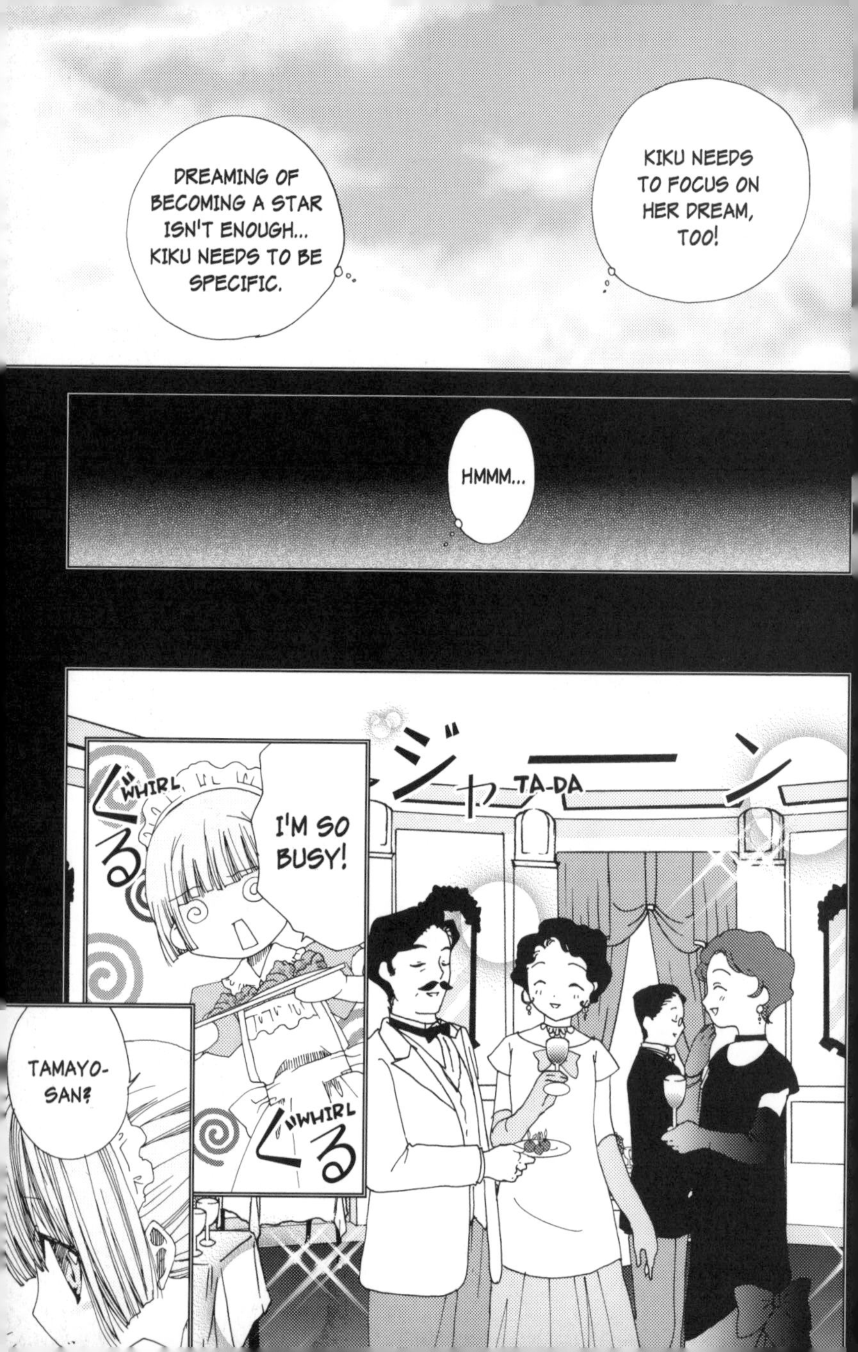
KIKU NEEDS TO FOCUS ON HER DREAM, TOO!
DREAMING OF BECOMING A STAR ISN'T ENOUGH... KIKU NEEDS TO BE SPECIFIC.
HMMM...
ジャーーン
TA-DA
くる
WHIRL
I'M SO BUSY!
くる
WHIRL
TAMAYO-SAN?

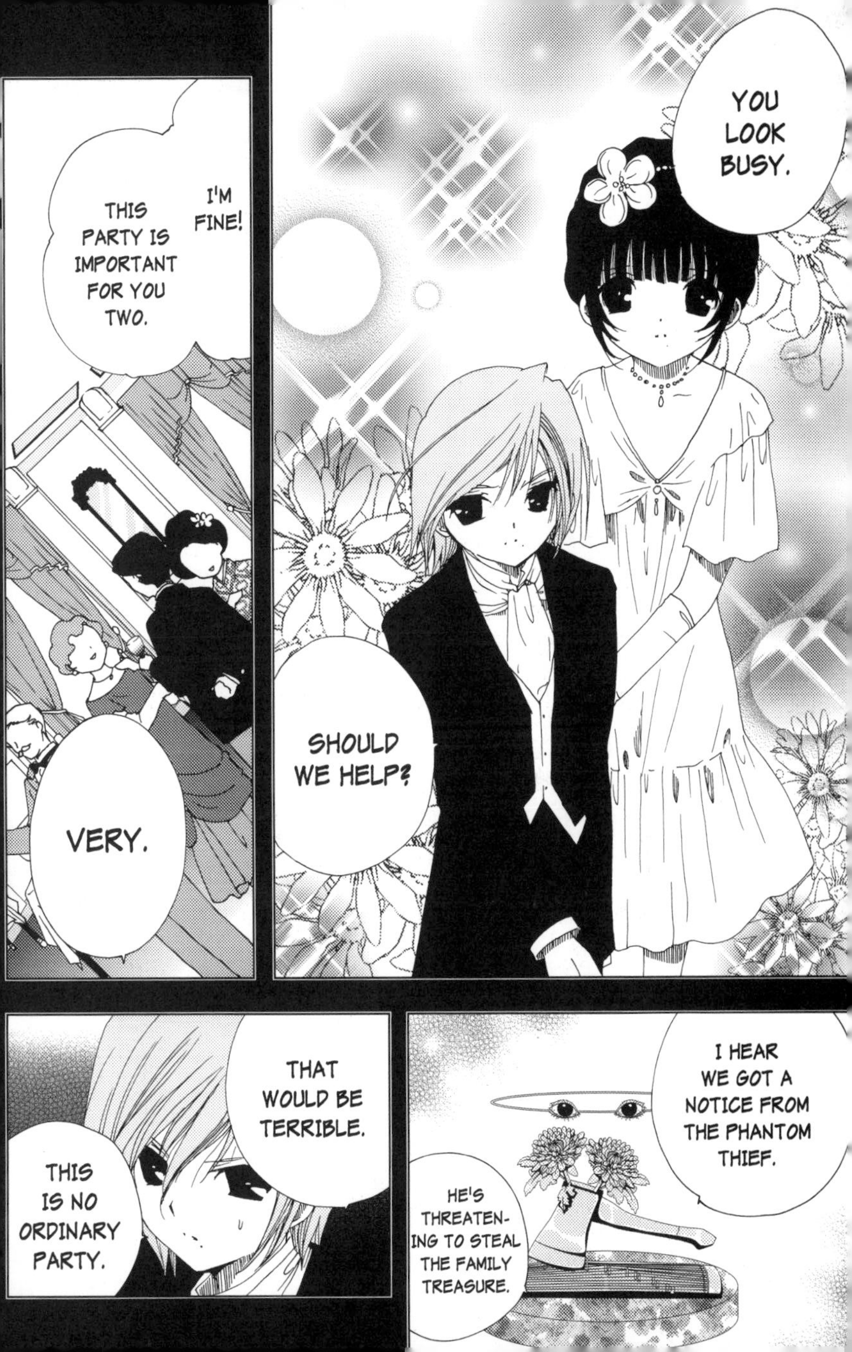
YOU LOOK BUSY.
SHOULD WE HELP?
I'M FINE!
THIS PARTY IS IMPORTANT FOR YOU TWO.
VERY.
I HEAR WE GOT A NOTICE FROM THE PHANTOM THIEF.
HE'S THREATEN-ING TO STEAL THE FAMILY TREASURE.
THAT WOULD BE TERRIBLE.
THIS IS NO ORDINARY PARTY.

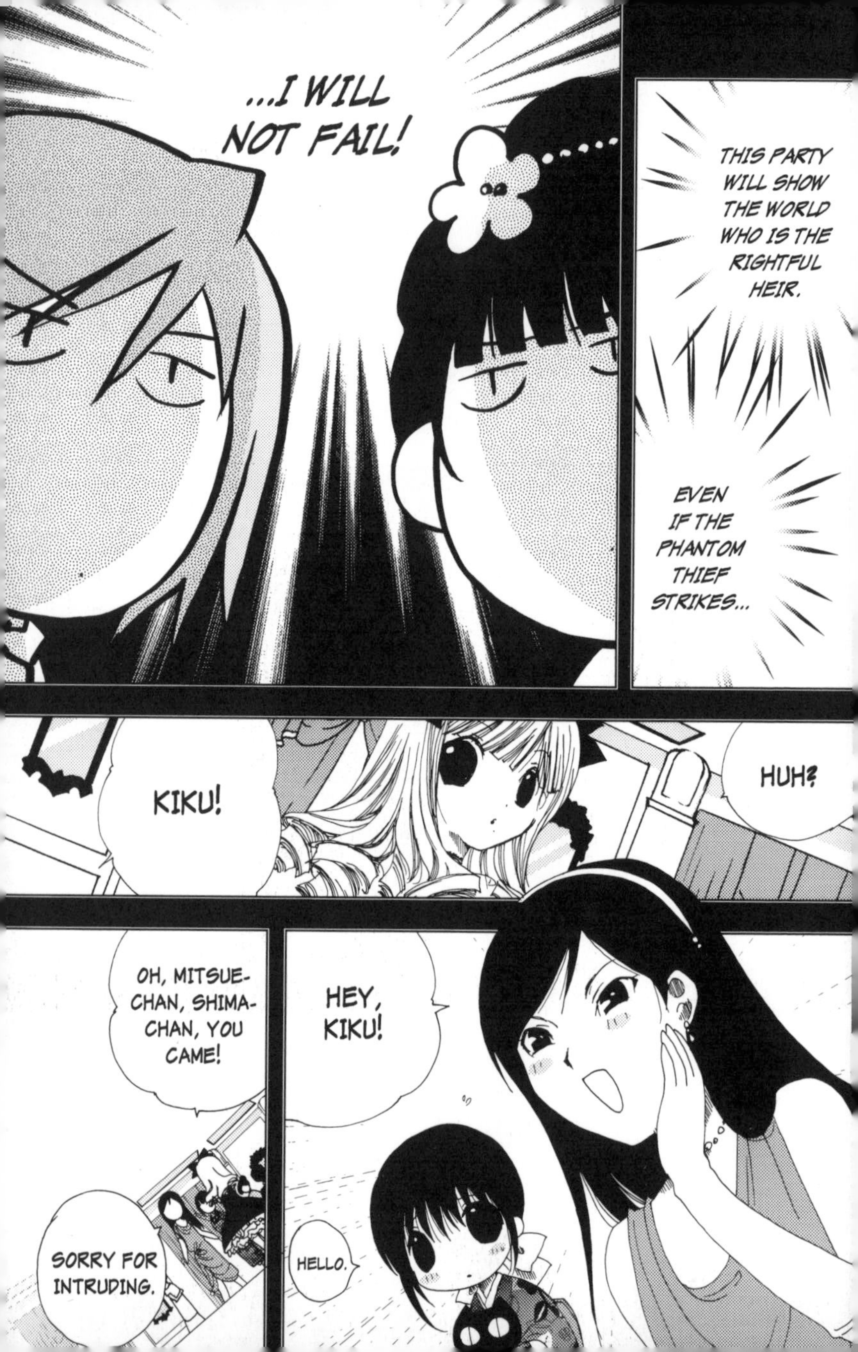
THIS PARTY WILL SHOW THE WORLD WHO IS THE RIGHTFUL HEIR.
EVEN IF THE PHANTOM THIEF STRIKES...
...I WILL NOT FAIL!
KIKU!
HUH?
HEY, KIKU!
HELLO.
OH, MITSUE-CHAN, SHIMA-CHAN, YOU CAME!
SORRY FOR INTRUDING.

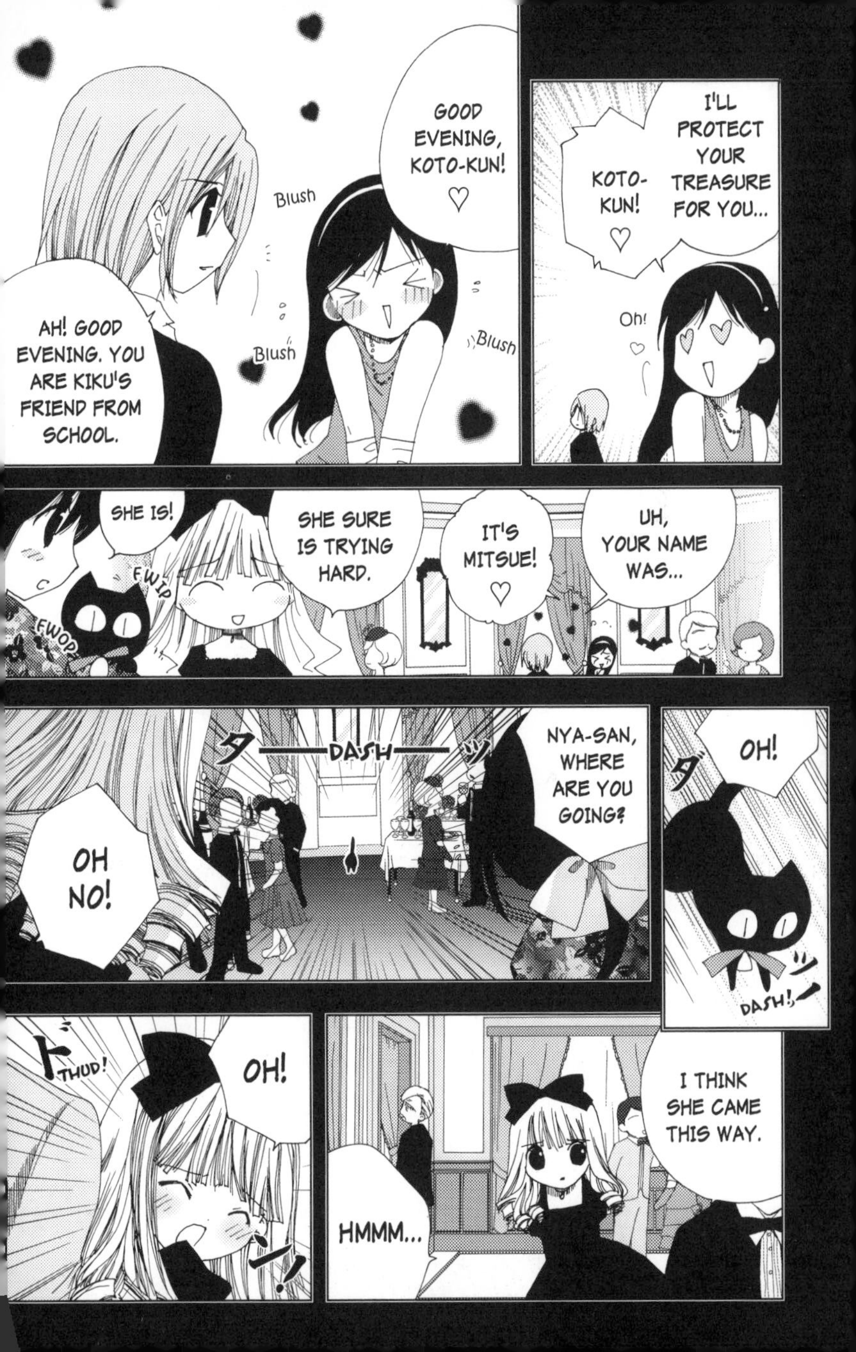
I'LL PROTECT YOUR TREASURE FOR YOU...
KOTO-KUN! ♡
Oh! ♡
GOOD EVENING, KOTO-KUN! ♡
Blush
Blush
Blush
AH! GOOD EVENING. YOU ARE KIKU'S FRIEND FROM SCHOOL.
UH, YOUR NAME WAS...
IT'S MITSUE! ♡
SHE SURE IS TRYING HARD.
SHE IS!
FWIP
FWOP
OH!
DASH!
NYA-SAN, WHERE ARE YOU GOING?
DASH
OH NO!
I THINK SHE CAME THIS WAY.
HMMM...
OH!
THUD!

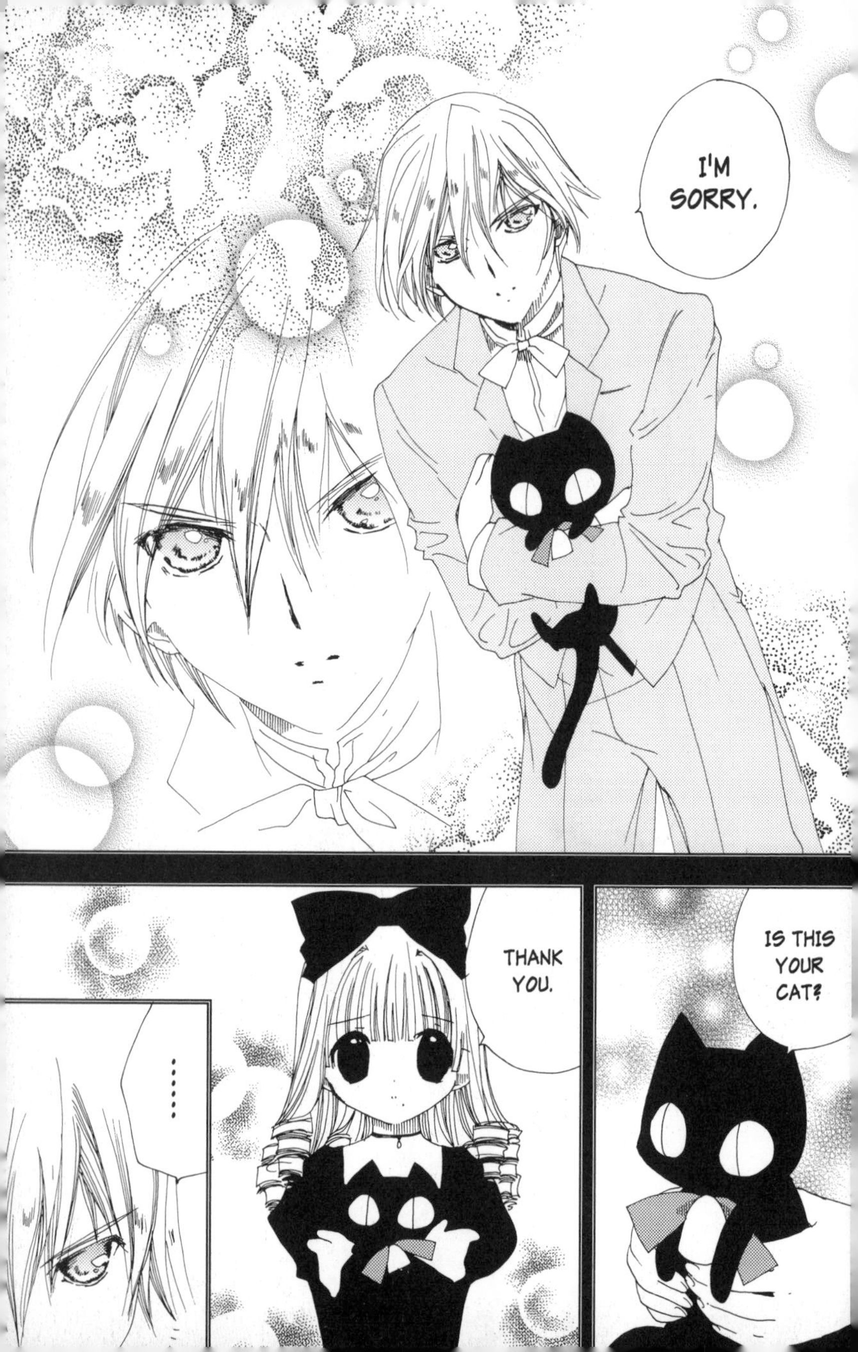
I'M SORRY.
IS THIS YOUR CAT?
THANK YOU.
......

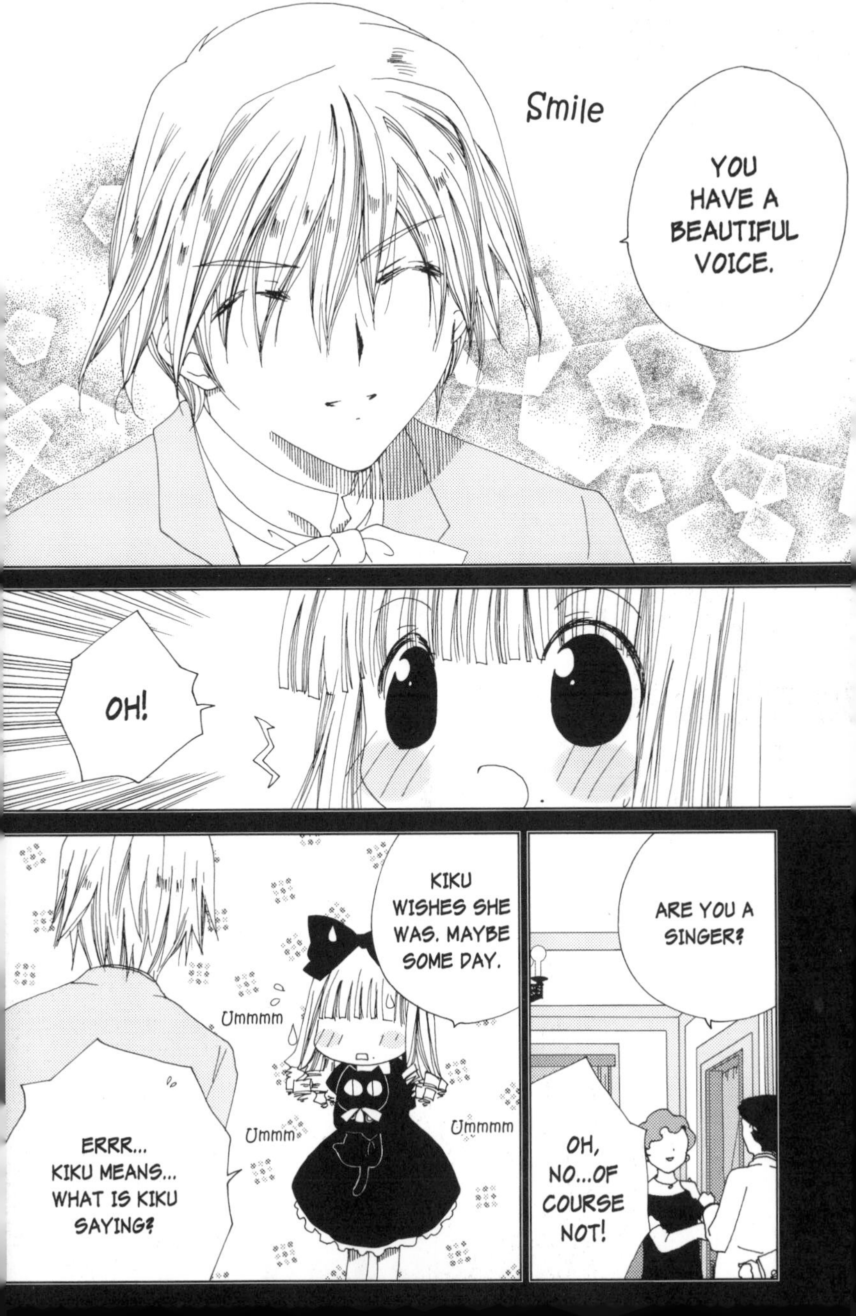
Smile
YOU HAVE A BEAUTIFUL VOICE.
OH!
ARE YOU A SINGER?
OH, NO...OF COURSE NOT!
KIKU WISHES SHE WAS. MAYBE SOME DAY.
Ummmm
Ummmm
Ummm
ERRR... KIKU MEANS... WHAT IS KIKU SAYING?

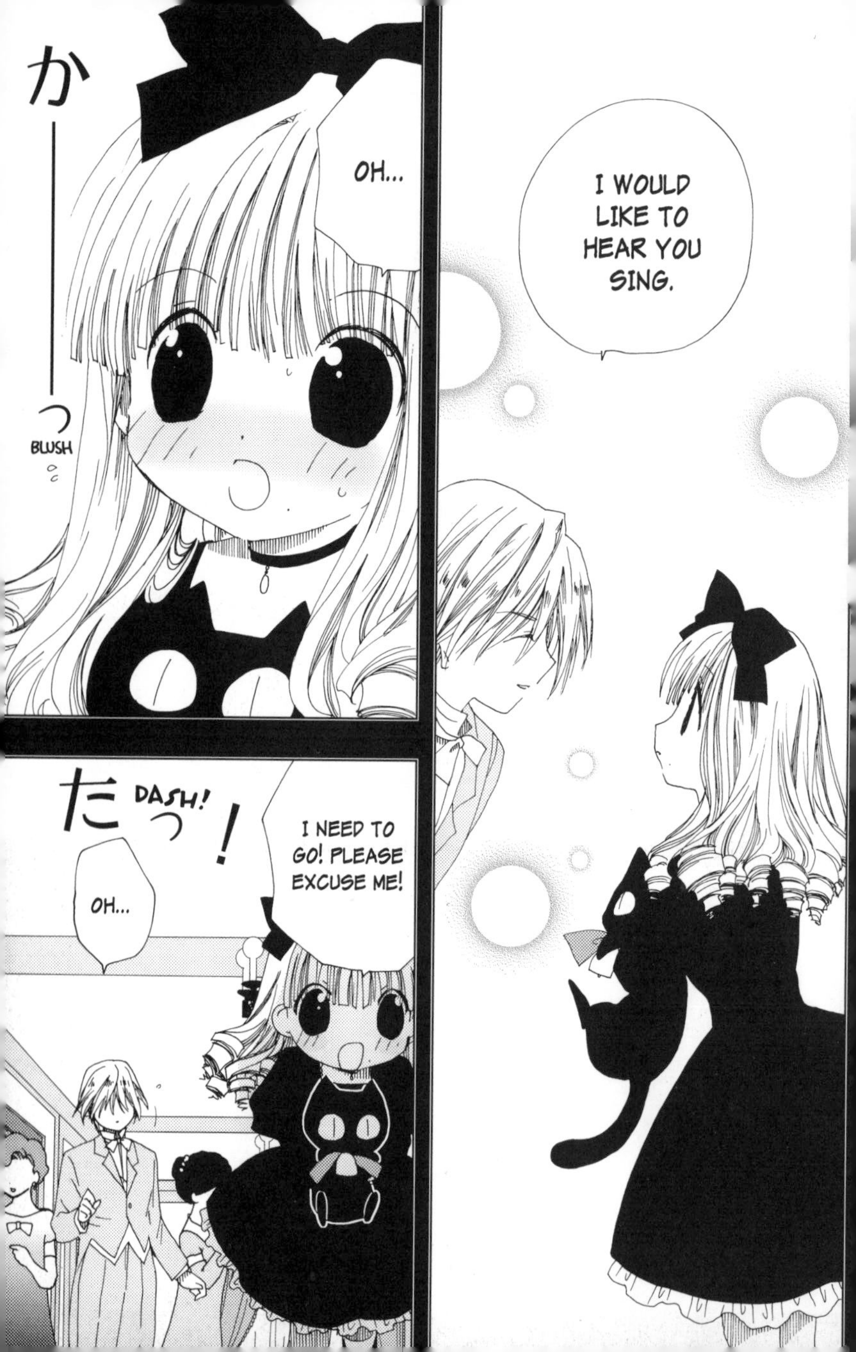
I WOULD LIKE TO HEAR YOU SING.
OH...
か――っ
BLUSH
I NEED TO GO! PLEASE EXCUSE ME!
たっ!
DASH!
OH...

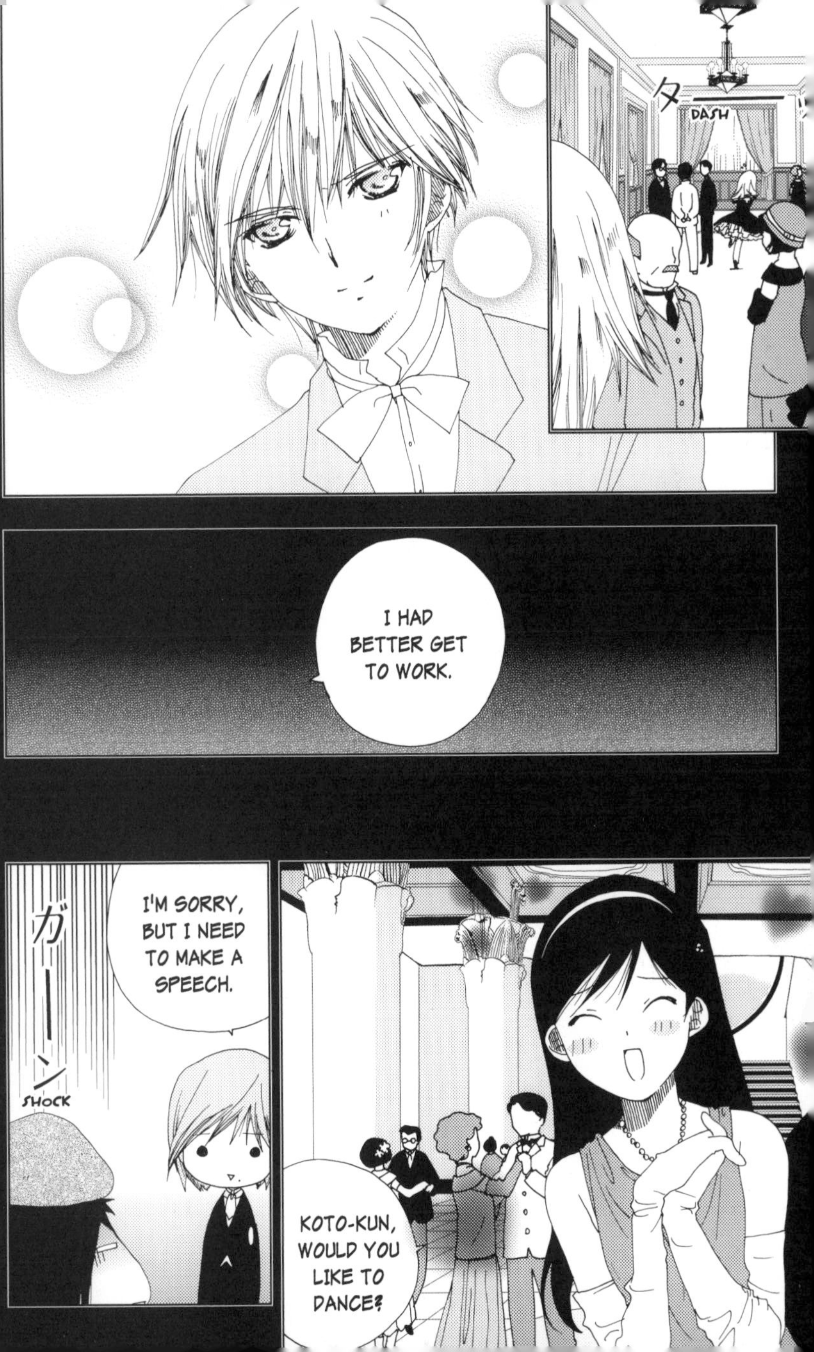
タ
DASH
I HAD BETTER GET TO WORK.
KOTO-KUN, WOULD YOU LIKE TO DANCE?
I'M SORRY, BUT I NEED TO MAKE A SPEECH.
ガーン
SHOCK

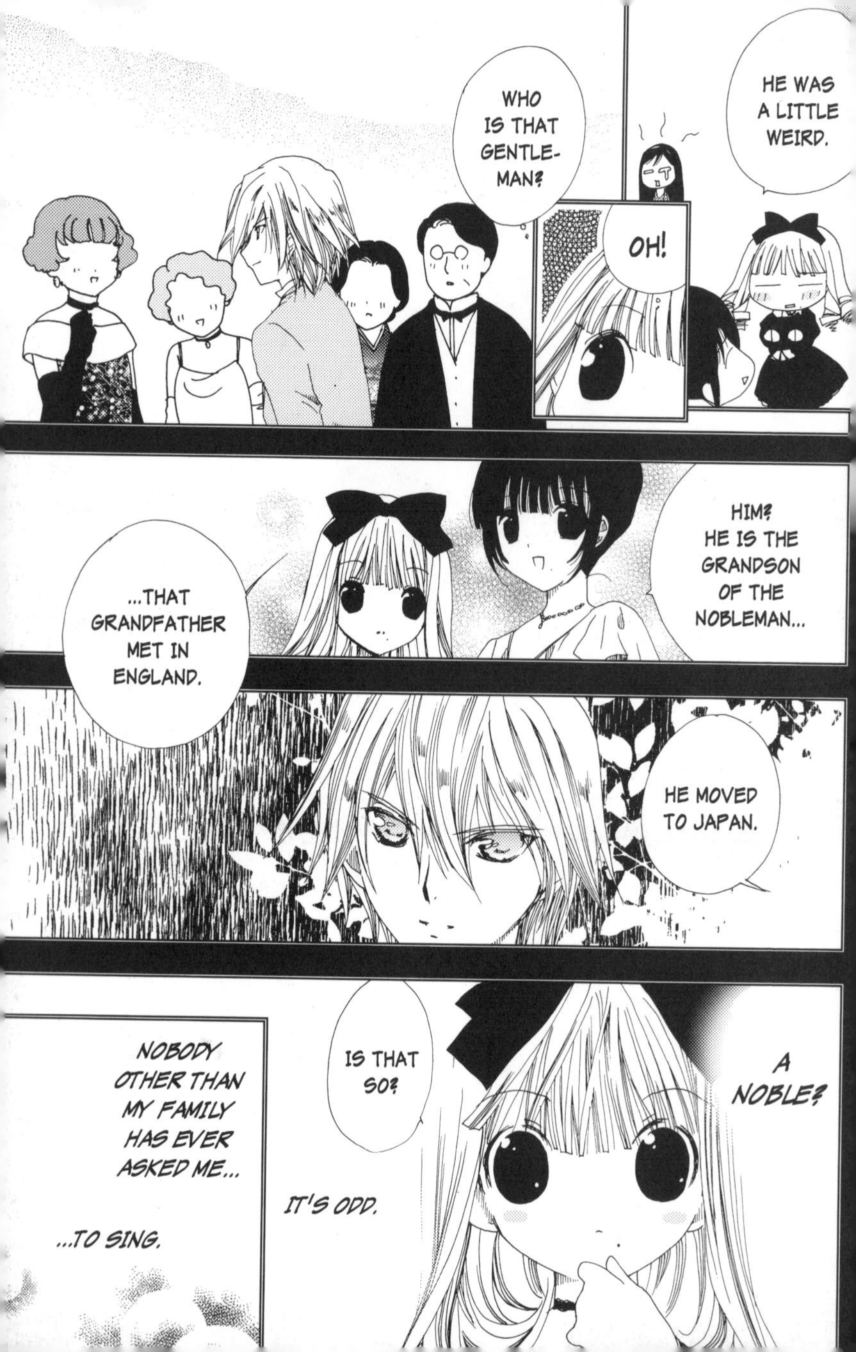
HE WAS A LITTLE WEIRD.
OH!
WHO IS THAT GENTLEMAN?
HIM? HE IS THE GRANDSON OF THE NOBLEMAN...
...THAT GRANDFATHER MET IN ENGLAND.
HE MOVED TO JAPAN.
A NOBLE?
IS THAT SO?
IT'S ODD.
NOBODY OTHER THAN MY FAMILY HAS EVER ASKED ME...
...TO SING.

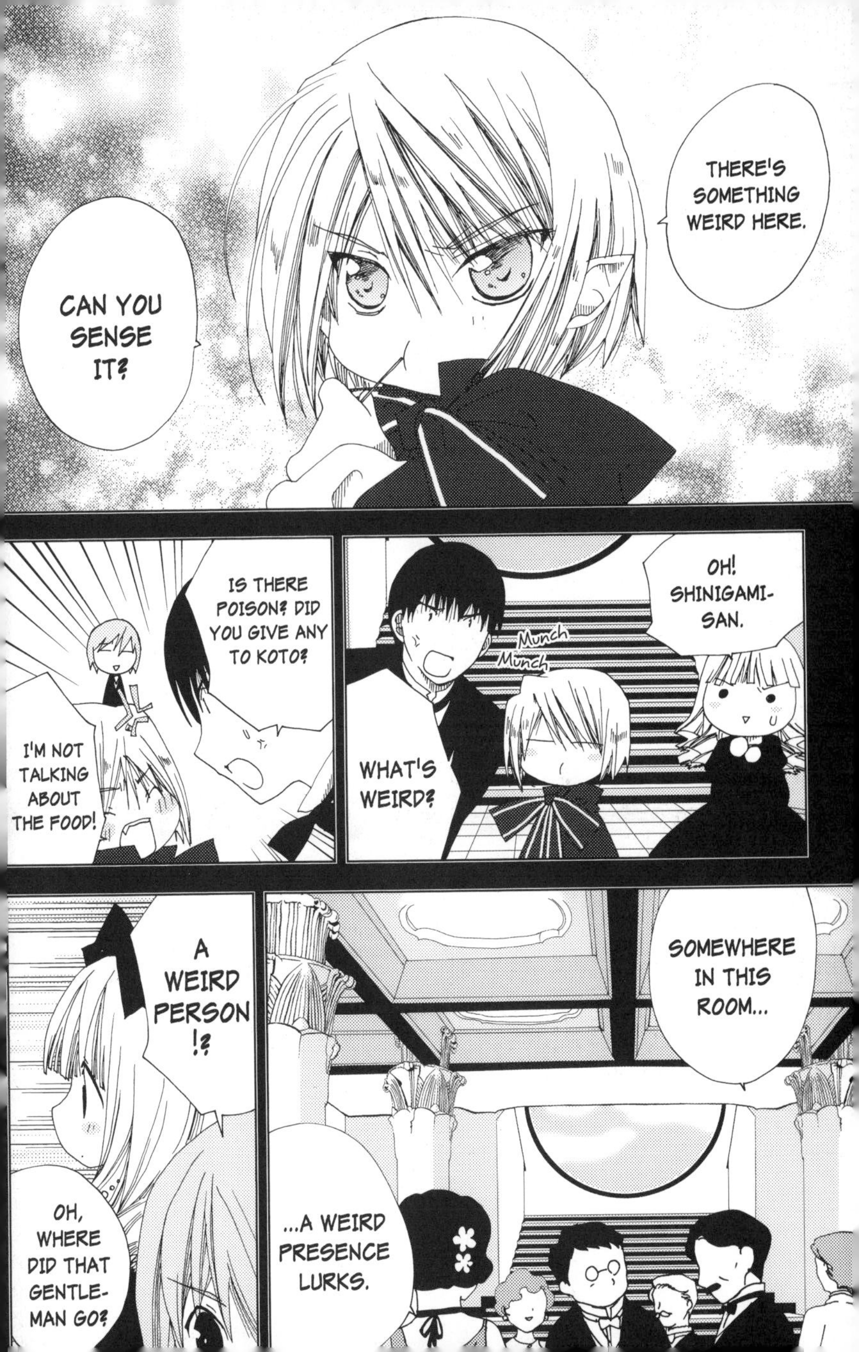
THERE'S SOMETHING WEIRD HERE.
CAN YOU SENSE IT?
OH! SHINIGAMI-SAN.
Munch Munch
WHAT'S WEIRD?
IS THERE POISON? DID YOU GIVE ANY TO KOTO?
I'M NOT TALKING ABOUT THE FOOD!
SOMEWHERE IN THIS ROOM...
...A WEIRD PRESENCE LURKS.
A WEIRD PERSON!?
OH, WHERE DID THAT GENTLEMAN GO?

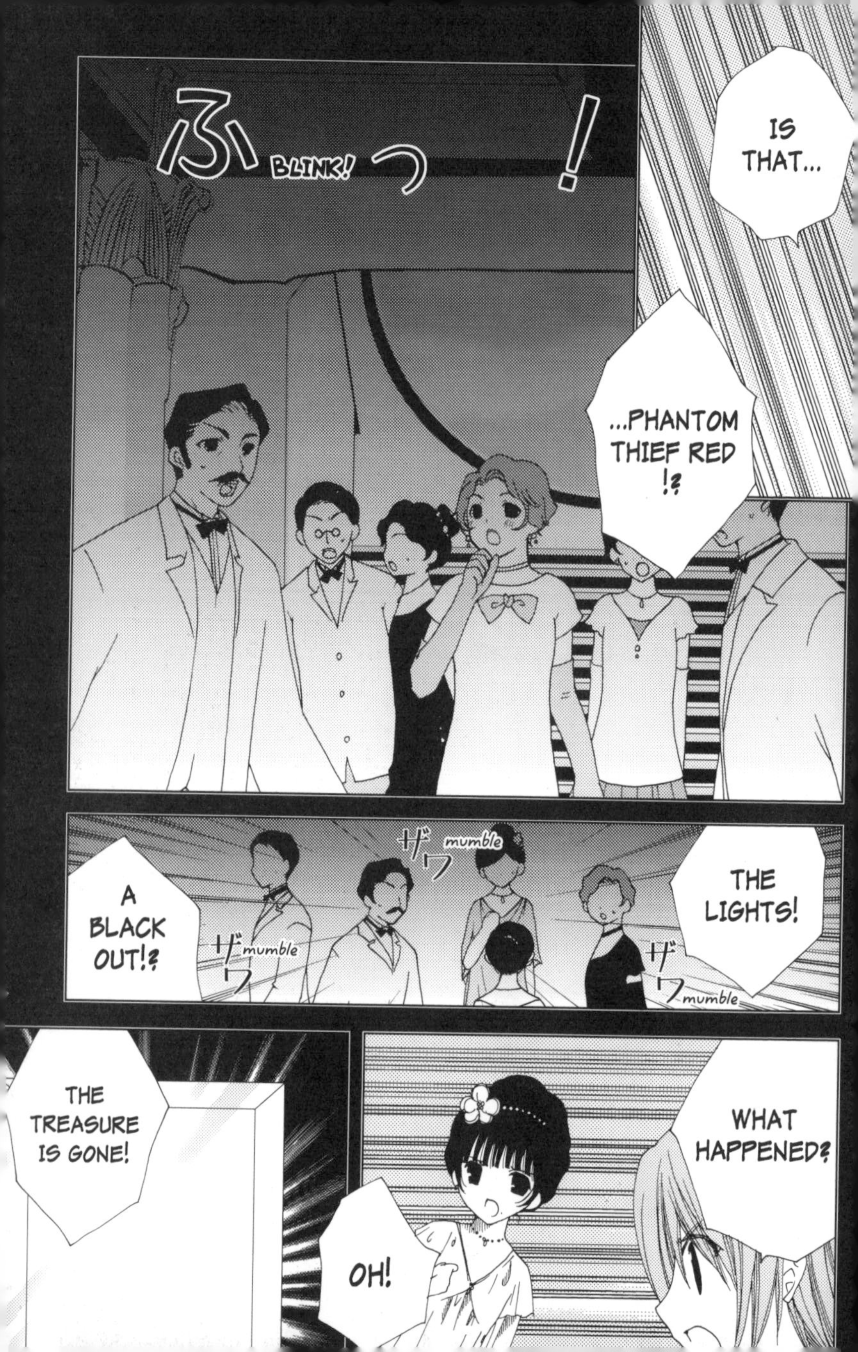
IS THAT...
...PHANTOM THIEF RED!?
ふっ
BLINK!
!
THE LIGHTS!
ザワ mumble
ザワ mumble
ザワ mumble
A BLACK OUT!?
WHAT HAPPENED?
OH!
THE TREASURE IS GONE!

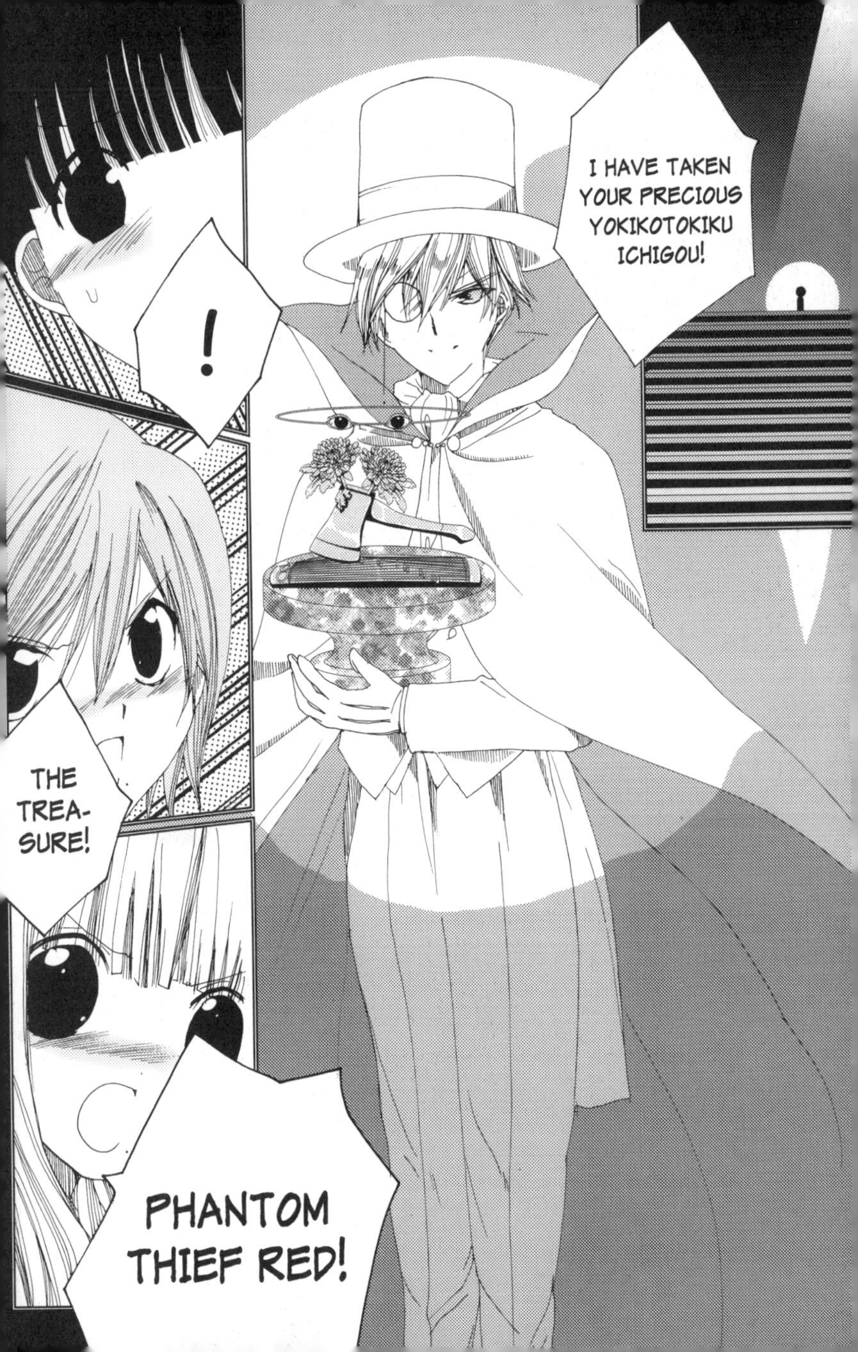
I HAVE TAKEN YOUR PRECIOUS YOKIKOTOKIKU ICHIGOU!
!
THE TREA-SURE!
PHANTOM THIEF RED!

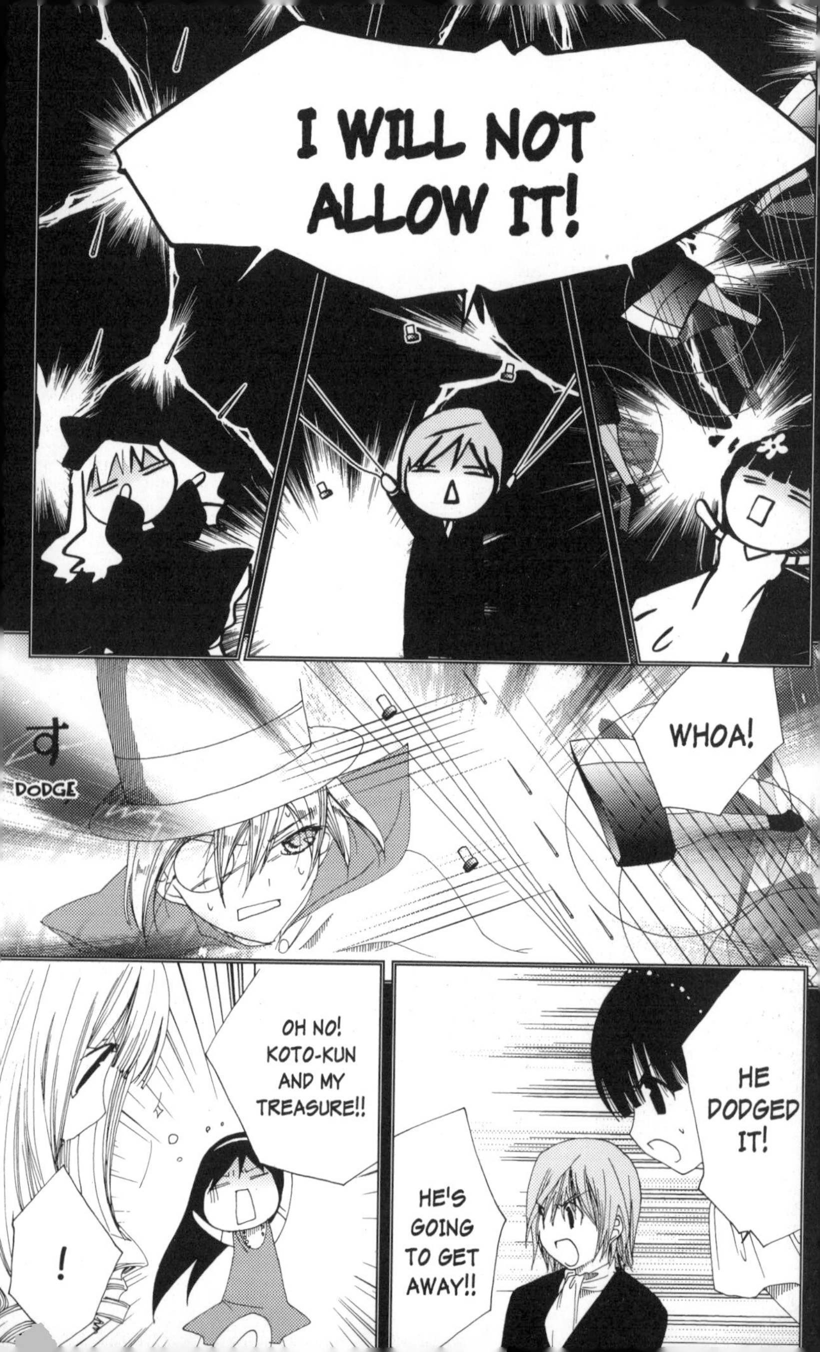
I WILL NOT ALLOW IT!
WHOA!
す
DODGE
HE DODGED IT!
HE'S GOING TO GET AWAY!!
OH NO! KOTO-KUN AND MY TREASURE!!
!

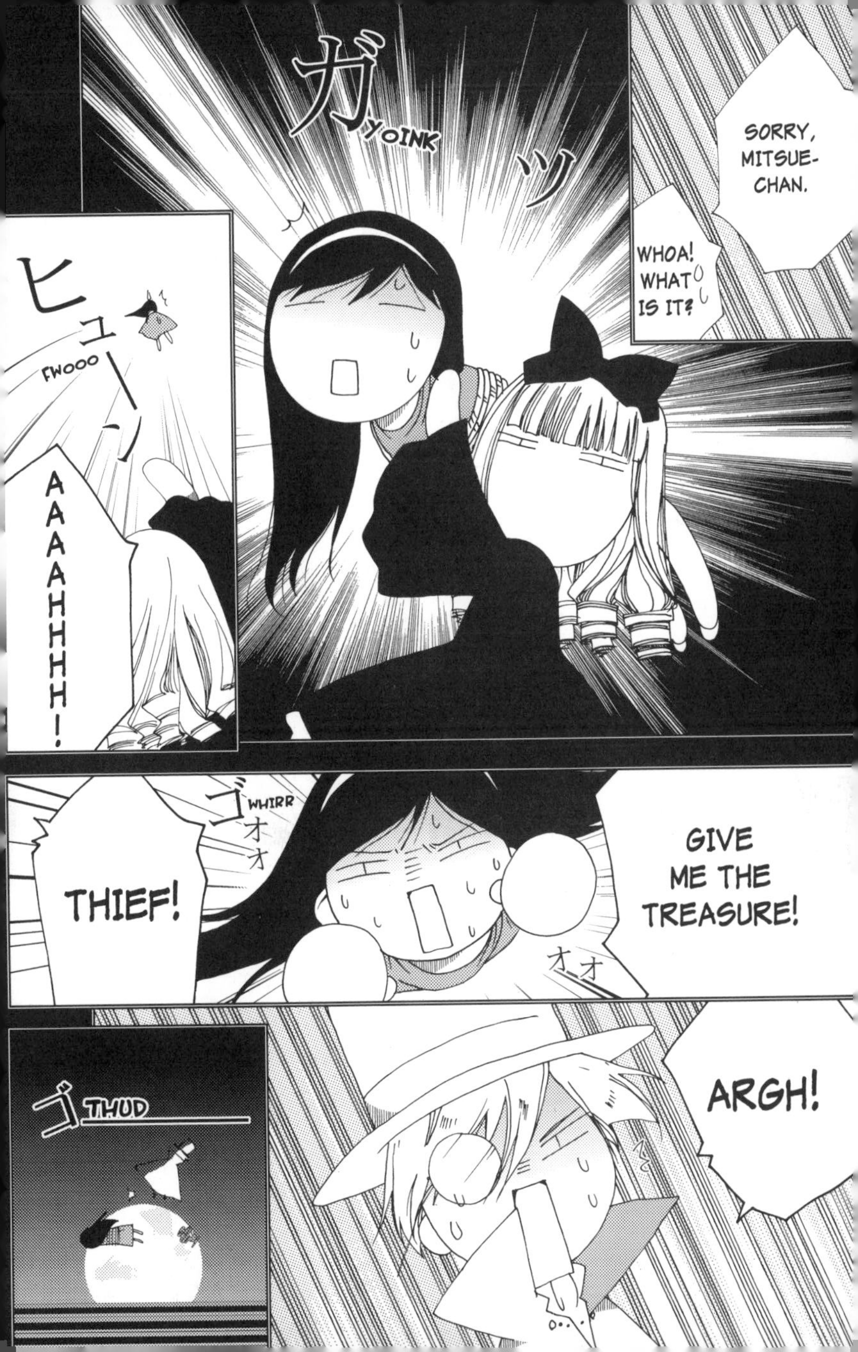
SORRY, MITSUE-CHAN.
WHOA! WHAT IS IT?
ガッ
YOINK
ヒュー
FWOOO
AAAAAHHHHH!
GIVE ME THE TREASURE!
ゴオオオオ
WHIRR
THIEF!
ARGH!
ゴ
THUD

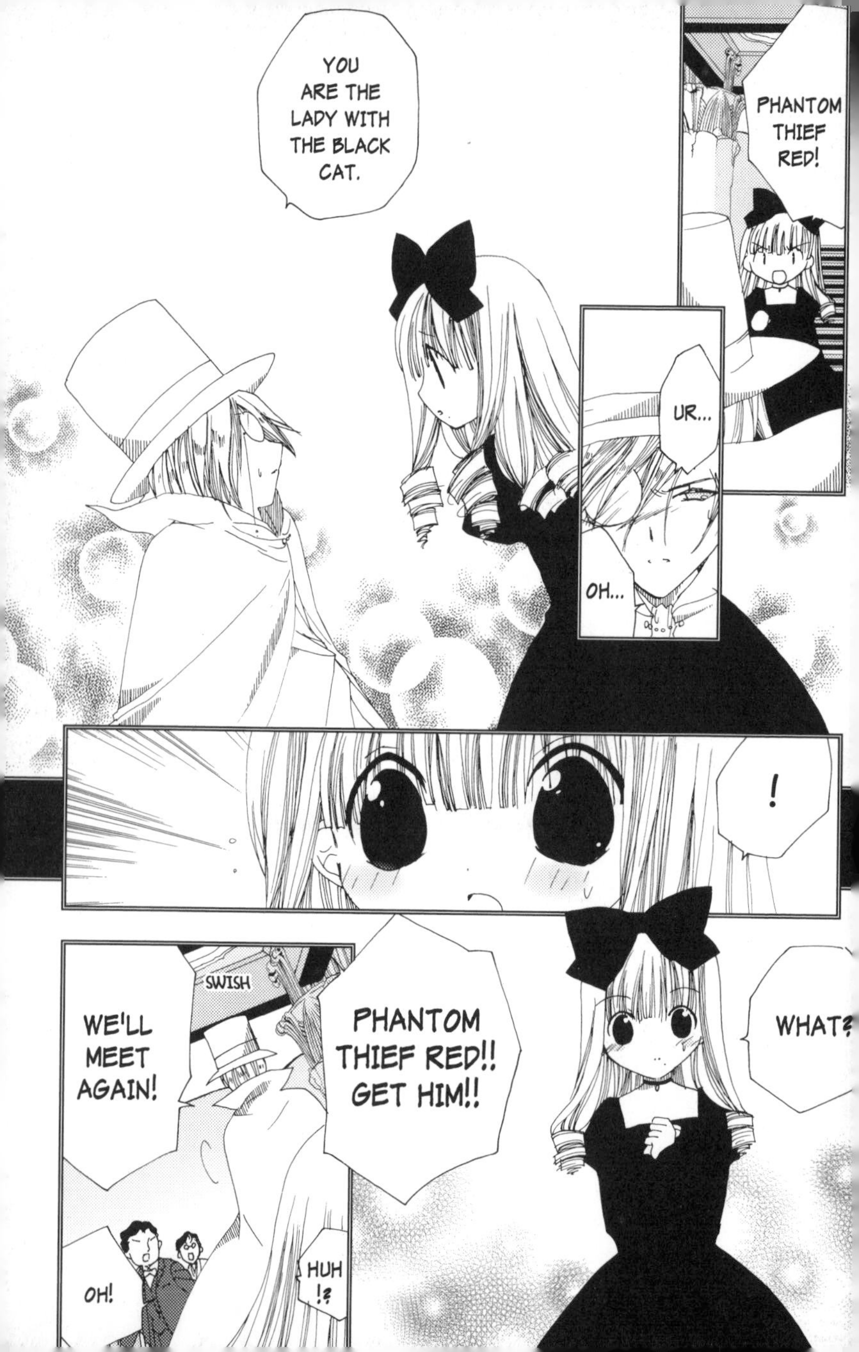
PHANTOM THIEF RED!
UR...
OH...
YOU ARE THE LADY WITH THE BLACK CAT.
!
WHAT?
PHANTOM THIEF RED!! GET HIM!!
SWISH
WE'LL MEET AGAIN!
HUH!?
OH!

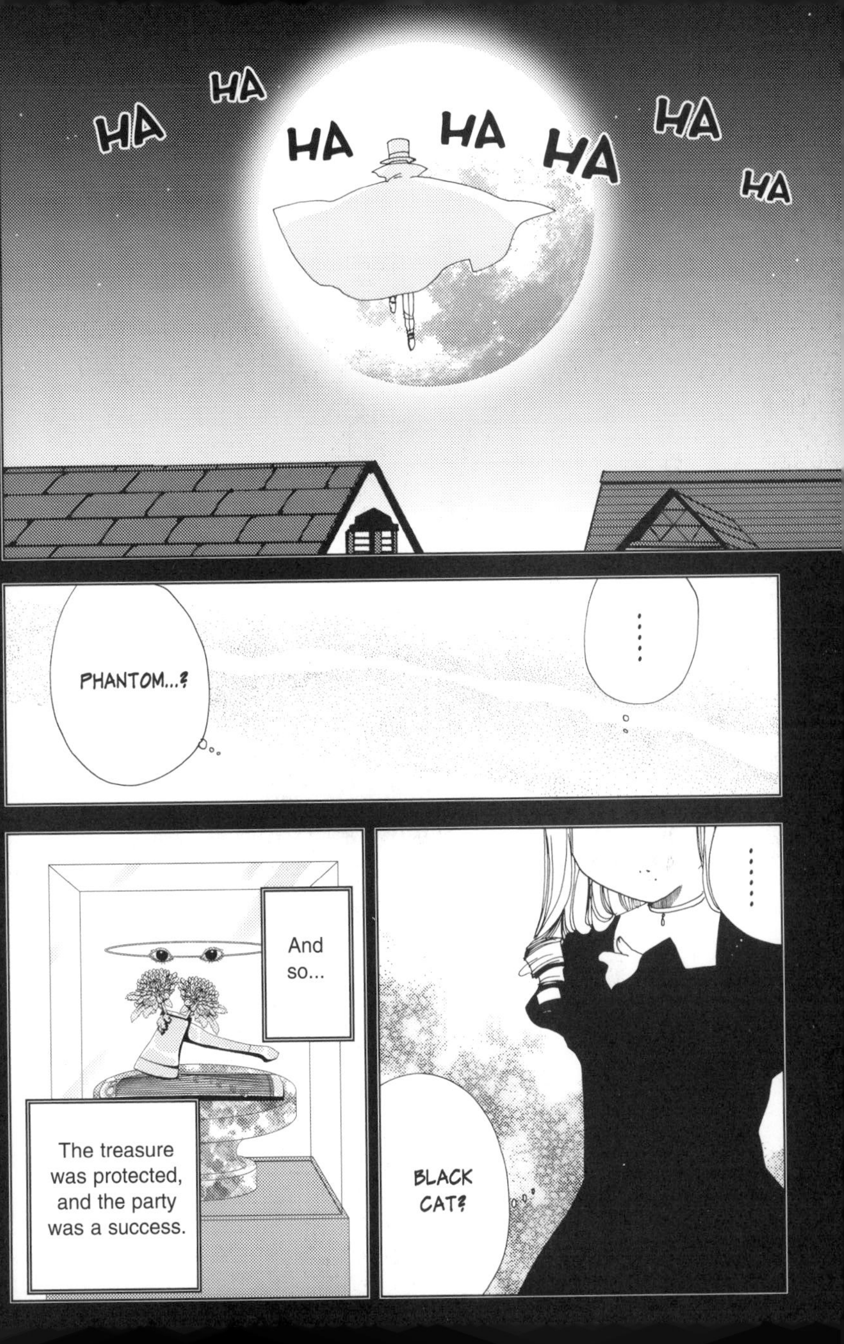
HA HA HA HA HA HA HA
......
PHANTOM...?
......
BLACK CAT?
And so...
The treasure was protected, and the party was a success.

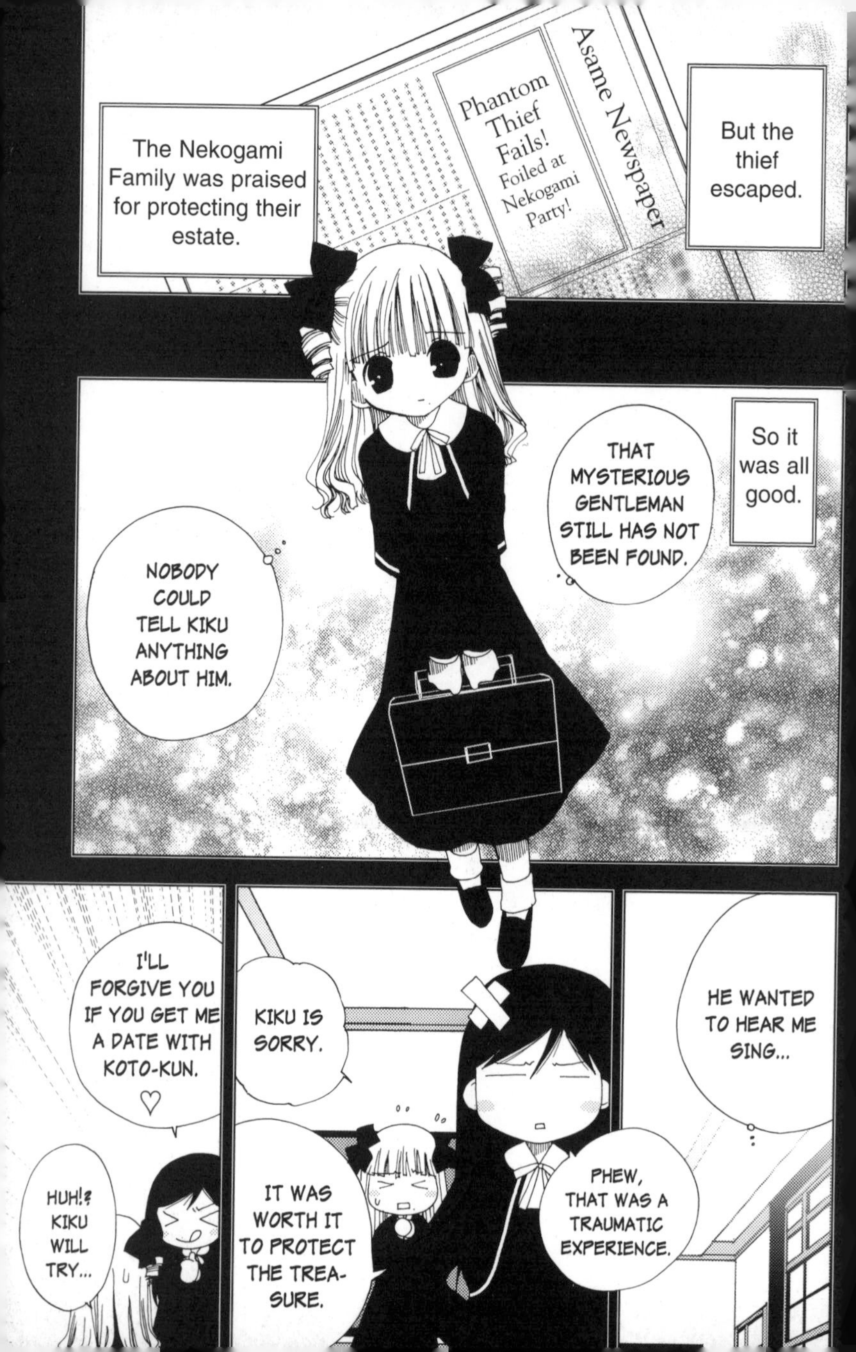
But the thief escaped.
Asame Newspaper
Phantom Thief Fails! Foiled at Nekogami Party!
The Nekogami Family was praised for protecting their estate.
So it was all good.
THAT MYSTERIOUS GENTLEMAN STILL HAS NOT BEEN FOUND.
NOBODY COULD TELL KIKU ANYTHING ABOUT HIM.
HE WANTED TO HEAR ME SING...
PHEW, THAT WAS A TRAUMATIC EXPERIENCE.
KIKU IS SORRY.
IT WAS WORTH IT TO PROTECT THE TREA-SURE.
I'LL FORGIVE YOU IF YOU GET ME A DATE WITH KOTO-KUN. ♡
HUH!? KIKU WILL TRY...

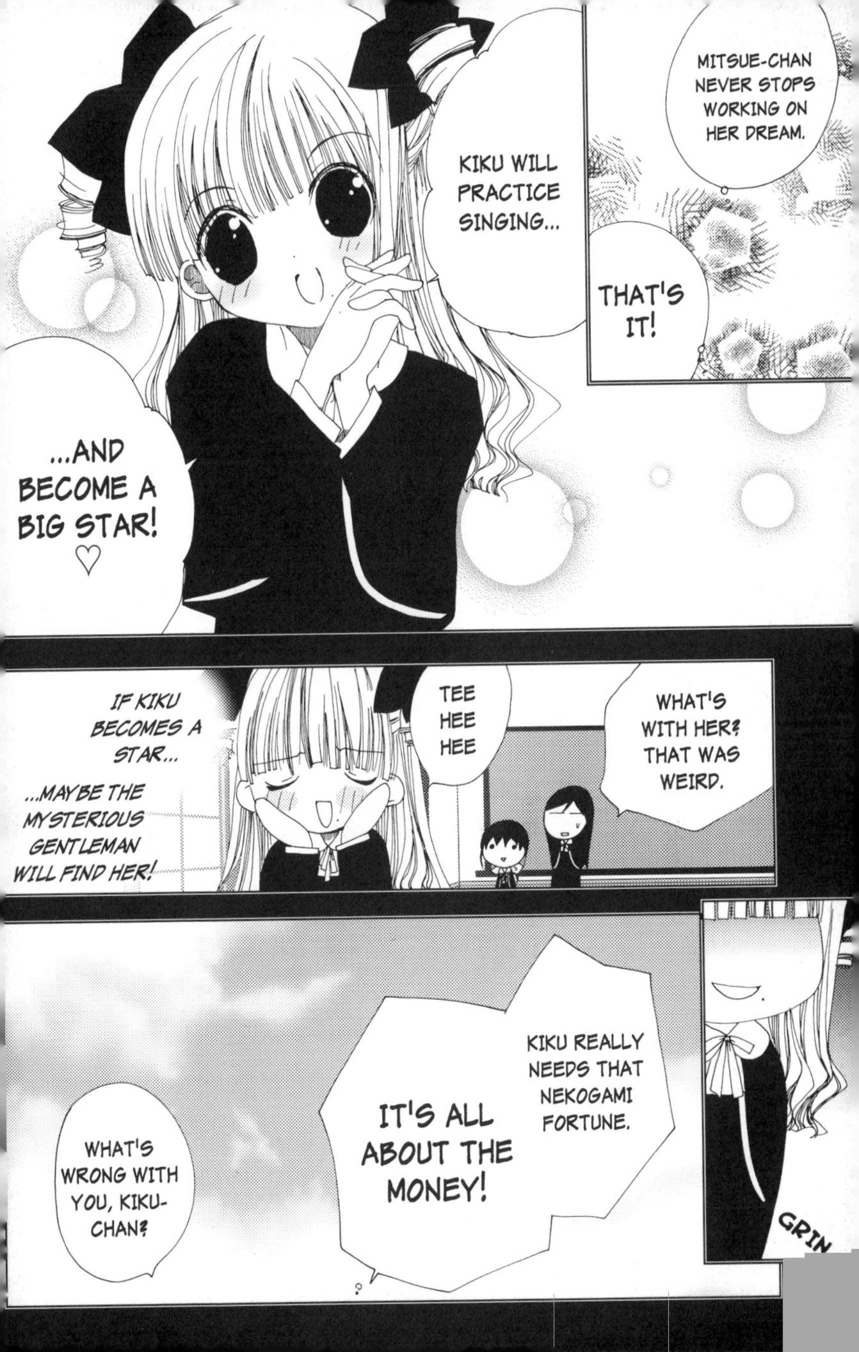
MITSUE-CHAN NEVER STOPS WORKING ON HER DREAM.
THAT'S IT!
KIKU WILL PRACTICE SINGING...
...AND BECOME A BIG STAR! ♡
WHAT'S WITH HER? THAT WAS WEIRD.
TEE HEE HEE
IF KIKU BECOMES A STAR...
...MAYBE THE MYSTERIOUS GENTLEMAN WILL FIND HER!
GRIN
KIKU REALLY NEEDS THAT NEKOGAMI FORTUNE.
IT'S ALL ABOUT THE MONEY!
WHAT'S WRONG WITH YOU, KIKU-CHAN?

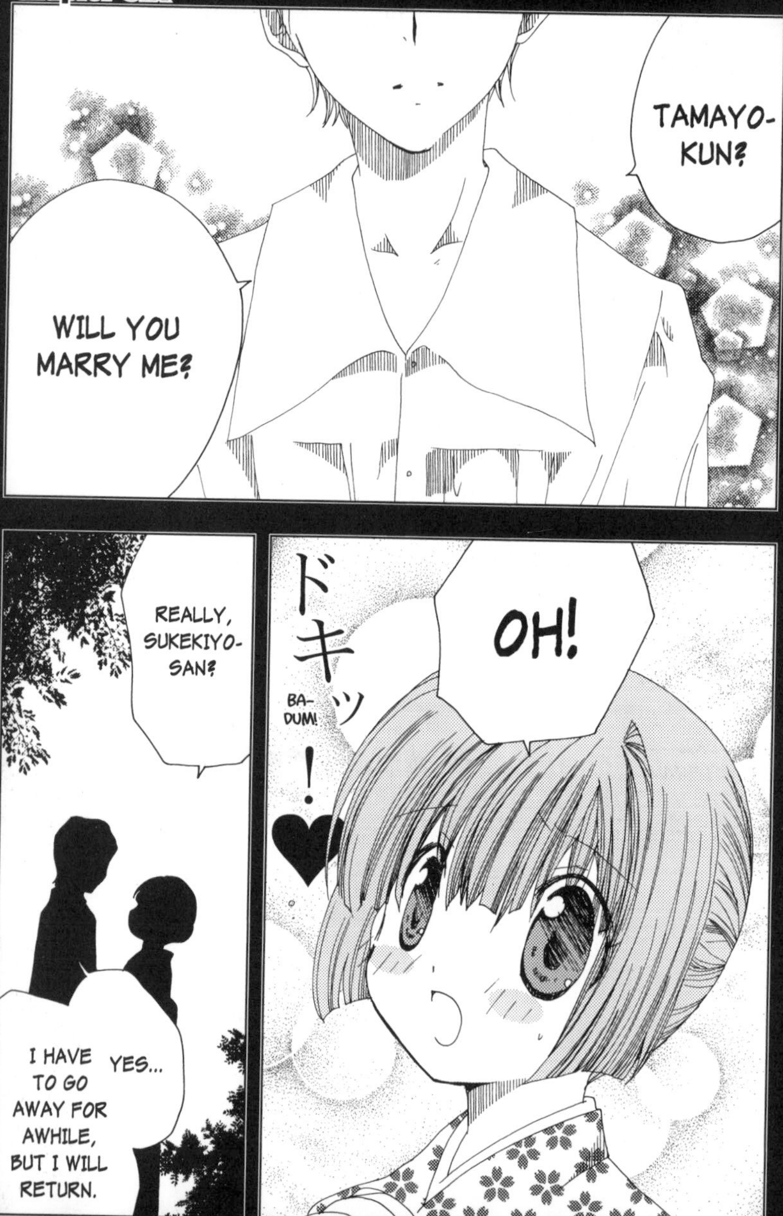
TAMAYO-KUN?
WILL YOU MARRY ME?
OH!
ドキッ!
BA-DUM!
REALLY, SUKEKIYO-SAN?
YES...
I HAVE TO GO AWAY FOR AWHILE, BUT I WILL RETURN.

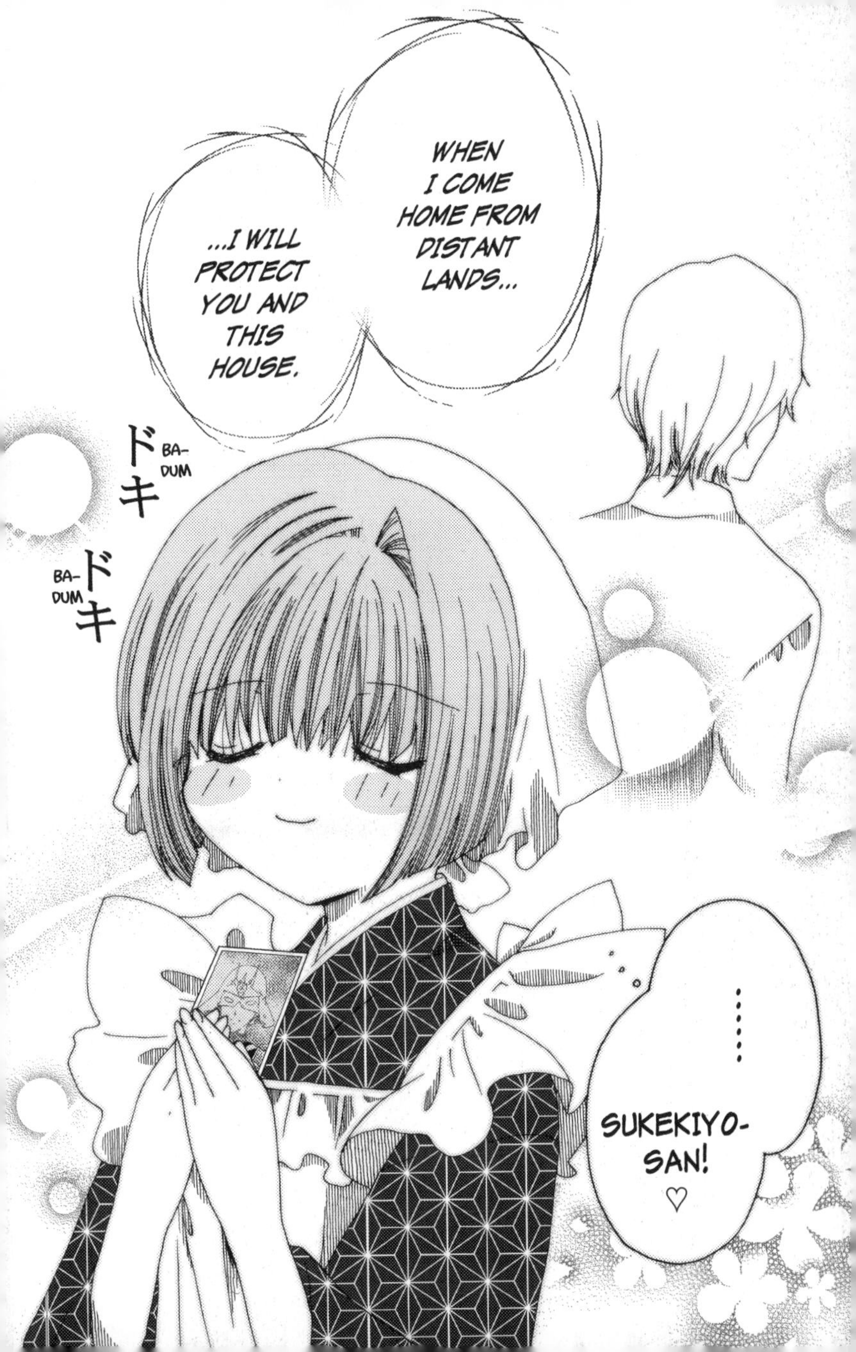
WHEN I COME HOME FROM DISTANT LANDS...
...I WILL PROTECT YOU AND THIS HOUSE.
ドキ BA-DUM
ドキ BA-DUM
......
SUKEKIYO-SAN! ♡

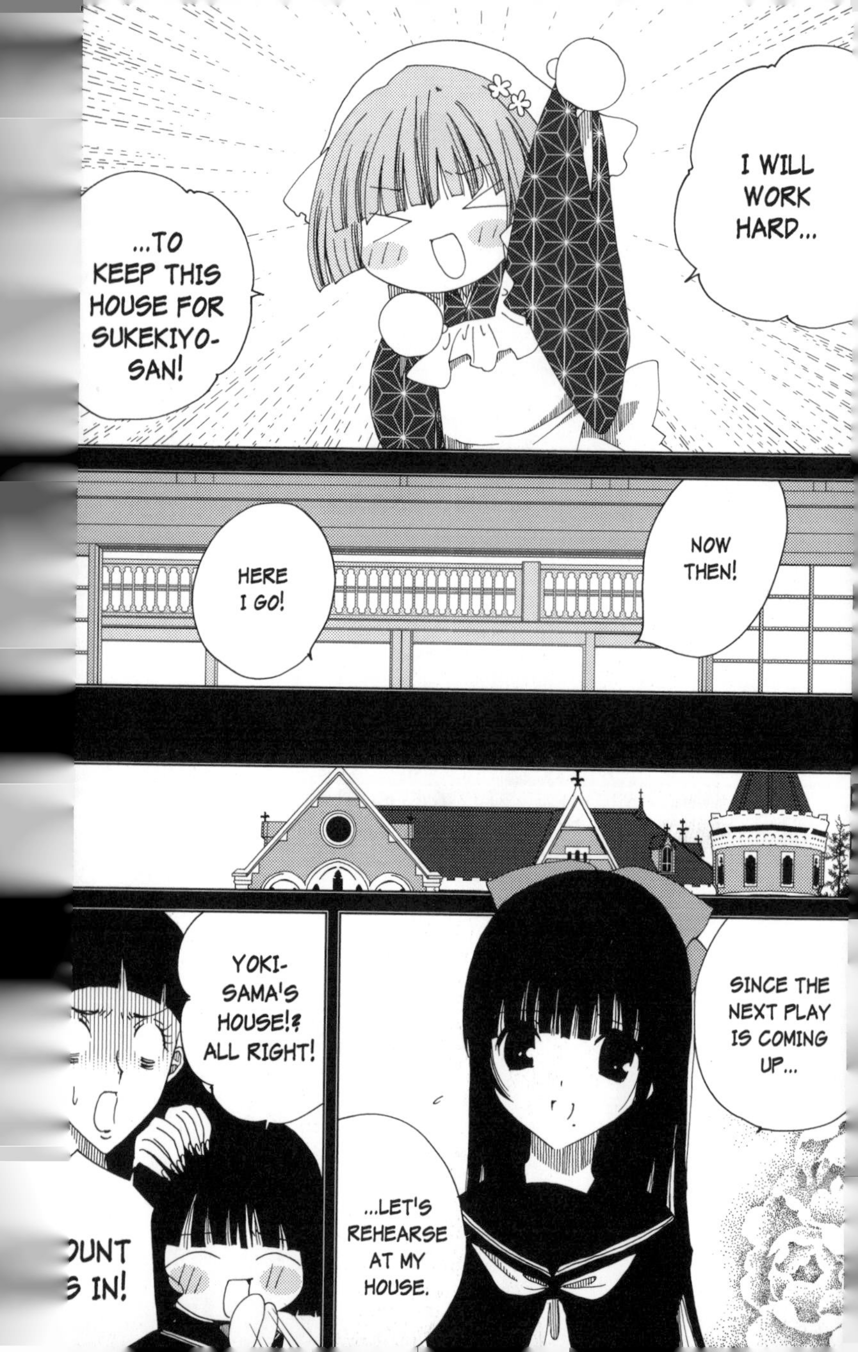
I WILL WORK HARD...
...TO KEEP THIS HOUSE FOR SUKEKIYO-SAN!
NOW THEN!
HERE I GO!
SINCE THE NEXT PLAY IS COMING UP...
...LET'S REHEARSE AT MY HOUSE.
YOKI-SAMA'S HOUSE!? ALL RIGHT!

TAMAYO-SAN! ♡

IT'S BEEN A WHILE SINCE I'VE BEEN TO YOUR HOUSE.

PLEASE WAIT FOR ME!

KOTO-KUN! KOTO-KUN! ♡

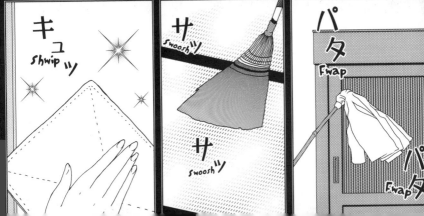

キュ
shwip ッ

サ
swoosh ッ

サ
swoosh ッ

パ
タ
Fwap

パ
Fwap ッ

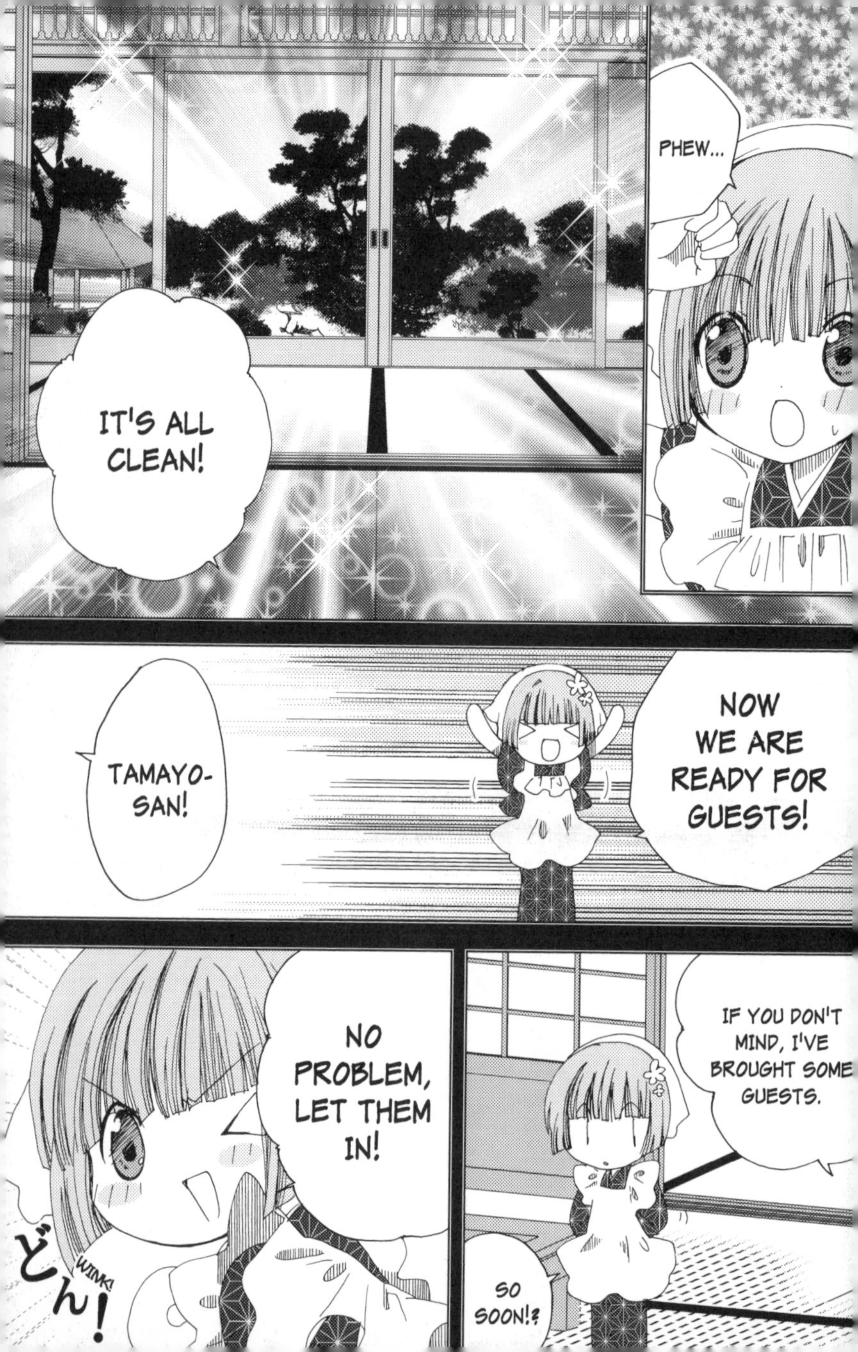
PHEW...
IT'S ALL CLEAN!
NOW WE ARE READY FOR GUESTS!
TAMAYO-SAN!
IF YOU DON'T MIND, I'VE BROUGHT SOME GUESTS.
SO SOON!?
NO PROBLEM, LET THEM IN!
WINK!
どん!

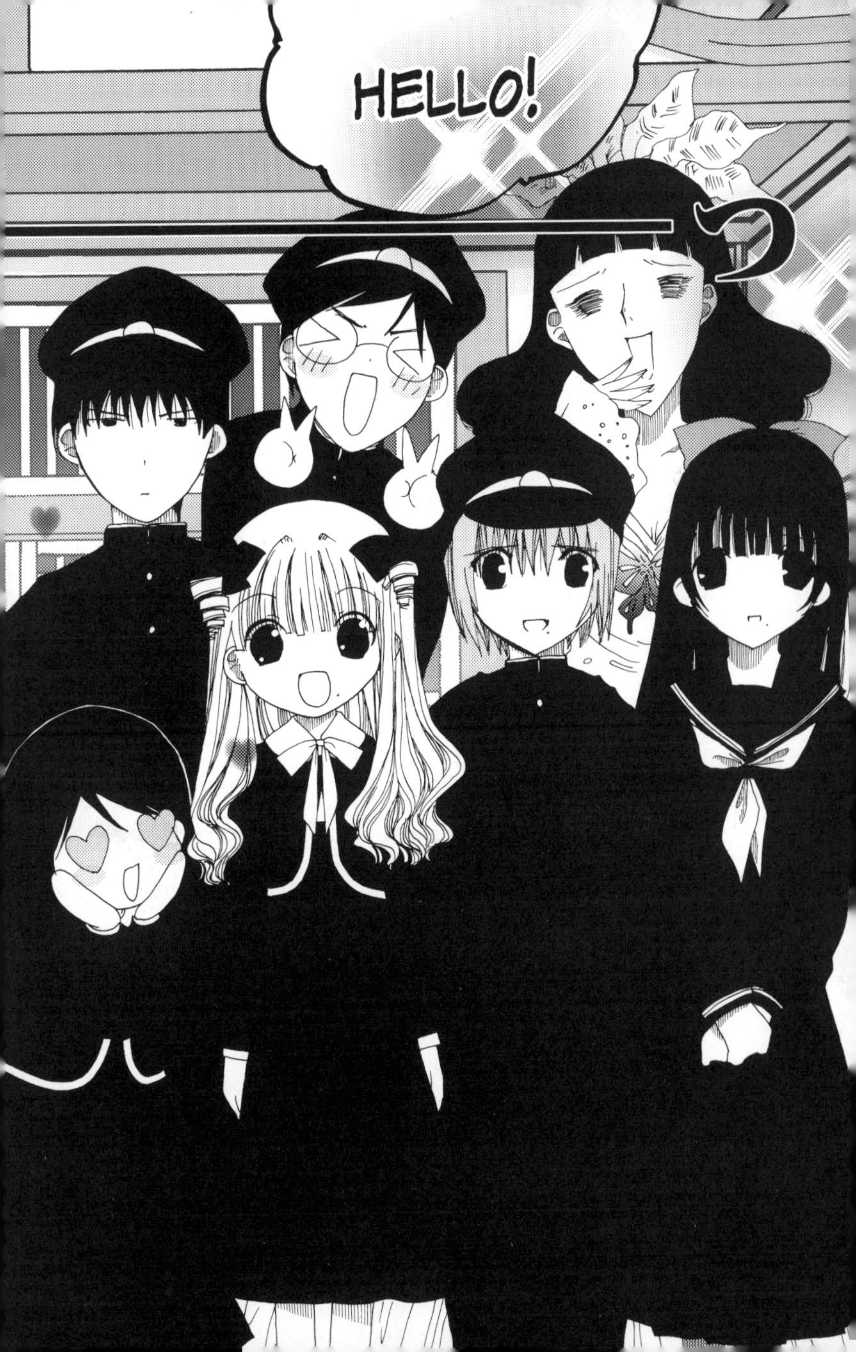
HELLO!

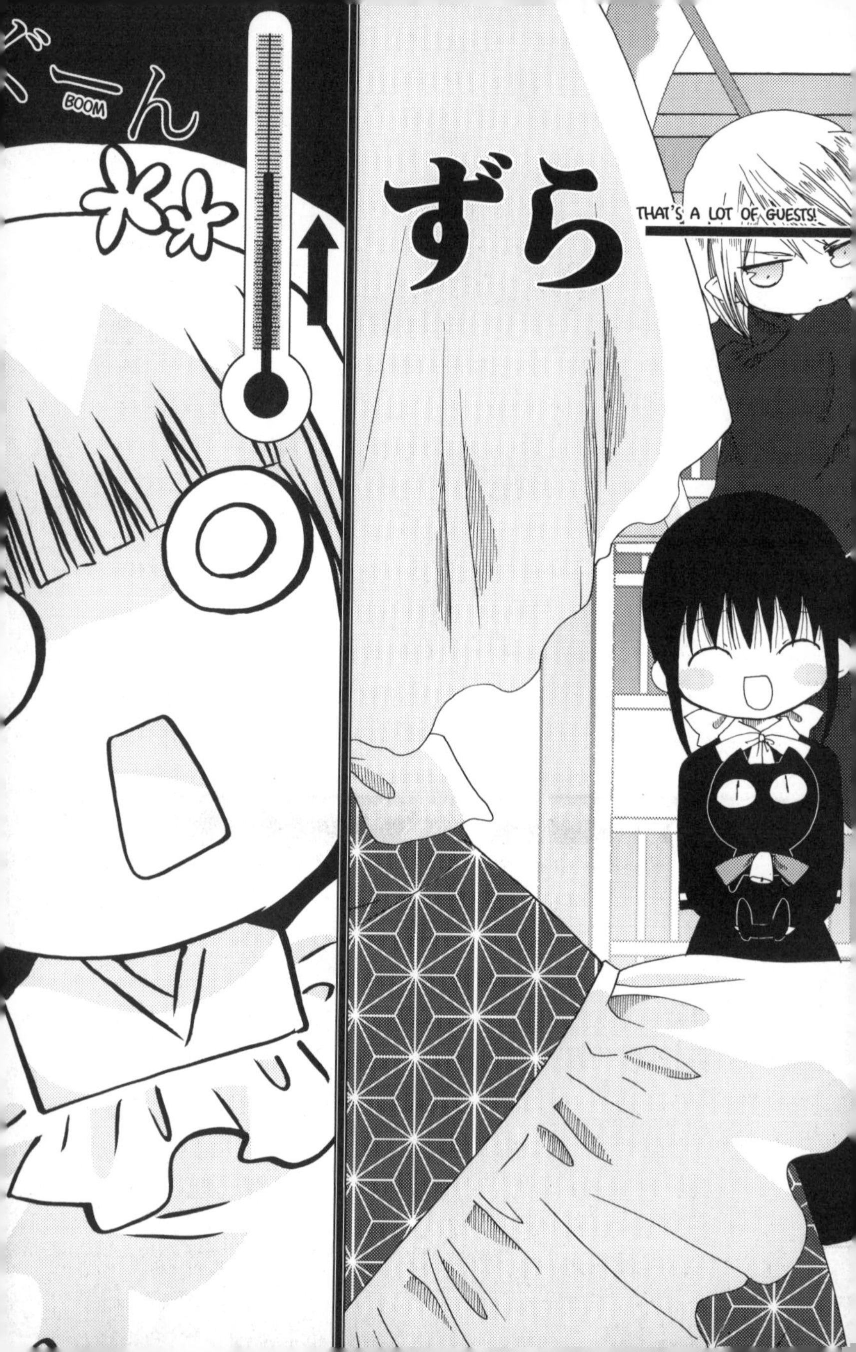
ずら
THAT'S A LOT OF GUESTS!
BOOM

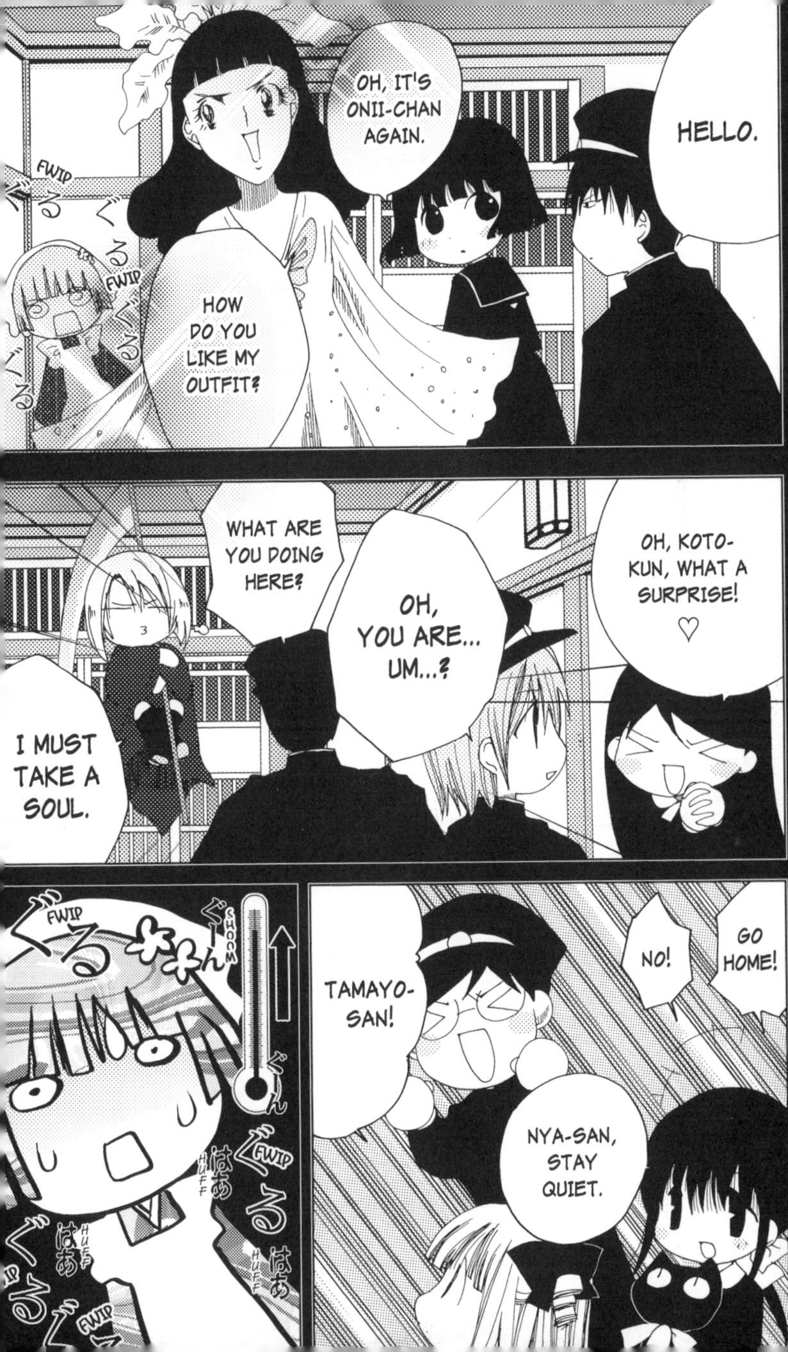
HELLO.
OH, IT'S ONII-CHAN AGAIN.
HOW DO YOU LIKE MY OUTFIT?
FWIP ぐるぐる
FWIP ぐるぐる
OH, KOTO-KUN, WHAT A SURPRISE! ♡
OH, YOU ARE... UM...?
WHAT ARE YOU DOING HERE?
I MUST TAKE A SOUL.
GO HOME!
NO!
TAMAYO-SAN!
NYA-SAN, STAY QUIET.
FWIP ぐる
SHOOM ぐーん
FWIP ぐる
HUFF はあ
HUFF はあ
FWIP ぐる

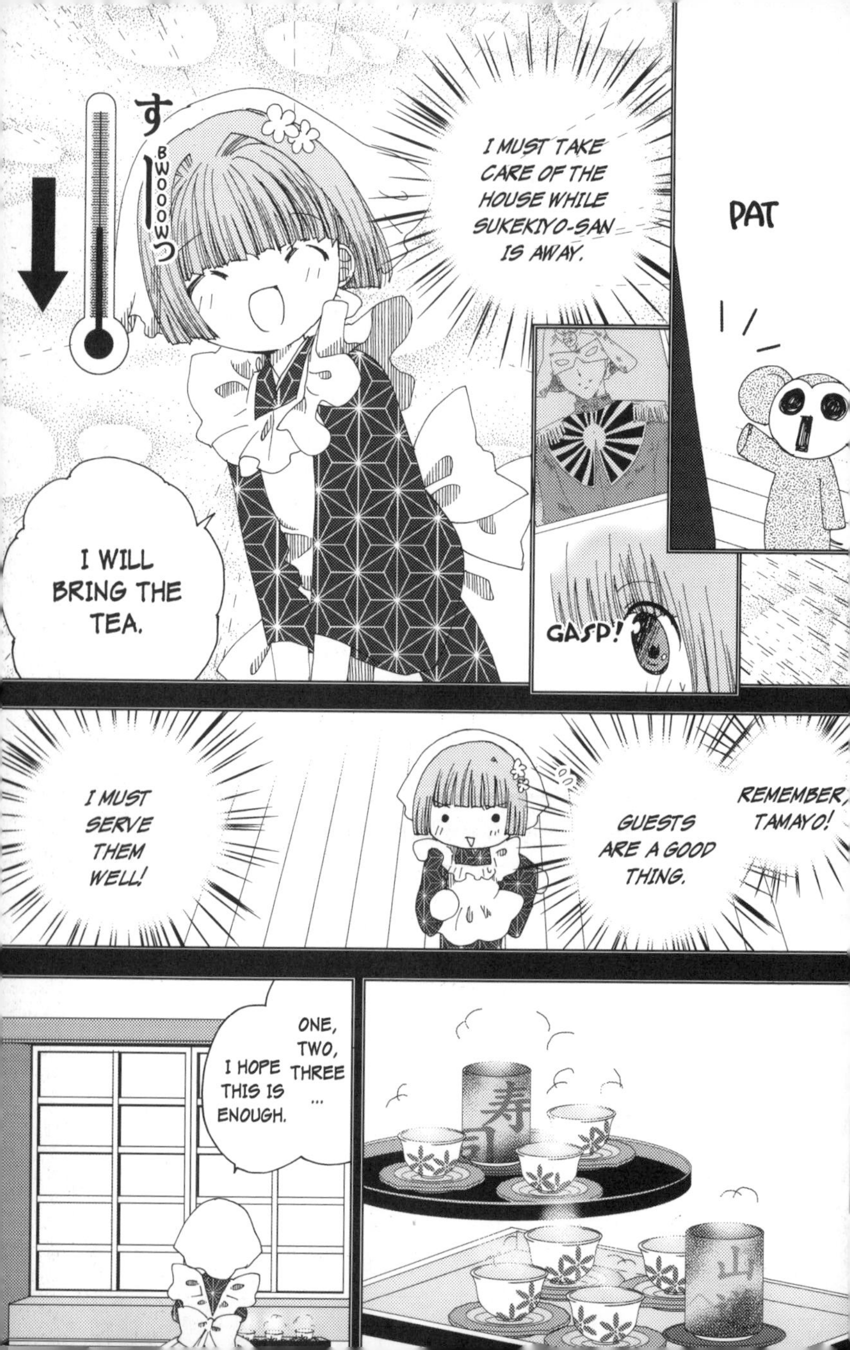
PAT
GASP!
I MUST TAKE CARE OF THE HOUSE WHILE SUKEKIYO-SAN IS AWAY.
すーっ
BWOOOW
I WILL BRING THE TEA.
REMEMBER, TAMAYO!
GUESTS ARE A GOOD THING.
I MUST SERVE THEM WELL!
ONE, TWO, THREE ...
I HOPE THIS IS ENOUGH.

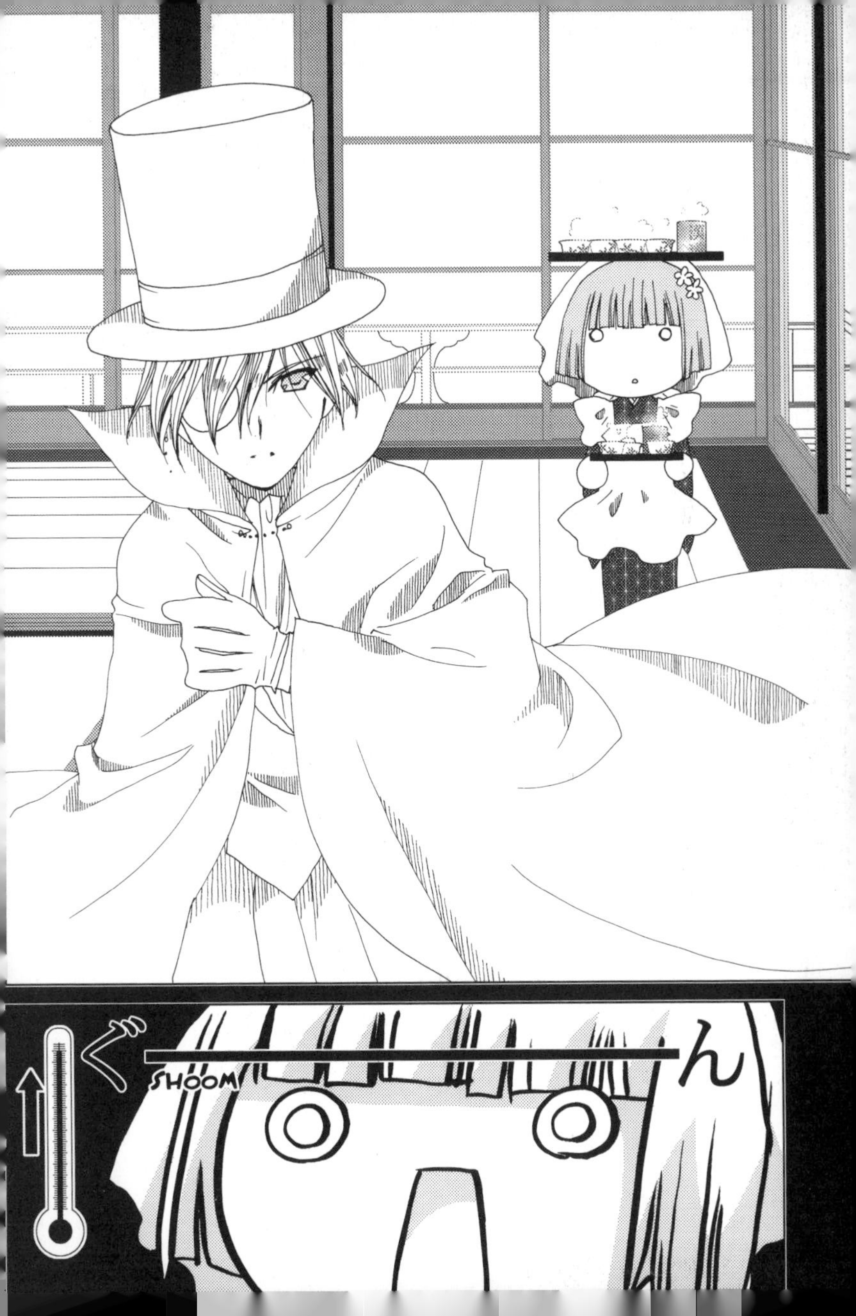
ぐ——ん
SHOOM

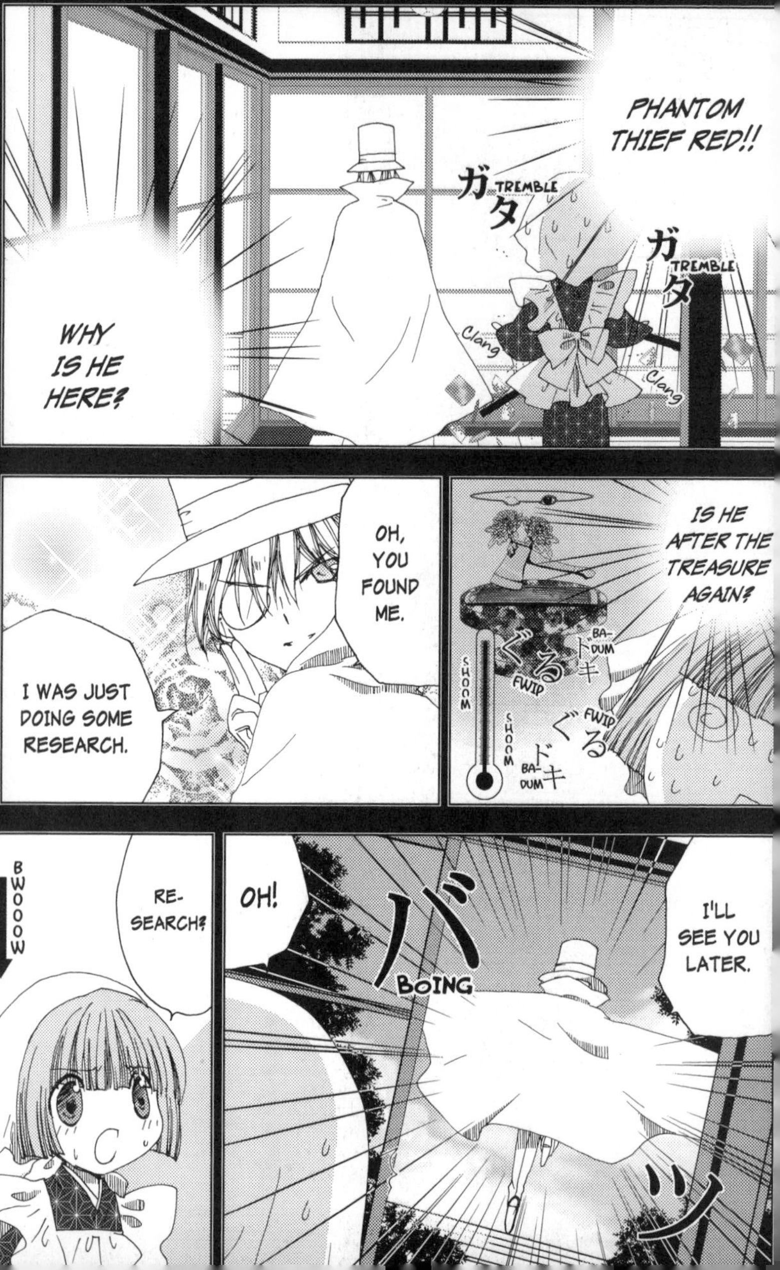
PHANTOM THIEF RED!!
ガタ TREMBLE
ガタ TREMBLE
Clang
Clang
WHY IS HE HERE?
IS HE AFTER THE TREASURE AGAIN?
ドキ BA-DUM
ぐる FWIP
ドキ BA-DUM
ぐる FWIP
SHOOM
SHOOM
OH, YOU FOUND ME.
I WAS JUST DOING SOME RESEARCH.
I'LL SEE YOU LATER.
バッ BOING
OH!
RE-SEARCH?
BWOOOOW

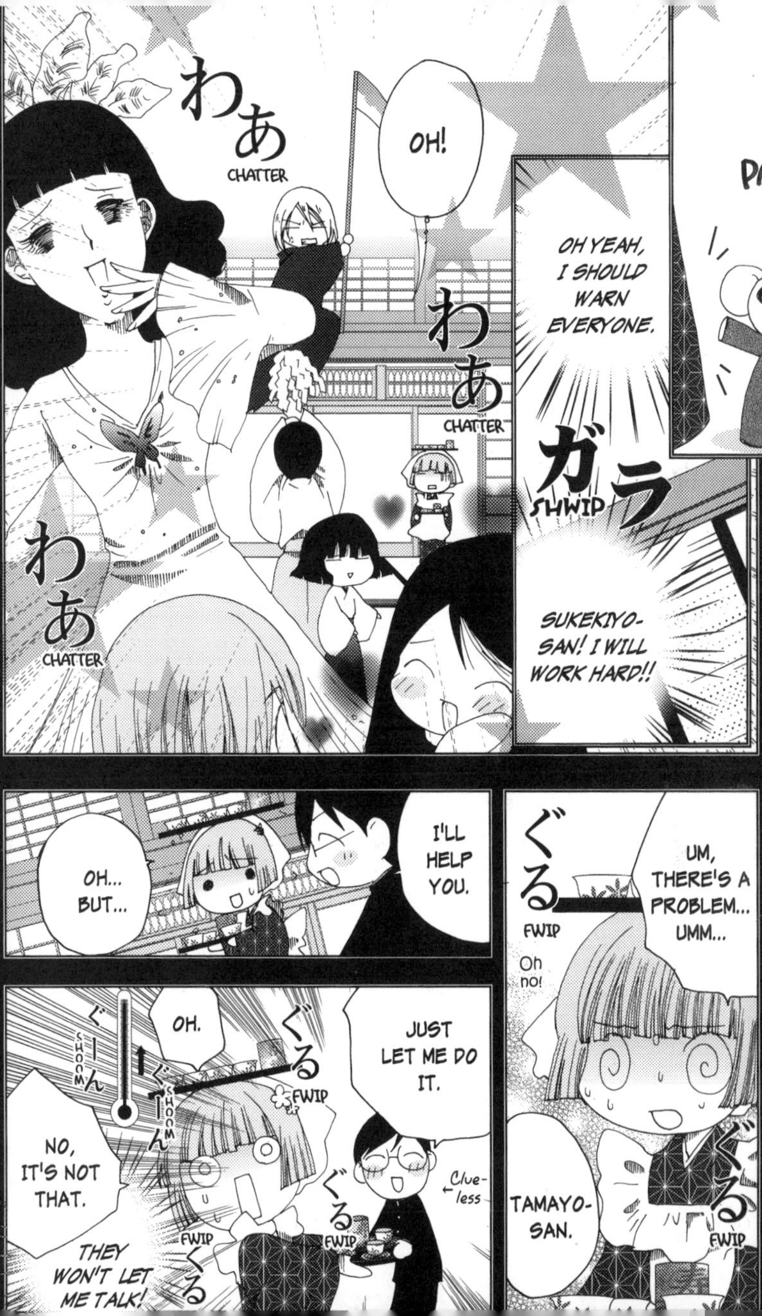
PAT
OH YEAH, I SHOULD WARN EVERYONE.
ガラ
SHWIP
SUKEKIYO-SAN! I WILL WORK HARD!!
わあ
CHATTER
OH!
わあ
CHATTER
わあ
CHATTER
ぐる
FWIP
UM, THERE'S A PROBLEM... UMM...
Oh no!
ぐる
FWIP
TAMAYO-SAN.
I'LL HELP YOU.
OH... BUT...
JUST LET ME DO IT.
← Clueless
ぐる
FWIP
ぐる
FWIP
OH.
ぐーん
SHOOM
ぐーん
SHOOM
NO, IT'S NOT THAT.
ぐる
FWIP
THEY WON'T LET ME TALK!

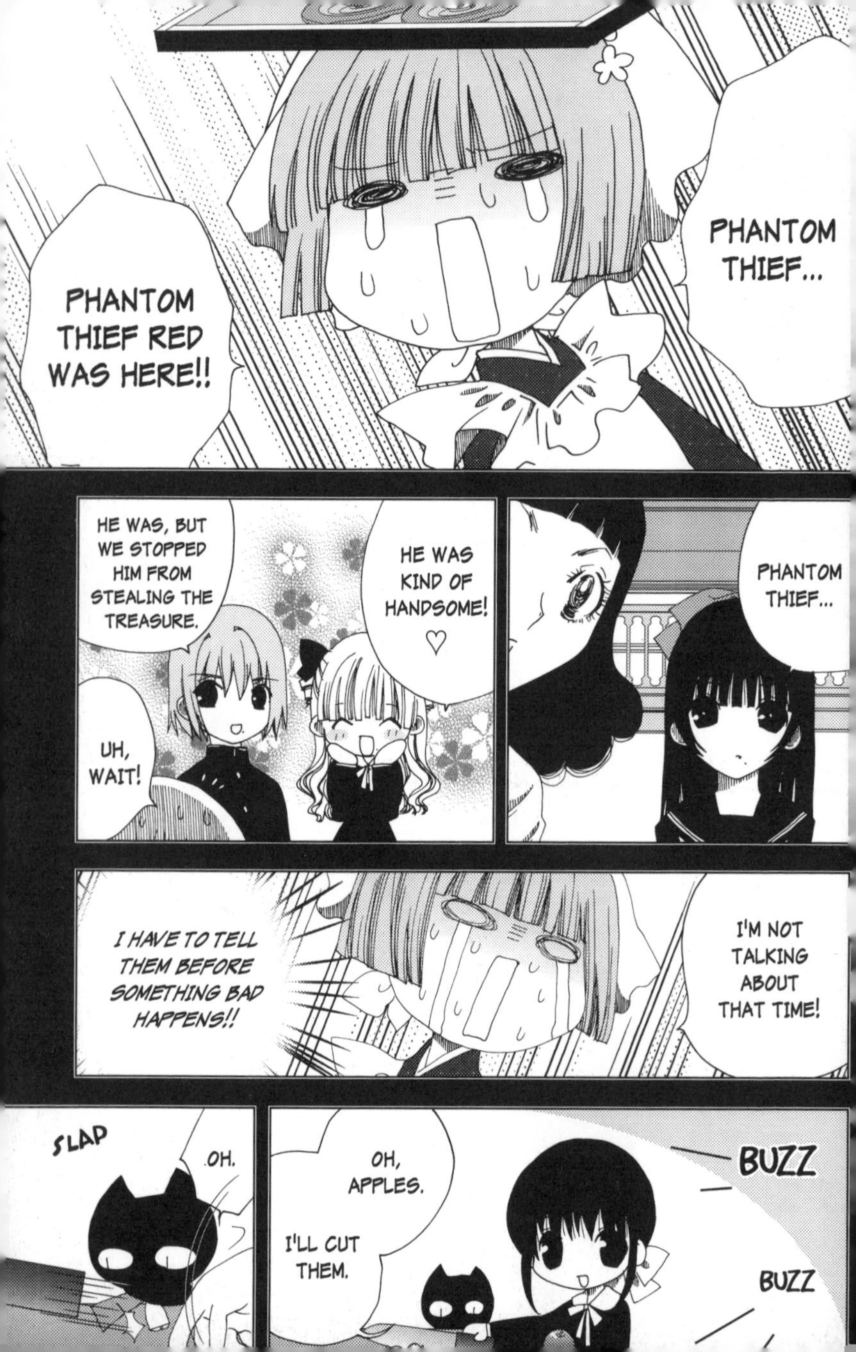
PHANTOM THIEF...
PHANTOM THIEF RED WAS HERE!!
PHANTOM THIEF...
HE WAS KIND OF HANDSOME! ♡
HE WAS, BUT WE STOPPED HIM FROM STEALING THE TREASURE.
UH, WAIT!
I'M NOT TALKING ABOUT THAT TIME!
I HAVE TO TELL THEM BEFORE SOMETHING BAD HAPPENS!!
BUZZ
OH, APPLES.
BUZZ
I'LL CUT THEM.
.OH.
SLAP

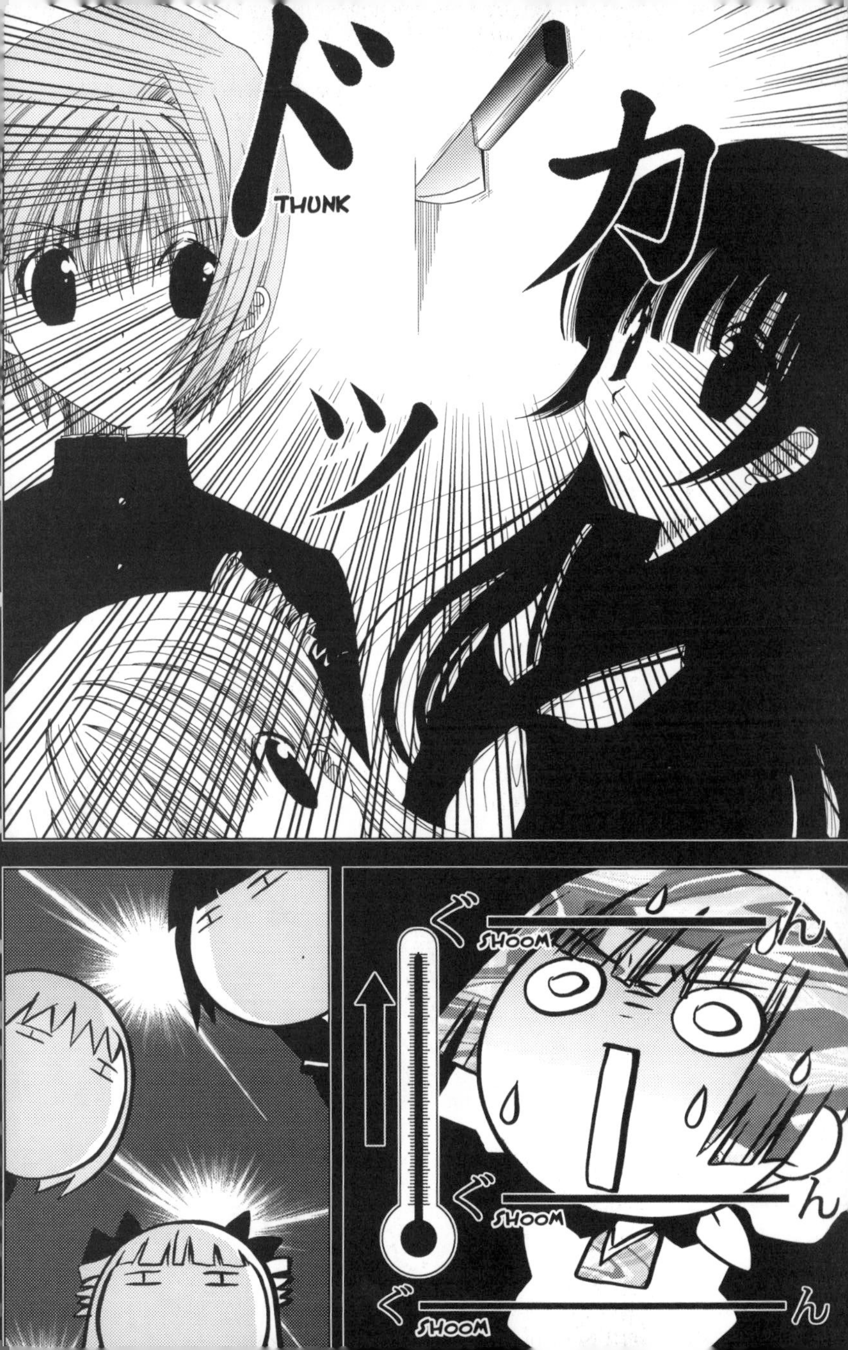
ドカッ
THUNK
ぐーん
SHOOM
ぐーん
SHOOM
ぐーん
SHOOM

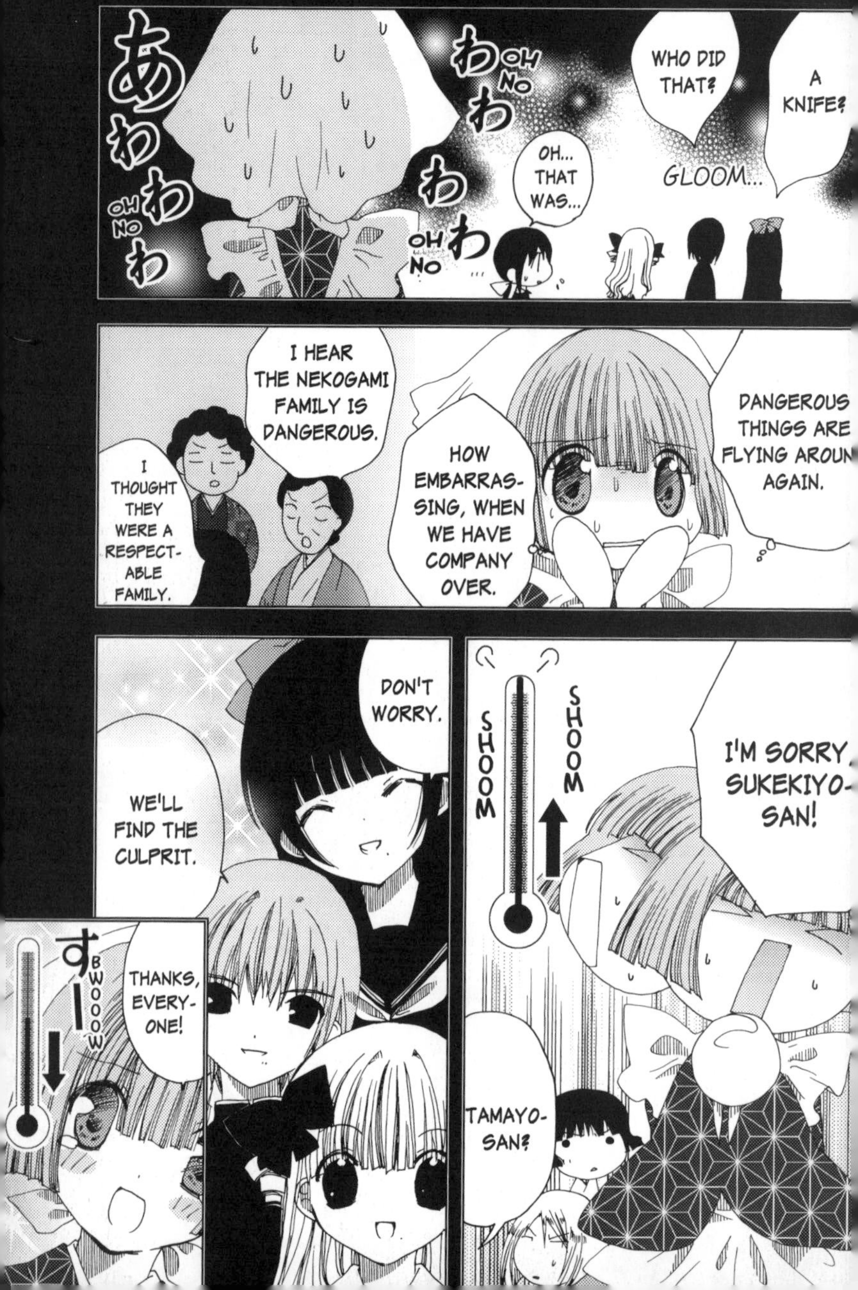
A KNIFE?
WHO DID THAT?
GLOOM...
OH... THAT WAS...
わ OH NO わ わ わ OH NO
あ わ OH NO わ わ
DANGEROUS THINGS ARE FLYING AROUN AGAIN.
HOW EMBARRAS-SING, WHEN WE HAVE COMPANY OVER.
I HEAR THE NEKOGAMI FAMILY IS DANGEROUS.
I THOUGHT THEY WERE A RESPECT-ABLE FAMILY.
I'M SORRY, SUKEKIYO-SAN!
SHOOM
SHOOM
TAMAYO-SAN?
DON'T WORRY.
WE'LL FIND THE CULPRIT.
すー BWOOOW
THANKS, EVERY-ONE!

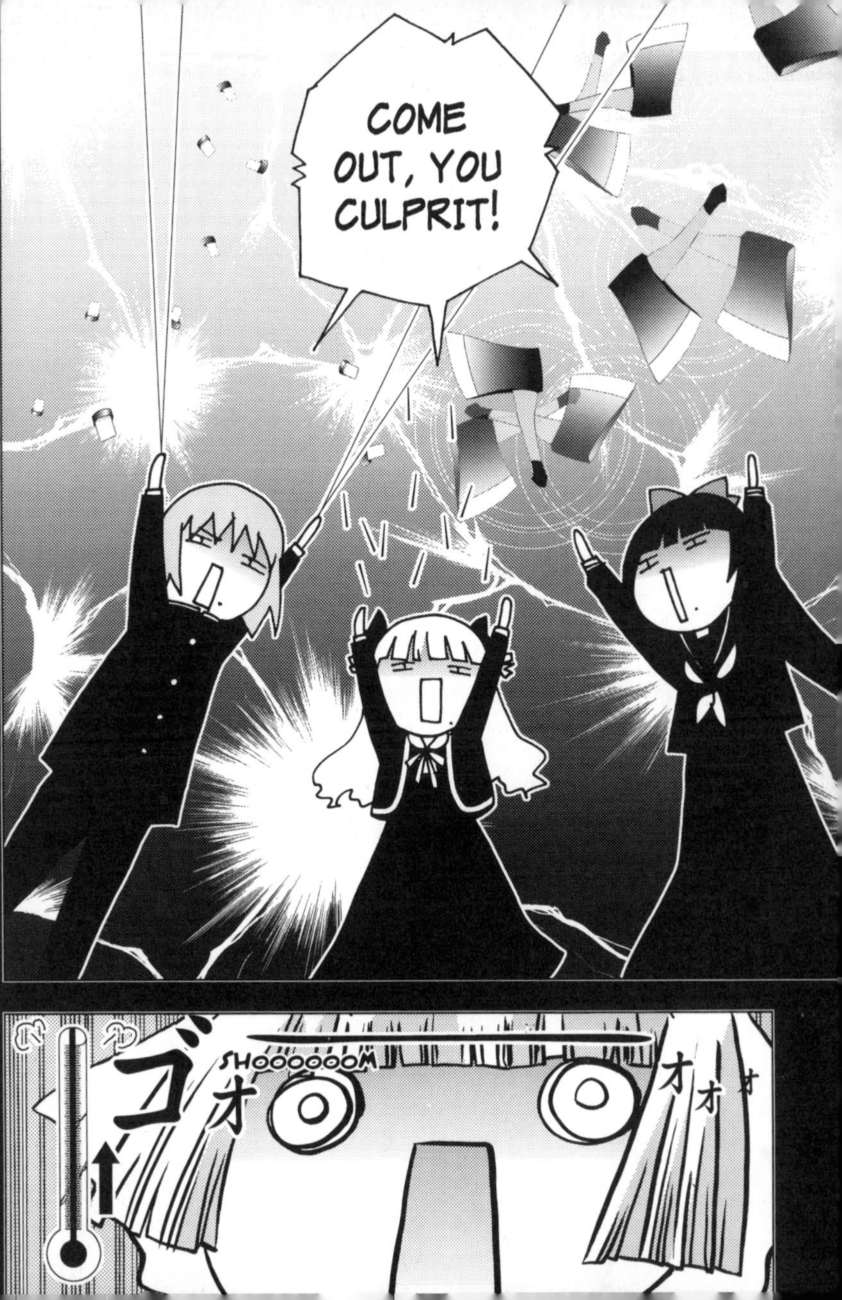
COME OUT, YOU CULPRIT!
SHOOOOOOM
ゴオ
オオオ

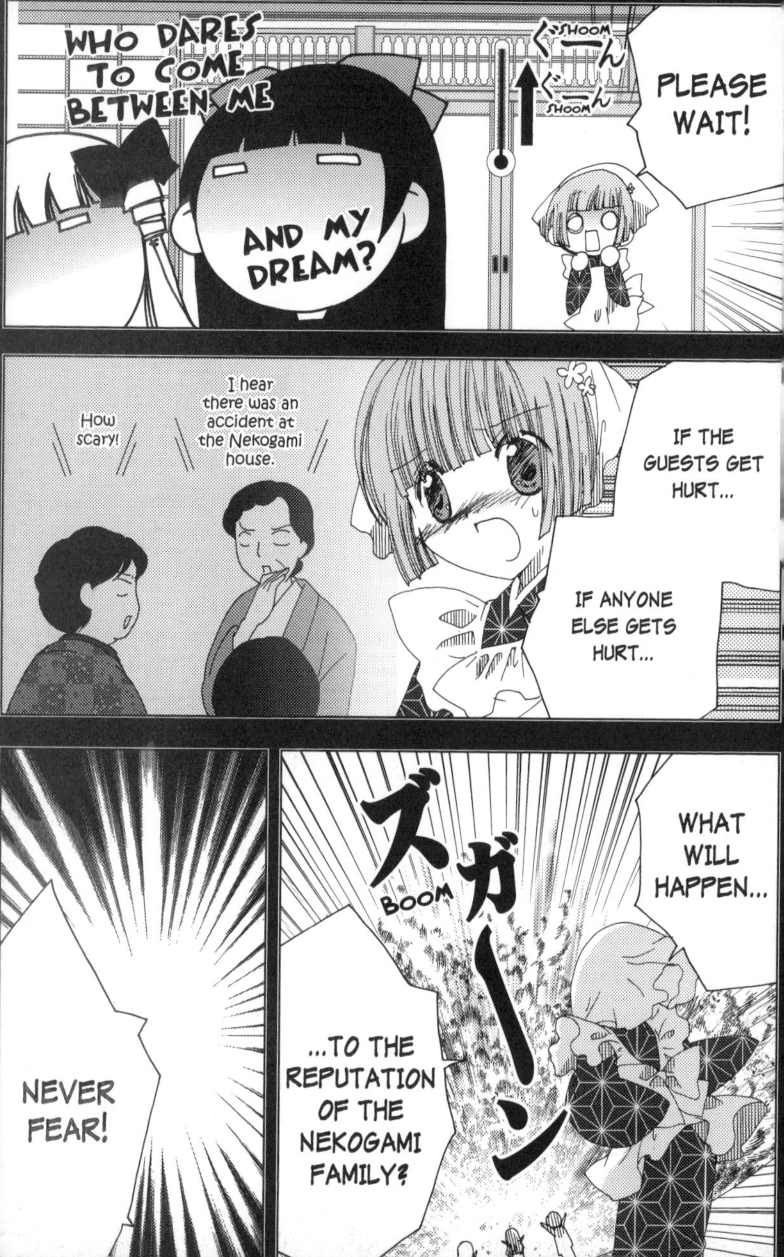
PLEASE WAIT!
ぐーん SHOOM
ぐーん SHOOM
WHO DARES TO COME BETWEEN ME
AND MY DREAM?
IF THE GUESTS GET HURT...
IF ANYONE ELSE GETS HURT...
I hear there was an accident at the Nekogami house.
How scary!
WHAT WILL HAPPEN...
ズガーン BOOM
...TO THE REPUTATION OF THE NEKOGAMI FAMILY?
NEVER FEAR!

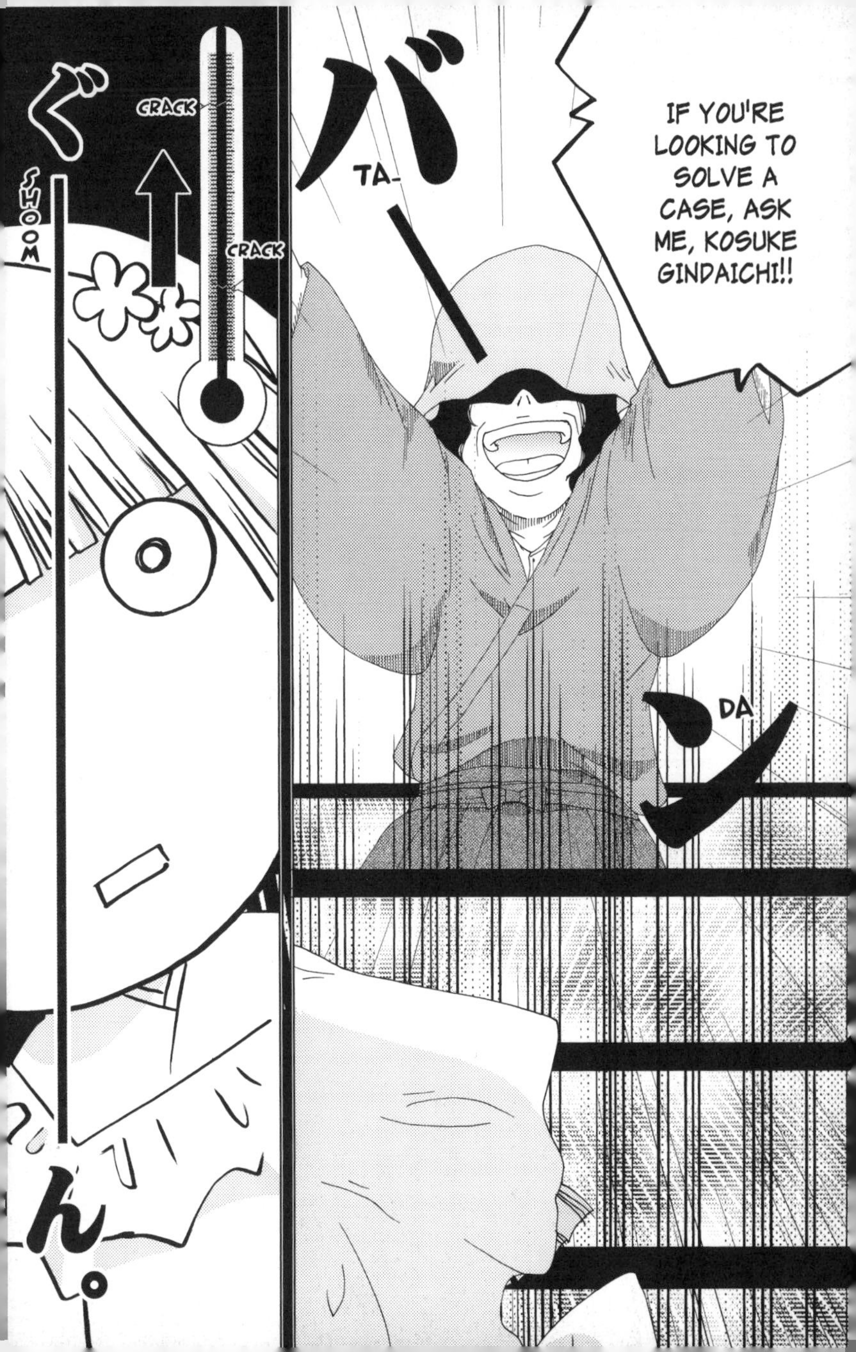
IF YOU'RE LOOKING TO SOLVE A CASE, ASK ME, KOSUKE GINDAICHI!!
バーン
TA-
DA
CRACK
CRACK
ぐーん。
SHOOM

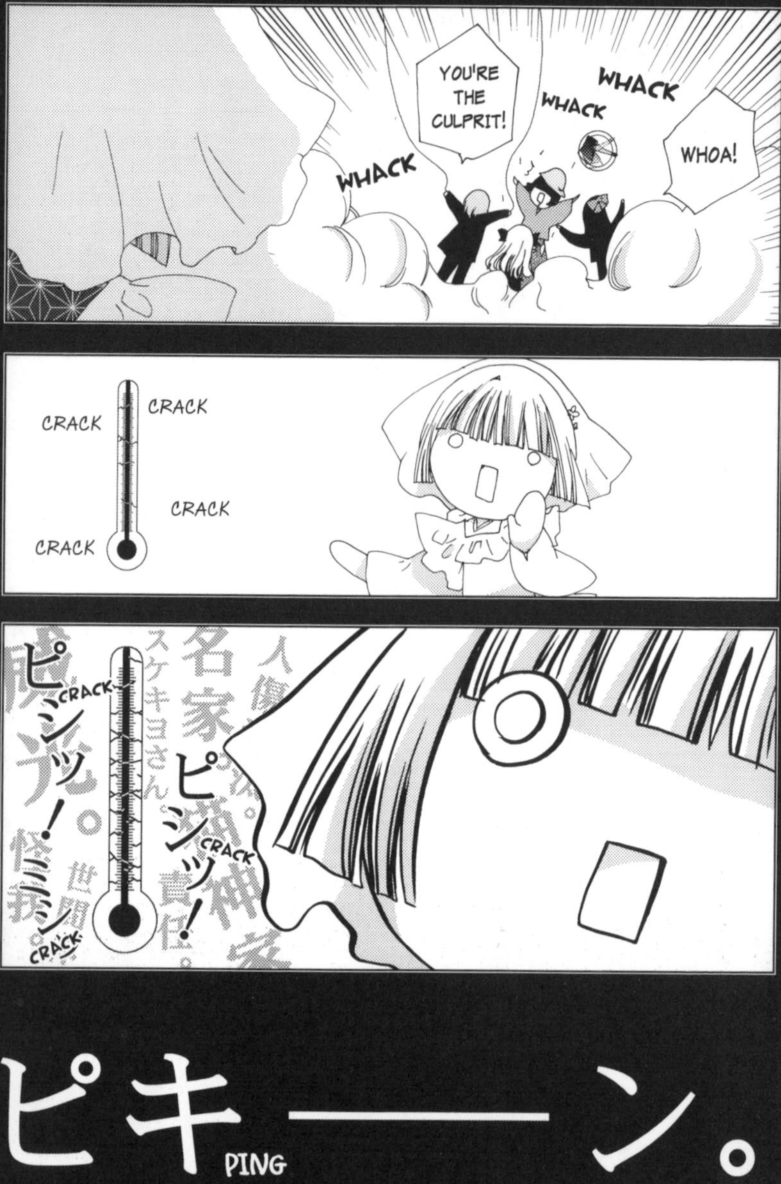

WHOA!
WHACK
WHACK
YOU'RE THE CULPRIT!
WHACK
CRACK
CRACK
CRACK
CRACK
ピシッ!
CRACK
ピシッ!
CRACK
ミシッ
CRACK
ピキーーン。
PING

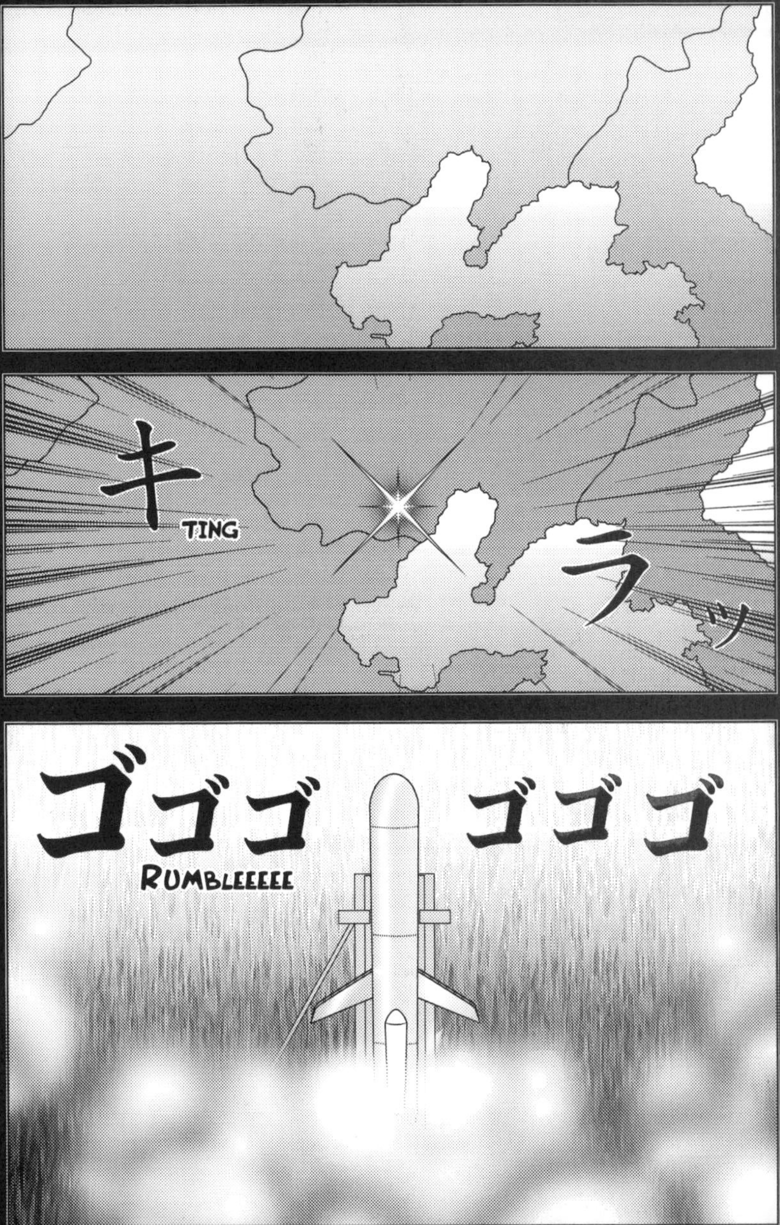
キ
TING
ラッ
ゴゴゴ
RUMBLEEEEE
ゴゴゴ

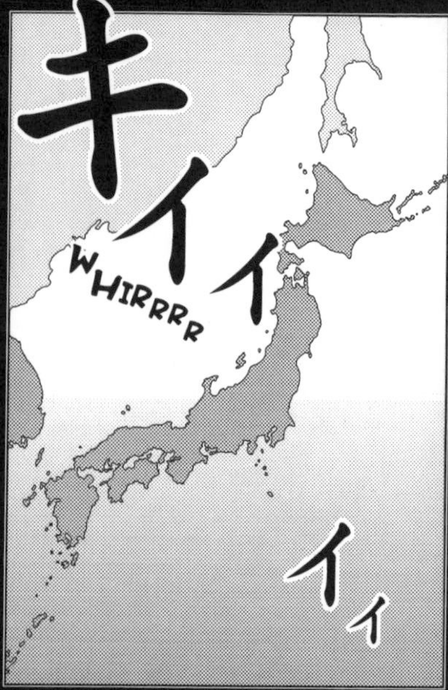
キイイ
WHIRRRR
イイ
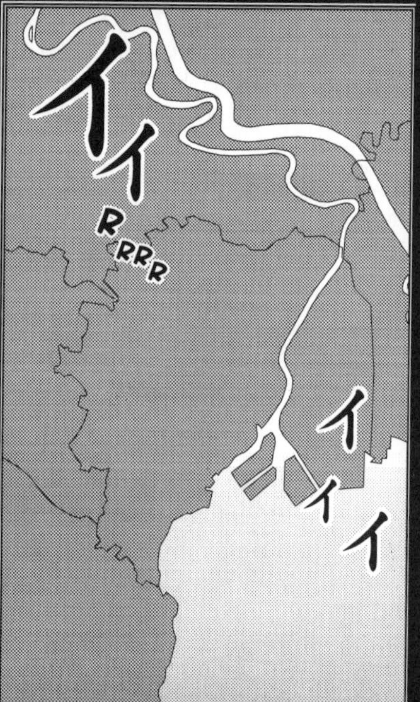
イイ
RRRR
イイイ
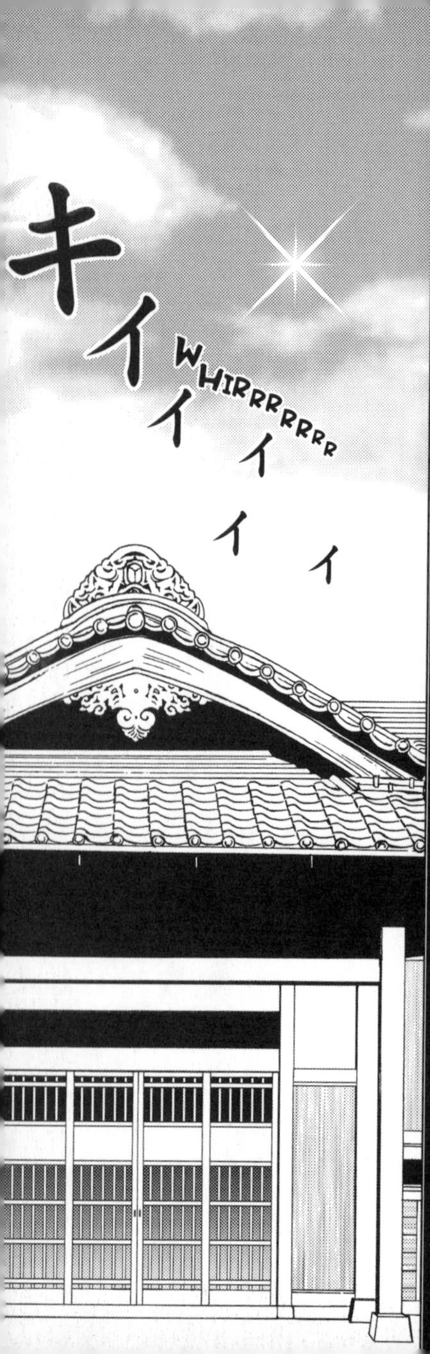
キイイイイイ
WHIRRRRRRRR

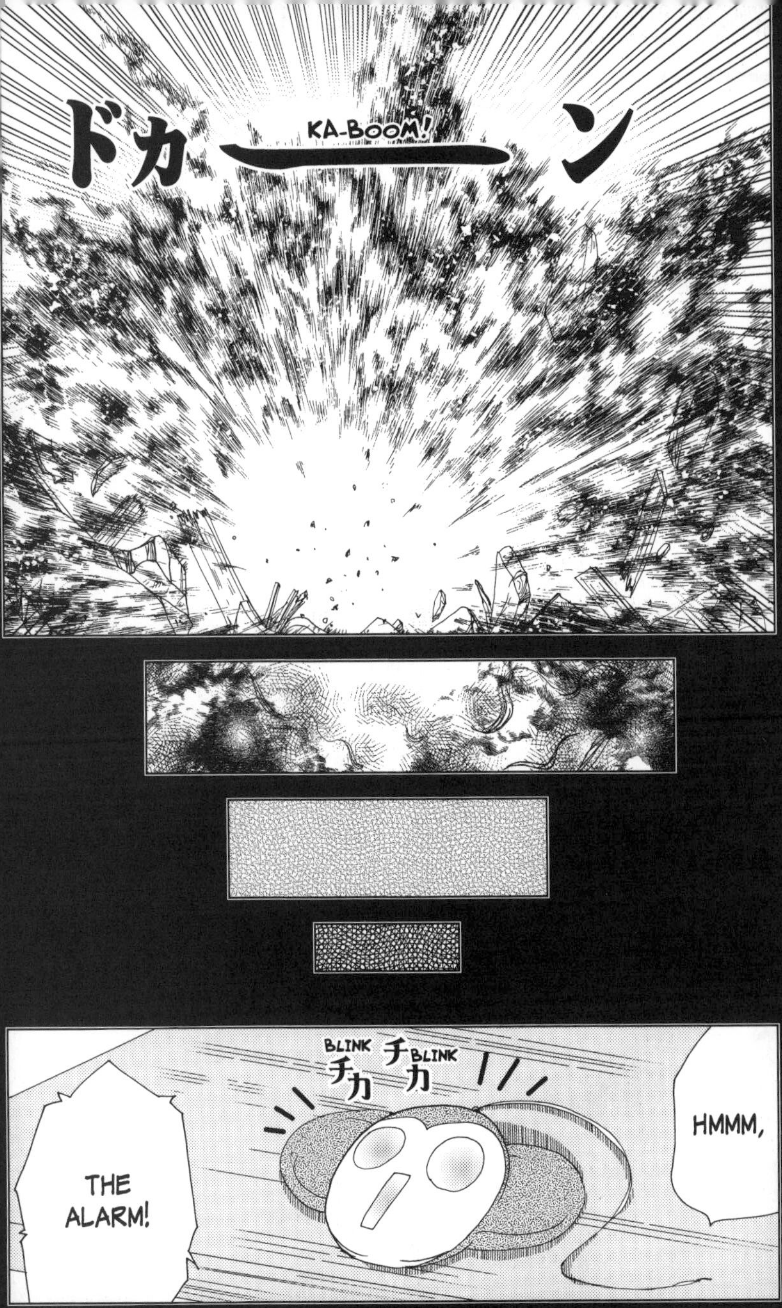
ドカーーーン
KA-BOOM!
HMMM,
チカ BLINK
BLINK チカ
THE ALARM!

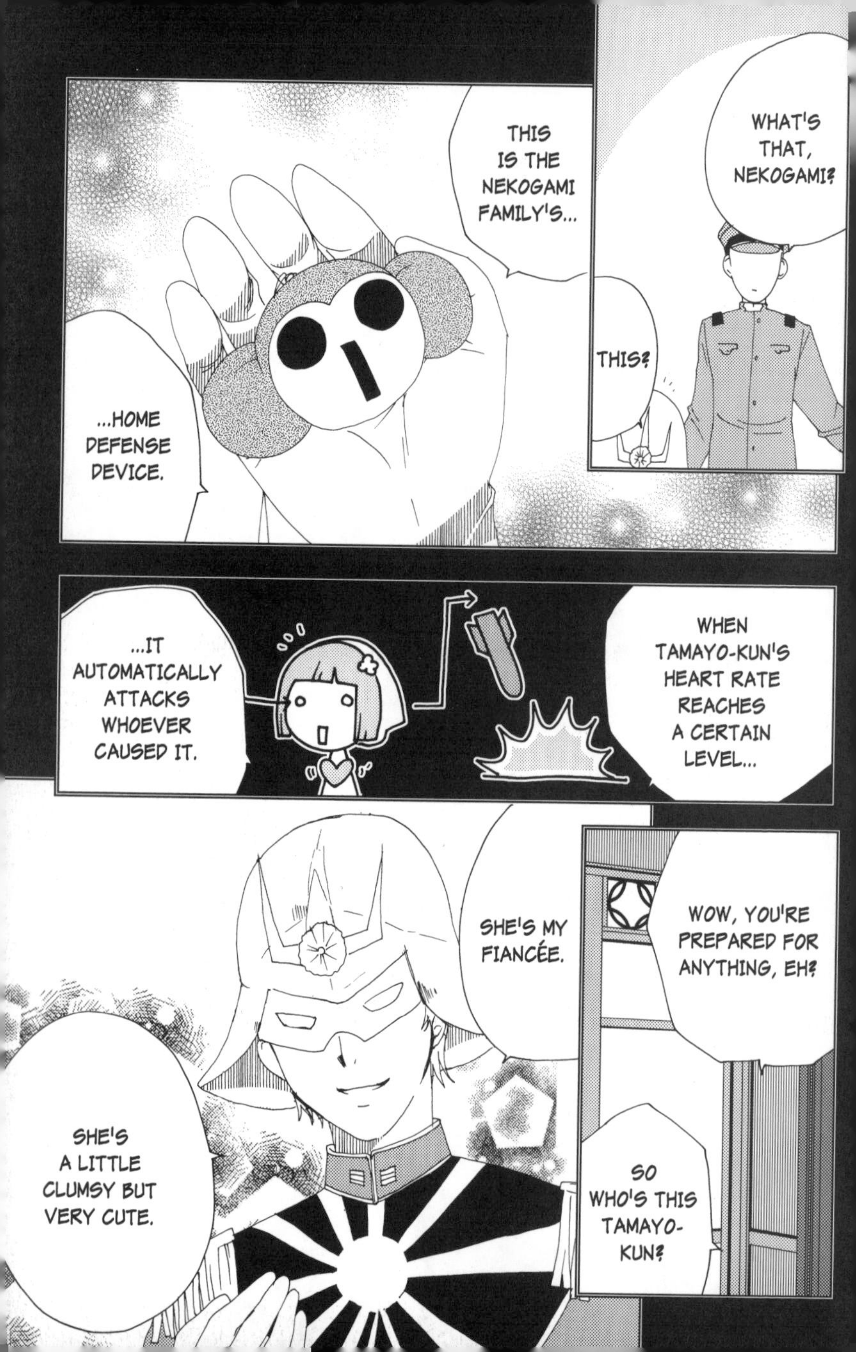
WHAT'S THAT, NEKOGAMI?
THIS?
THIS IS THE NEKOGAMI FAMILY'S...
...HOME DEFENSE DEVICE.
WHEN TAMAYO-KUN'S HEART RATE REACHES A CERTAIN LEVEL...
...IT AUTOMATICALLY ATTACKS WHOEVER CAUSED IT.
WOW, YOU'RE PREPARED FOR ANYTHING, EH?
SO WHO'S THIS TAMAYO-KUN?
SHE'S MY FIANCÉE.
SHE'S A LITTLE CLUMSY BUT VERY CUTE.

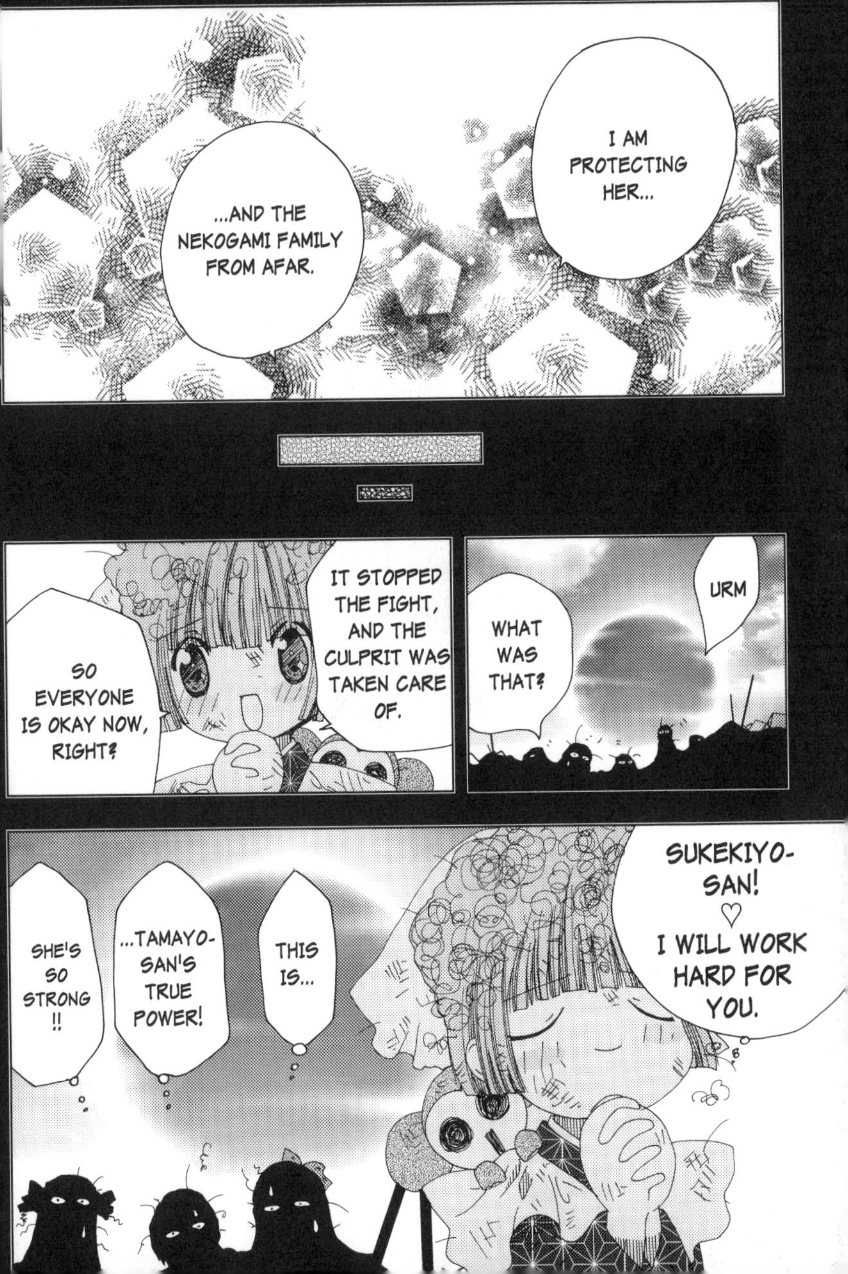
I AM PROTECTING HER...
...AND THE NEKOGAMI FAMILY FROM AFAR.
URM
WHAT WAS THAT?
IT STOPPED THE FIGHT, AND THE CULPRIT WAS TAKEN CARE OF.
SO EVERYONE IS OKAY NOW, RIGHT?
SUKEKIYO-SAN! ♡ I WILL WORK HARD FOR YOU.
THIS IS...
...TAMAYO-SAN'S TRUE POWER!
SHE'S SO STRONG !!

Chapter SEVEN

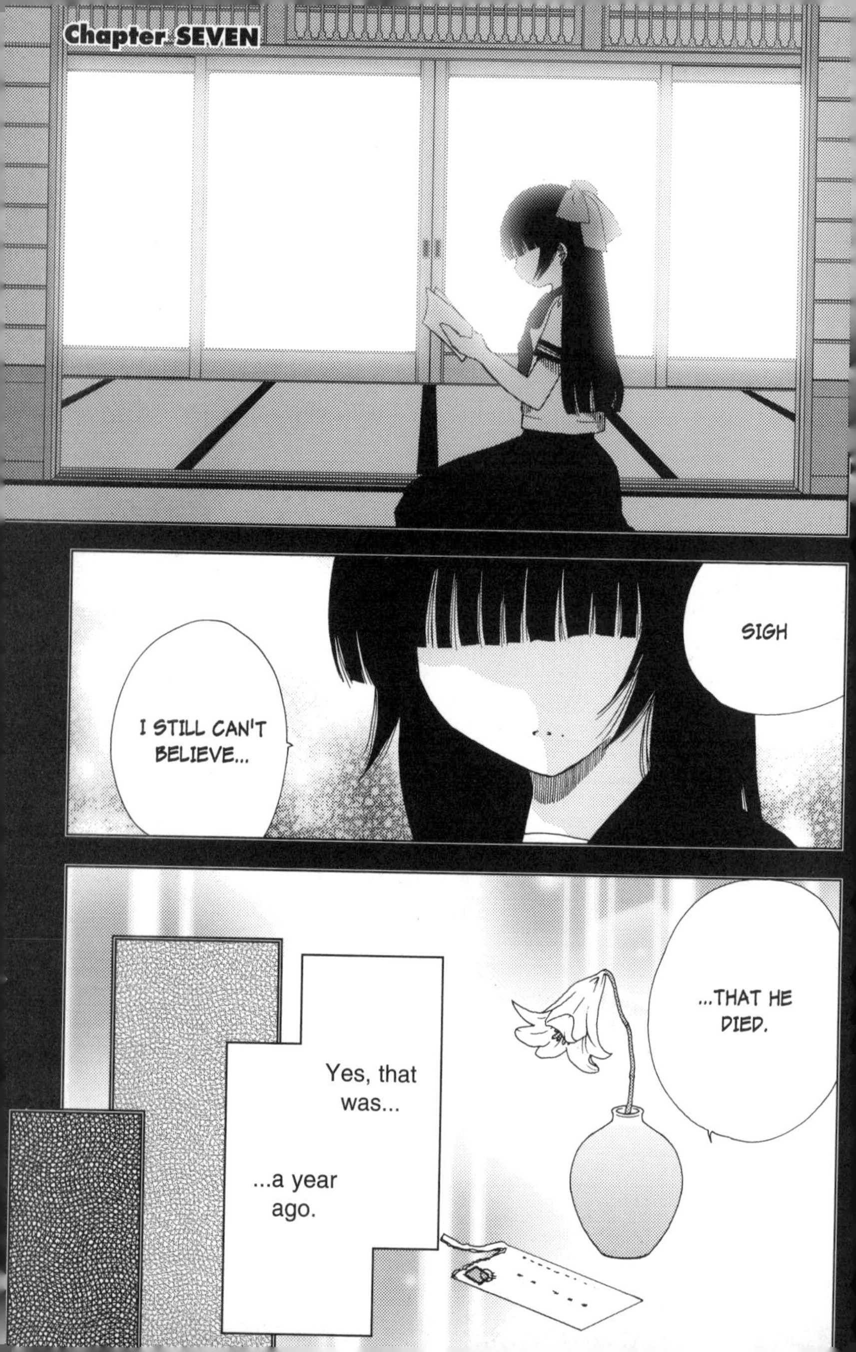
SIGH
I STILL CAN'T BELIEVE...
...THAT HE DIED.
Yes, that was...
...a year ago.

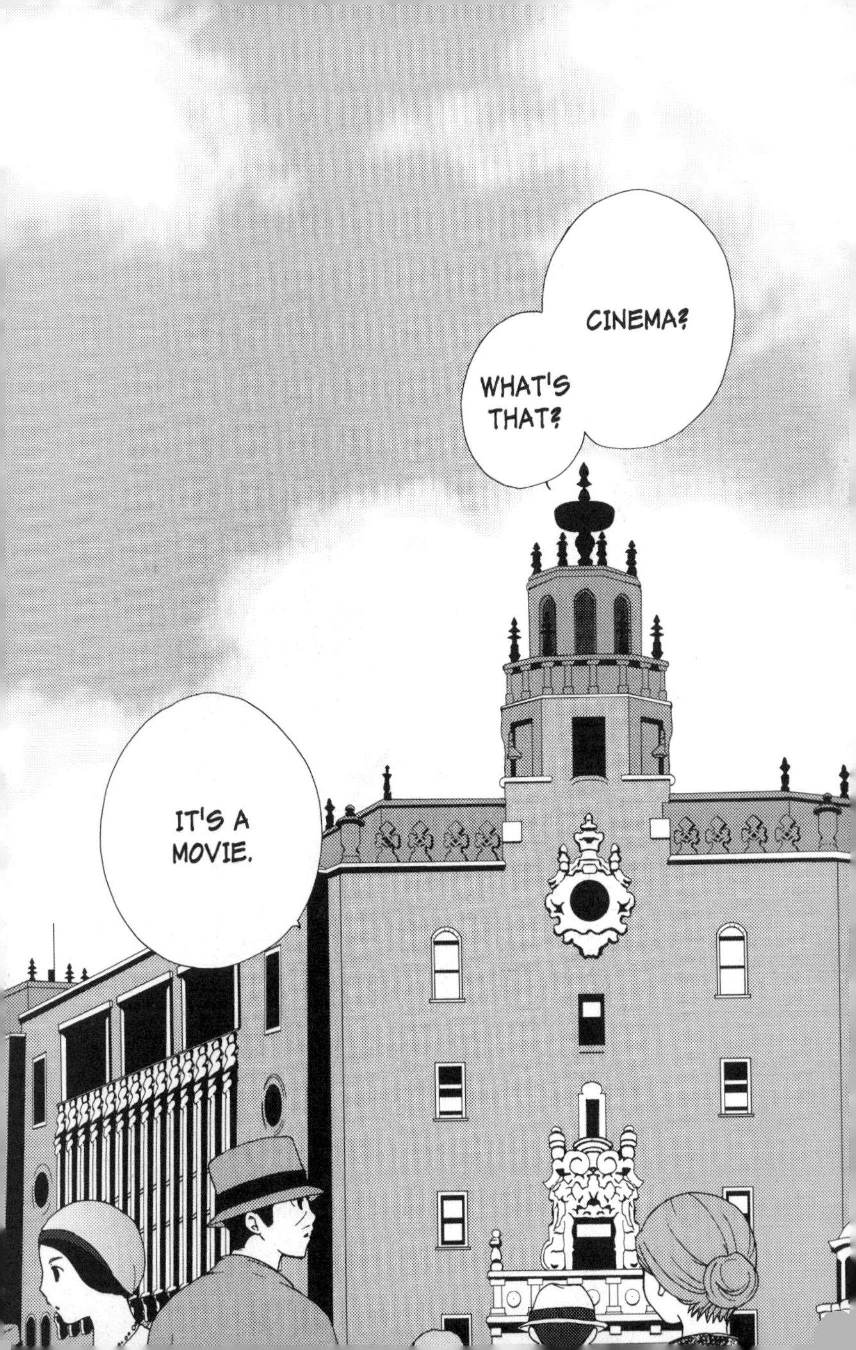
CINEMA?
WHAT'S THAT?
IT'S A MOVIE.

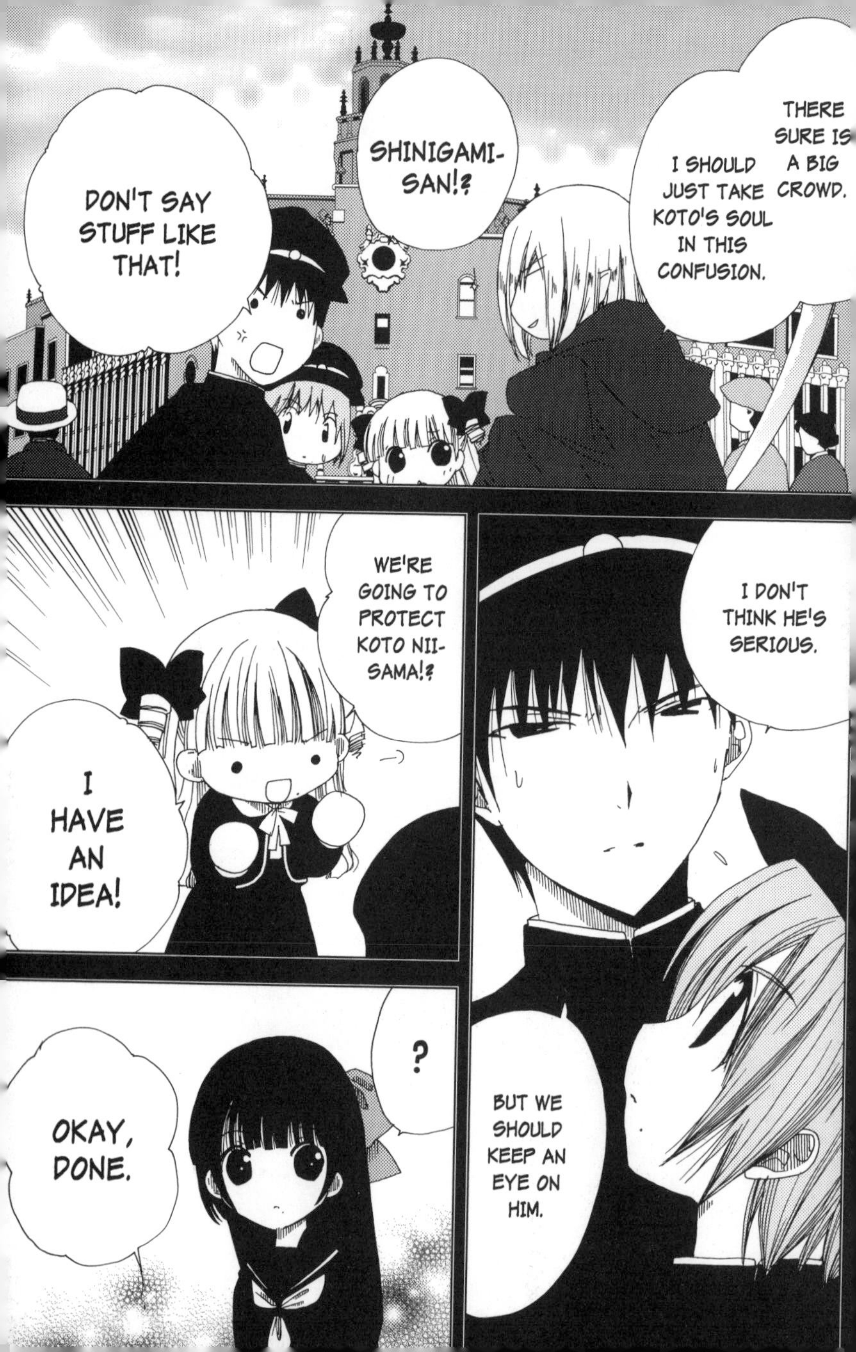
THERE SURE IS A BIG CROWD.
I SHOULD JUST TAKE KOTO'S SOUL IN THIS CONFUSION.
SHINIGAMI-SAN!?
DON'T SAY STUFF LIKE THAT!
I DON'T THINK HE'S SERIOUS.
BUT WE SHOULD KEEP AN EYE ON HIM.
WE'RE GOING TO PROTECT KOTO NII-SAMA!?
I HAVE AN IDEA!
?
OKAY, DONE.

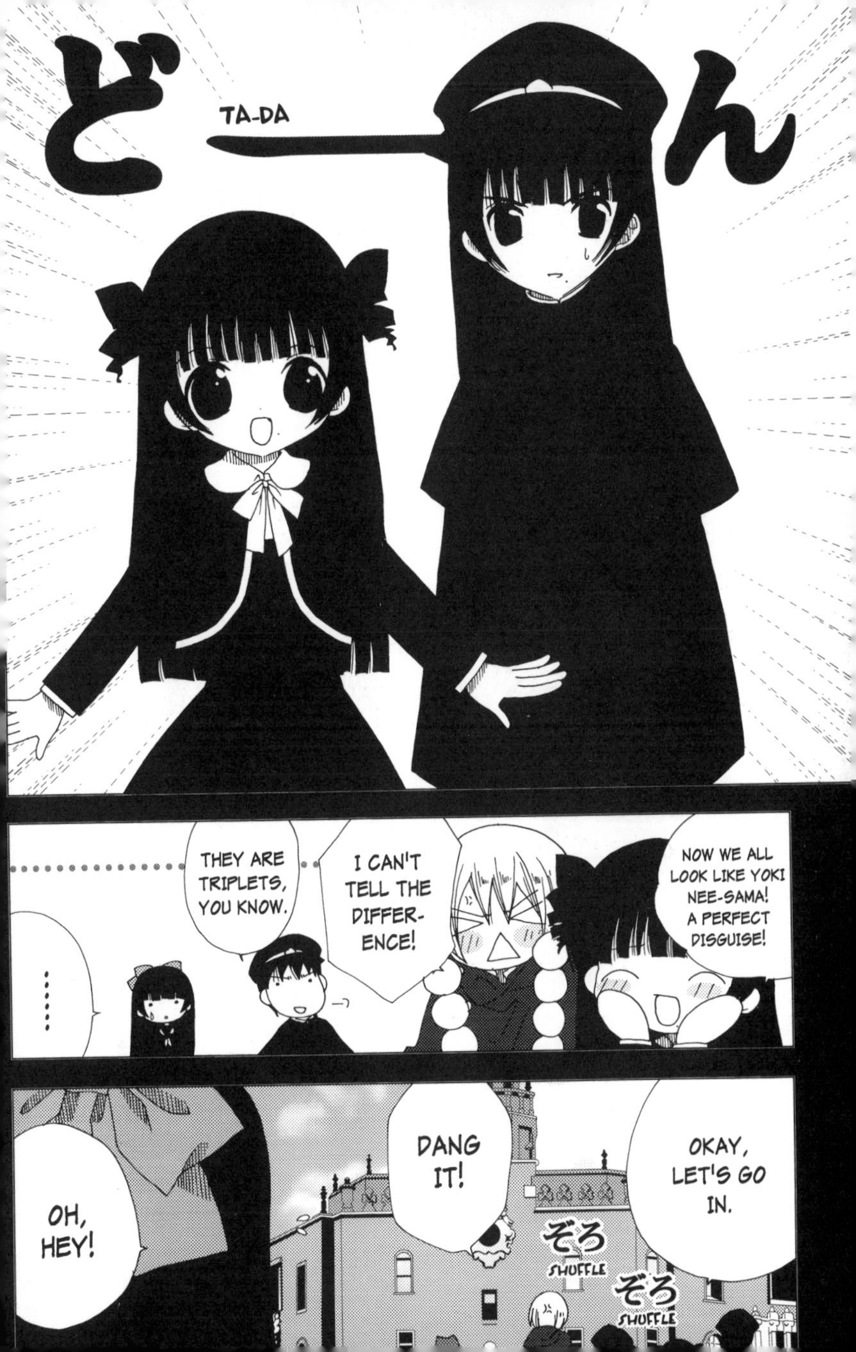
どーん
TA-DA
NOW WE ALL LOOK LIKE YOKI NEE-SAMA! A PERFECT DISGUISE!
I CAN'T TELL THE DIFFER-ENCE!
THEY ARE TRIPLETS, YOU KNOW.
......
OKAY, LET'S GO IN.
DANG IT!
ぞろ
SHUFFLE
ぞろ
SHUFFLE
OH, HEY!

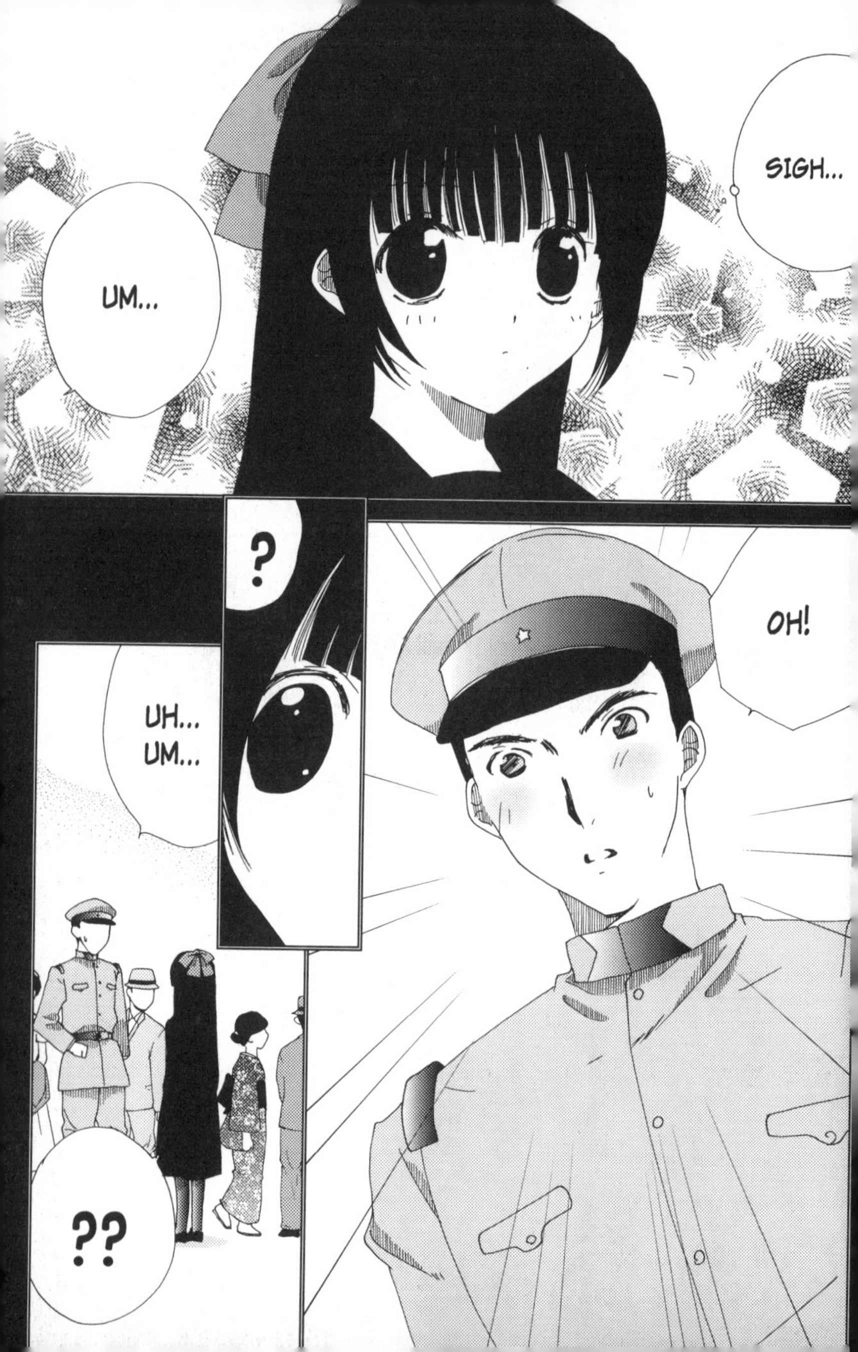
SIGH...
UM...
OH!
?
UH... UM...
??

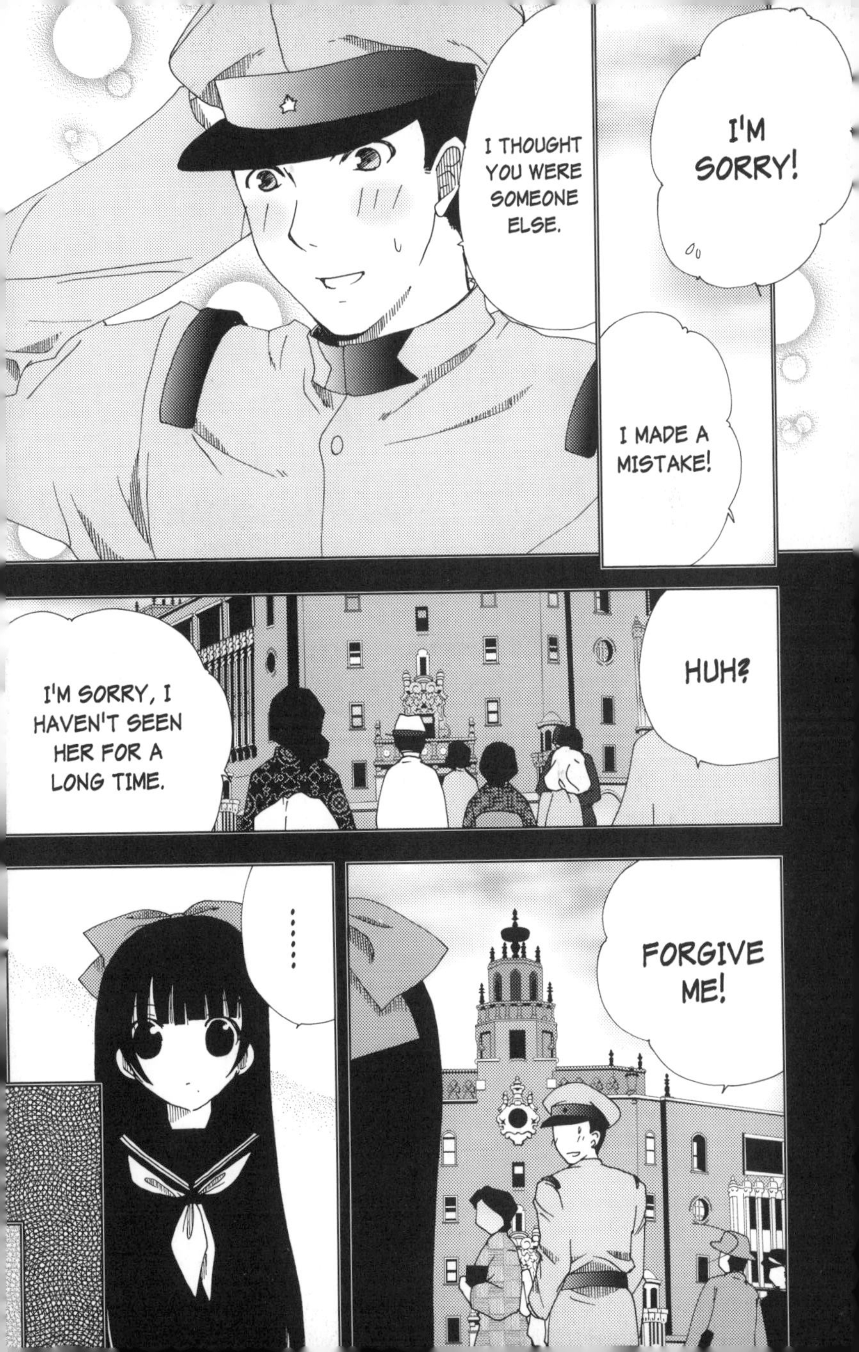
I'M SORRY!
I MADE A MISTAKE!
I THOUGHT YOU WERE SOMEONE ELSE.
HUH?
I'M SORRY, I HAVEN'T SEEN HER FOR A LONG TIME.
FORGIVE ME!
......

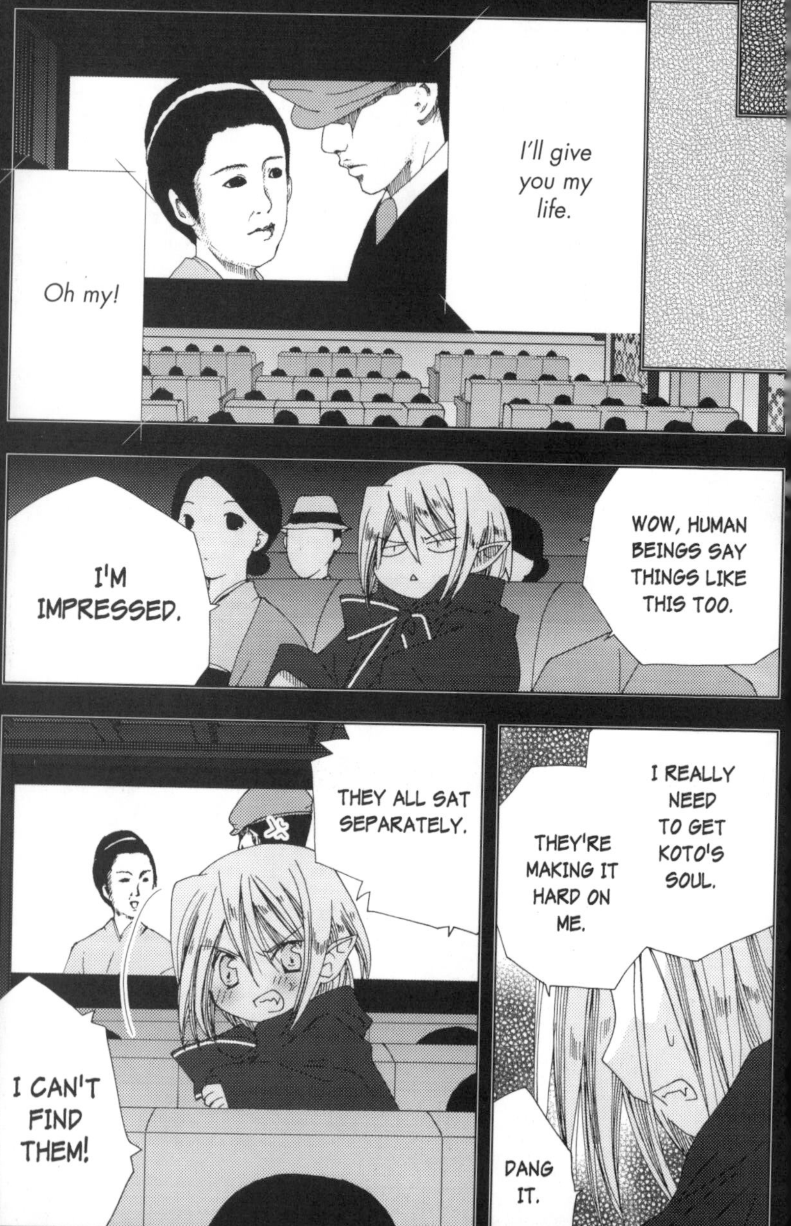
I'll give you my life.
Oh my!
WOW, HUMAN BEINGS SAY THINGS LIKE THIS TOO.
I'M IMPRESSED.
I REALLY NEED TO GET KOTO'S SOUL.
THEY'RE MAKING IT HARD ON ME.
DANG IT.
THEY ALL SAT SEPARATELY.
I CAN'T FIND THEM!

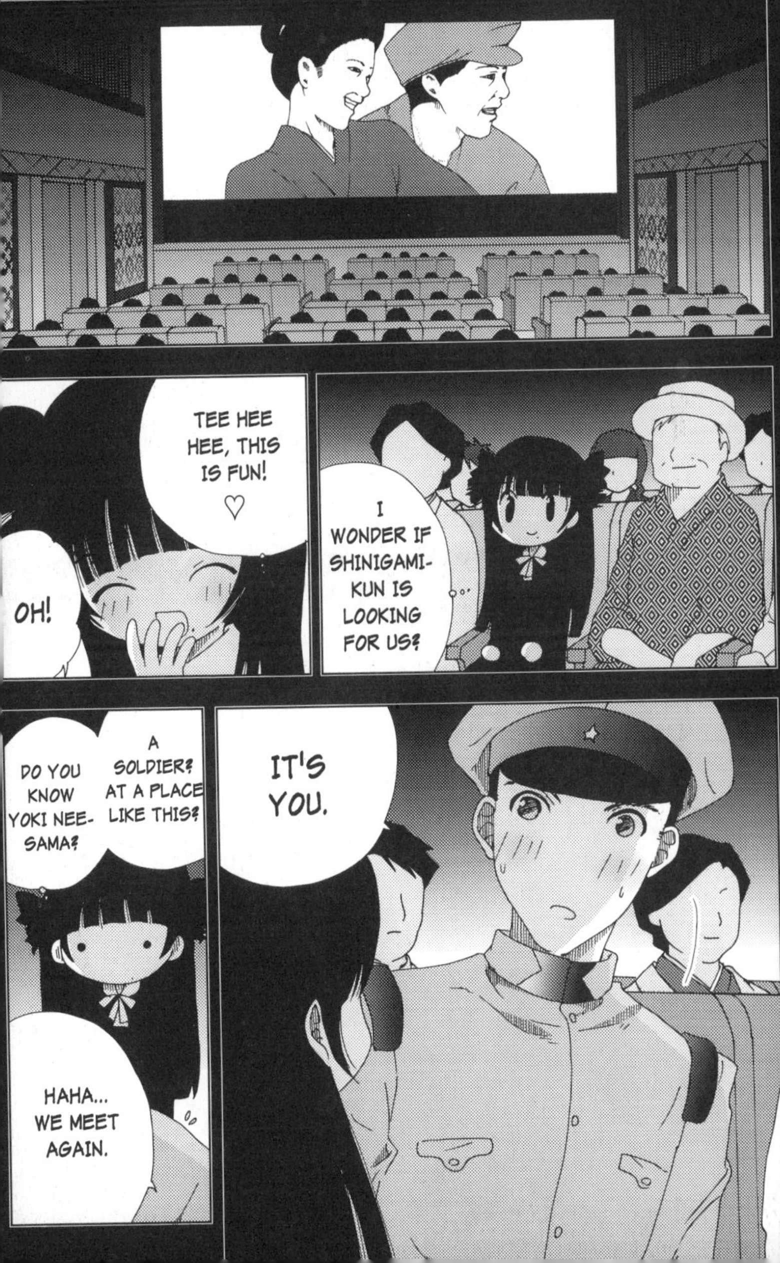
I WONDER IF SHINIGAMI-KUN IS LOOKING FOR US?
TEE HEE HEE, THIS IS FUN! ♡
OH!
IT'S YOU.
A SOLDIER? AT A PLACE LIKE THIS?
DO YOU KNOW YOKI NEE-SAMA?
HAHA... WE MEET AGAIN.

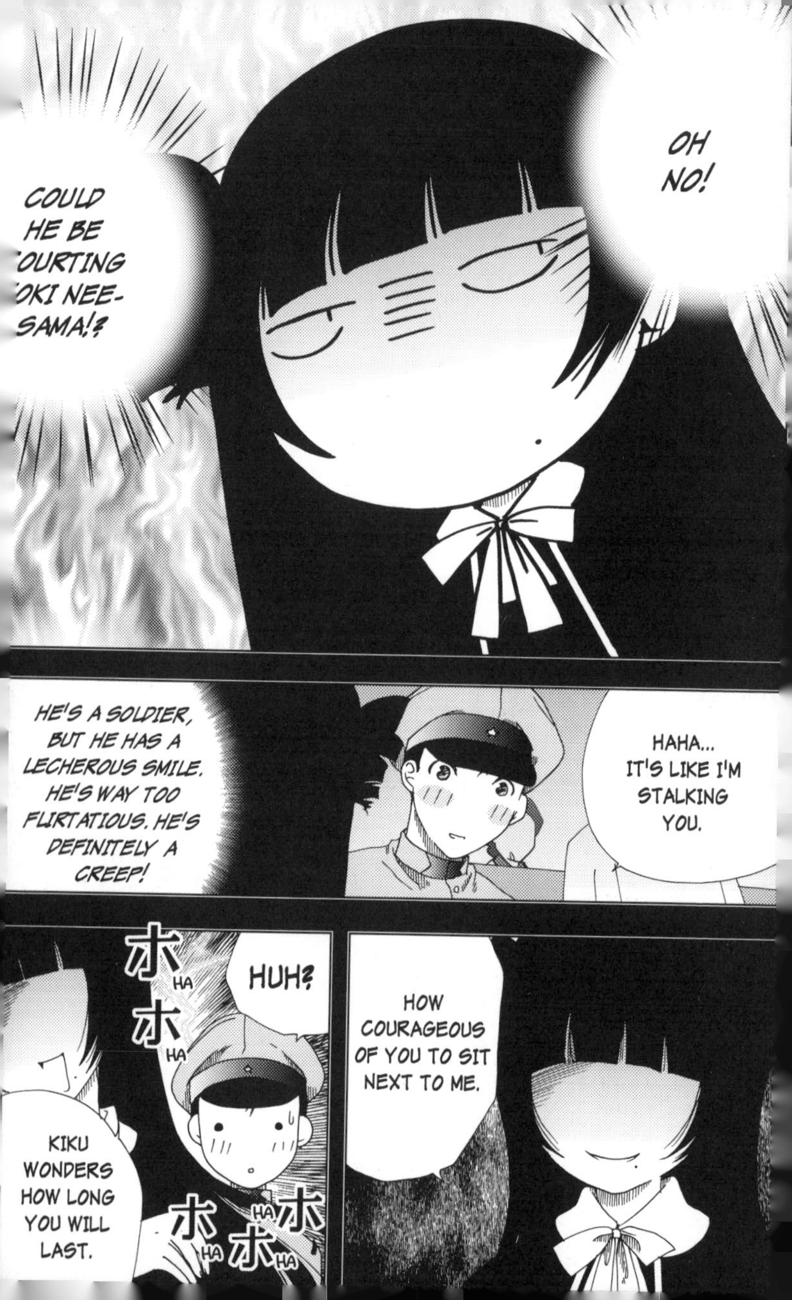
OH NO!
COULD HE BE COURTING OKI NEE-SAMA!?
HAHA... IT'S LIKE I'M STALKING YOU.
HE'S A SOLDIER, BUT HE HAS A LECHEROUS SMILE. HE'S WAY TOO FLIRTATIOUS. HE'S DEFINITELY A CREEP!
HOW COURAGEOUS OF YOU TO SIT NEXT TO ME.
HUH?
ホ HA ホ HA
KIKU WONDERS HOW LONG YOU WILL LAST.
ホ HA ホ HA ホ HA

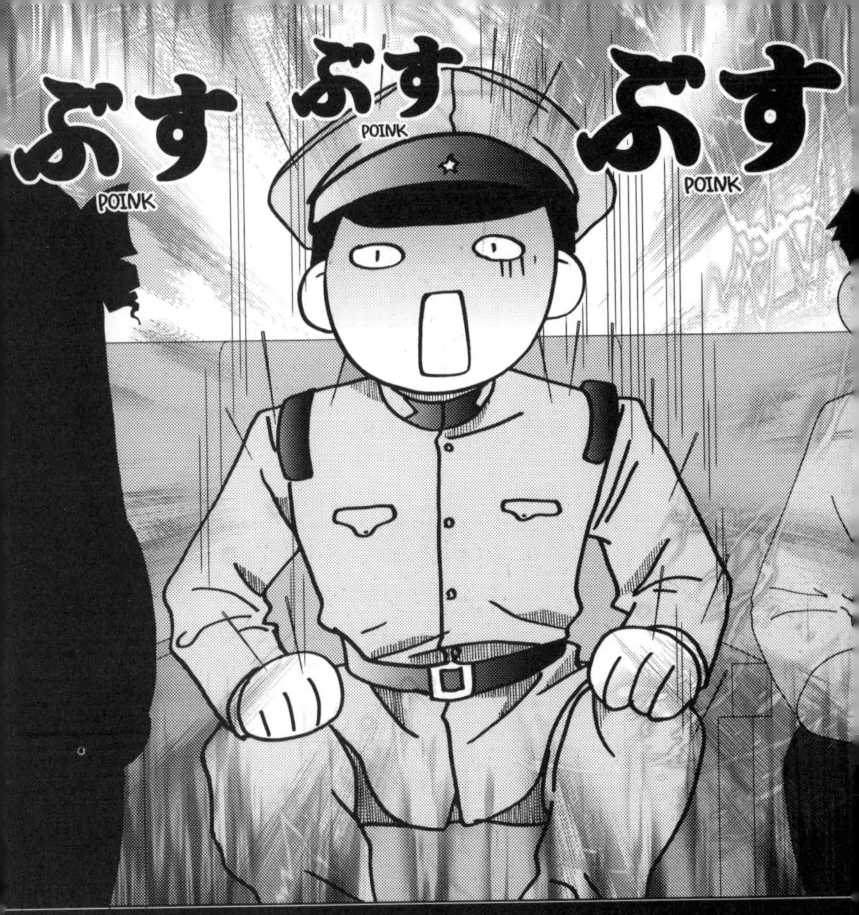
ぶす
POINK
ぶす
POINK
ぶす
POINK

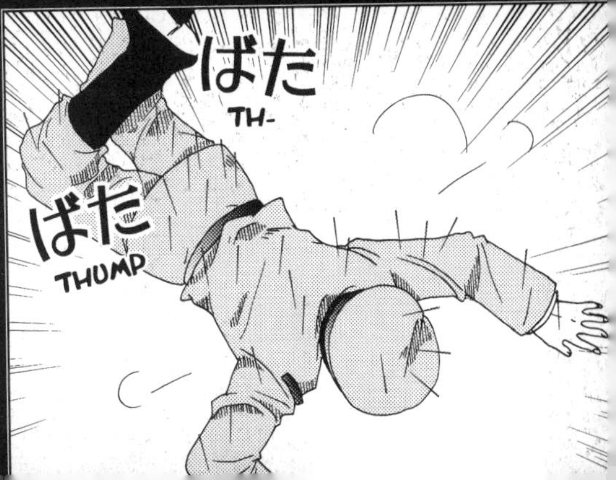
ばた
TH-
ばた
THUMP

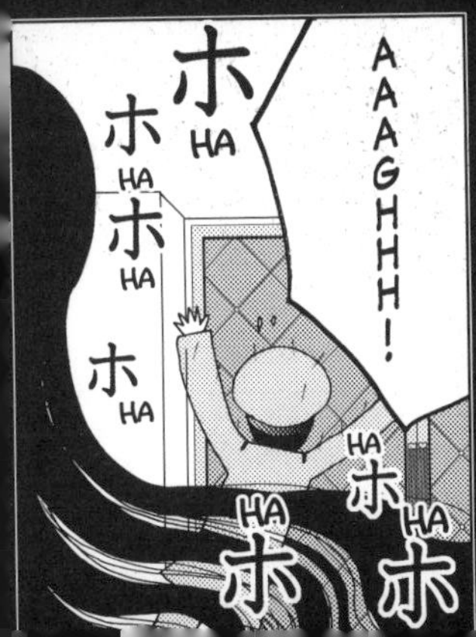
AAAGHHH!
ホ HA
ホ HA
ホ HA
ホ HA
HA ホ
HA ホ
HA ホ

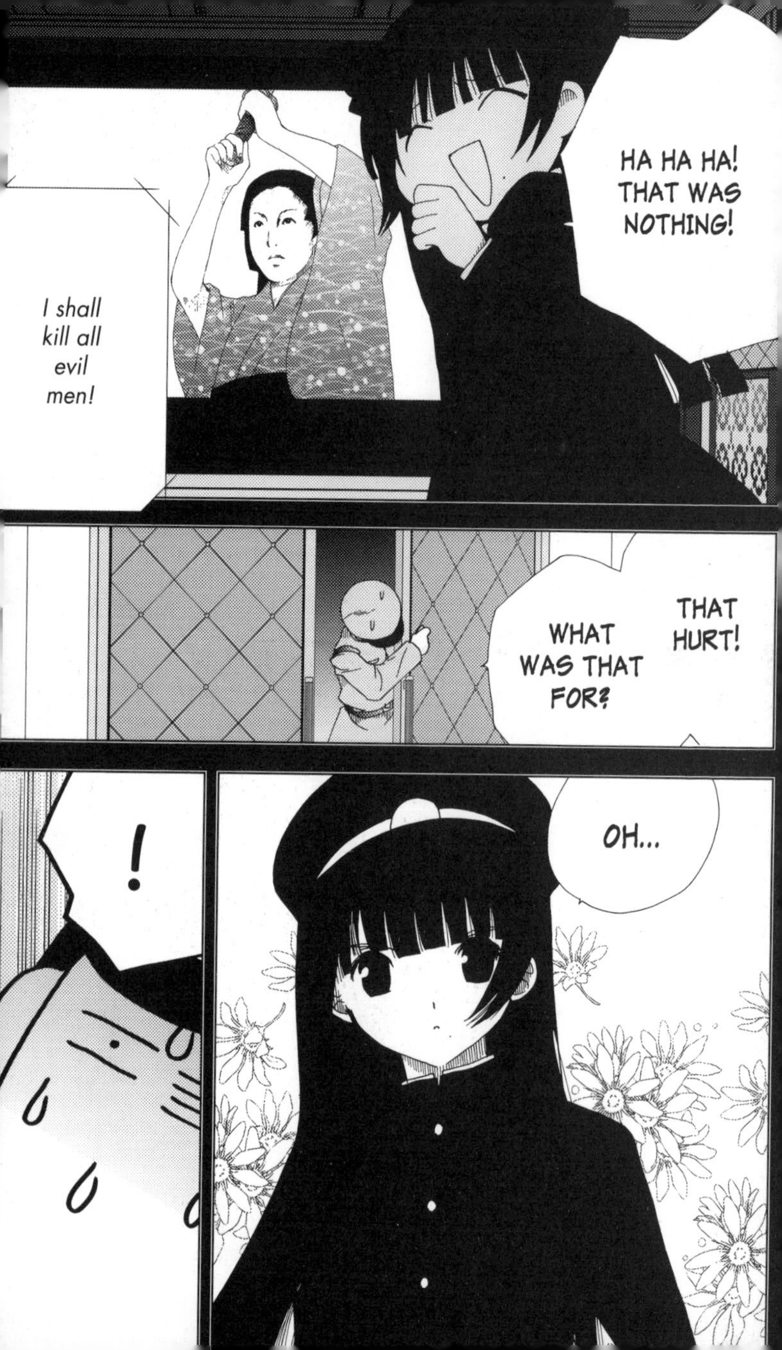
HA HA HA! THAT WAS NOTHING!
I shall kill all evil men!
THAT HURT!
WHAT WAS THAT FOR?
OH...
!

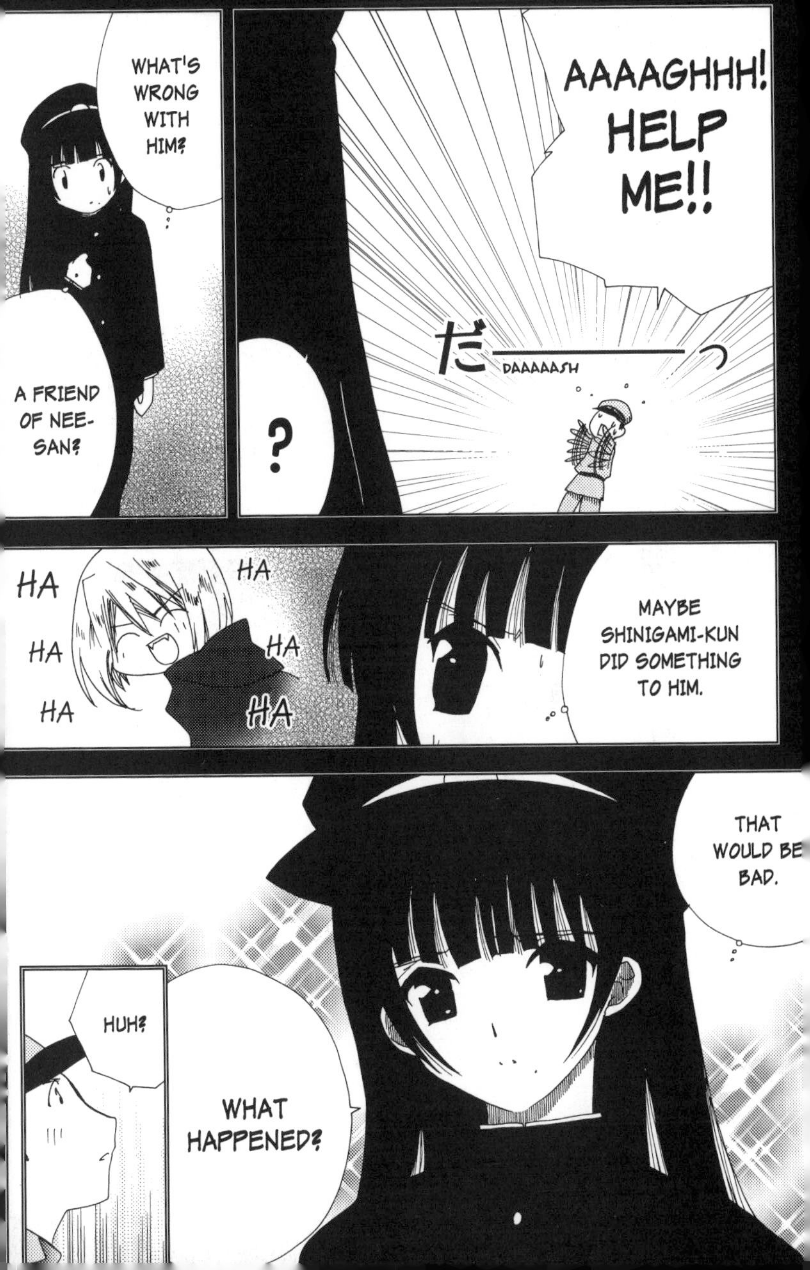
AAAAGHHH! HELP ME!!
だーーっ
DAAAAAASH
?
WHAT'S WRONG WITH HIM?
A FRIEND OF NEE-SAN?
MAYBE SHINIGAMI-KUN DID SOMETHING TO HIM.
HA
HA
HA
HA
HA
HA
THAT WOULD BE BAD.
HUH?
WHAT HAPPENED?

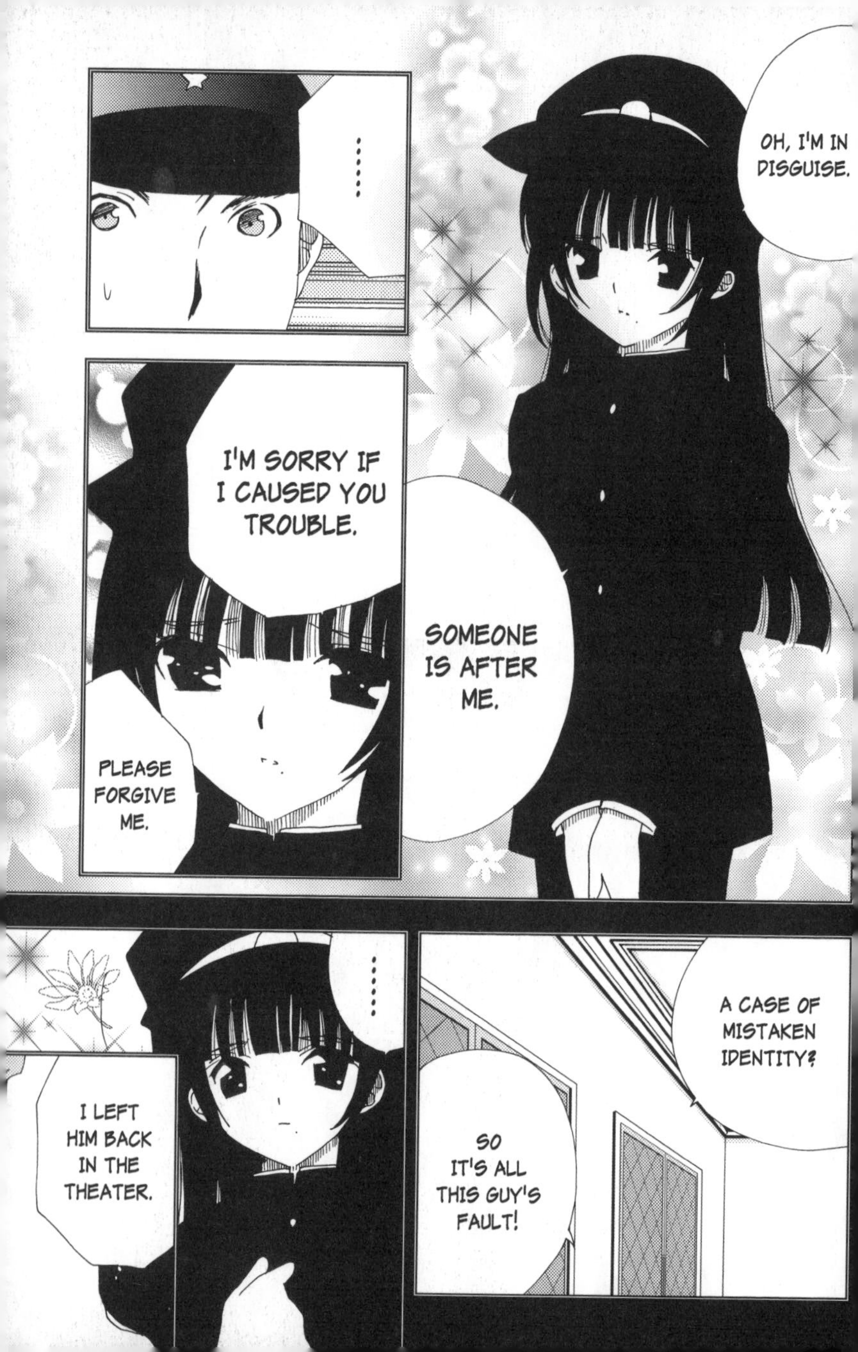
OH, I'M IN DISGUISE.
SOMEONE IS AFTER ME.
......
I'M SORRY IF I CAUSED YOU TROUBLE.
PLEASE FORGIVE ME.
A CASE OF MISTAKEN IDENTITY?
SO IT'S ALL THIS GUY'S FAULT!
......
I LEFT HIM BACK IN THE THEATER.

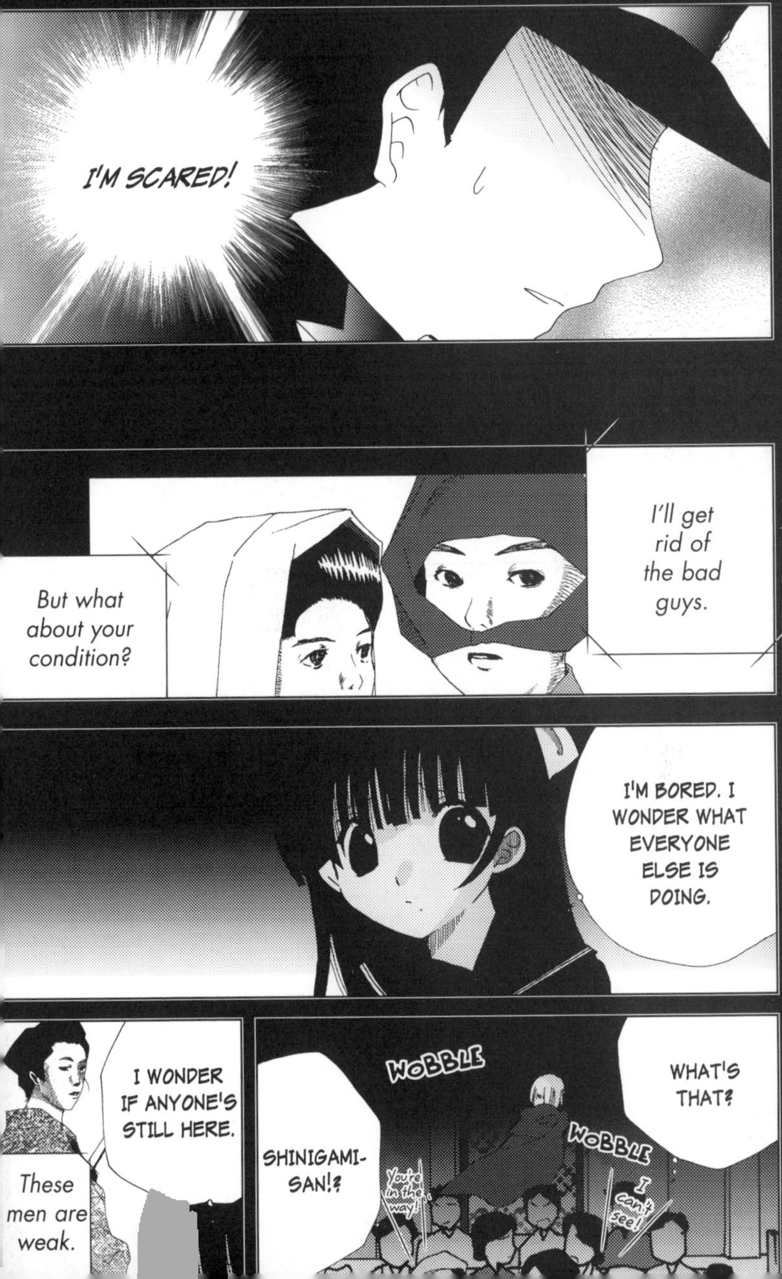
I'M SCARED!
I'll get rid of the bad guys.
But what about your condition?
I'M BORED. I WONDER WHAT EVERYONE ELSE IS DOING.
WHAT'S THAT?
WOBBLE
WOBBLE
I can't see!
You're in the way!
SHINIGAMI-SAN!?
I WONDER IF ANYONE'S STILL HERE.
These men are weak.

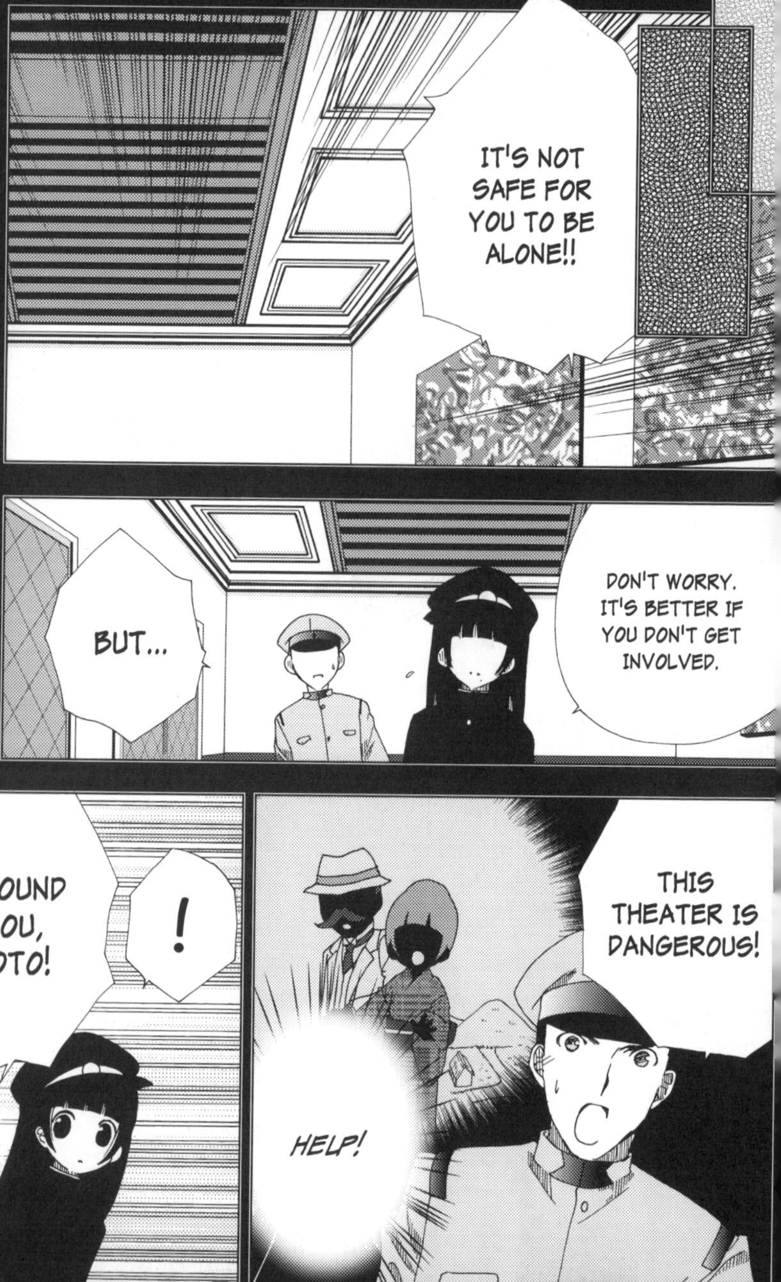
IT'S NOT SAFE FOR YOU TO BE ALONE!!
DON'T WORRY. IT'S BETTER IF YOU DON'T GET INVOLVED.
BUT...
THIS THEATER IS DANGEROUS!
HELP!
!
I FOUND YOU, KOTO!

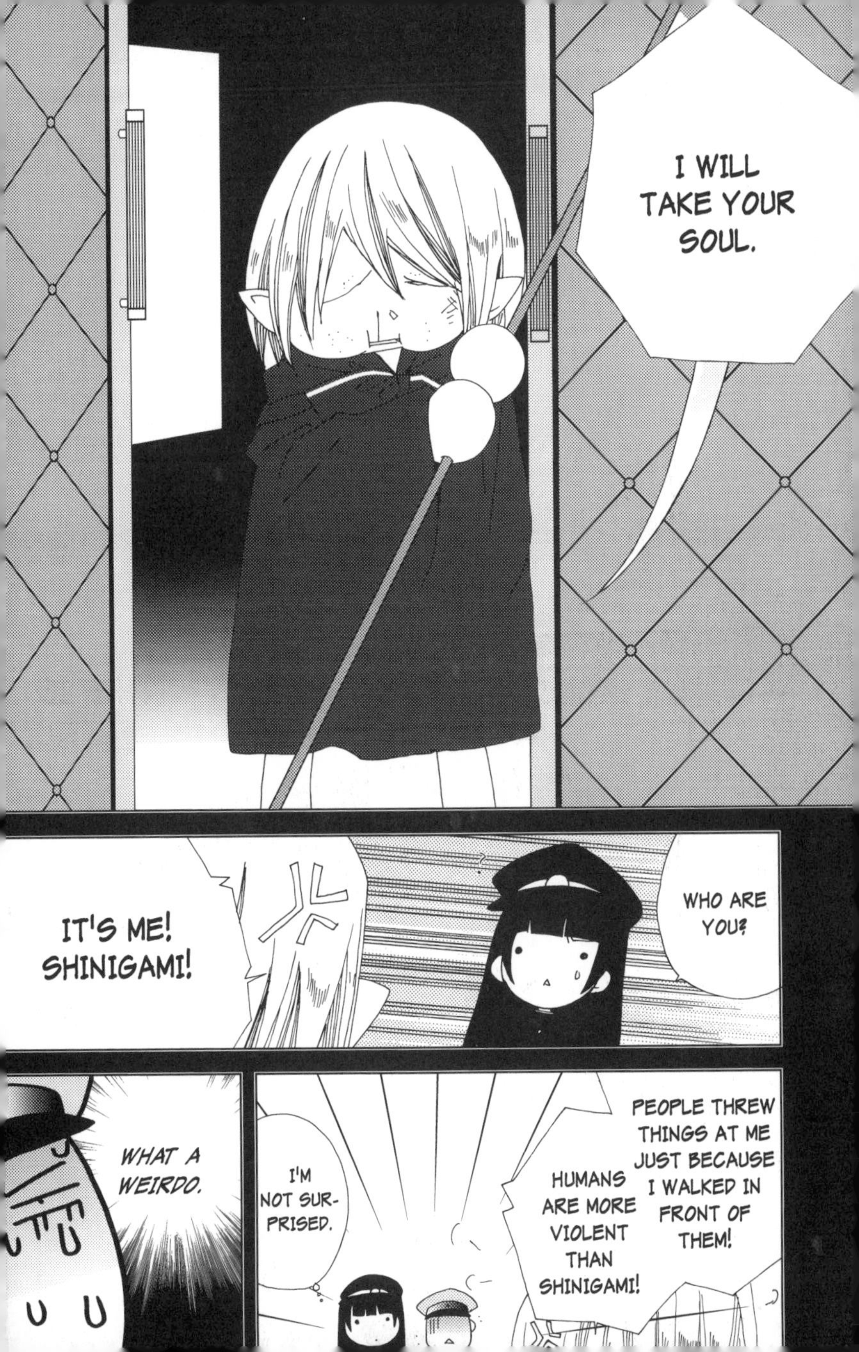
I WILL TAKE YOUR SOUL.
WHO ARE YOU?
IT'S ME! SHINIGAMI!
PEOPLE THREW THINGS AT ME JUST BECAUSE I WALKED IN FRONT OF THEM!
HUMANS ARE MORE VIOLENT THAN SHINIGAMI!
I'M NOT SUR-PRISED.
WHAT A WEIRDO.

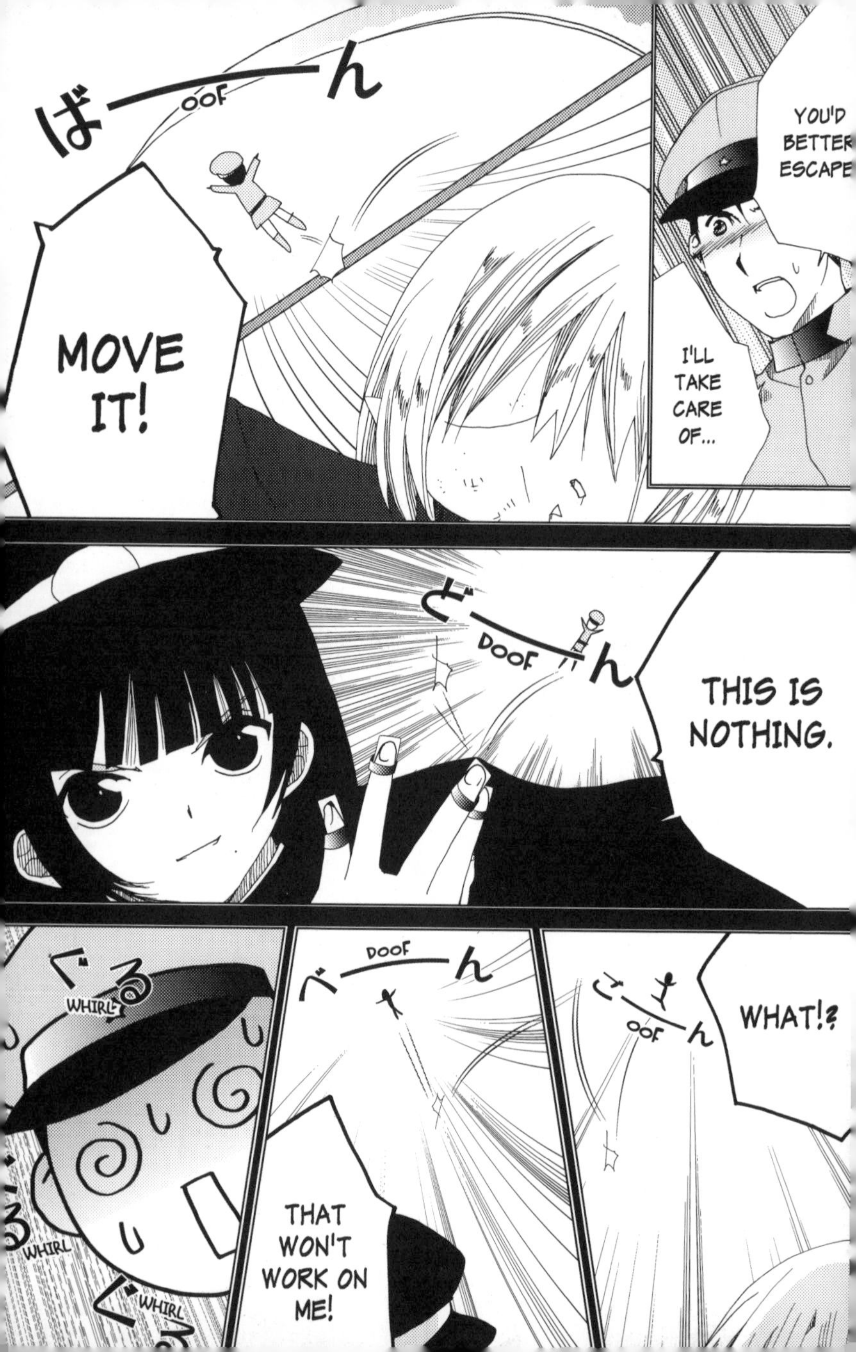
YOU'D BETTER ESCAPE
I'LL TAKE CARE OF...
ばーーん
OOF
MOVE IT!
どーん
DOOF
THIS IS NOTHING.
ごーん
OOF
WHAT!?
べーん
DOOF
THAT WON'T WORK ON ME!
ぐる
WHIRL
WHIRL
WHIRL

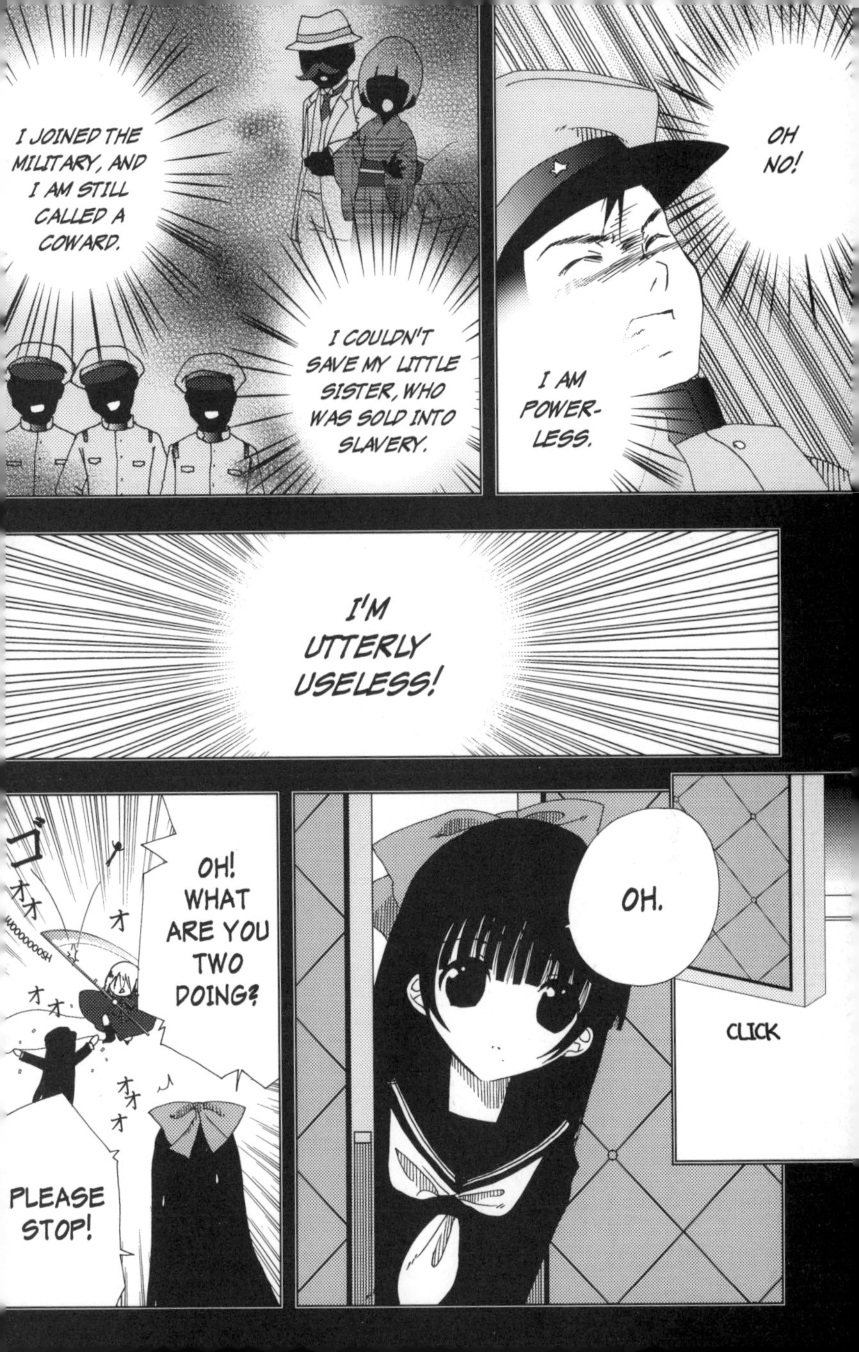
OH NO!
I AM POWER-LESS.
I JOINED THE MILITARY, AND I AM STILL CALLED A COWARD.
I COULDN'T SAVE MY LITTLE SISTER, WHO WAS SOLD INTO SLAVERY.
I'M UTTERLY USELESS!
OH.
CLICK
OH! WHAT ARE YOU TWO DOING?
WOOOOOOOOSH
PLEASE STOP!

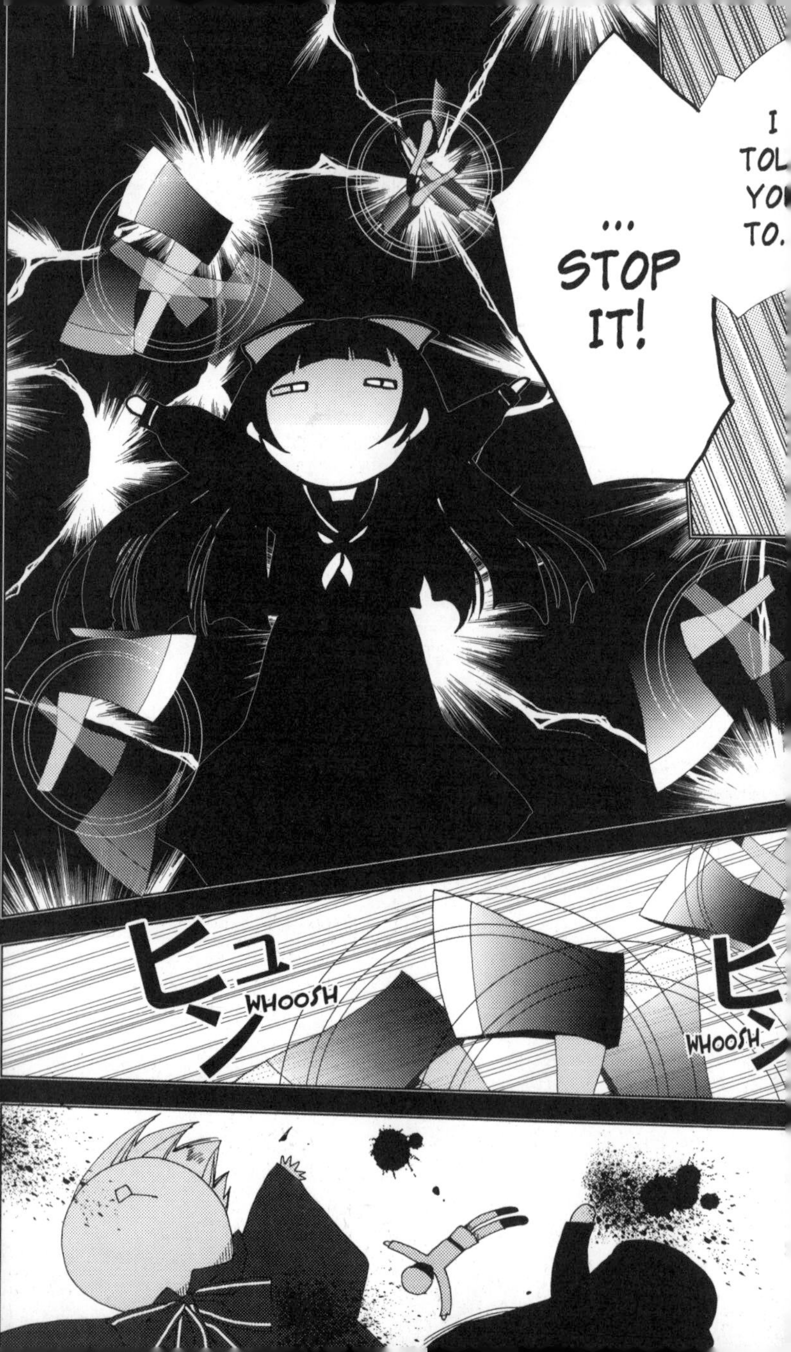
I TOL YO TO.
... STOP IT!
ヒン
WHOOSH
ヒュン
WHOOSH

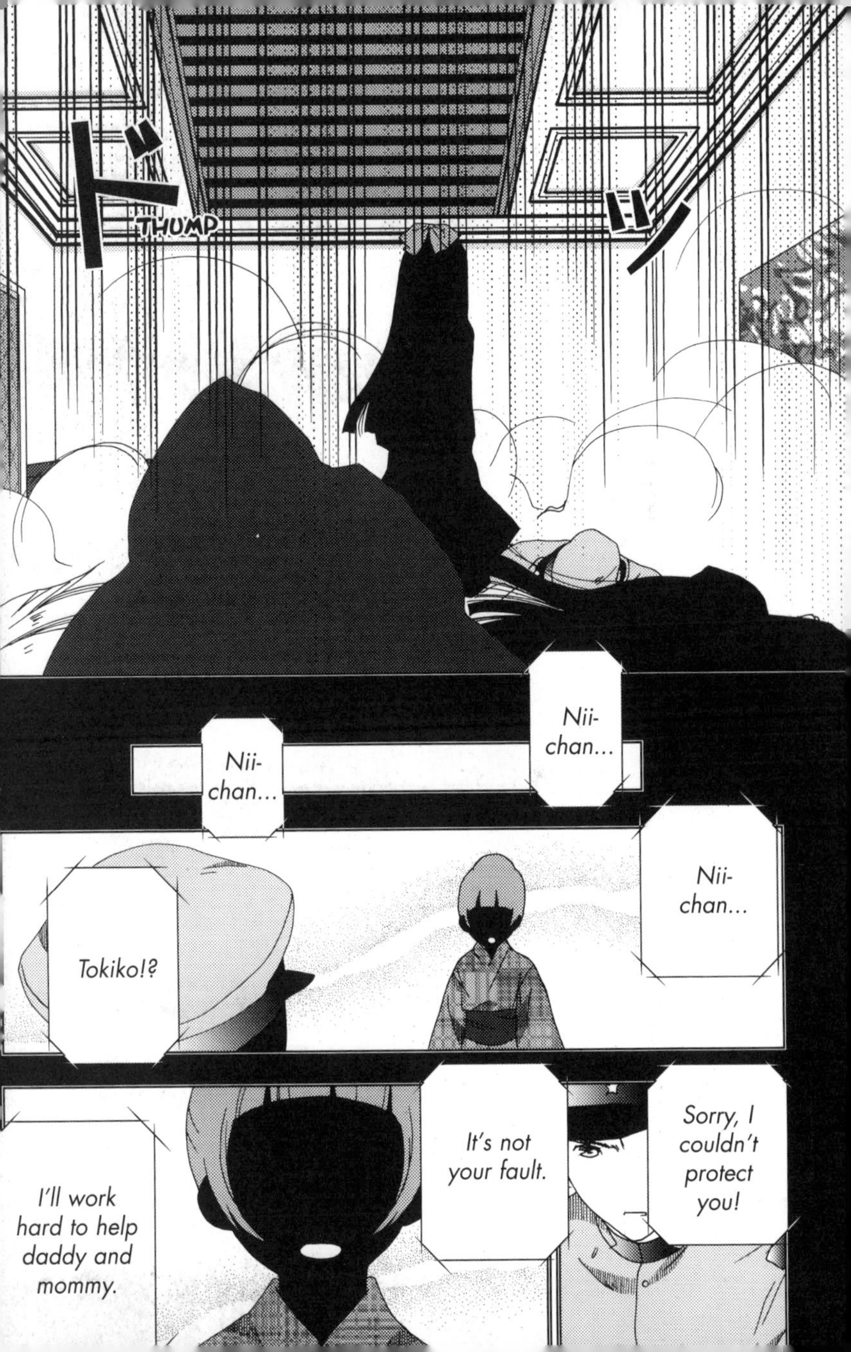
THUMP
Nii-chan...
Nii-chan...
Nii-chan...
Tokiko!?
Sorry, I couldn't protect you!
It's not your fault.
I'll work hard to help daddy and mommy.

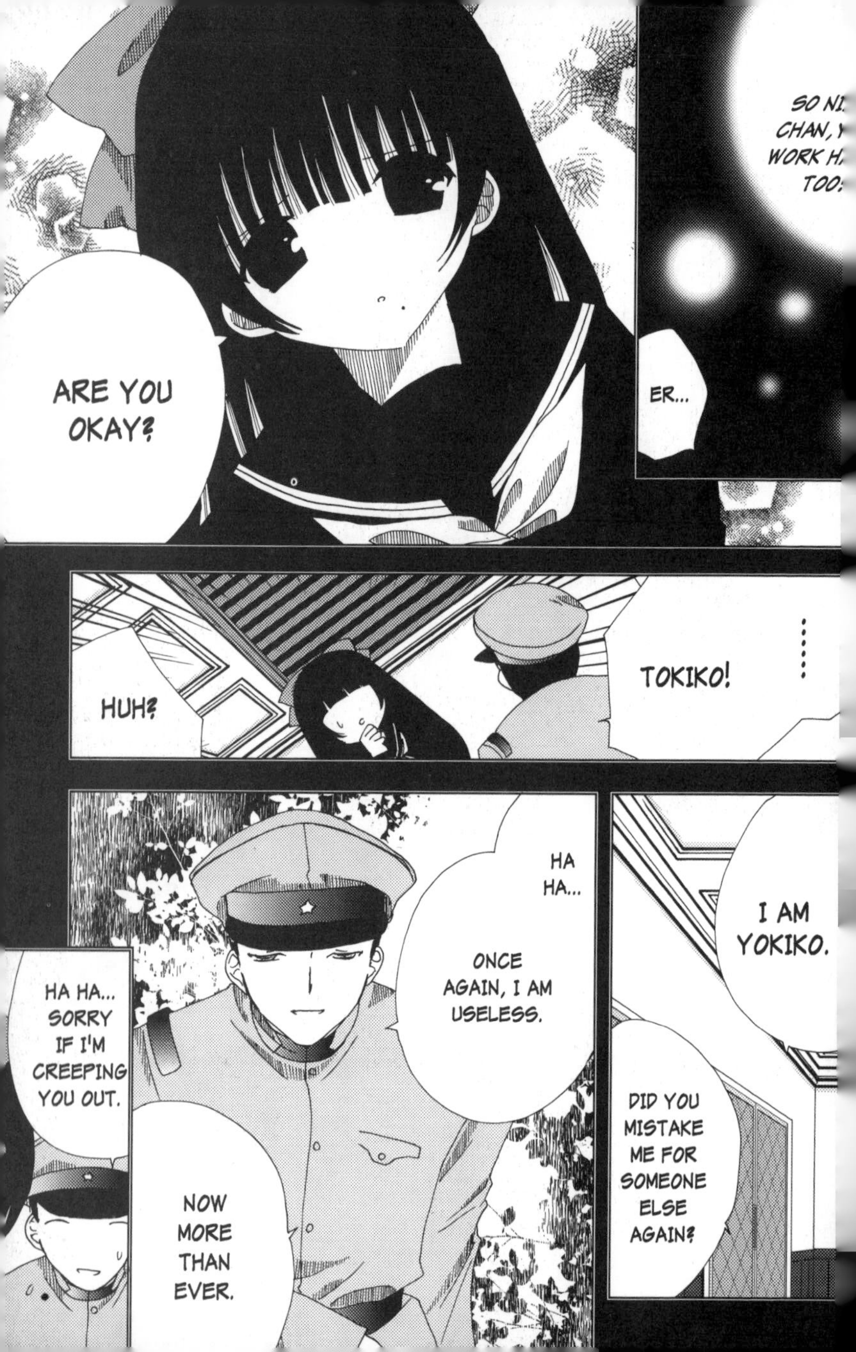
SO NI
CHAN, Y
WORK HA
TOO
ER...
ARE YOU OKAY?
......
TOKIKO!
HUH?
I AM YOKIKO.
DID YOU MISTAKE ME FOR SOMEONE ELSE AGAIN?
HA HA...
ONCE AGAIN, I AM USELESS.
HA HA... SORRY IF I'M CREEPING YOU OUT.
NOW MORE THAN EVER.

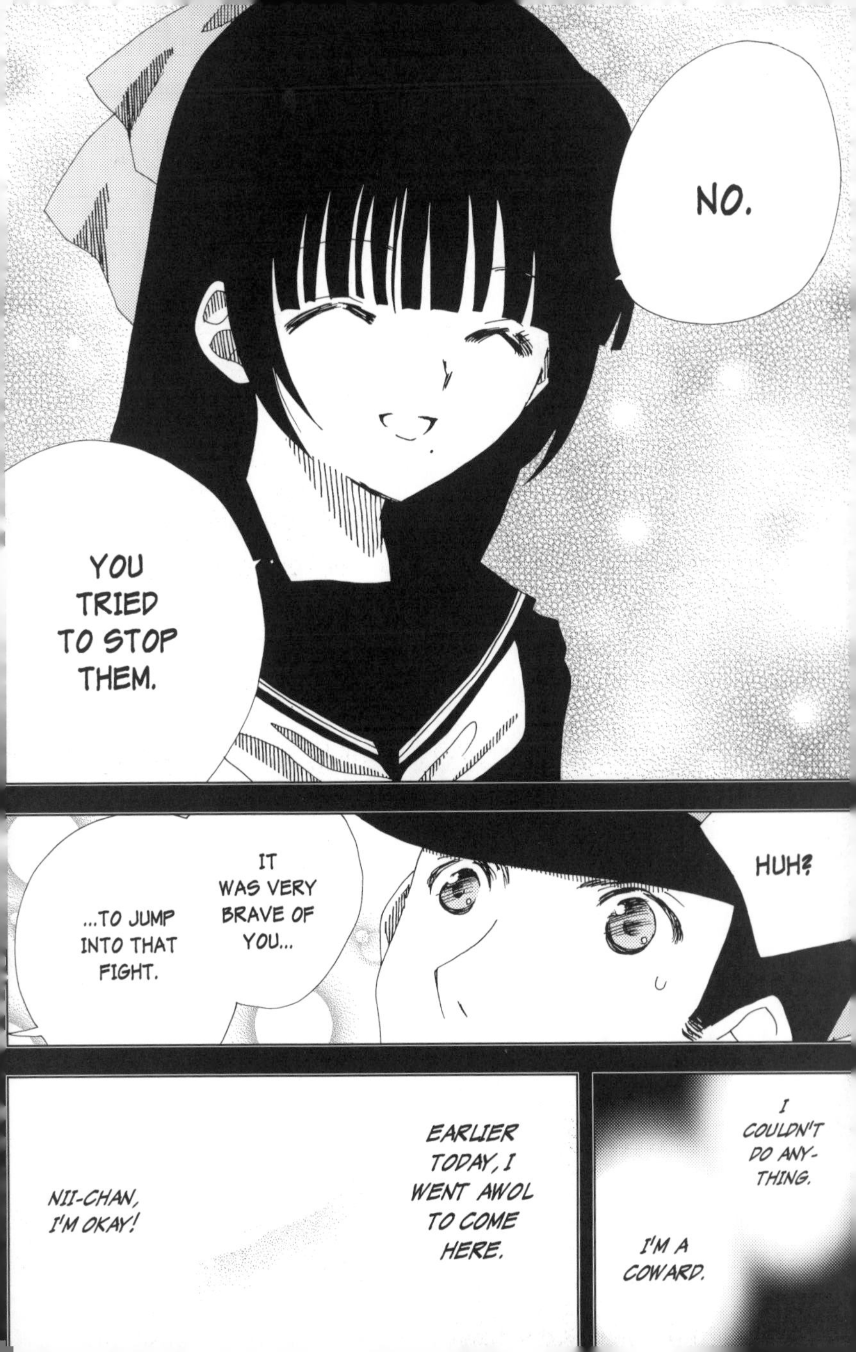
NO.
YOU TRIED TO STOP THEM.
HUH?
IT WAS VERY BRAVE OF YOU...
...TO JUMP INTO THAT FIGHT.
I COULDN'T DO ANY-THING.
I'M A COWARD.
EARLIER TODAY, I WENT AWOL TO COME HERE.
NII-CHAN, I'M OKAY!

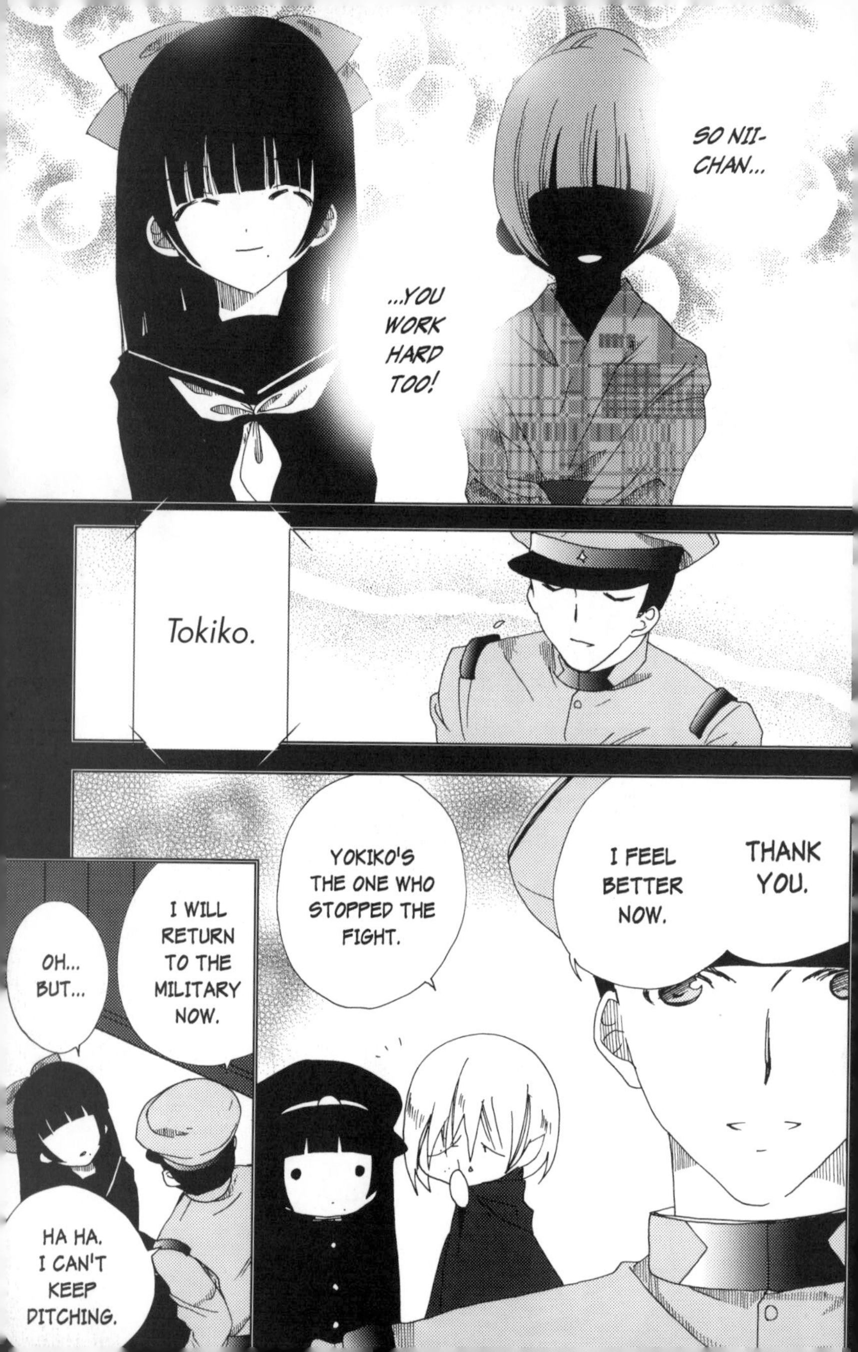

SO NII-CHAN...
...YOU WORK HARD TOO!
Tokiko.
THANK YOU.
I FEEL BETTER NOW.
YOKIKO'S THE ONE WHO STOPPED THE FIGHT.
I WILL RETURN TO THE MILITARY NOW.
OH... BUT...
HA HA. I CAN'T KEEP DITCHING.

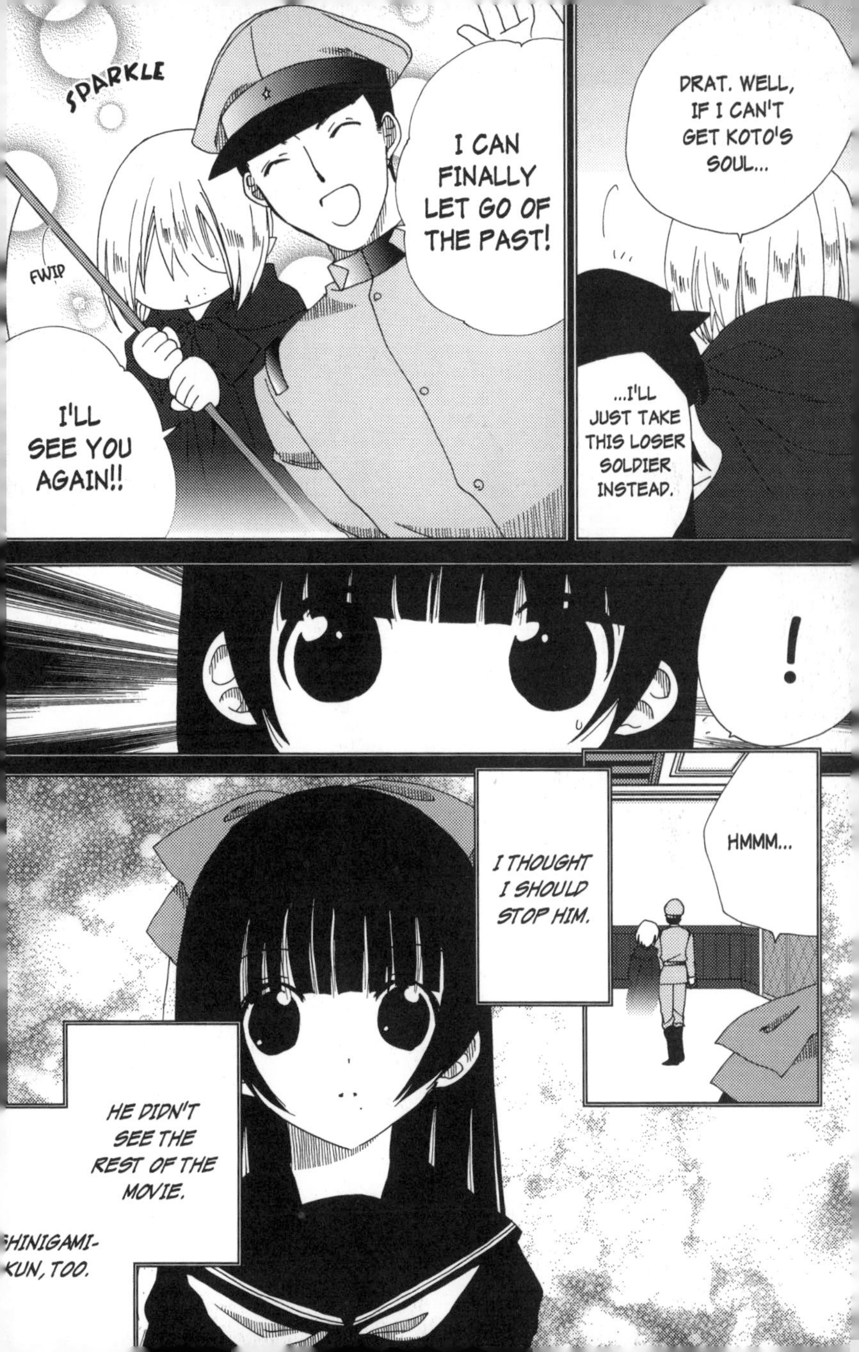
DRAT. WELL, IF I CAN'T GET KOTO'S SOUL...
...I'LL JUST TAKE THIS LOSER SOLDIER INSTEAD.
I CAN FINALLY LET GO OF THE PAST!
SPARKLE
FWIP
I'LL SEE YOU AGAIN!!
!
HMMM...
I THOUGHT I SHOULD STOP HIM.
HE DIDN'T SEE THE REST OF THE MOVIE.
SHINIGAMI-KUN, TOO.

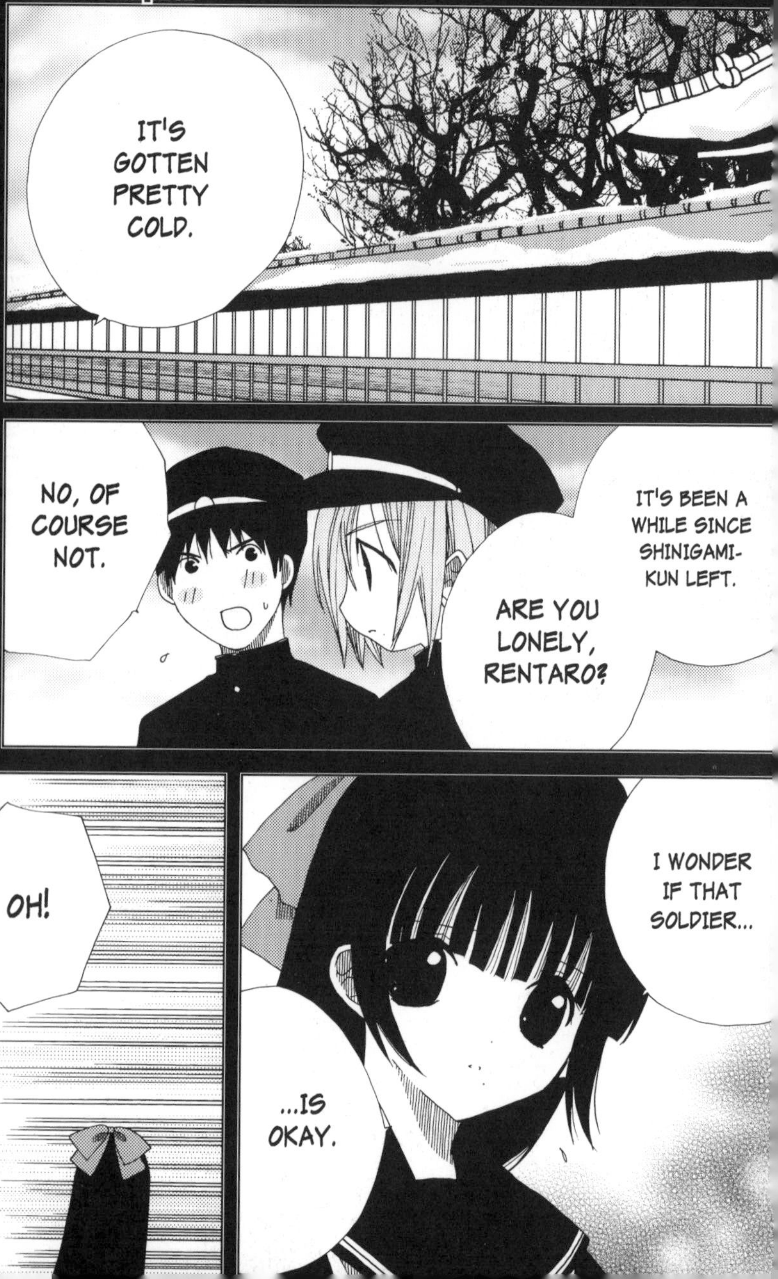
IT'S GOTTEN PRETTY COLD.
IT'S BEEN A WHILE SINCE SHINIGAMI-KUN LEFT.
ARE YOU LONELY, RENTARO?
NO, OF COURSE NOT.
I WONDER IF THAT SOLDIER...
...IS OKAY.
OH!

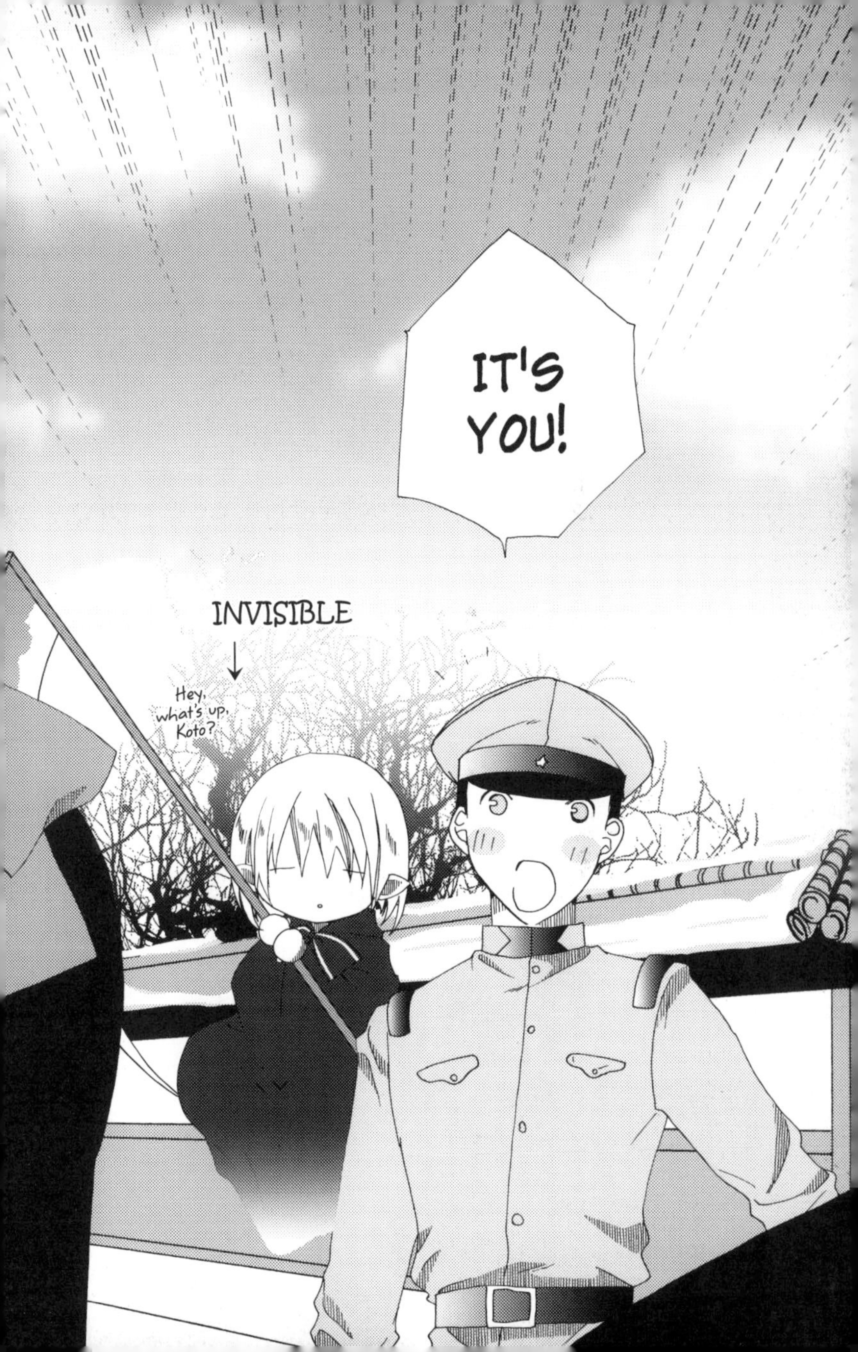
IT'S YOU!
INVISIBLE
Hey, what's up, Koto?

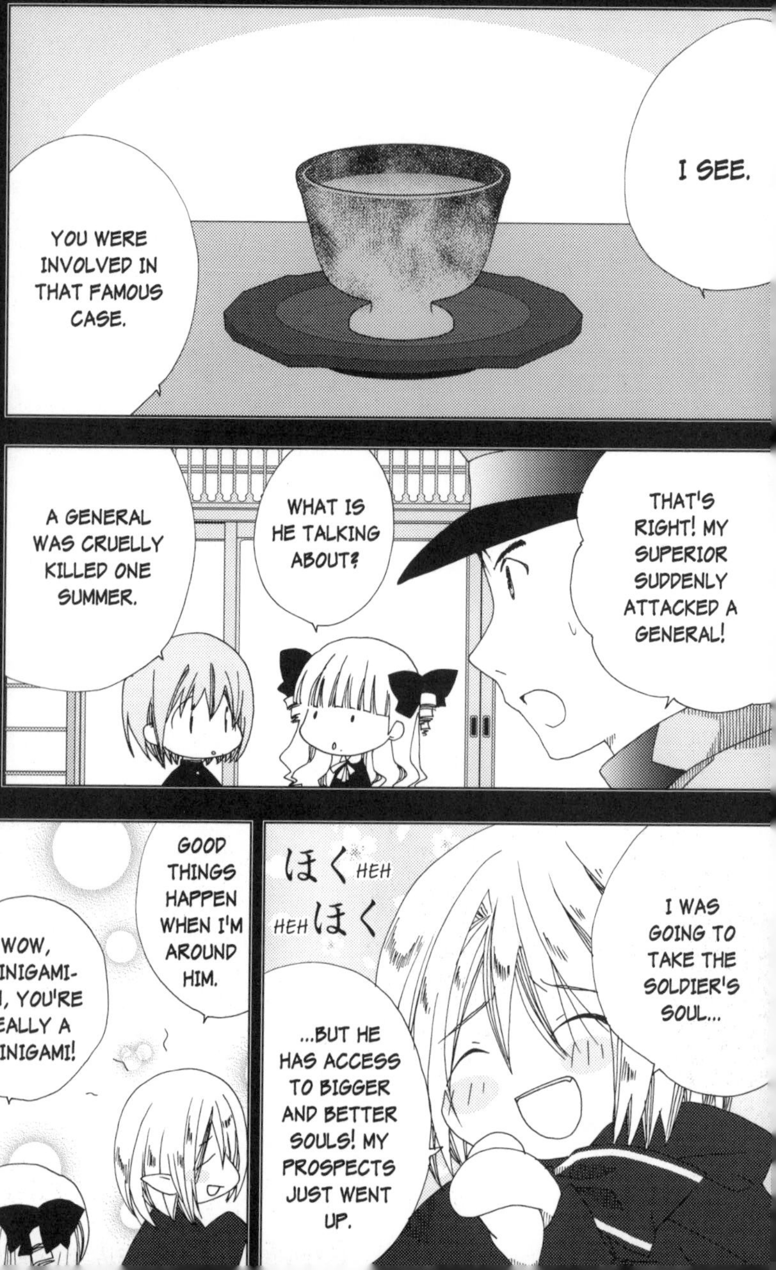
I SEE.
YOU WERE INVOLVED IN THAT FAMOUS CASE.
THAT'S RIGHT! MY SUPERIOR SUDDENLY ATTACKED A GENERAL!
WHAT IS HE TALKING ABOUT?
A GENERAL WAS CRUELLY KILLED ONE SUMMER.
I WAS GOING TO TAKE THE SOLDIER'S SOUL...
ほく HEH
HEH ほく
...BUT HE HAS ACCESS TO BIGGER AND BETTER SOULS! MY PROSPECTS JUST WENT UP.
GOOD THINGS HAPPEN WHEN I'M AROUND HIM.
WOW, SHINIGAMI-KUN, YOU'RE REALLY A SHINIGAMI!

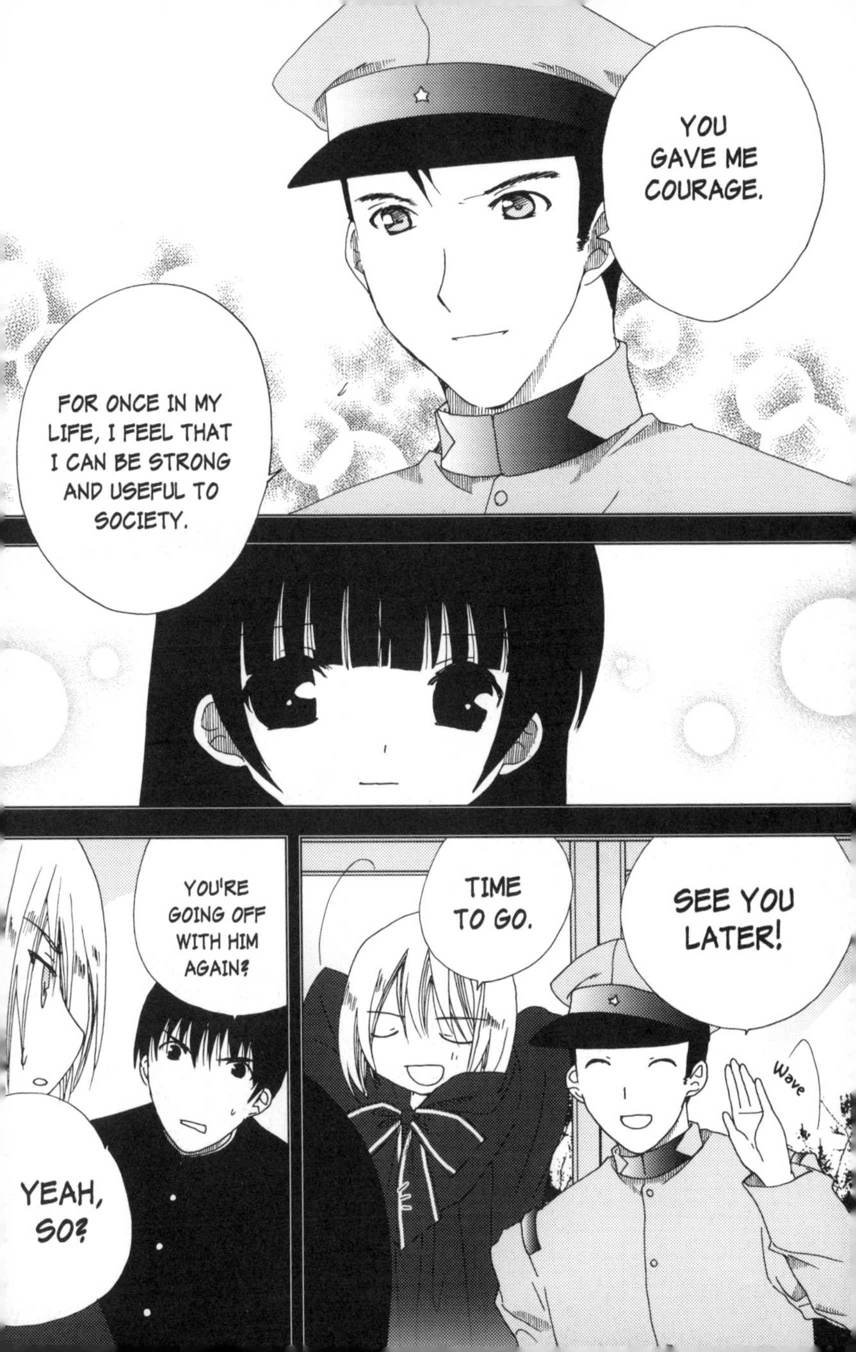
YOU GAVE ME COURAGE.
FOR ONCE IN MY LIFE, I FEEL THAT I CAN BE STRONG AND USEFUL TO SOCIETY.
SEE YOU LATER!
TIME TO GO.
Wave
YOU'RE GOING OFF WITH HIM AGAIN?
YEAH, SO?

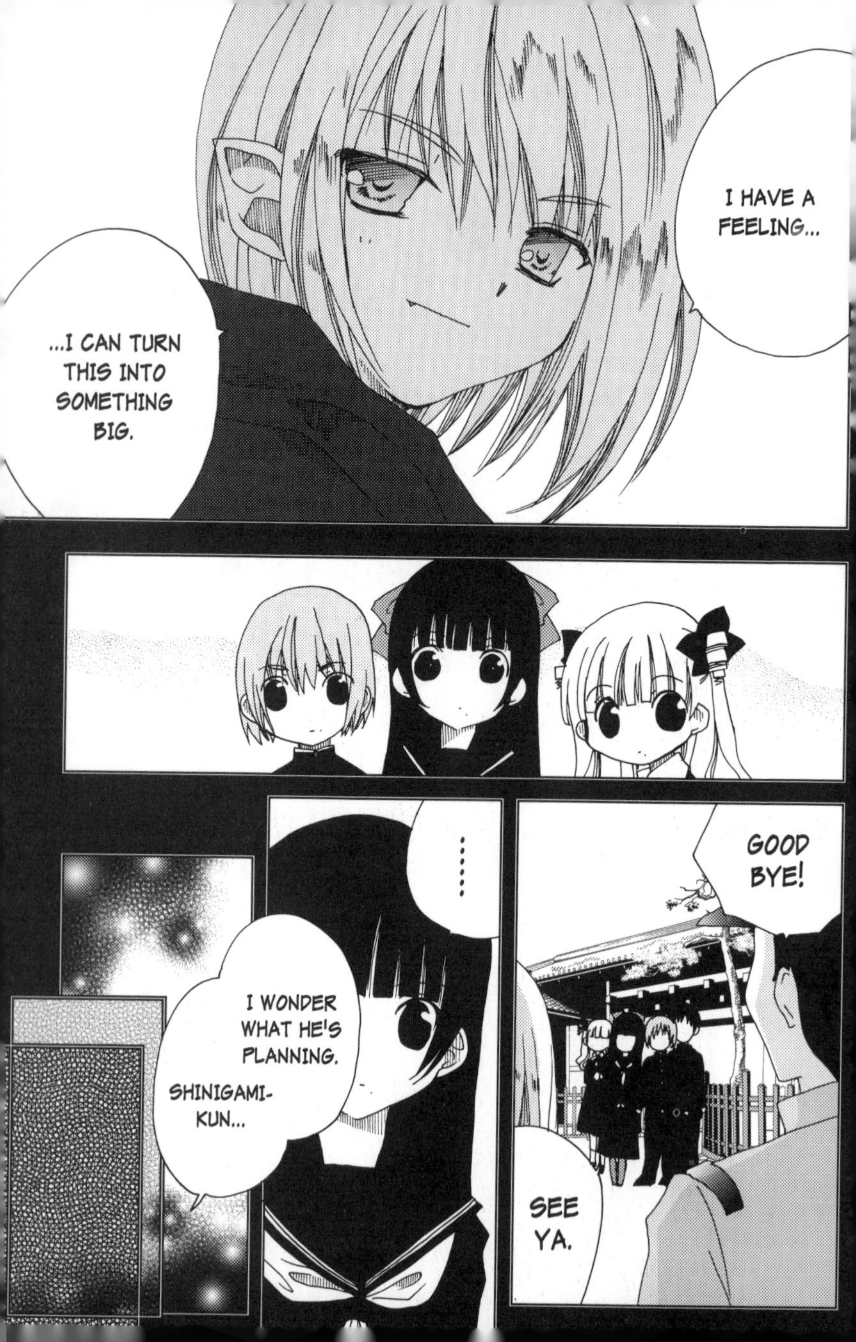
I HAVE A FEELING...
...I CAN TURN THIS INTO SOMETHING BIG.
GOOD BYE!
SEE YA.
......
I WONDER WHAT HE'S PLANNING.
SHINIGAMI-KUN...

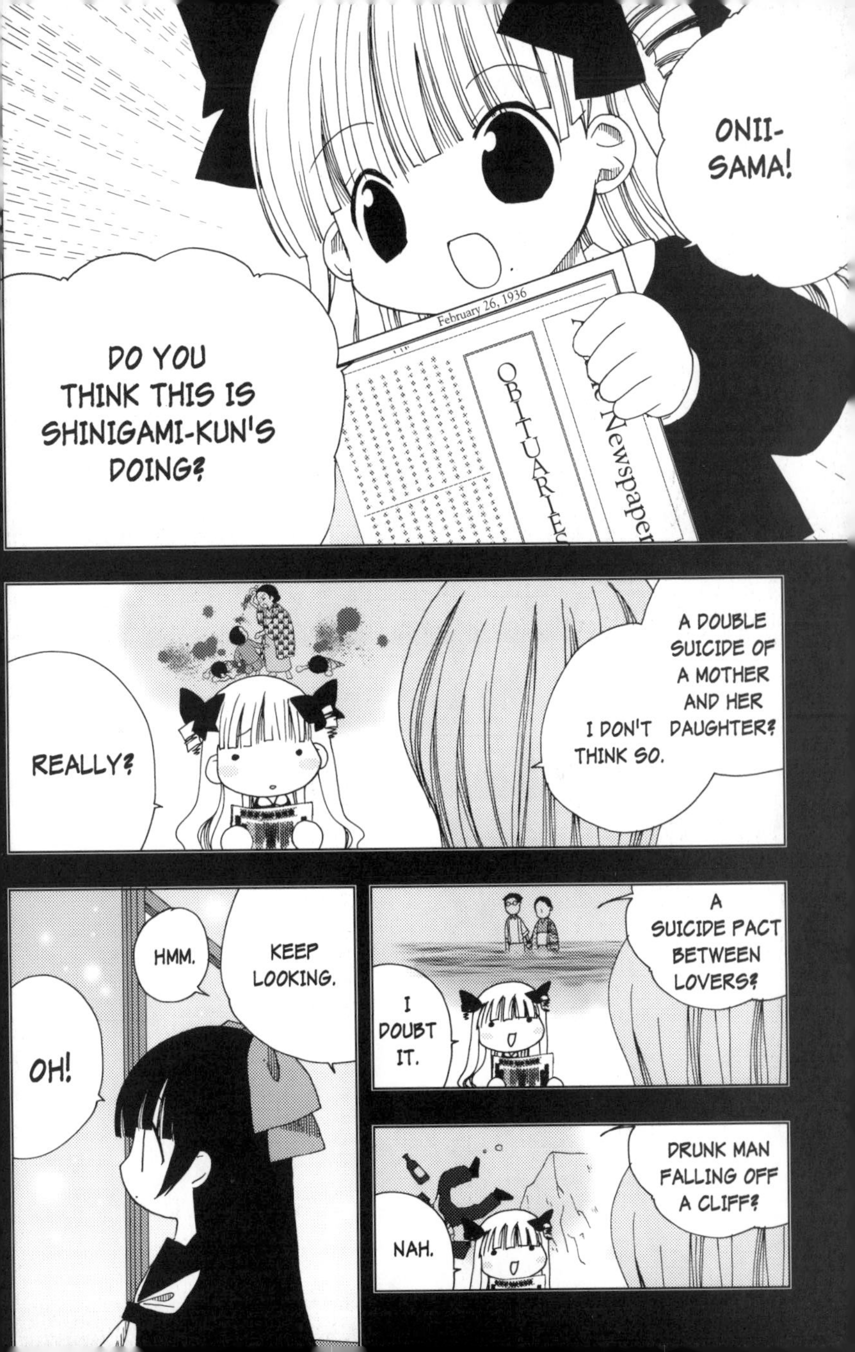
ONII-SAMA!
DO YOU THINK THIS IS SHINIGAMI-KUN'S DOING?
February 26, 1936
A DOUBLE SUICIDE OF A MOTHER AND HER DAUGHTER?
I DON'T THINK SO.
REALLY?
A SUICIDE PACT BETWEEN LOVERS?
I DOUBT IT.
DRUNK MAN FALLING OFF A CLIFF?
NAH.
KEEP LOOKING.
HMM.
OH!

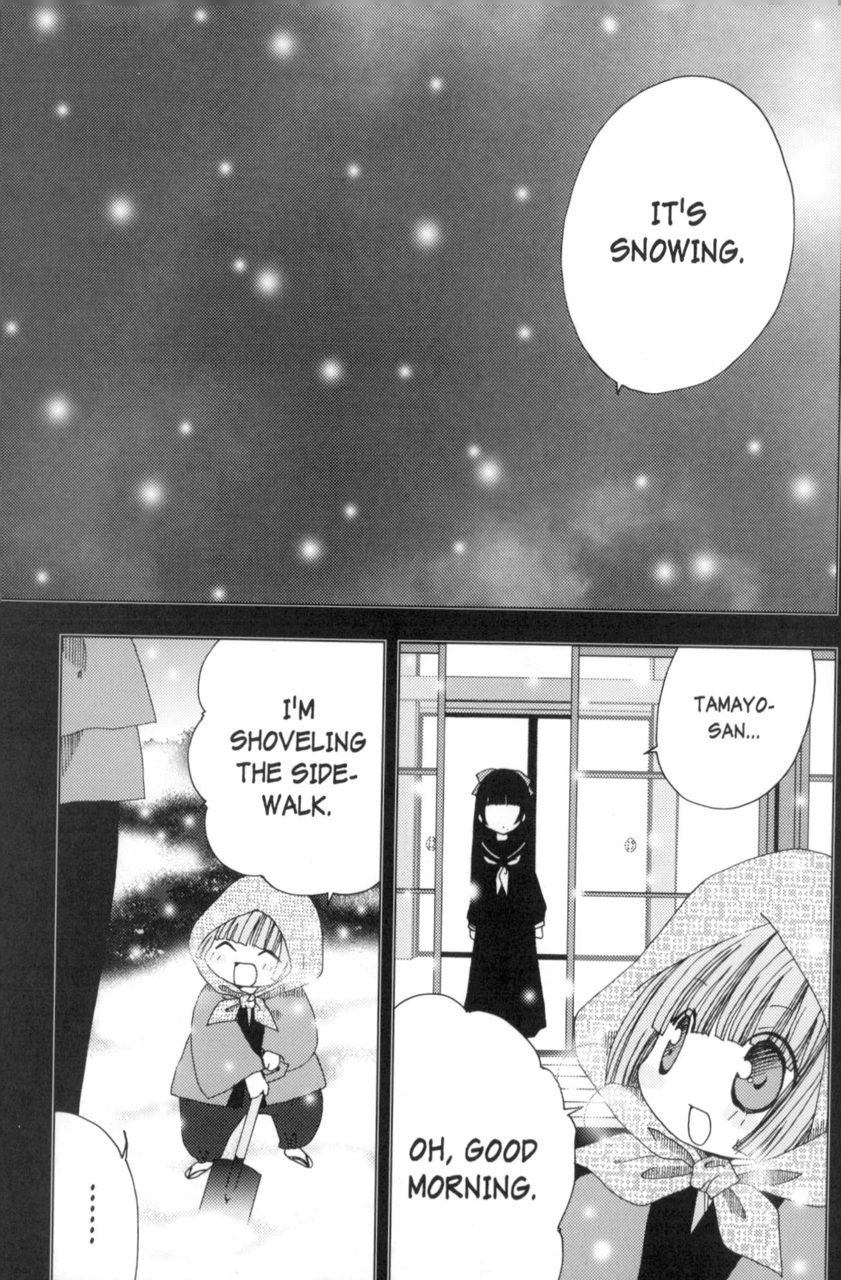
IT'S SNOWING.
TAMAYO-SAN...
OH, GOOD MORNING.
I'M SHOVELING THE SIDE-WALK.
......

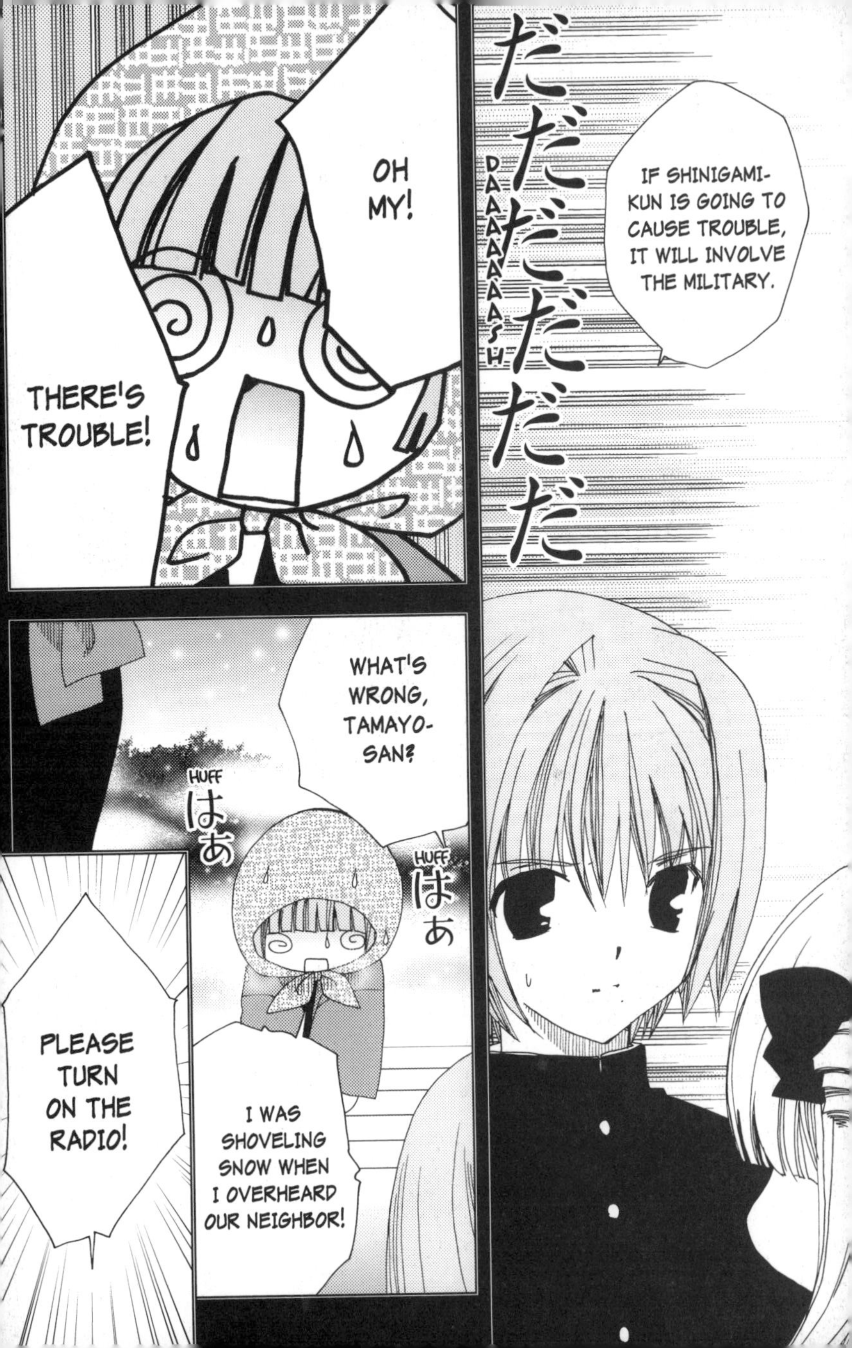
IF SHINIGAMI-KUN IS GOING TO CAUSE TROUBLE, IT WILL INVOLVE THE MILITARY.
だだだだだだ
DAAAAAAAASH
OH MY!
THERE'S TROUBLE!
WHAT'S WRONG, TAMAYO-SAN?
HUFF
はぁ
HUFF
はぁ
I WAS SHOVELING SNOW WHEN I OVERHEARD OUR NEIGHBOR!
PLEASE TURN ON THE RADIO!

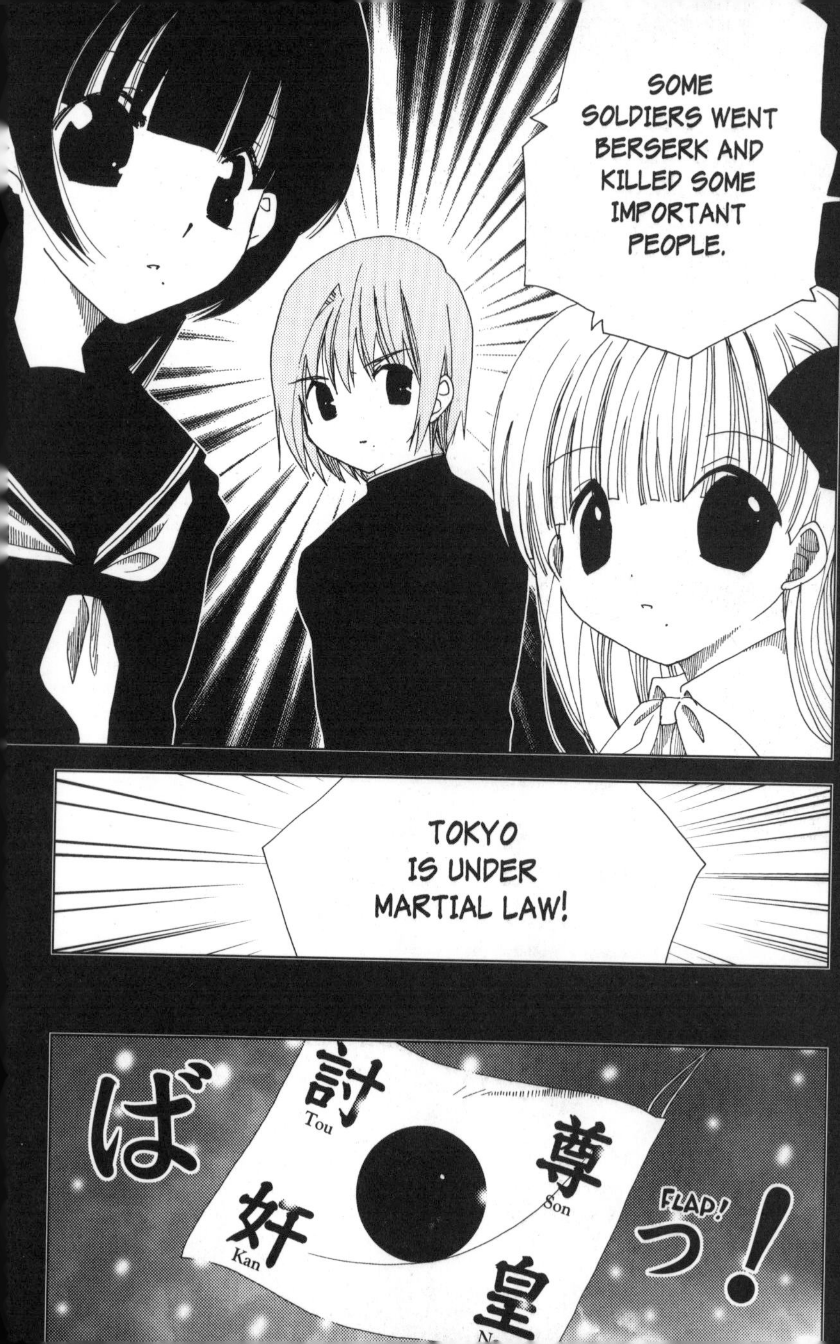
SOME SOLDIERS WENT BERSERK AND KILLED SOME IMPORTANT PEOPLE.
TOKYO IS UNDER MARTIAL LAW!
ばっ！
FLAP!
尊 Son
皇
討 Tou
奸 Kan

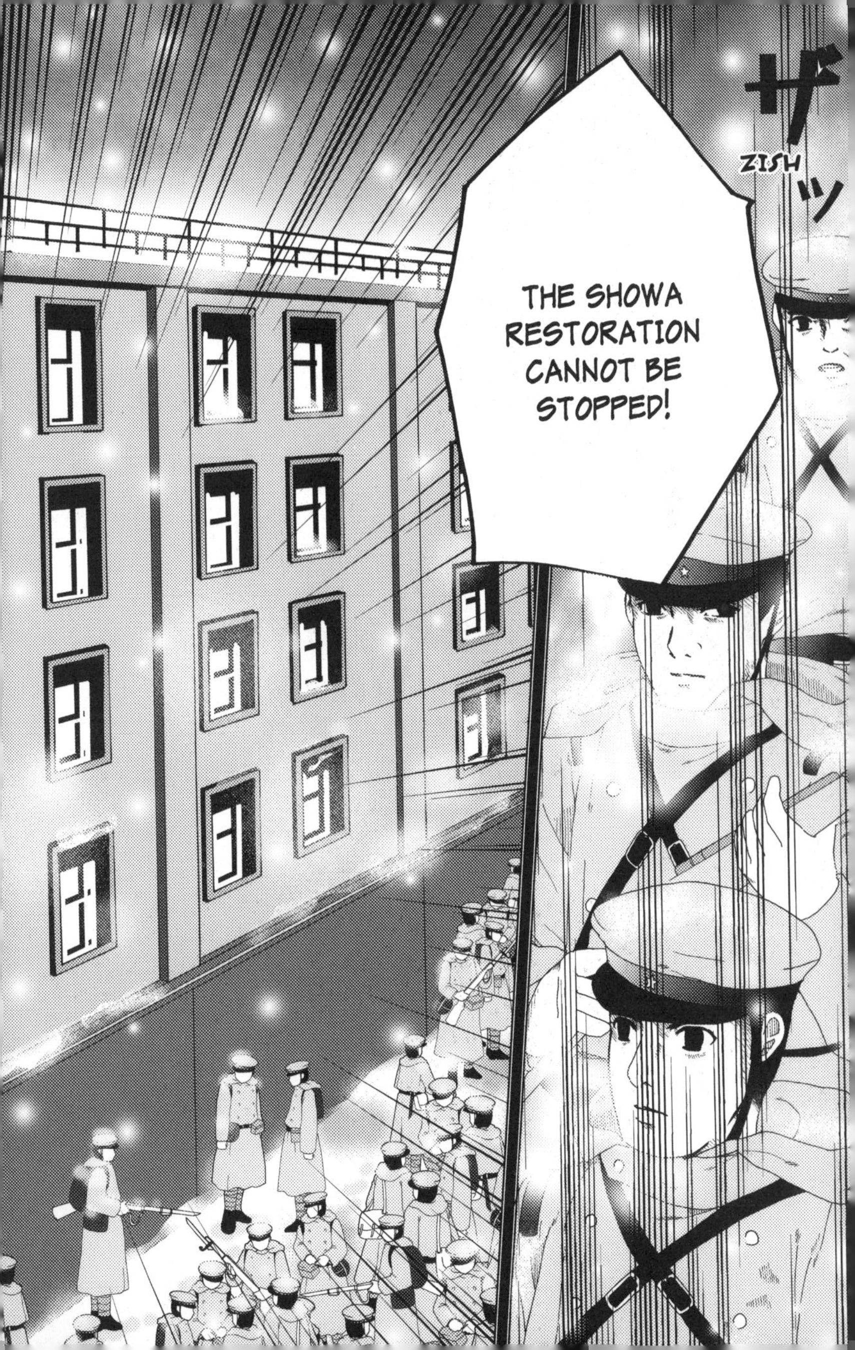
ザッ
ZISH
THE SHOWA RESTORATION CANNOT BE STOPPED!

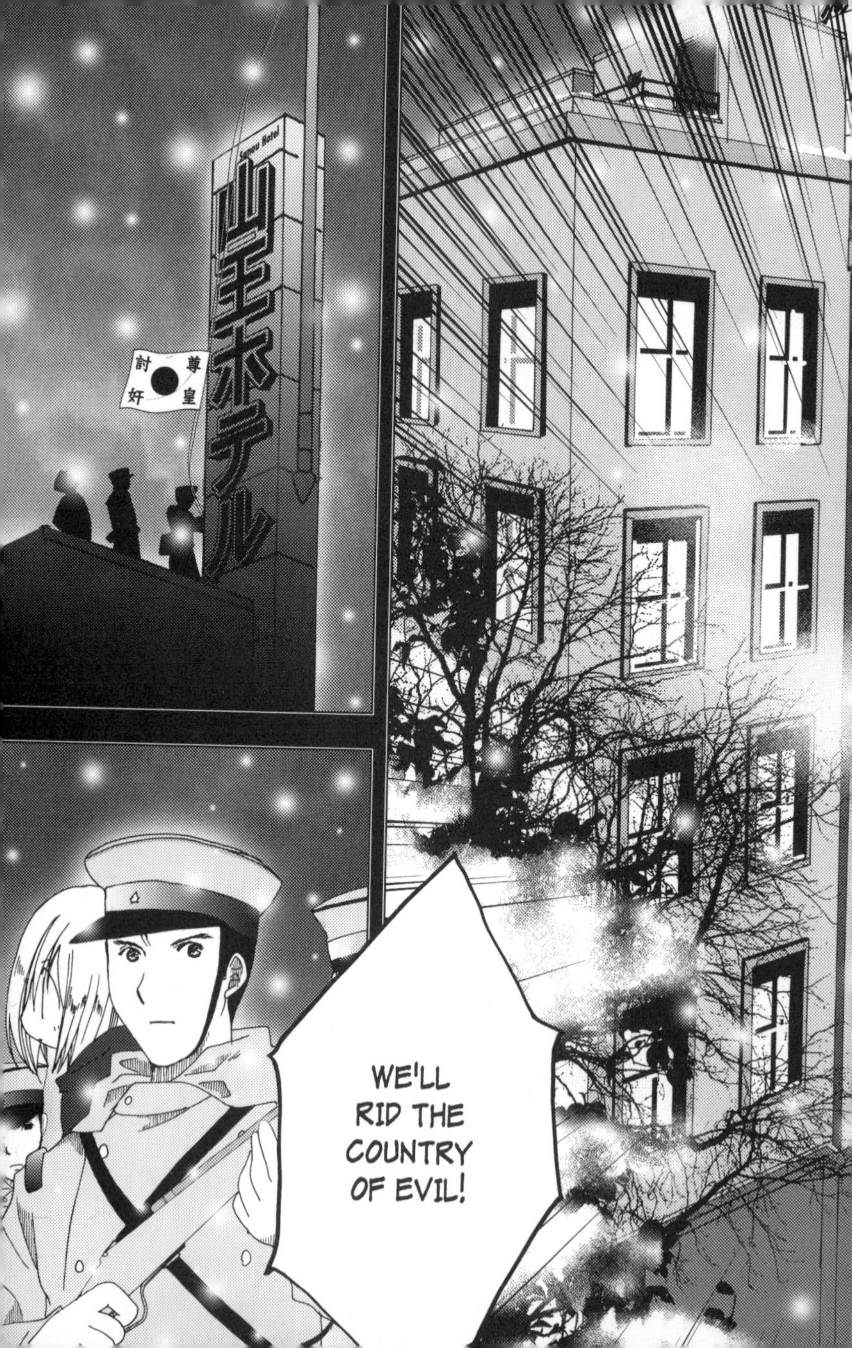
山王ホテル
尊皇討奸
WE'LL RID THE COUNTRY OF EVIL!

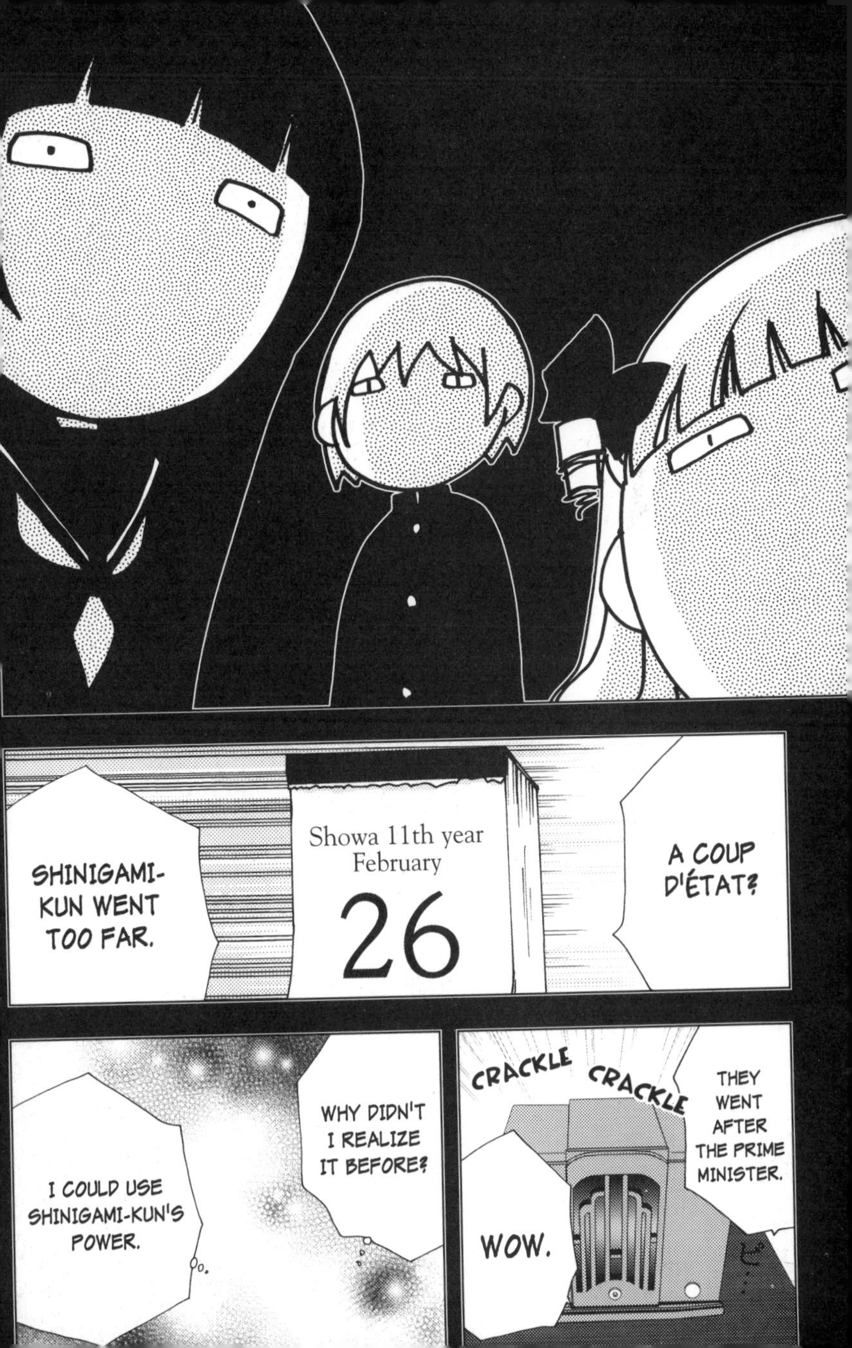
A COUP D'ÉTAT?
Showa 11th year February 26
SHINIGAMI-KUN WENT TOO FAR.
CRACKLE CRACKLE
THEY WENT AFTER THE PRIME MINISTER.
WOW.
WHY DIDN'T I REALIZE IT BEFORE?
I COULD USE SHINIGAMI-KUN'S POWER.

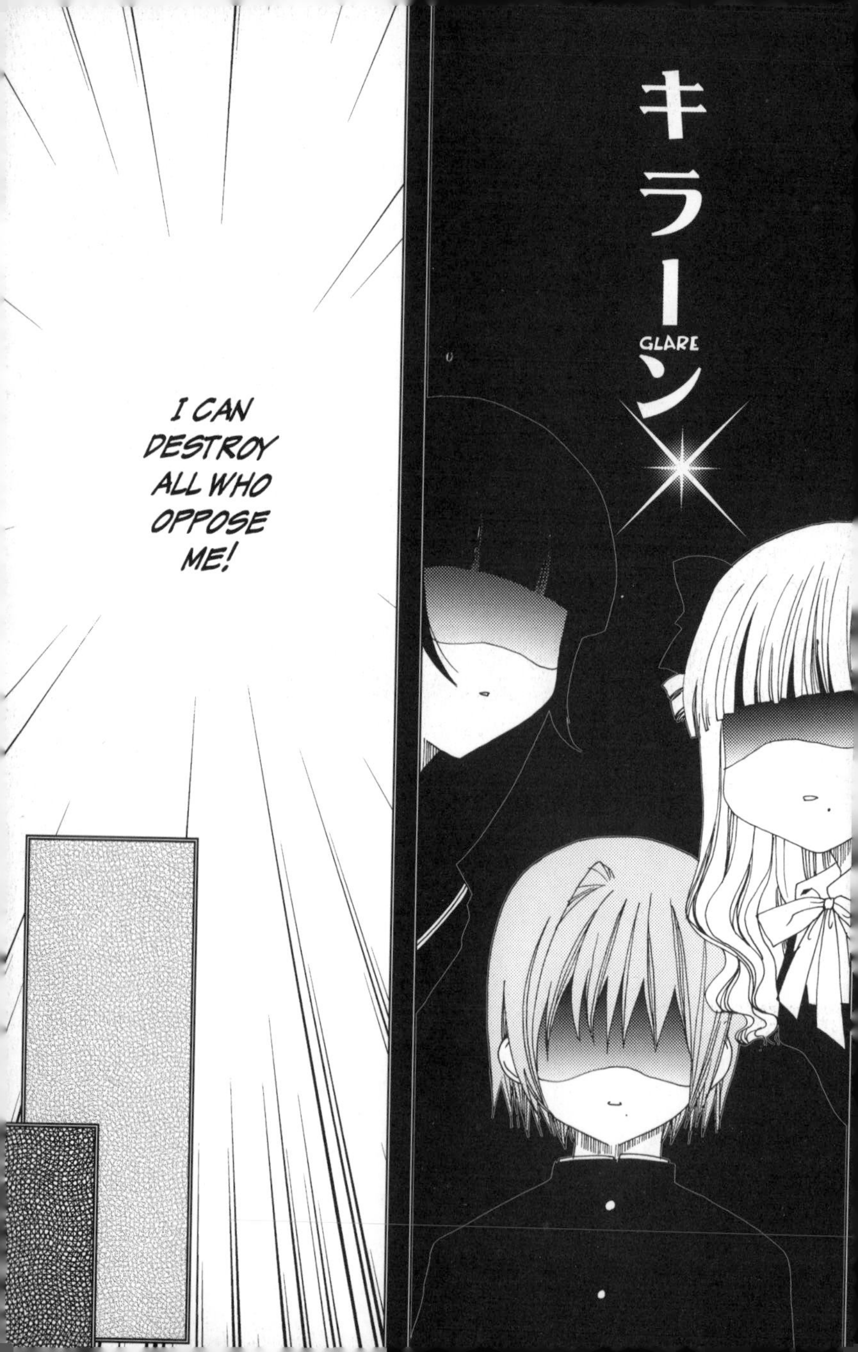
キラーン
GLARE
I CAN DESTROY ALL WHO OPPOSE ME!

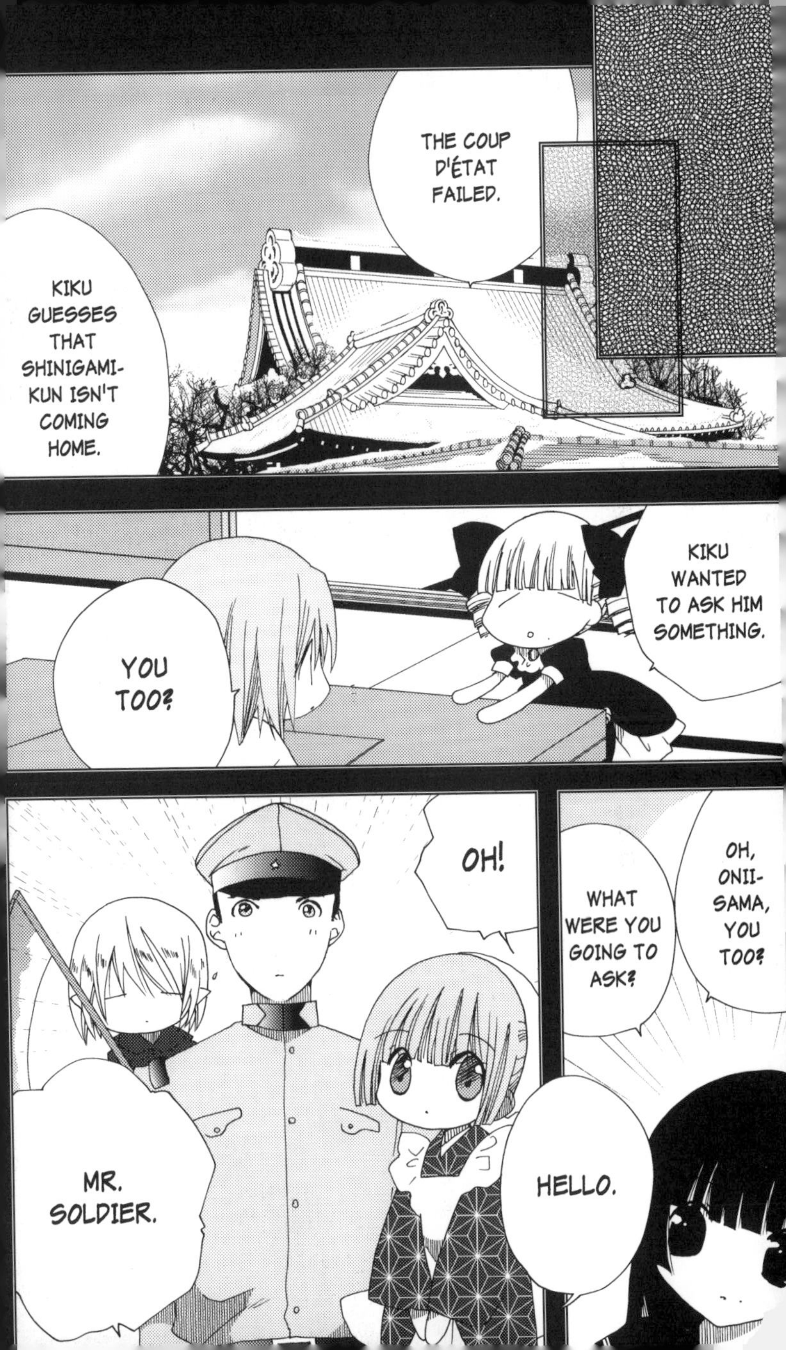
THE COUP D'ÉTAT FAILED.
KIKU GUESSES THAT SHINIGAMI-KUN ISN'T COMING HOME.
KIKU WANTED TO ASK HIM SOMETHING.
YOU TOO?
OH, ONII-SAMA, YOU TOO?
WHAT WERE YOU GOING TO ASK?
OH!
HELLO.
MR. SOLDIER.

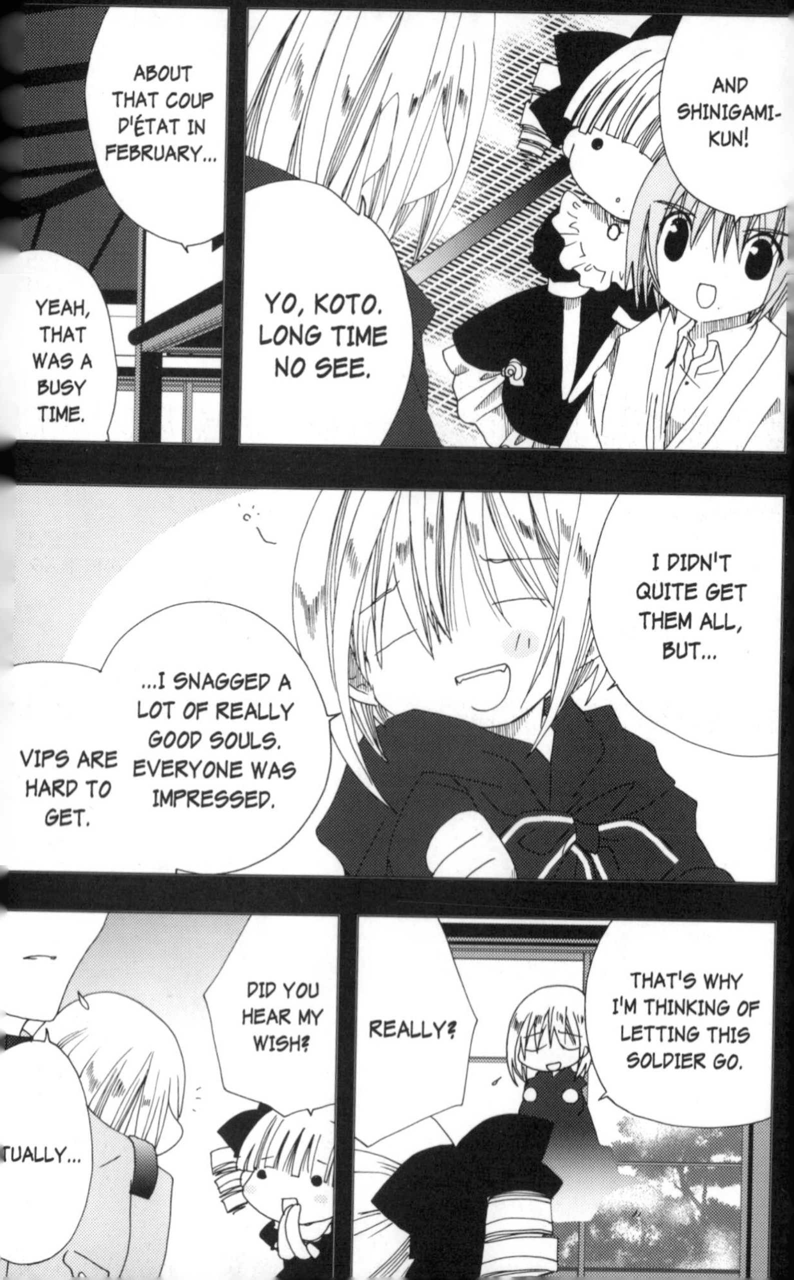
AND SHINIGAMI-KUN!
YO, KOTO. LONG TIME NO SEE.
ABOUT THAT COUP D'ÉTAT IN FEBRUARY...
YEAH, THAT WAS A BUSY TIME.
I DIDN'T QUITE GET THEM ALL, BUT...
...I SNAGGED A LOT OF REALLY GOOD SOULS. EVERYONE WAS IMPRESSED.
VIPS ARE HARD TO GET.
THAT'S WHY I'M THINKING OF LETTING THIS SOLDIER GO.
REALLY?
DID YOU HEAR MY WISH?
TUALLY...

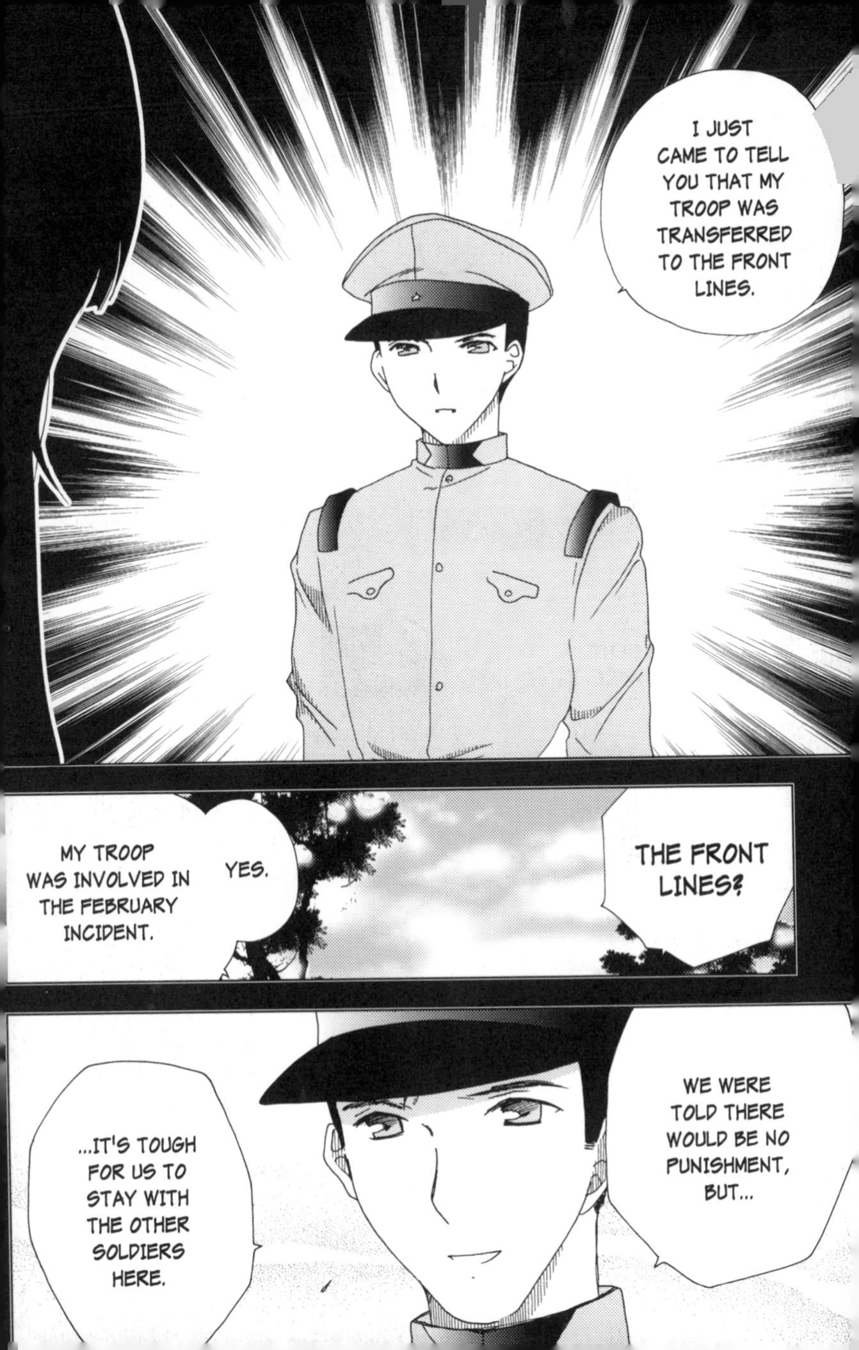
I JUST CAME TO TELL YOU THAT MY TROOP WAS TRANSFERRED TO THE FRONT LINES.
THE FRONT LINES?
YES.
MY TROOP WAS INVOLVED IN THE FEBRUARY INCIDENT.
WE WERE TOLD THERE WOULD BE NO PUNISHMENT, BUT...
...IT'S TOUGH FOR US TO STAY WITH THE OTHER SOLDIERS HERE.

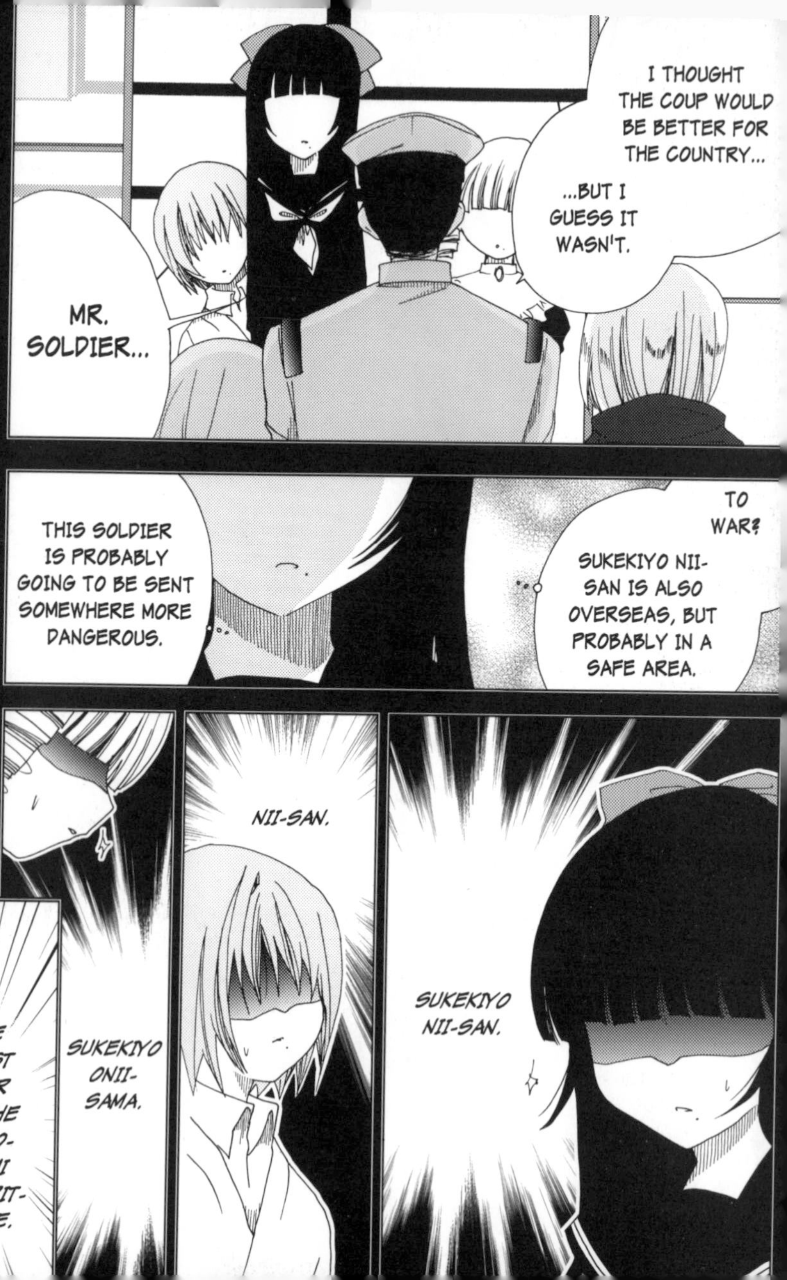
I THOUGHT THE COUP WOULD BE BETTER FOR THE COUNTRY...
...BUT I GUESS IT WASN'T.
MR. SOLDIER...
TO WAR?
SUKEKIYO NII-SAN IS ALSO OVERSEAS, BUT PROBABLY IN A SAFE AREA.
THIS SOLDIER IS PROBABLY GOING TO BE SENT SOMEWHERE MORE DANGEROUS.
SUKEKIYO NII-SAN.
NII-SAN.
SUKEKIYO ONII-SAMA.
THE FIRST HEIR TO THE NEKO-GAMI INHERIT-ANCE.

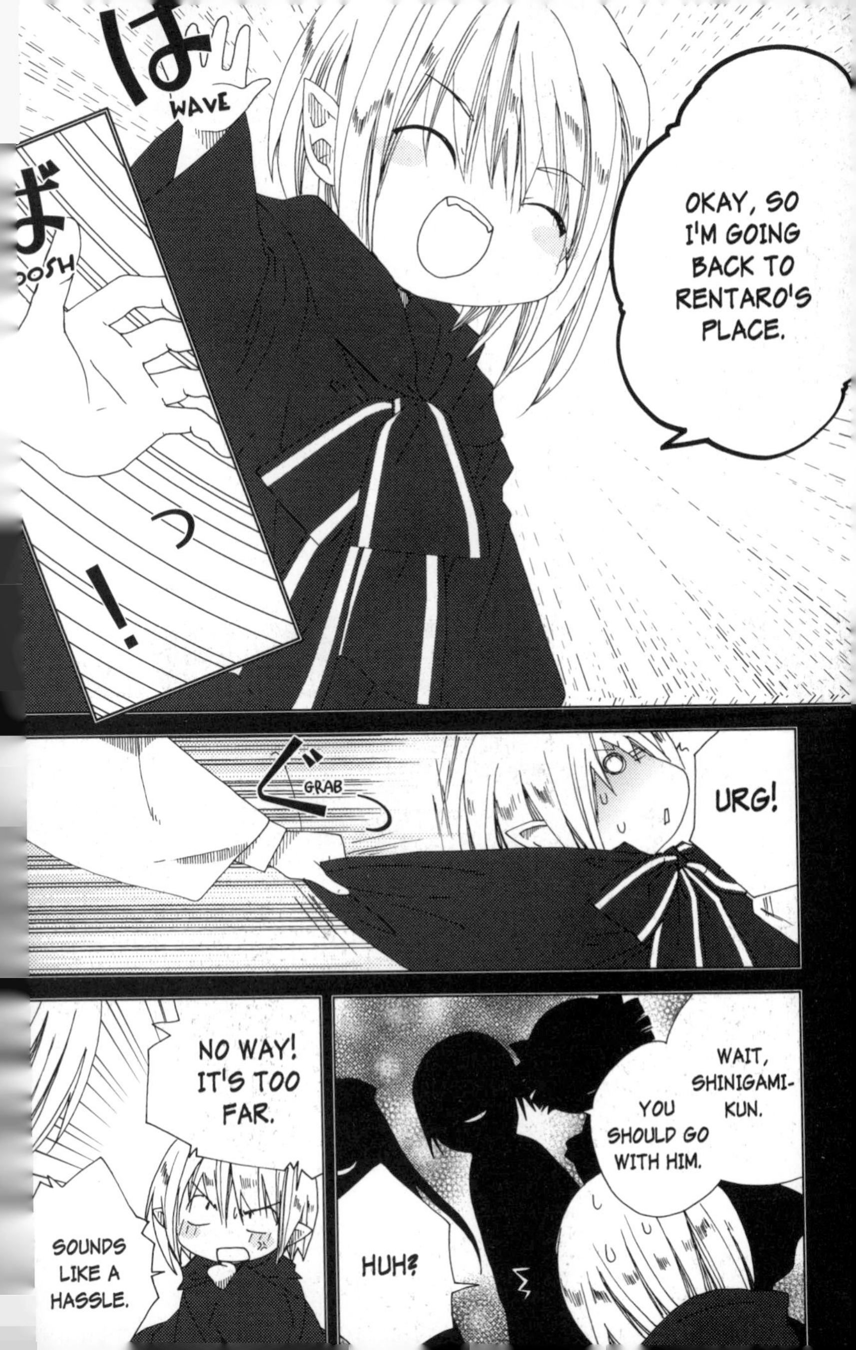
OKAY, SO I'M GOING BACK TO RENTARO'S PLACE.
ぱ
WAVE
ざ
OOSH
っ!
URG!
ぐ
GRAB
WAIT, SHINIGAMI-KUN.
YOU SHOULD GO WITH HIM.
HUH?
NO WAY! IT'S TOO FAR.
SOUNDS LIKE A HASSLE.

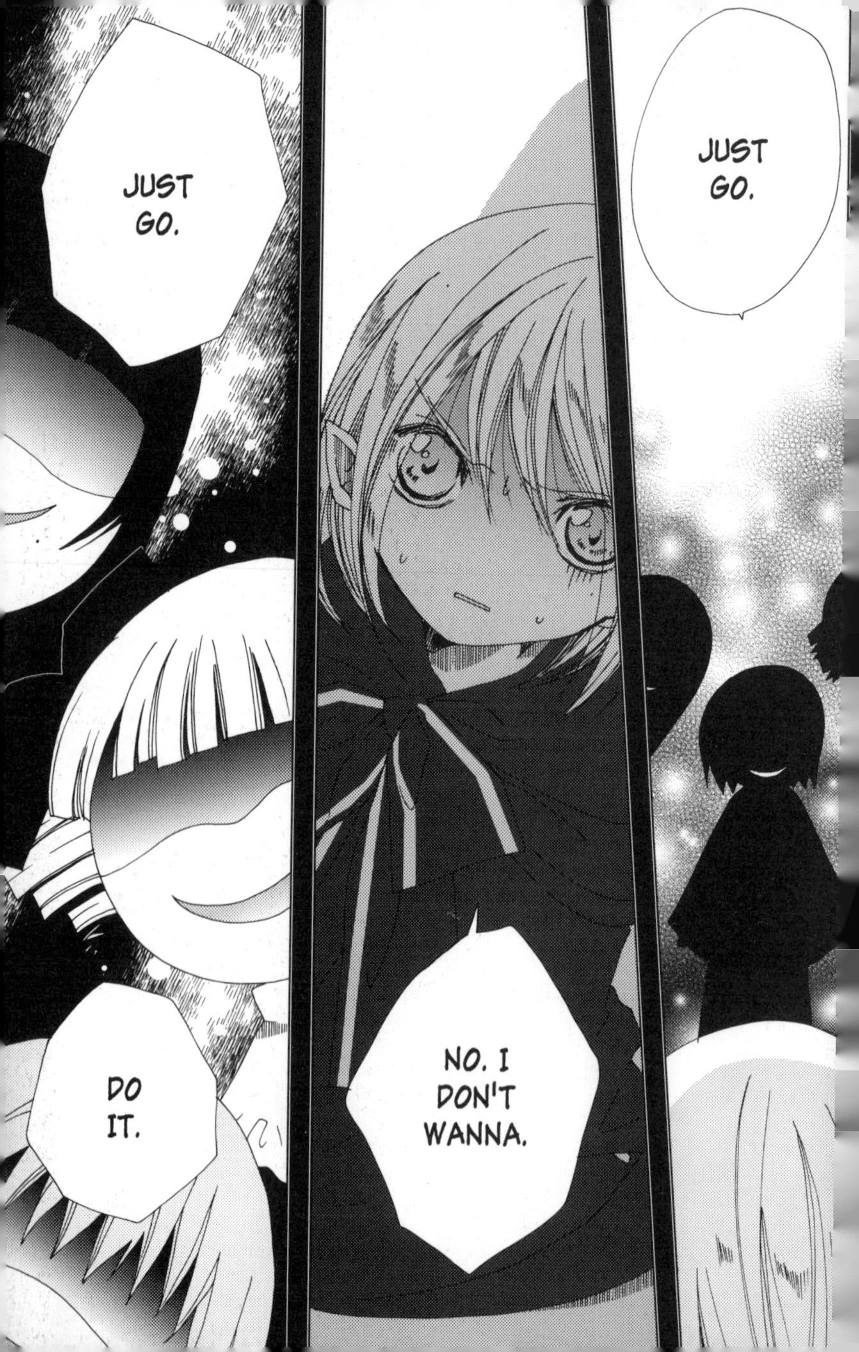
JUST GO.
NO. I DON'T WANNA.
JUST GO.
DO IT.

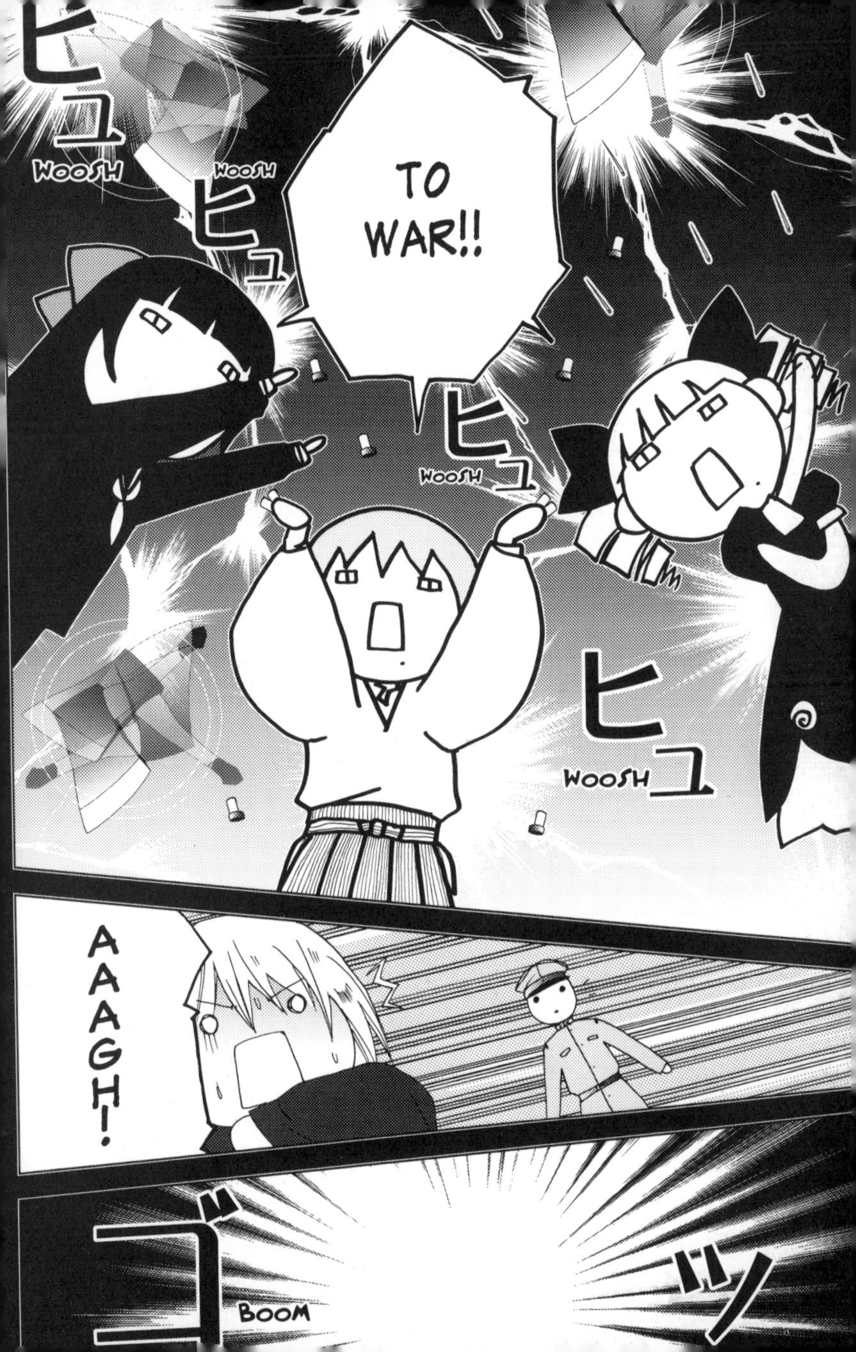
TO WAR!!
ヒュ
WOOSH
ヒュ
WOOSH
ヒュ
WOOSH
ヒュ
WOOSH
AAAGH!
ゴッ
BOOM

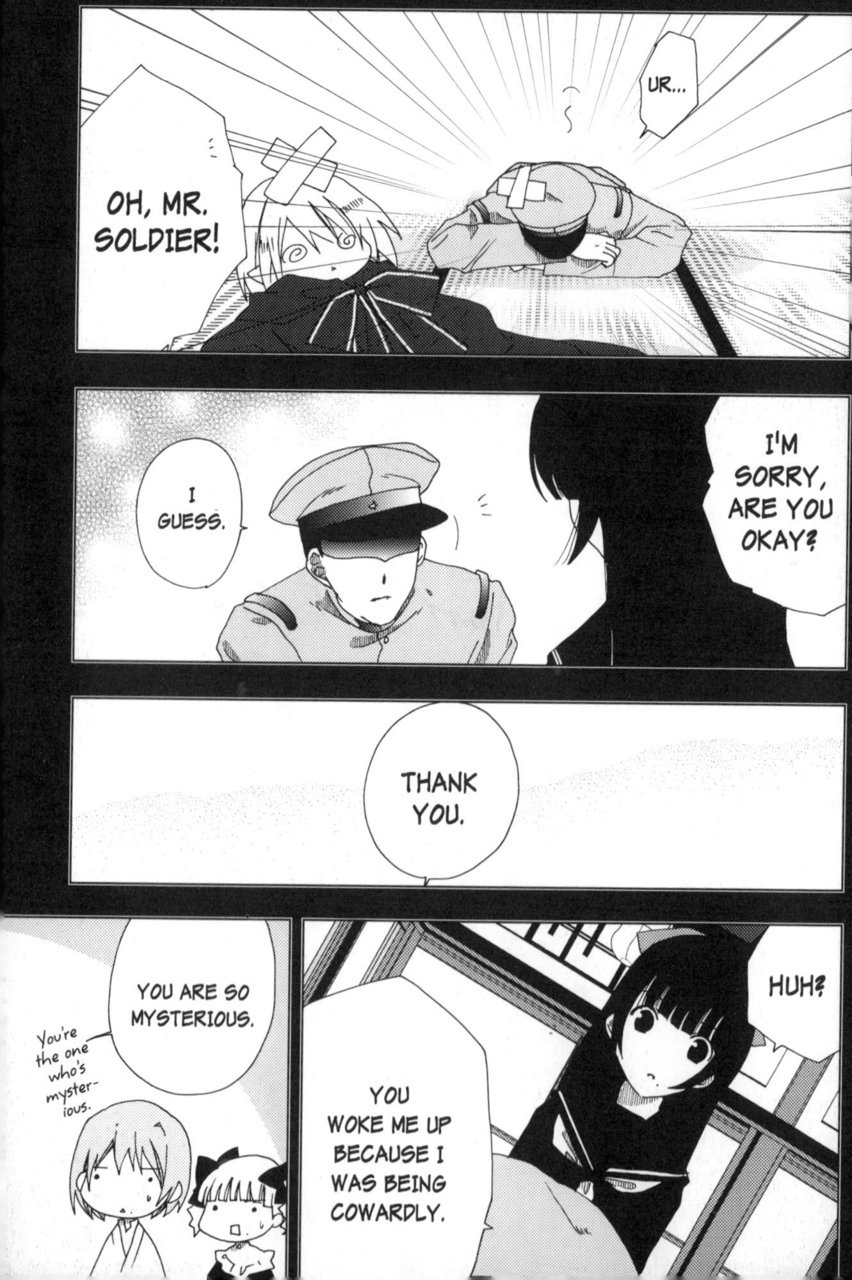
UR...
OH, MR. SOLDIER!
I'M SORRY, ARE YOU OKAY?
I GUESS.
THANK YOU.
HUH?
YOU WOKE ME UP BECAUSE I WAS BEING COWARDLY.
YOU ARE SO MYSTERIOUS.
You're the one who's mysterious.

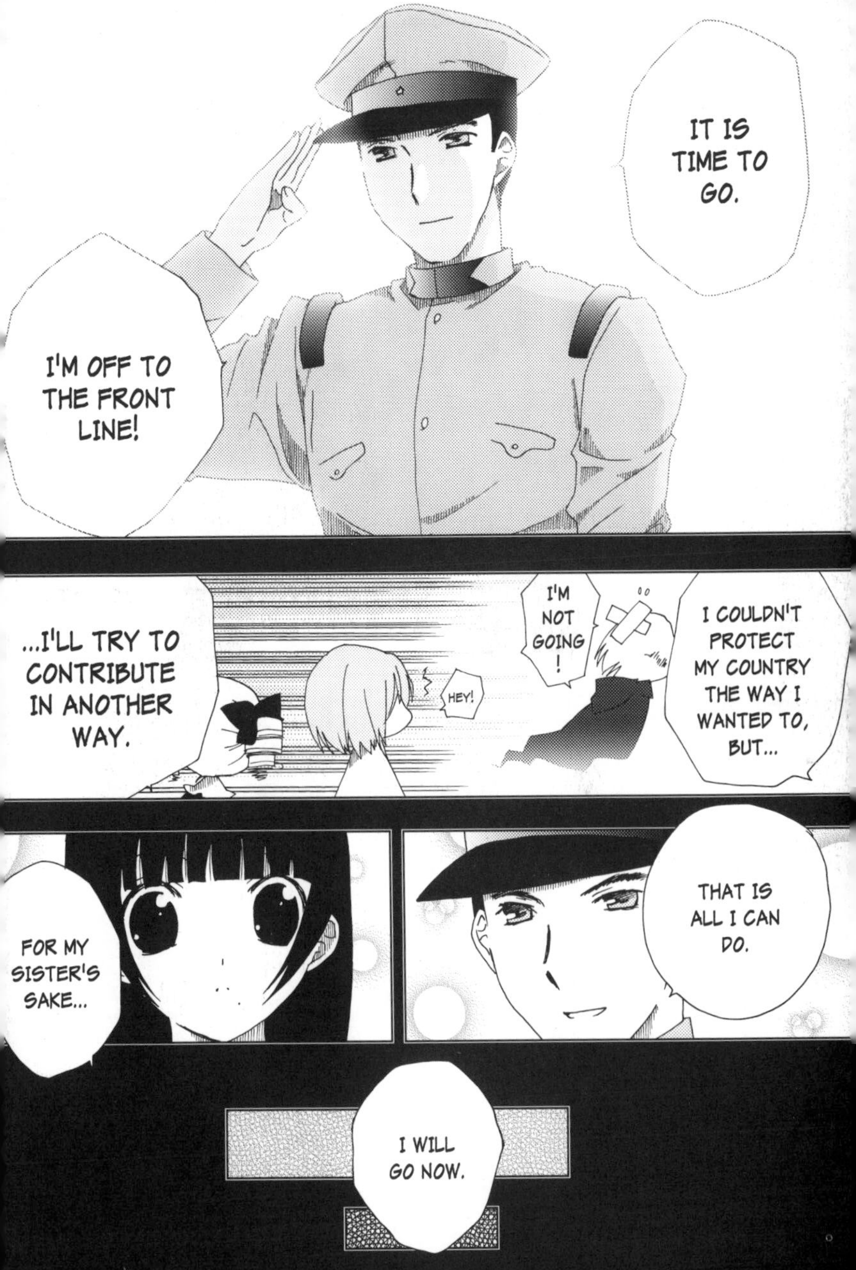
IT IS TIME TO GO.
I'M OFF TO THE FRONT LINE!
I COULDN'T PROTECT MY COUNTRY THE WAY I WANTED TO, BUT...
I'M NOT GOING!
HEY!
...I'LL TRY TO CONTRIBUTE IN ANOTHER WAY.
THAT IS ALL I CAN DO.
FOR MY SISTER'S SAKE...
I WILL GO NOW.

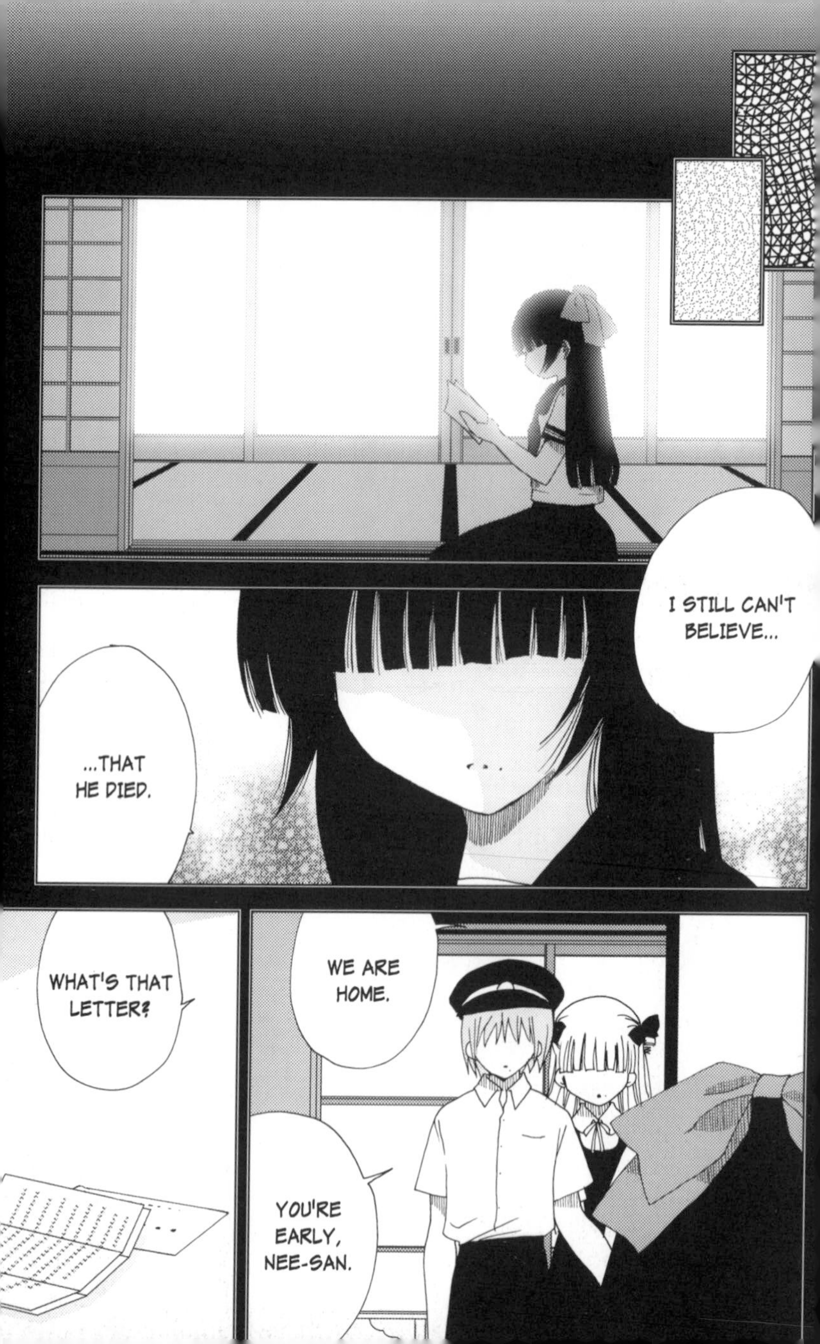
I STILL CAN'T BELIEVE...
...THAT HE DIED.
WE ARE HOME.
YOU'RE EARLY, NEE-SAN.
WHAT'S THAT LETTER?

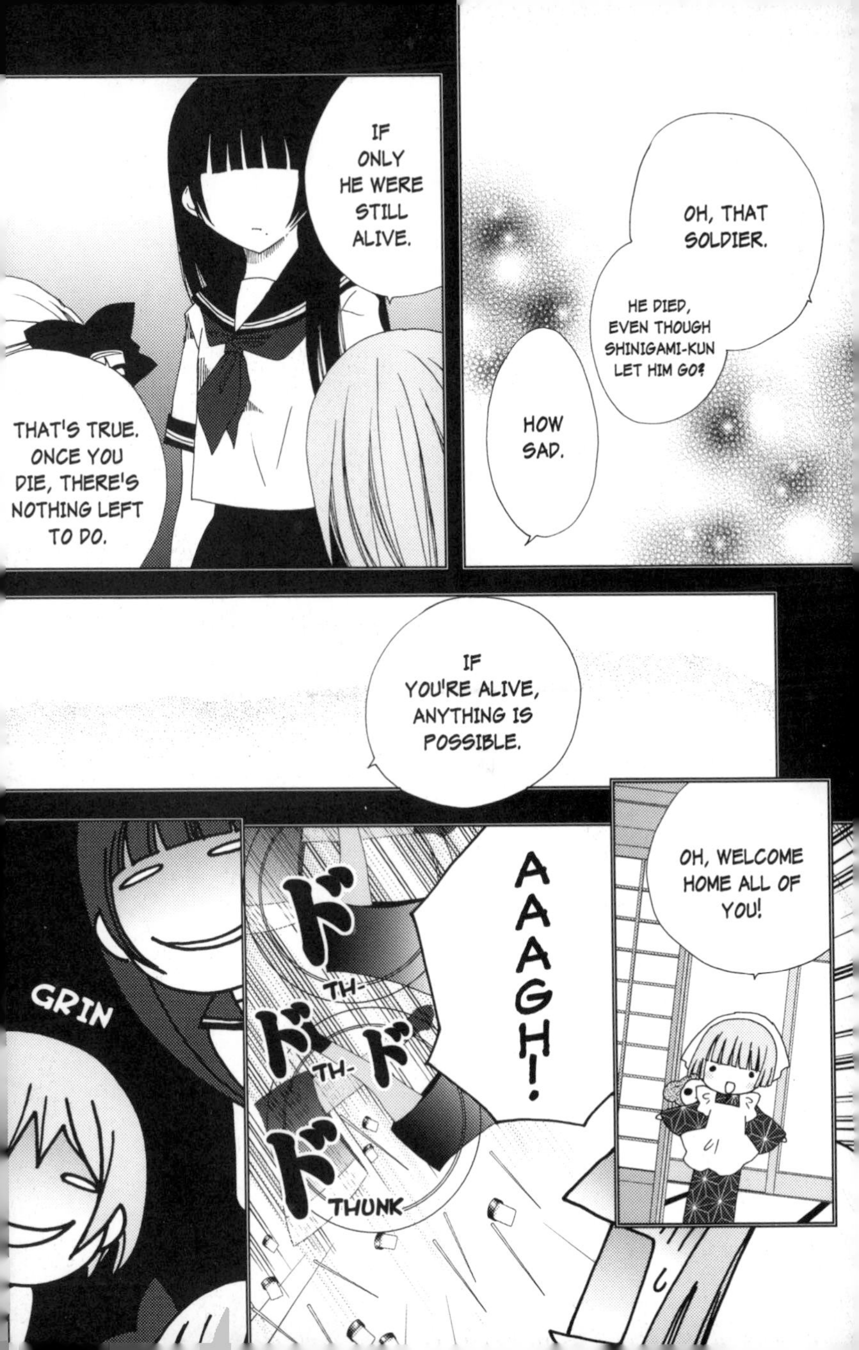
OH, THAT SOLDIER.
HE DIED, EVEN THOUGH SHINIGAMI-KUN LET HIM GO?
HOW SAD.
IF ONLY HE WERE STILL ALIVE.
THAT'S TRUE. ONCE YOU DIE, THERE'S NOTHING LEFT TO DO.
IF YOU'RE ALIVE, ANYTHING IS POSSIBLE.
OH, WELCOME HOME ALL OF YOU!
AAAGH!
ド TH-
ド TH-
ド
ド THUNK
GRIN

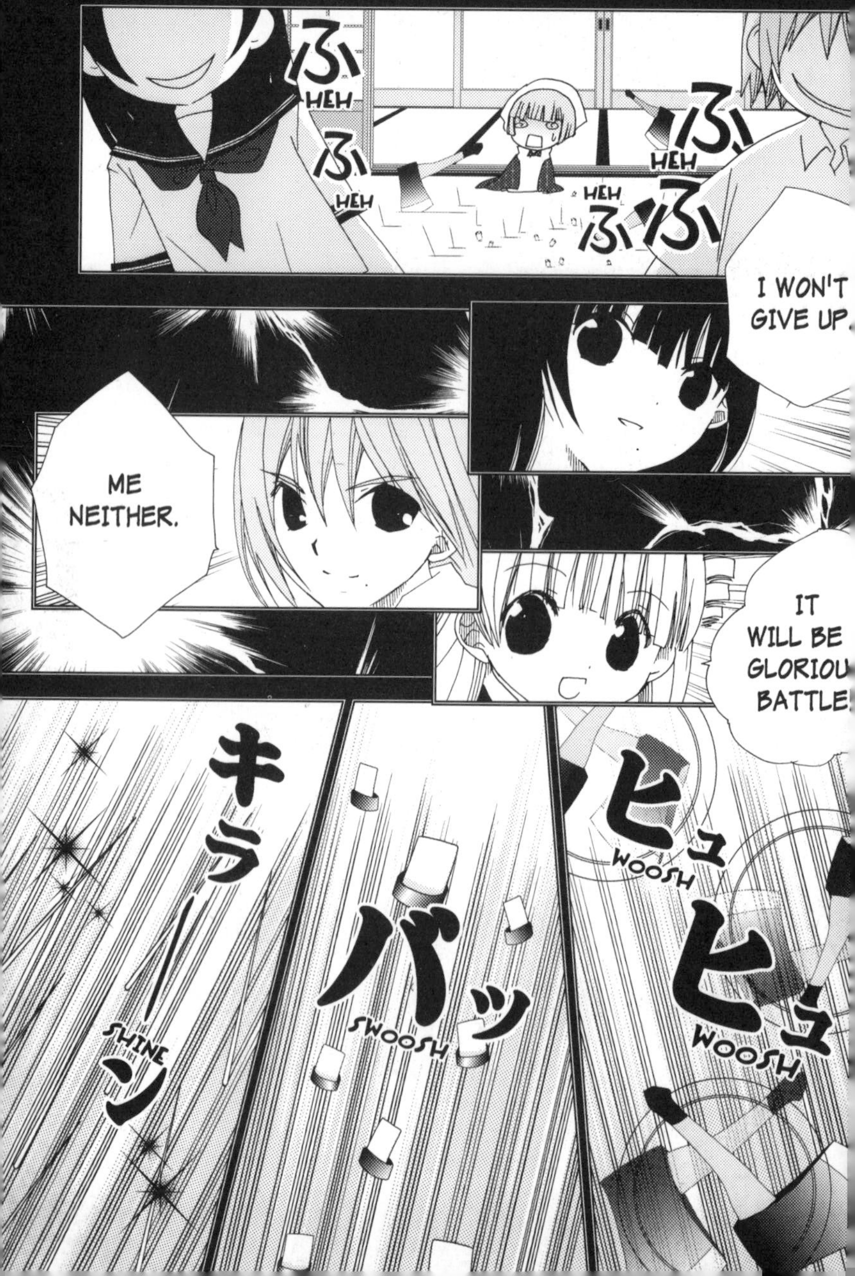
ふ
HEH
ふ
HEH
ふ
HEH
ふ
HEH
ふ
ふ
HEH
I WON'T GIVE UP.
ME NEITHER.
IT WILL BE GLORIOU BATTLE!
ヒュ
WOOSH
ヒュ
WOOSH
バッ
SWOOSH
キラーン
SHINE

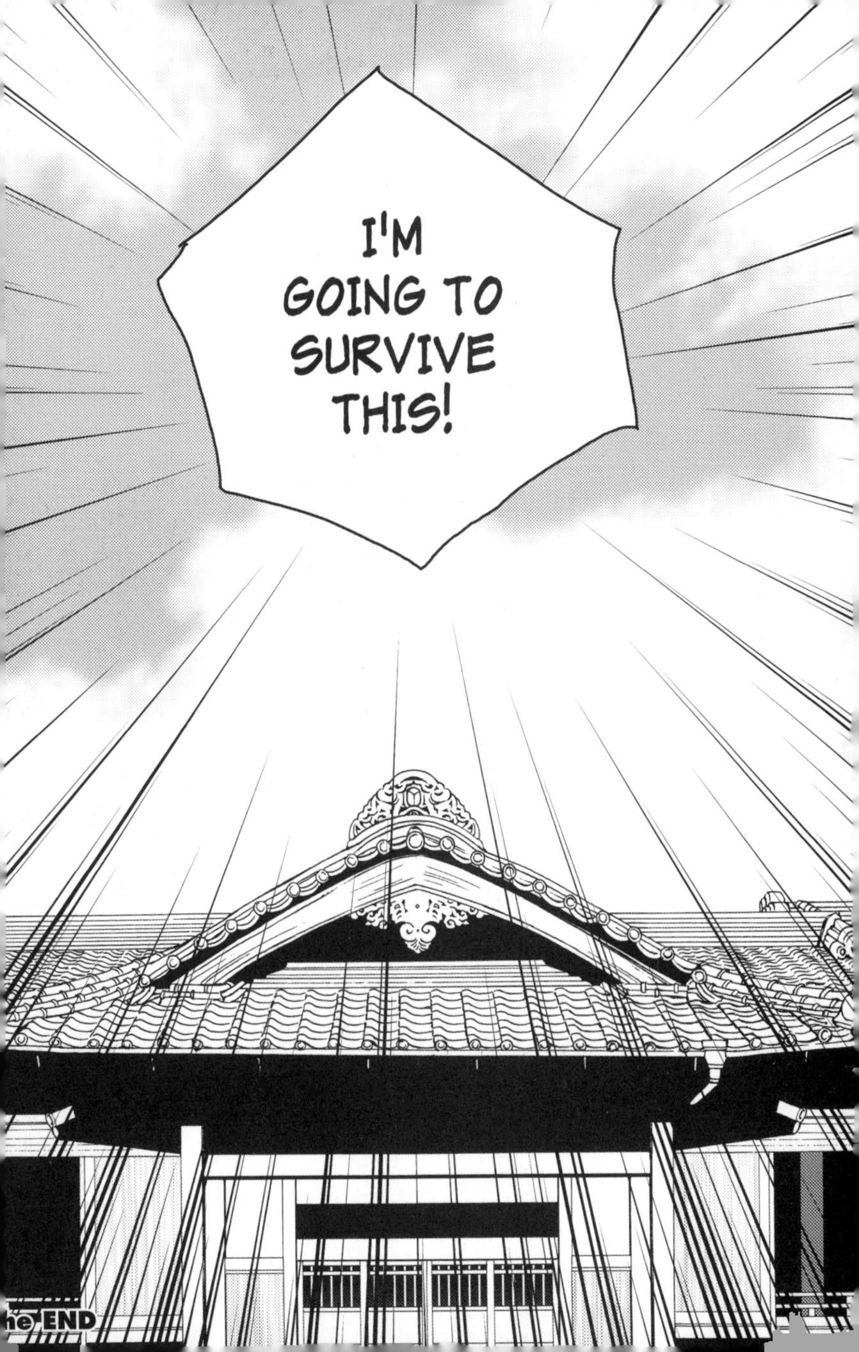
I'M GOING TO SURVIVE THIS!
he END

Yoki Koto Kiku

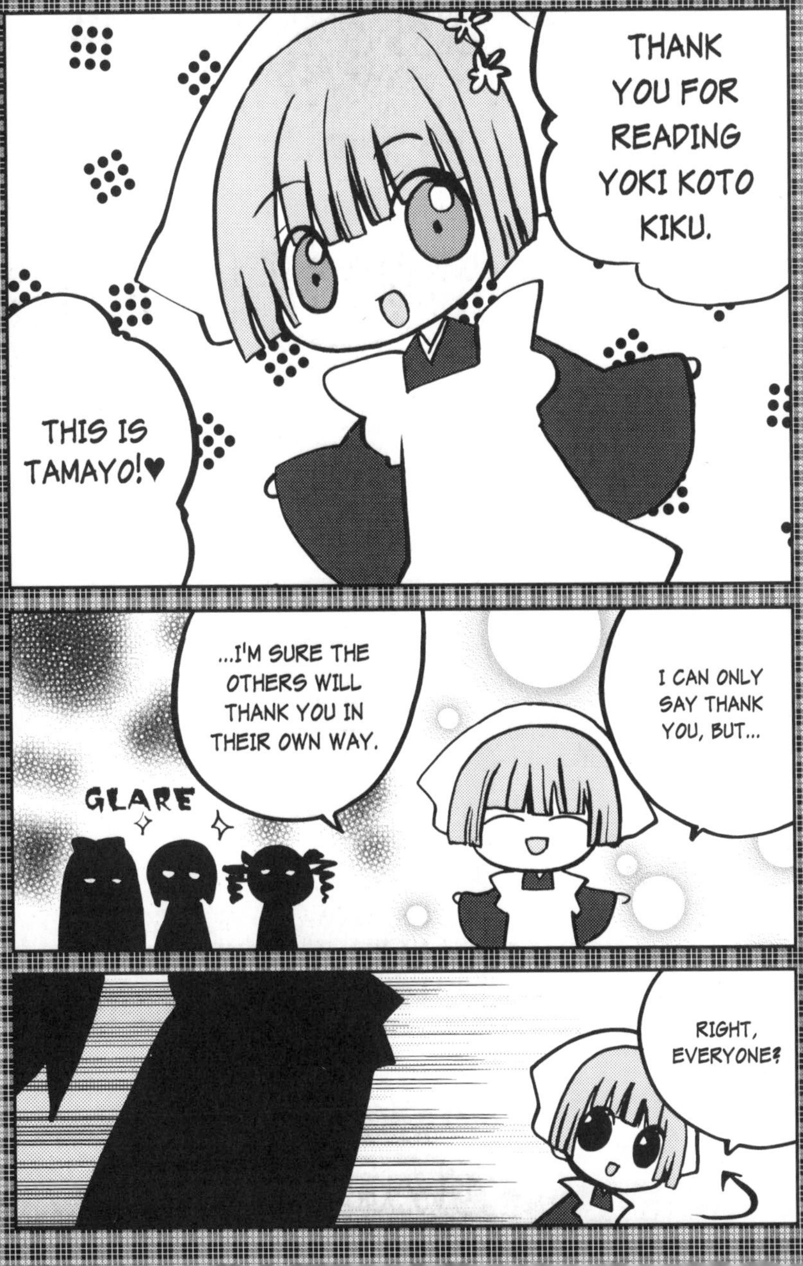
THANK YOU FOR READING YOKI KOTO KIKU.
THIS IS TAMAYO!♥
I CAN ONLY SAY THANK YOU, BUT...
...I'M SURE THE OTHERS WILL THANK YOU IN THEIR OWN WAY.
GLARE
RIGHT, EVERYONE?

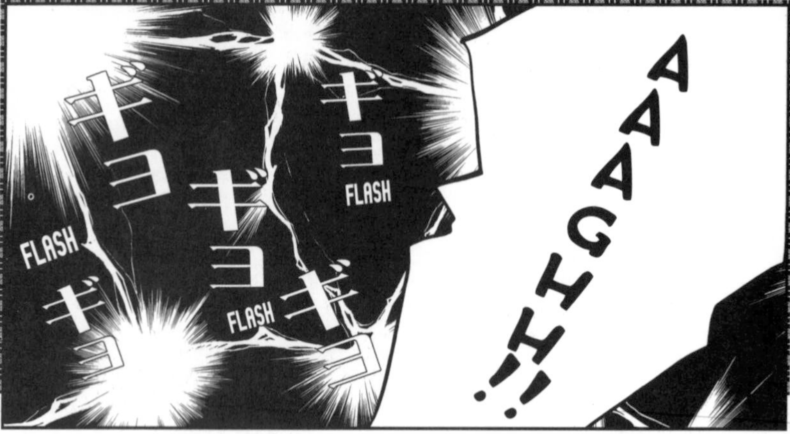
AAAGHH!!
ギョ
FLASH
ギョ
ギョ
FLASH
ギョ
FLASH
ギョ
FLASH

· Afterword ·

- Thank you for reading Yoki Koto Kiku.
  This is Koge-Donbo.

- I drew this manga because I wanted to draw something darkly humorous but with cute and innocent-looking characters. I was given a lot of creative freedom on this manga, but I'll be happy as long as you enjoy it.

- It would be nice if I could draw these characters again.

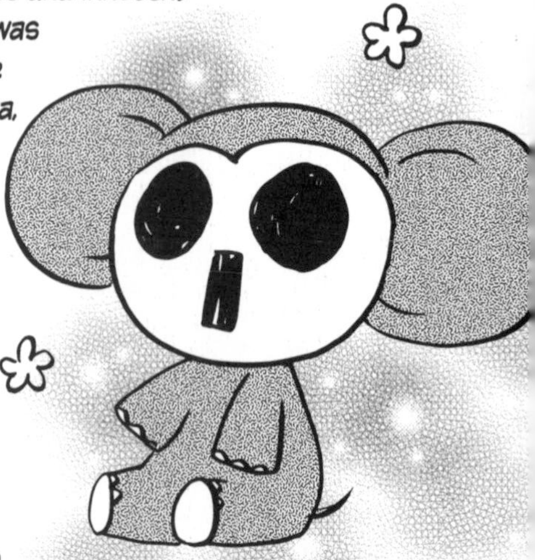

I will see you soon!

2006.1. Koge-Donbo

Yoki Koto Kiku is largely a parody of the Japanese mystery novel, *Inugami-ke no Ichizoku*, known in English as *The Inugami Clan* (there is a translation by Yumiko Yamazaki, published by ICG Muse, Inc., available). It is just one installment in the many adventures of detective Kosuke Kindaichi, created by author Seishi Yokomizu (1902-1981).

Kosuke Kindaichi is a private detective with some rather unusual idiosyncrasies. He is characterized by his tousled hair and wears a rumpled kimono (a Japanese robe) and hakama (Japanese-style pants). When he is excited he scratches his head and stutters. Despite his appearance, he is a shrewd and capable detective.

The Inugami Clan is his most famous case, in which he follows a string of macabre murders involving the Inugami family. When Sahei Inugami, the wealthy head of a silk magnate, dies and leaves behind a large fortune, Kindaichi is called to the family's home in order to prevent any unfortunate events. But as soon as he arrives, a series of strange incidents is set in motion starting with the death of the very person who requested him. Without much information to go on, Kindaichi waits for the reading of the rich man's will.

When the will is finally read, it is revealed to be an intricately woven web of conditions upon which various members of the family stand to inherit portions of the Inugami business and fortune. The one who stands to benefit the most is Tamayo, the granddaughter of the benefactor of Sahei Inugami. None of Sahei Inugami's direct children are eligible to inherit, and his three grandsons can only inherit a portion of the fortune contingent upon their marriage to Tamayo or her death. Added to this is the possibility that a fifth person, Sahei Inugami's illegitimate son Shizuma, is also eligible for the inheritance granted that he is still living.

The contents of the will trigger the events that follow, as members of the family plot against each other and are killed off in fantastic fashion. With each new death, more secrets of the Inugami are revealed, and the more intriguing the mystery becomes.

While *Yoki Koto Kiku* shares many similarities with *The Inugami Clan*, there are some notable differences. There are no triplets in *The Inugami Clan*, and there are no characters named Yoki or Koto, although there is a character named Kikuno (not related to the family).

There is also a manga called *The Kindaichi Case Files* that follows the investigations of teenage detective Hajime Kindaichi, the grandson of Kosuke Kindaichi.

Translation Notes

Yoki Koto Kiku - The phrase "yoki koto kiku" is layered with meaning. Aside from being the names of the main protagonists, also it is the family treasures in both *The Inugami Clan* and *Yoki Koto Kiku*. "Yoki" is Japanese for an ax, koto is a type of Japanese stringed instrument similar to a zither, and "kiku" is Japanese for a chrysanthemum flower. Each of the triplets also use weapons based on their names. Yoki hurls hatchets, Koto wields koto strings with finger picks, and Kiku throws the needles used for flower arrangement. The phrase can also mean, "We hear good tidings."

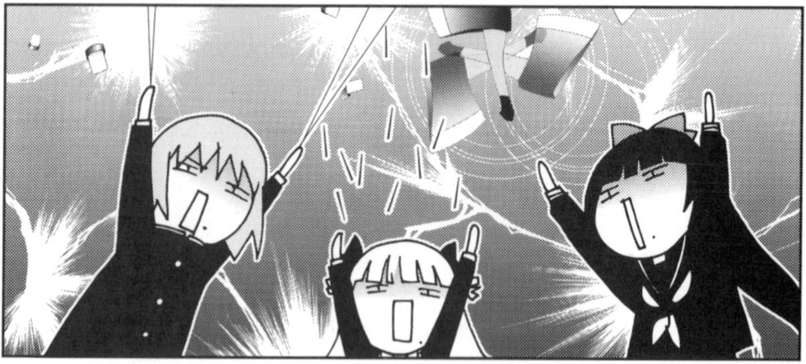

Nekogami - A parody of Inugami. "Nekogami" literally translates to "cat god," and "inugami" translates to "dog god."

Color Insert

Yamato Nadeshiko - This is a term used to refer to the ideal Japanese woman. A Yamato Nadeshiko is the epitome of femininity and grace. It is also the name of a flower called the "Fringed Pink" in English.

Sukekiyo - A parody of the eldest grandson of Sahei Inugami from *The Inugami Clan*.

☠ Translation Notes ☠

Saruzou - Tamayo's pet and protector, Saruzou, is a parody of a character of the same name in *The Inugami Clan*. In the novel, Saruzou is a strong burly man whose face resembles a monkey's. In the manga, he is a creature with the head of a monkey and the body of an elephant. His name is actually a nickname that combines the Japanese words for monkey, "saru," and elephant, "zou." He is Tamayo's friend who watches over her and protects her.

Pg. 8
San - A suffix; can be put after any name indicating respect.

Pg. 9
Nii-sama - A formal Japanese term for brother.

Chan - A suffix; usually used after a girl's name. Can also be used for young children, or someone you are close to.

Sama - A suffix; used for someone who is higher ranking.

Pg. 11
Onee-sama - A formal Japanese term for "big sister."

Pg. 18
Ojii-sama - A formal Japanese term for grandfather.

Pg. 19
Kun - A suffix, usually goes after a boy's name.

Pg. 22
Sahei Nekogami - A parody of Sahei Inugami from *The Inugami Clan*.

Translation Notes

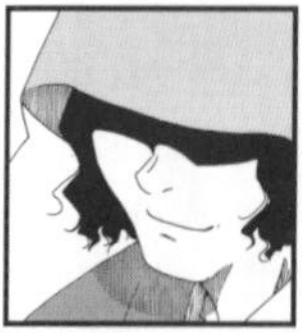

Pg. 28
Kosuke Gindaichi - A parody of detective Kosuke Kindaichi from *The Inugami Clan.* In Japanese "kin" is gold and "gin" is silver.

Pg. 36
Namu Amida Butsu - A Buddhist mantra known as the Nembutsu.

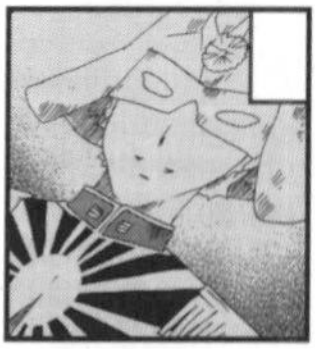

Pg. 55
Sukekiyo's photograph - Sukekiyo bears an uncanny resemblance to the Gundam series' lead antagonist, Char Aznable. In the original novel, Sukekiyo had his face badly burned during the war, and took to wearing a rubber mask upon his return home.

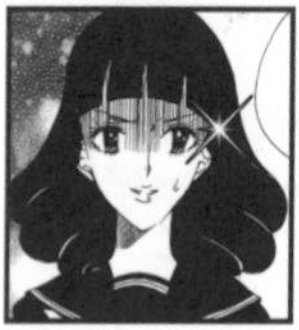

Pg. 60
Chiyoko - A parody of 1970's female antagonist shoujo manga characters such as those from the manga *Glass Mask*, *Aim for the Ace*, and *Rose of Versailles.*

Princess Ibaraki - Probably a word play on "Ibara-hime" ("Sleeping Beauty") and Ibaraki prefecture. Ibaraki is located in the south of Honshu, the mainland part of Japan. Prefectures are very similar to America's state system of government.

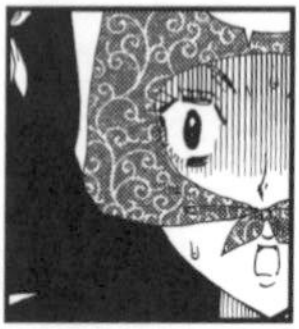

Pg. 67
Chiyoko wearing a hood - Chiyoko is wearing a hood made out of a wrapping cloth called furoshiki. In Japanese plays and comedy sketches, robbers are depicted wearing these hoods.

Translation Notes

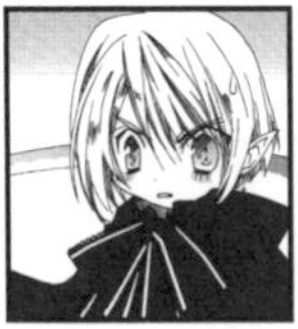

Pg. 71
Shinigami - Japanese for "Death God," shinigami is more or less Death or the Grim Reaper in Japanese culture. Unlike the Grim Reaper, who is usually referred to as one being, there can be many different Shinigami.

Pg. 83
Onii-chan - An informal Japanese term for "big brother."

Pg. 95
Shima - Shima is a character from Koge-Donbo's manga title, *Pita-Ten.*

Pg. 97
Yokikotokiku Ichigou - A parody of the family treasures from The Inugami Clan. "Ichigou" is Japanese for "number one."

Asame Newspaper - A parody of the Asahi Newspaper, one of Japan's leading newspapers. There is one line of difference between the Japanese character for "hi" (日) and "me" (目).

Phantom Thief Red - A parody of Kaito Kid from the manga by Gosho Aoyama.

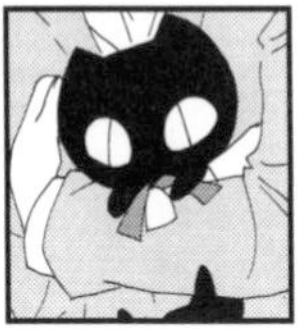

Pg. 104
Nya-san - The black cat in Koge-Donbo's manga, *Pita-Ten*, is also named Nya-san.

Pg. 164
AWOL - A military term that stands for "absent without official leave."

Translation Notes

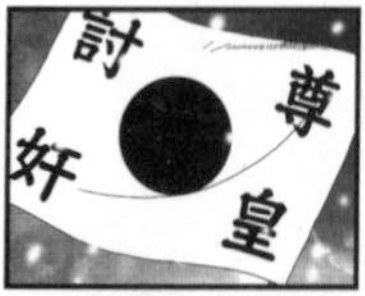
尊皇
討奸

Pg. 175

Son nou tou kan - A slogan used during the Showa Restoration which translates to "Respect the emperor, get rid of evil."

Showa restoration - The Showa period began with Emperor Hirohito's installment in December of 1926 and ended in January of 1989. The Showa Restoration of the 1930s saw a rise in right-wing patriotism, militarism, and a revival of Shintoism all leading up to World War II.

Pg. 178

Showa 11th year February 26 - Japanese years are listed according to the year of the current reigning emperor, so Showa 11 is the 11th year of the Showa period which began in 1926. On February 26, 1936, the 226 Incident occurred in which a group of young Japanese military officers led approximately 1,500 troops in an unsuccessful coup d' état attempt.

Interview with Koge-Donbo

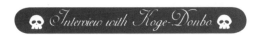

Following the successful release of *Yoki Koto Kiku* in the US, Broccoli Books had the opportunity to ask creator Koge-Donbo some questions about the book and the thought that went into it. Here's what she had to say about working on *Yoki Koto Kiku.*

What inspired you to do a parody of *The Inugami Clan*?

Actually, my editor at Broccoli was the one who suggested making a parody of *The Inugami Clan*, so I didn't know that much about the series in the beginning.

What kind of novels did you read as a child? What kind of novels do you like to read now?

I never liked reading, so I didn't read much as a child. I don't read much now either, so I'm very slow at reading.

***Yoki Koto Kiku* explores a humor that's darker than *Di Gi Charat*, and rarely seen in your other works. Do you enjoy writing dark humor?**

I used to draw very dark manga like this a long time ago, so really old fans who have known my work before *Di Gi Charat* told me that it made them feel nostalgic.

Do you have a favorite character in *Yoki Koto Kiku*?

I really liked drawing the boy characters, so I really like Koto.

Of the triplets, which are you most similar to?

Hmm. All three of them are terrible people, so I hope I'm not like them at all. (LOL)

Who was your favorite character to draw?

Tamayo was fun to draw because she got flustered so easily.

We've seen some characters from *Pita-Ten* in this series. Do you have plans for some of the characters in *Yoki Koto Kiku* to appear in your other manga?

Well, *Yoki Koto Kiku* takes place 70 years ago in Japan, so if I ever write a story during that time period I will most likely have one of the characters appear again.

Final words for your fans in North America?

Yoki Koto Kiku has a very strong Japanese taste, so I'm a little worried that some of the US readers might not get some of the parts. I just hope that the readers will laugh at the really dark humor parts of the story, and not think too much about the difficult parts.

BROCCOLI BOOKS™ *FAN QUIZ!*

How much of a Broccoli Books fan are you? Try taking this test and see what kind of a fan you are! (Answers follow at the end. Try not to peek!)

1. *Yoki Koto Kiku* takes place during a tumultuous time in Japan's history. What is the name of this period?

a) Showa Restoration
b) Meiji Restoration
c) Kemmu Restoration
d) Tokugawa Restoration

2. *Murder Princess*' Anna and Yuna serve as both Professor Akamashi's mouth and hands, issuing demands and punches to those unlucky enough to face them. It's obvious they're not your average girls. What are they?

a) androids
b) aliens
c) monsters
d) monkeys

3. Before *Yoki Koto Kiku*, there was *Di Gi Charat*! It's heroine, Dejiko packs a wallop that's far more destructive than anything the triplets can dish out. Especially with her special attack, ___________.

a) Getter Tomahawk
b) Rocket Punch
c) Laser Eye Beam
d) Zambot Buster

4. In *Galaxy Angel*, each of the lovely angels pilots her own personal emblem frame, suited to her fighting style. What emblem frame does Forte pilot?

a) Gun Crazy
b) Happy Trigger
c) Bullet Ballet
d) The Big Bang

5. The attractive cast of *KAMUI* may look like something out of a primetime soap, and they're equally dysfunctional. Much of the story takes place at a school called NOA, which stands for?

a) Noble Offensive Academy
b) Neutral Organization for Aggression
c) National Order of the Arts
d) Native Office for Achievement

6. No one ever said being psychic was easy. Kai, from the series *E'S*, may have many special powers, but lacks which of the following abilities?

a) flight
b) teleportation
c) telekinesis
d) telepathy

7. *Until the Full Moon* is an excellent blend of gothic horror and light-hearted yaoi. Besides vampires, what other legendary monsters does it draw from?

a) werewolves
b) mummies
c) zombies
d) golems

8. Koge-Donbo's design of Saruzou is based on his name which is a combination of what two types of animals?

a) gorilla and whale
b) giraffe and anteater
c) koala and hippopotamus
d) monkey and elephant

9. Laharl had better look out! Seraph Lamington has sent a "young" angel-trainee on a mission to assassinate the overlord of the Netherworld in *Disgaea*. Who is the would-be assassin?

a) Etna
b) Rozalin
c) Flonne
d) Hanako

10. Some girls would love to trade places with Mana Kirihara in *Aquarian Age – Juvenile Orion*. After all, she's being protected by five hot young guys, one of whom is her childhood friend. Which one is he?

a) Naoya Itsuki
b) Kaname Kusakabe
c) Isshin Shiba
d) Tsukasa Amou

Answers: 1. a, 2. a, 3. c, 4. b, 5. a, 6. d, 7. a, 8. d, 9. c, 10. b.

1-2 questions right: Pass the butter, please.
3-4 questions right: The florets get caught in my teeth.
5-7 questions right: Give me Broccoli anyday!
8-10 questions right: Broccoli's tops!

For more information and the latest news on Broccoli Books, check out the Broccoli Books website:

www.broccolibooks.com

Introducing a new manga from **Koge-Donbo**, the creator of
Di Gi Charat and **Yoki Koto Kiku**, coming soon to the Broccoli Books line!

Kon kon KOKON

Ren just wants to be one of the cool kids, but it doesn't help that secretly he's just a nerdy monster fanatic. That is, until a young girl named Kokon shows up. She claims to be a fox that he had helped years ago and now she wants to return the favor. With the fox girl Kokon by his side, will Ren be able to become the most popular kid in school?

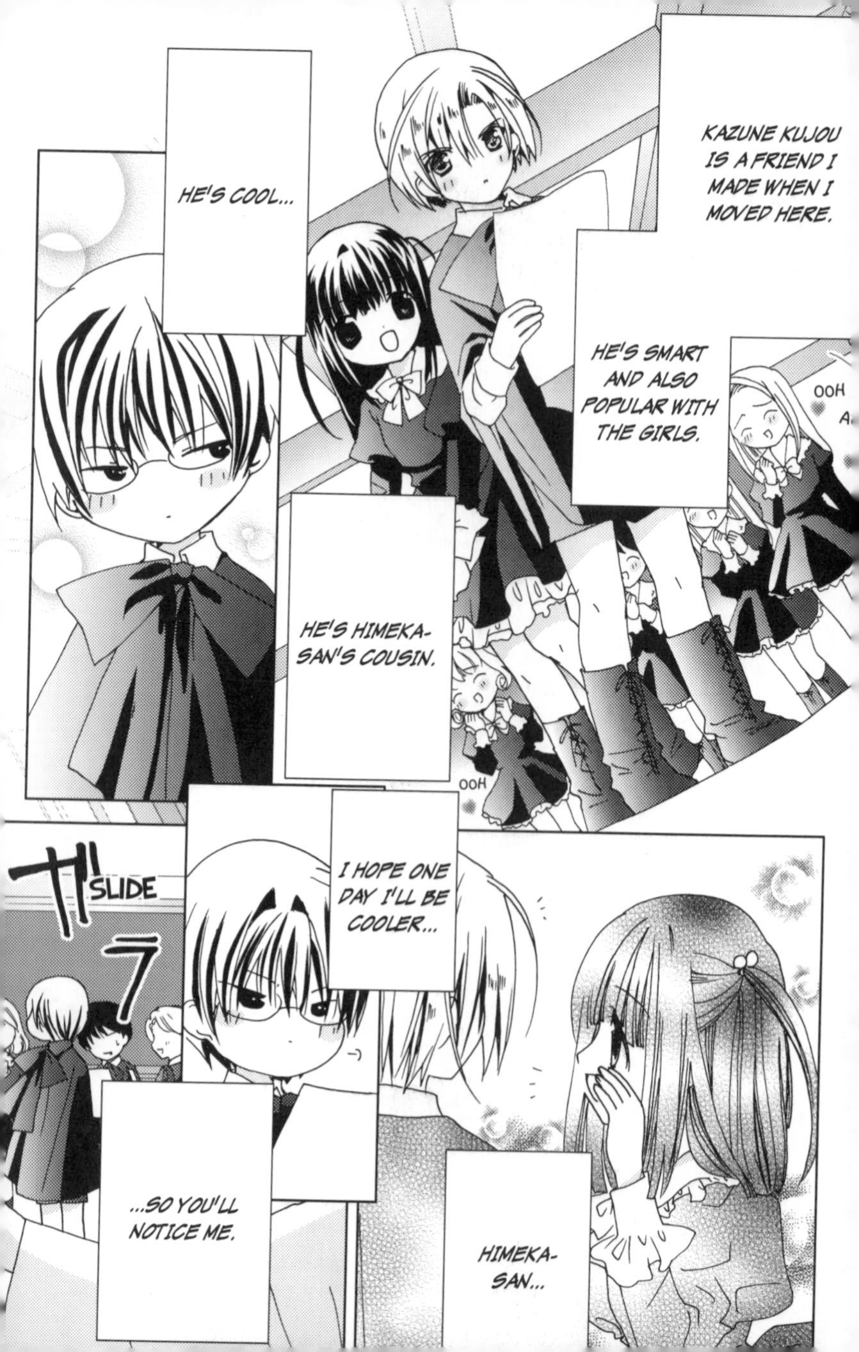
KAZUNE KUJOU IS A FRIEND I MADE WHEN I MOVED HERE.
HE'S SMART AND ALSO POPULAR WITH THE GIRLS.
OOH
HE'S HIMEKA-SAN'S COUSIN.
OOH
HE'S COOL...
I HOPE ONE DAY I'LL BE COOLER...
HIMEKA-SAN...
...SO YOU'LL NOTICE ME.
SLIDE

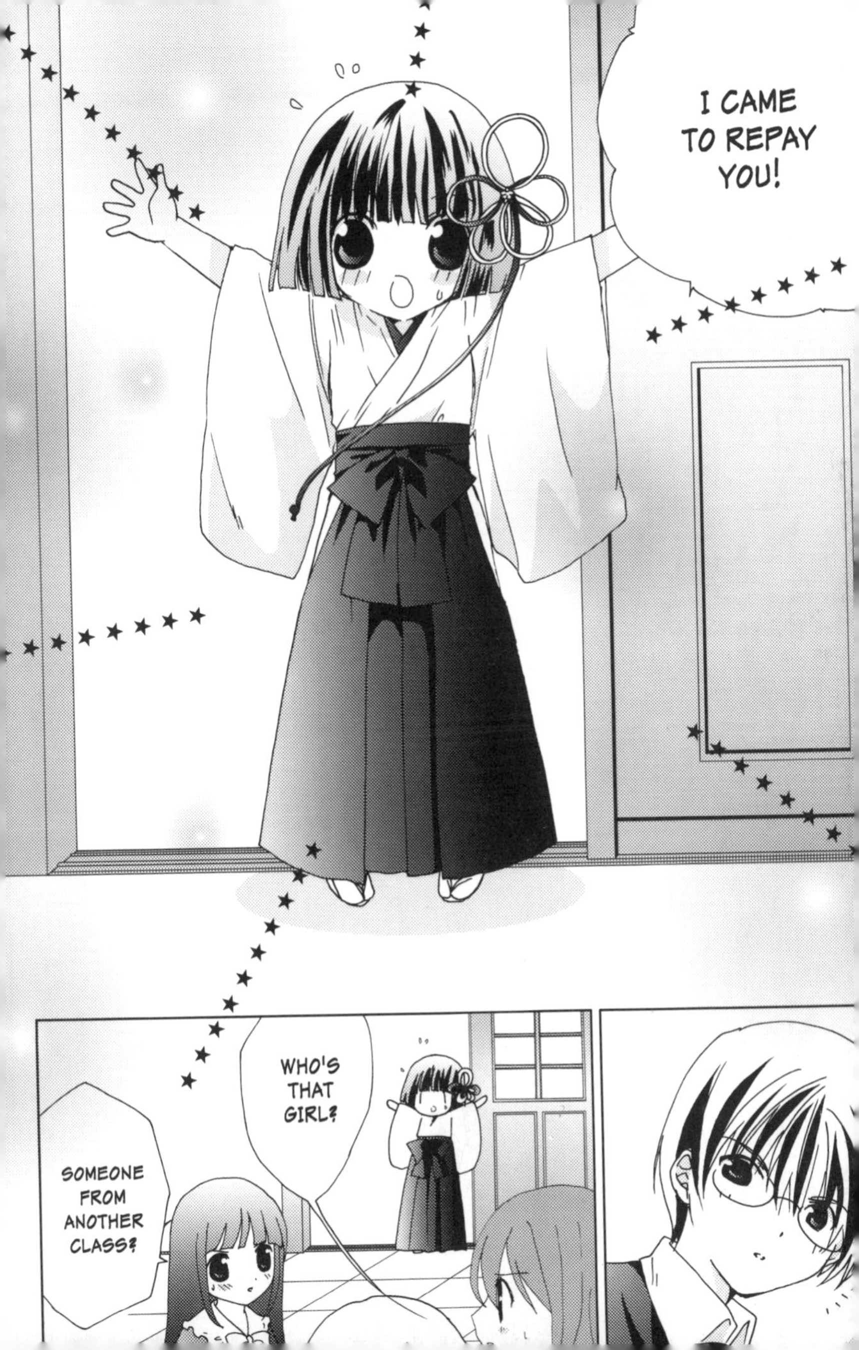
I CAME TO REPAY YOU!
WHO'S THAT GIRL?
SOMEONE FROM ANOTHER CLASS?

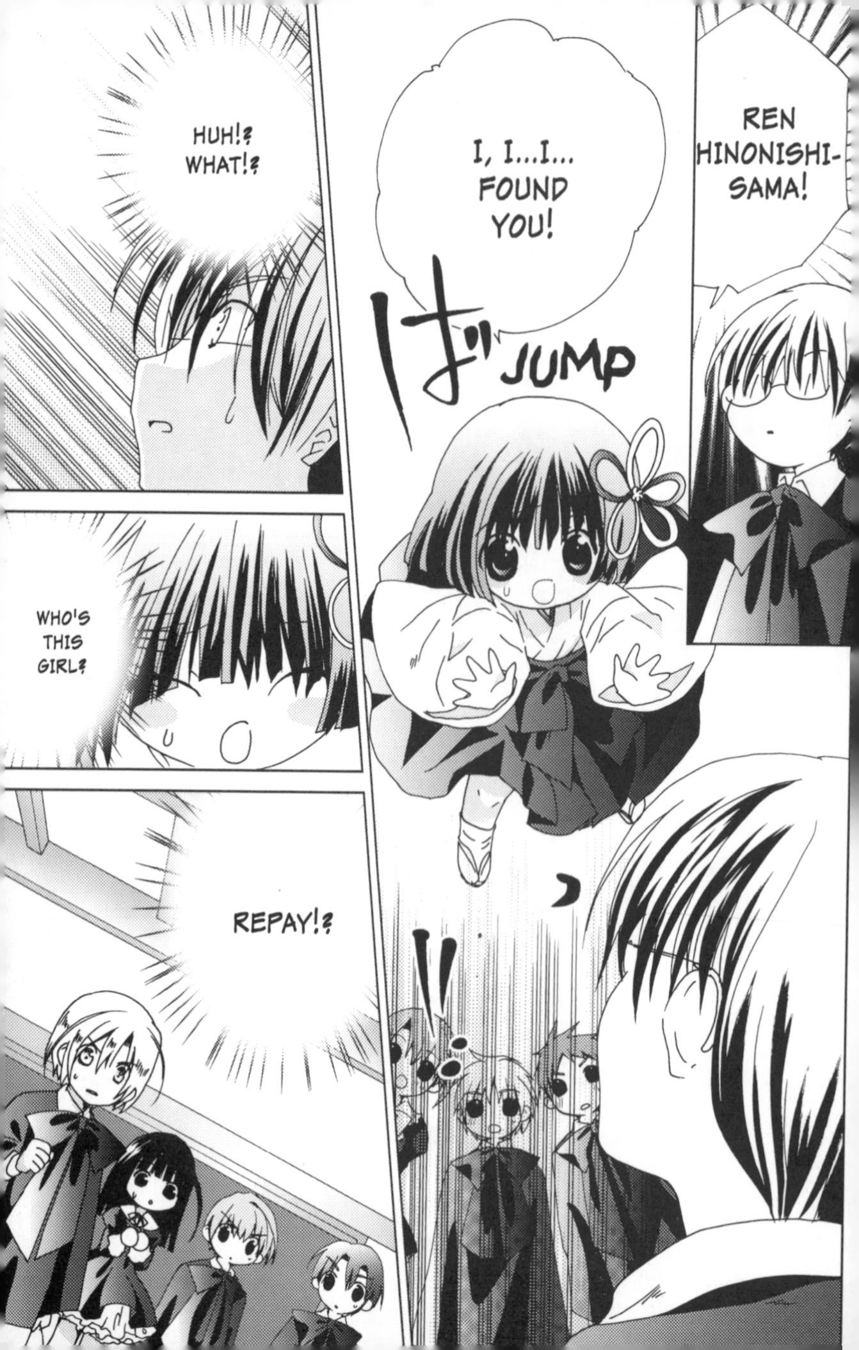
REN HINONISHI-SAMA!
I, I...I... FOUND YOU!
JUMP
HUH!? WHAT!?
WHO'S THIS GIRL?
REPAY!?

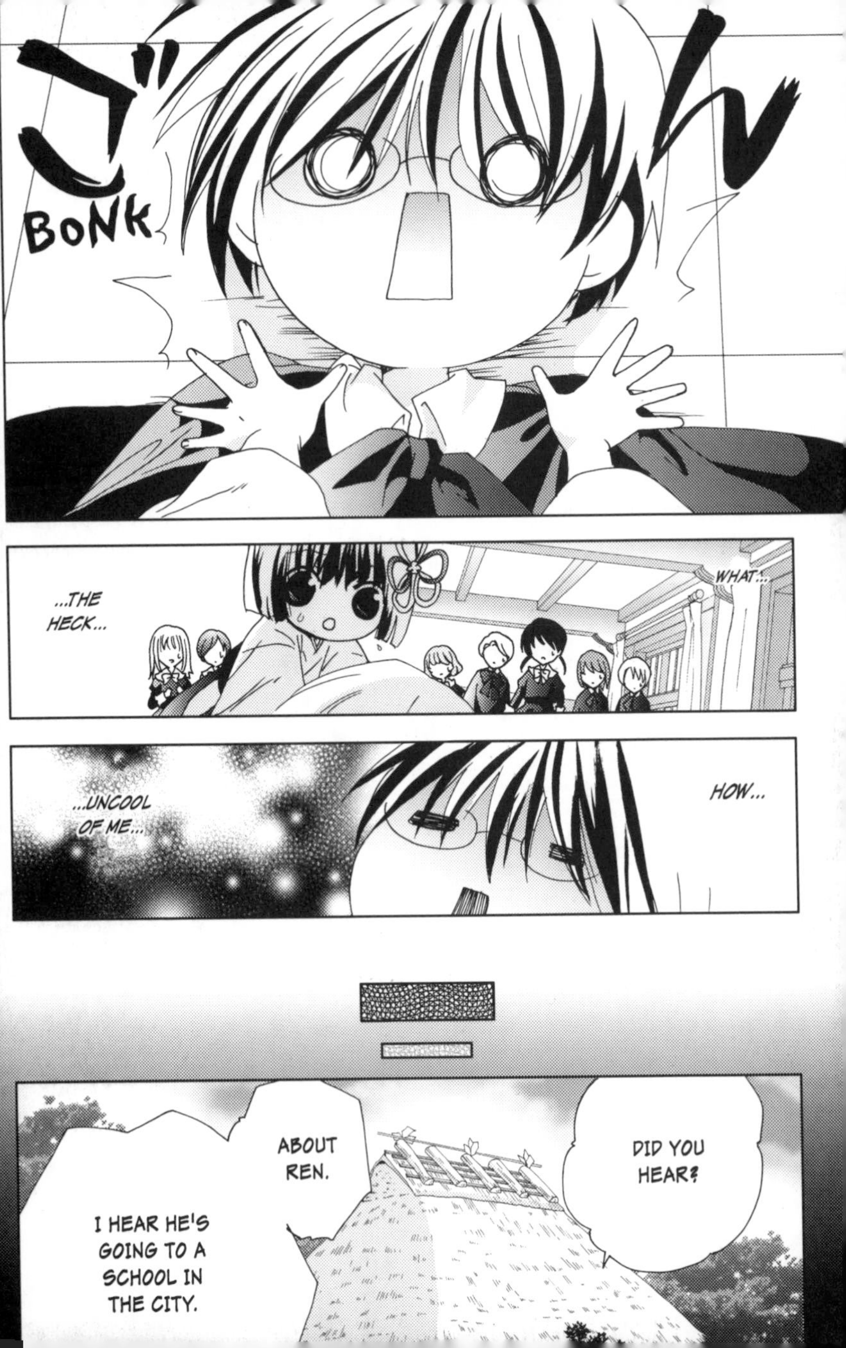
ゴん
BONK
WHAT...
...THE HECK...
HOW...
...UNCOOL OF ME...
DID YOU HEAR?
ABOUT REN.
I HEAR HE'S GOING TO A SCHOOL IN THE CITY.

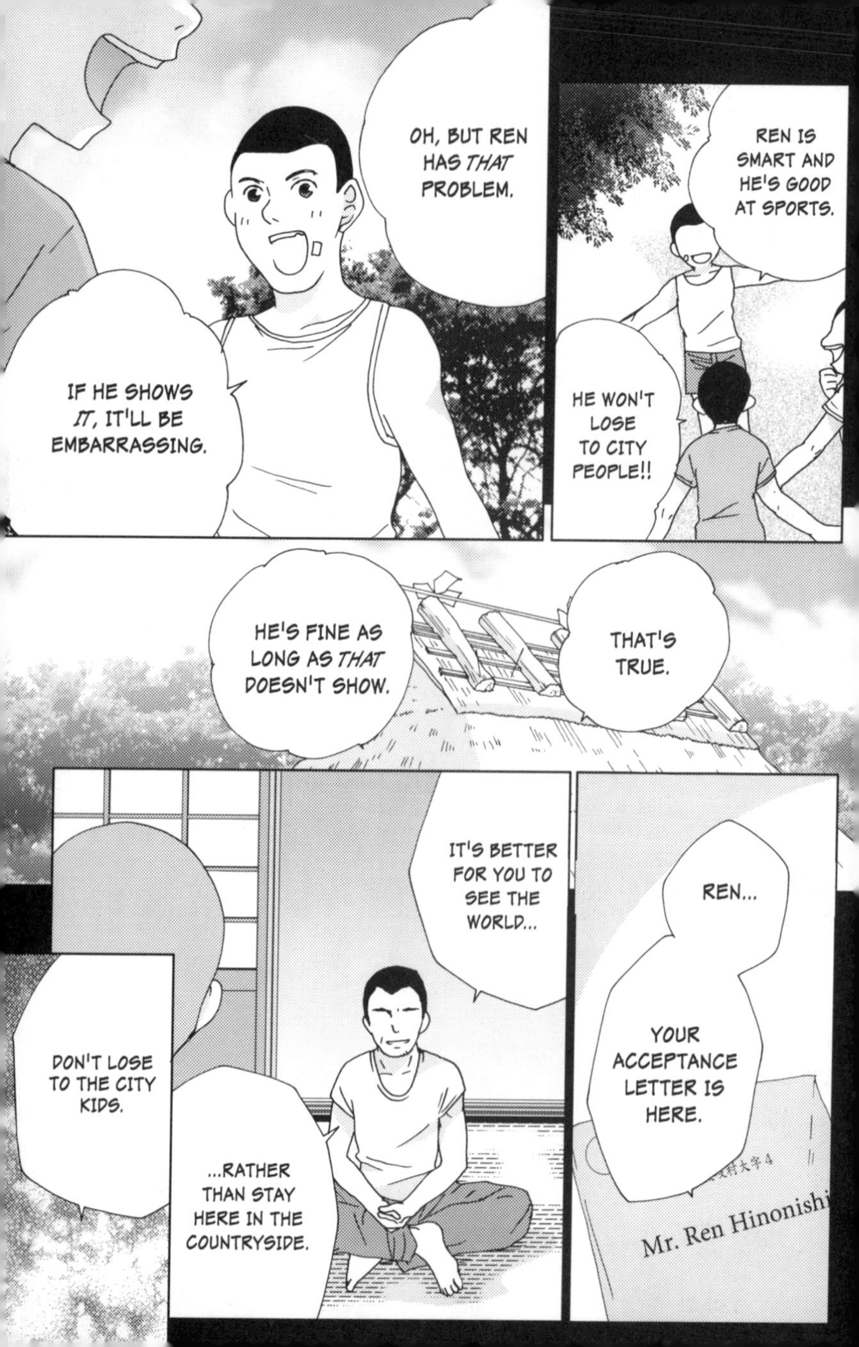
REN IS SMART AND HE'S GOOD AT SPORTS.
HE WON'T LOSE TO CITY PEOPLE!!
OH, BUT REN HAS *THAT* PROBLEM.
IF HE SHOWS *IT*, IT'LL BE EMBARRASSING.
HE'S FINE AS LONG AS *THAT* DOESN'T SHOW.
THAT'S TRUE.
REN...
YOUR ACCEPTANCE LETTER IS HERE.
Mr. Ren Hinonishi
IT'S BETTER FOR YOU TO SEE THE WORLD...
...RATHER THAN STAY HERE IN THE COUNTRYSIDE.
DON'T LOSE TO THE CITY KIDS.

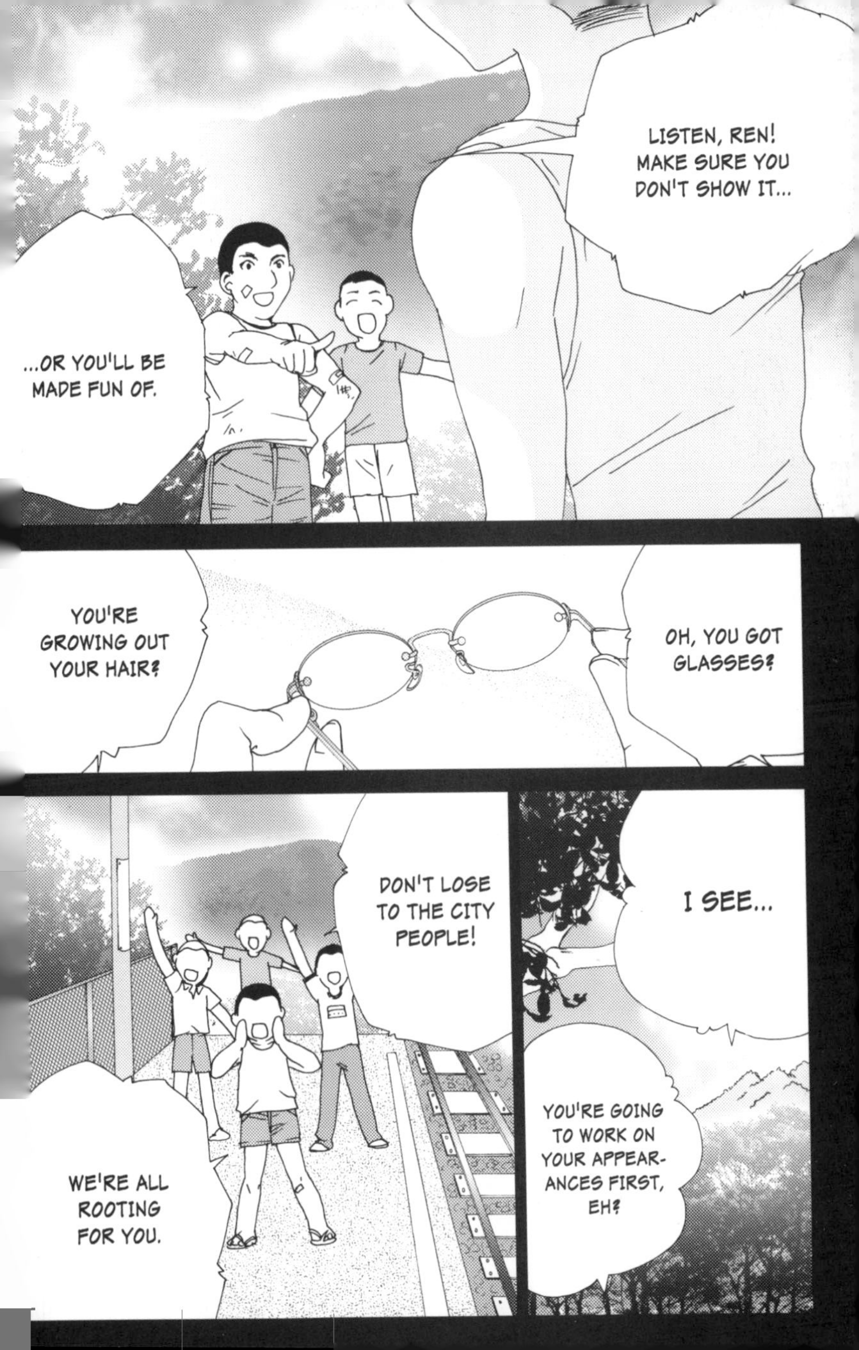
LISTEN, REN! MAKE SURE YOU DON'T SHOW IT...
...OR YOU'LL BE MADE FUN OF.
OH, YOU GOT GLASSES?
YOU'RE GROWING OUT YOUR HAIR?
I SEE...
YOU'RE GOING TO WORK ON YOUR APPEAR-ANCES FIRST, EH?
DON'T LOSE TO THE CITY PEOPLE!
WE'RE ALL ROOTING FOR YOU.

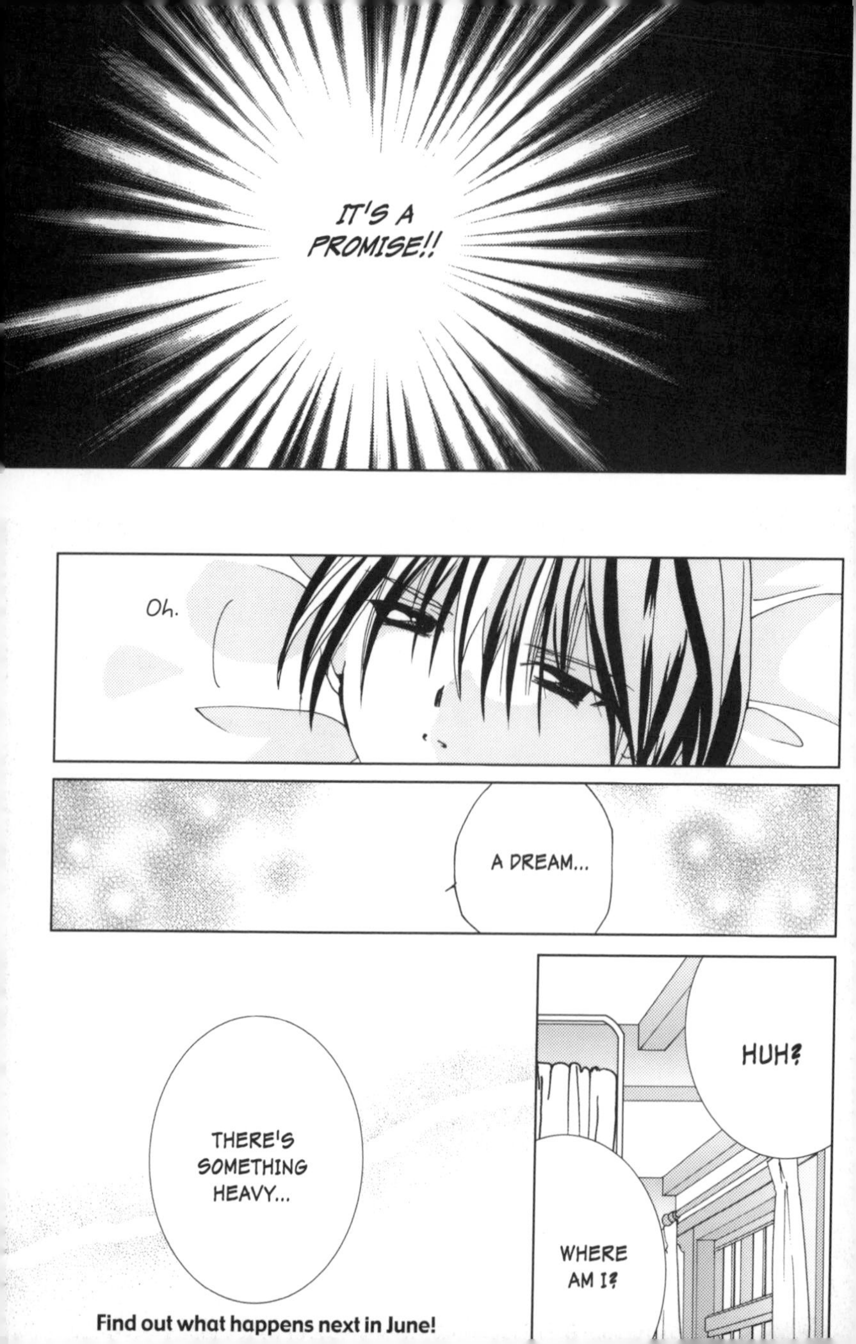
IT'S A PROMISE!!
Oh.
A DREAM...
HUH?
WHERE AM I?
THERE'S SOMETHING HEAVY...

Find out what happens next in June!

THE *DEVIL* IS IN THE *DETAILS.*

A box that grants three wishes might seem like a dream come true. At least that's what Keita thought, but inside the box he finds a girl. And this girl is no genie—Maki's a devil princess and she's come to take Keita's soul! But she can only take his soul after he makes his third wish. So, as a sheltered demon with little knowledge of how to be evil, Maki must rely on her trusty guidebook to teach herself the ways of the nefarious arts and trick Keita into using up his wishes. Until then, Maki's going to live with Keita until he can't stand living anymore.

My Dearest
DEVIL PRINCESS

*logo not finalized

IN BOOKSTORES EVERYWHERE THIS SUMMER!

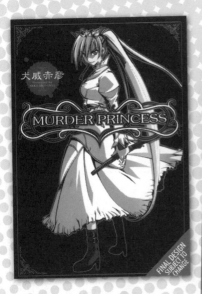

STOP!
YOU'RE READING THE WRONG WAY!

This is the end of the book! In Japan, manga is generally read from right to left. All reading starts on the upper right corner, and ends on the lower left. American comics are generally read from left to right, starting on the upper left of each page. In order to preserve the true nature of the work, we printed this book in a right to left fashion. Those who are unfamiliar with manga may find this confusing at first, but once you start getting into the story, you will wonder how you ever read manga any other way!

YKK

BB

THIS QUESTIONNAIRE IS REDEEMABLE FOR:

Yoki Koto Kiku Dust Jacket

Broccoli Books Questionnaire
Fill out and return to Broccoli Books to receive your corresponding dust jacket!*

PLEASE MAIL THE COMPLETE FORM, ALONG WITH UNUSED UNITED STATES POSTAGE
STAMPS WORTH $1.50 ENCLOSED IN THE ENVELOPE TO:**

Broccoli International
Attn: Broccoli Books Dust Jacket Committee
1728 S. La Cienega Blvd.
Los Angeles, CA 90035

(Please write legibly)

Name: _____

Address: _____

City, State, Zip: _____

E-mail: _____

Gender: ☐ Male ☐ Female   **Age:** _____

(If you are under 13 years old, parental consent is required)

Parent/Guardian signature: _____

Where did you hear about this title?

☐ Magazine   ☐ Convention

☐ Internet   ☐ Club

☑ At a Store   ☐ Other

☐ Word of Mouth

Where was this title purchased? (If known)

_____

Why did you buy this title?

It was a manga
_____
_____
_____

How would you rate the following features of this manga?

	Excellent	Good	Satisfactory	Poor
Translation	☑	☐	☐	☐
Art quality	☑	☐	☐	☐
Cover	☑	☐	☐	☐
Extra/Bonus Material	☑	☐	☐	☐

What would you like to see improved in Broccoli Books manga?

Would you like to join the Broccoli Books Mailing List? ☐ Yes ☑ No

Would you recommend this manga to someone else? ☑ Yes ☐ No

What related products would you be interested in? (Check all that apply)

- ☑ Apparel
- ☑ Posters
- ☑ Figures
- ☑ Plushies
- ☑ Art Books
- ☐ Stationery
- ☐ Trinkets
- ☑ Other

Favorite manga style/genre: (Check all that apply)

- ☐ Shoujo
- ☐ Shounen
- ☐ Yaoi
- ☑ Anime-based
- ☐ Video game-based

Final comments about this manga:

amazing

Thank you!

* While supplies last.

** For residents of Canada, please send an International Reply Coupon (IRC) of $3.00 US made out to "Broccoli International."

All information provided will be used for internal purposes only. We will not sell or otherwise divulge any of the information.

Requests not in compliance with all terms of this form will not be acknowledged or returned. All submissions are subject to verification and become the property of Broccoli International USA. Fraudulent submission, including use of multiple addresses or P.O. boxes to obtain additional Broccoli International USA information or offers may result in prosecution. Broccoli International USA reserves the right to withdraw or modify any terms of this form. Void where prohibited, taxed, or restricted by law. Broccoli International USA will not be liable for lost, misdirected, mutilated, illegible, incomplete, or postage-due mail. Sticker offer is only available to residents of the United States and Canada. For updates to the rules and regulations, please see www.broccolibooks.com.